Management Basics for Information Professionals

Instructors adopting this textbook for a course
may request supplementary case studies by emailing
editionsmarketing@ala.org.

Management Basics for Information Professionals

FOURTH EDITION

G. EDWARD EVANS
STACEY GREENWELL

ALA
Neal-Schuman

CHICAGO :: 2020

Extensive effort has gone into ensuring the reliability of the information in this book; however, the publisher makes no warranty, express or implied, with respect to the material contained herein.

ISBNs
978-0-8389-1873-9 (paper)
978-0-8389-4637-4 (PDF)
978-0-8389-4635-0 (ePub)
978-0-8389-4636-7 (Kindle)

Library of Congress Cataloging-in-Publication Data
Names: Evans, G. Edward, 1937- author. | Greenwell, Stacey, author.
Title: Management basics for information professionals / G. Edward Evans, Stacey Greenwell.
Description: 4th edition. | Chicago : ALA Neal-Schuman, 2020. | Includes bibliographical references and
    index.
Identifiers: LCCN 2019025745 (print) | LCCN 2019025746 (ebook) | ISBN 9780838946374 (pdf) |
    ISBN 9780838946350 (epub) | ISBN 9780838946367 (kindle edition) | ISBN 9780838918739
    (paperback)
Subjects: LCSH: Library administration—United States. | Information services—United States—
    Management.
Classification: LCC Z678 (ebook) | LCC Z678 .E9 2019 (print) | DDC 025.1—dc23
LC record available at https://lccn.loc.gov/2019025745

Cover design by Kimberly Thornton; imagery © Adobe Stock. Text design and composition by Karen Sheets de Gracia in the Cardea and Acumin Pro typefaces.

♾ This paper meets the requirements of ANSI/NISO Z39.48-1992 (Permanence of Paper).

Printed in the United States of America
24 23 22 21 20   5 4 3 2 1

ALA Neal-Schuman purchases fund advocacy, awareness,
and accreditation programs for library professionals worldwide.

CONTENTS

PART IV Managing Things

ILLUSTRATIONS

TABLES

FIGURE

PREFACE

This edition has a three-fold purpose. The first is to introduce a new coauthor, Stacey Greenwell, who was a great collaborator in preparing the second edition of *Academic Librarianship,* another ALA Neal-Schuman publication. The second purpose is to make clear that an organization's operational sector—for-profit, nonprofit, or public—plays a determining role in how you carry out basic management functions. The final purpose is to be more concise while adding new ideas and examples.

The second purpose is perhaps the most significant. As with many introductory texts, prior editions of this book failed to seriously address the critical role that the library's context plays in how basic management functions operate. Almost all libraries, with the exception of corporate libraries, are in either the public or nonprofit sectors (and some are in both). Those sectors have a major influence on what the basic elements of management will be and how they can be applied and remain within the law. (Indeed, as chapter 3 will explore, laws play a significant role in library operations.) Chapter 1 outlines, in broad strokes, the sector differences. The later chapters provide details of how those differences impact the application of basic management concepts.

More often than not, when you read something in the library literature about a new idea related to managerial practice, it arose from work done in the for-profit sector. To be sure, there is research done on public and nonprofit organizations; however, it is not as extensive and often only applies to a narrow segment of the sector being investigated.

In this edition, the book's chapters have been restructured into five broad sections. Part I, the opening section, looks at general issues in managing a library—background, leadership, environment, legal, and ethical issues. Part II discusses seven of the basic managerial functions—accountability; vision, mission, and planning; assessment; decision making; change management; communication; and advocacy and marketing. Part III looks at "people" considerations—staffing; staff development and team building; diversity; and motivation. Part IV discusses "things"—money, technology, and facilities. Finally, Part V focuses on managing yourself and your career.

Although this edition has substantially reduced the number of printed pages, there is new material in all of the chapters. The page count reduction was achieved through tighter, more concise language. The use of sidebars that present real work experiences, suggestions for further reading, and things to think about have been retained and updated.

As was true with prior editions, we were lucky to have several seasoned managers and teachers who provided essential guidance and thinking regarding the content of this edition. Special thanks go to:

Holland Christie is Manager of the Battle Ground Community Library, one of the libraries in the Fort Vancouver Regional Library District in Vancouver, Washington. She has worked in a multitude of roles within public libraries, including Programming Librarian, Youth Services Librarian, Public Services Manager, and Deputy Director. She received her MLS from the University of Arizona and a bachelor's degree in English from Northern Arizona University. She has worked as a contributing editor and coauthor on several fiction and nonfiction titles; her most recent book project was as coauthor of *Managerial Leadership for Librarians* (Libraries Unlimited, 2017).

Maggie Farrell is Dean of Libraries at the University of Nevada, Las Vegas. She previously served as Dean of Libraries at Clemson University and the University of Wyoming. She writes the quarterly column "Leadership Reflections" for the *Journal of Library Administration*. She also is active in the American Library Association, serving in various leadership roles. She received a BA from the University of Missouri-Kansas City, an MLS from the University of Arizona, and a Master's in Public Administration from Arizona State University.

Patricia Layzell Ward is semi-retired. Currently she is Hon. Archivist Modern Collections to the Ffestiniog Railway Company. She has worked in public and special libraries and enjoyed a long-time involvement in teaching and research. This included posts at North-Western Polytechnic, Loughborough University, Curtin University Western Australia, and the University of Wales Aberystwyth. She is Emeritus Editor of *Library Management*; author of conference papers, journal articles, and reports; examiner to a number of universities; a consultant in Europe, South America, South-East Asia, and Australia; and formerly active in IFLA. She is a Fellow of the Chartered Institute of Library and Information Professionals and holds a master's degree and PhD in Library, Archives and Information Studies from University College London.

Joseph Mika is Professor Emeritus at the School of Information Sciences, Wayne State University, Detroit, where he twice served as Director of the School during his twenty-five-year tenure at the University. He was also Assistant Dean at the School of Library and Information Science at the University of Southern Mississippi, Hattiesburg; Assistant Library Director at Johnson State College, Vermont; and Assistant Library Director at the Ohio State University, Mansfield Campus. His teaching areas included administration, customer service, personnel management, and collection development. He was co-owner of Hartzell-Mika Consulting, a firm in operation from 1999 to 2019, which provided assistance with library director searches, strategic planning facilitation, facility development and planning, and staff and board training sessions. Mika is a retired Colonel in the U.S. Army, having served twenty-nine years in the Army Reserves.

Maggie Saponaro is Director of Collection Development Strategies at the University of Maryland Libraries, where she is responsible for the leadership and vision for the content of purchased and licensed collections across all disciplinary areas and formats. In this position, she directs the collection development work of the Libraries' subject specialist liaison librarians, with primary responsibility for content and budgeting of the UMD Libraries' general collections. She also serves on the Collection Strategies and Services administrative team for policy creation and strategic planning across the entire division. She was formerly Associate Director of Learning Resources at the Alexandria Campus of Northern Virginia Community College and a librarian for the College of Human Resources at Virginia Polytechnic Institute and State University. She is currently interim chair of the NorthEast Regional Library (NERL) Program Council Executive Committee and is a member of the Nexis Uni Advisory Committee. She holds a master's degree in library science from the University of California, Los Angeles, with postgraduate work in the areas of personnel programs and public administration.

A special acknowledgement is due for Camila Alire, coauthor of the prior edition, for allowing the use of some of her managerial experiences that were part of the last edition.

G. Edward Evans, *Flagstaff, Arizona*
Stacey Greenwell, *Lexington, Kentucky*

PART I

Background

CHAPTER 1

Introduction

Management is a role more and more librarians are finding themselves in with little preparation or guidance . . . . Preparing librarians for management roles enhances skills that may be applied in any area throughout their careers.

Mary Ann Venner, 2017

Public libraries have acquiesced to public and government criticism in some ways . . . . As a result of pressure to become more businesslike, public libraries have adopted a "new managerialism."

Masanori Koizumi and Michael M. Widdersheim, 2016

Whether you work in an academic or public library (or another type of library altogether), you will be familiar with the management model of a librarian supervising paraprofessional staff . . . . But does that assumption still hold true when a relatively inexperienced librarian is supervising paraprofessional staff of long tenure?

Autumn Faulkner, 2016

I would argue that it should be required of all students. Instead I propose being more honest about the introductory nature of such courses. No claims should be made that this course will provide students with the skills needed to be successful managers or provide absolute answers.

Robert Holley, 2015

Some of you who are reading this as part of a required management course may be thinking something like, "I do not expect, nor do I want, to be a manager. All I want to do is be a good _____ librarian." You fill in the blank. You are the not the first to have such thoughts, nor are you likely to be the last. Many of us do not think about, or recognize, the pervasiveness of basic management elements (planning, budgeting, and decision making, for example) in our daily lives. And, it is surprising how fast we begin to have to manage when we become librarians.

Patricia Katopol (2016) highlighted the point that many LIS students, including herself, do not expect nor want to be managers: "I don't want to deal with people" and "I don't want to be in authority, I just want a job" (p. 1). She later became a teacher of management in an SLIS program. Those of us involved in preparing this edition likewise had no managerial aspirations as students, but it happened. Odds are high that it will happen to you as well.

For most of us, the workplace takes up a major part of our time. As result, that environment has a significant role in our outlook on life. Don Cohen and Laurence Prusak (2001) stated, "We experience work as a human, social activity that engages the same social needs and responses as the other parts of our lives; the need for connection and cooperation, support, and trust, a sense of belonging, fairness, and recognition" (p. x). Many of those workplace needs are directly influenced by those above us in the organizational structure. In a very real sense, being a good managerial leader is much more than helping make the organization effective.

Perry and Christensen (2015) identified six skill sets a manager in the public sphere should develop— technical, human, conceptual, interpersonal, responsiveness, and focus on results and ethics. We cover such skills in later chapters. However, there are other managerial concerns not directly covered by those skills. The six skills do not address money matters like budgeting, but we will. Also, libraries exist as a place, even in this digital age, and we look at the "place aspect" in one of the chapters. There is also a final chapter focusing on career development, networking, and collaboration.

There are those who claim management is just common sense. They are only marginally correct. What is often labeled "common sense" is, in reality, something one learns, to a greater or lesser degree, over time. Some people believe that because management is "just common sense"—there is nothing to be learned, or taught, about the activity. However, even those who have such beliefs do receive an education of sorts, largely achieved through trial and error, while they try to employ common sense. Also, it is safe to assume that these are the individuals who engage in the most muddling managerial styles

👥 AUTHOR AND ADVISORY BOARD EXPERIENCE

AUTHORS

On Evans's first day as a full-time librarian he was given an assistant. Had he not had some undergraduate coursework in public administration he probably would have made a mess of that responsibility. The library school program he graduated from had no management and administration course requirement. He had taken the academic library course, which had a very modest emphasis on basic management knowledge and much less on skills.

Greenwell should have known that management would be in her future. At seventeen years old, she was left "in charge" of a public library for an hour each Saturday while the librarian took a lunch break. Thankfully, no harm ensued. In her first full-time librarian position, within a few short months she found herself supervising a department of four seasoned librarians. While in library school she grumbled frequently about the required management course, but she became grateful for it not long after graduation.

ADVISORY BOARD

Joe Mika, who taught the basic management course at Wayne State University in Detroit, also points out that students should take the management and administration course because they themselves will have managers. Such coursework will help them to understand their managers and directors and how different administrative styles will affect their careers.

||||| **CHECK THIS OUT**

An interesting article that looks at what library directors do is Douglas Crane's 2015 report on interviews he conducted after he thought he might like to become a director. He undertook the sixteen interviews because he had little idea about what a director actually did. The article, "May I Ask You a Question? Lesson Learned from Interviewing Public Library Leaders," appeared in *Public Libraries* 54, no. 6: 34–38, 2015.

and generally cause the most grief for their colleagues because they seem not to employ a system for their "managing."

Reading about management, taking a course, or attending some workshops on the subject improves your chances of being a better manager. Poor managers hurt their organizations and the people they work with, as well as themselves. Coursework and workshops will not ensure you will be a good manager, but these tools can improve your skills. There is no magic bullet in terms of managerial success; what was effective yesterday may not be tomorrow. Management, at its most basic level, is about people (those you work with as well as yourself), and people are unpredictable. Everyone engages in a little "muddling" regardless of training; however, the amount of muddling decreases as the amount of training and experience increases.

You will have at least some supervisory or managerial responsibilities at least once during your career. Such duties will arise much sooner than you might imagine, if not from day one. The Faulkner quotation at the beginning of this chapter is from an article in which she describes how, within a few months of getting her MLS, she was assigned some project management duties (p. 2). Both the authors and Advisory Board members experienced a similar rapid move into managerial responsibilities (see the sidebar on page 4).

For some individuals, management is a negative concept—manipulative, coercive, anti-employee, and authoritarian are a few words that may come to mind. These thoughts can be accurate at times, especially when managers have little background in basic management methods. Julian Birkinshaw (2010) wrote, "I think that the corruption of management as a word is partly the result of a 100-year period of trying to make sense of the big, industrial, hierarchical, bureaucratic company. All of the words we use around management now are essentially words about how you manage dehumanized, standardized machines that pump out millions and millions of identical products." In the case of libraries, his thoughts are doubly on target. There is the size factor and for-profit nature of the organizations, and then there is the fact that most libraries are in the public and nonprofit sectors, further skewing the application of managerial concepts.

WHAT IS MANAGEMENT?

Perhaps the shortest definition of management is one attributed to Mary Parker Follett (1941): "management is the art of getting things done through people." This definition belies the complexity of management yet concisely sums up management. A longer and more complex definition is Daniel Wren's: "management is an activity essential to organized endeavors that perform certain functions to obtain the effective acquisition, allocation, and utilization of human efforts and physical resources for the purpose of accomplishing some goal" (1979, p. 3). There are literally hundreds of other definitions of the term. All contain two essential elements—people and activities.

There is generally something of a pyramid shape to any organization, with more people involved in working directly with "customers" than in performing solely managerial duties. Most organizations consist of a "top" (few people), a "middle" (several people), and a "bottom" (many people). Certainly, there has been significant flattening of this structure, but a person would be hard-pressed to identify an organization with fewer than three levels. Even in a fully team-based organization there will be some type of team supervisor(s), team leader(s), and team members.

Just what do managers do? There are many answers to this question, and the question actually deals with two issues: function and behavior. Some managerial functions are planning, directing, and budgeting, while the behavioral aspects involve roles such as negotiator or group spokesperson. Management writers tend to emphasize one side or the other. This book is organized according to functions; however, we also explore behavioral aspects and place great emphasis on user needs.

The standard concepts of a manager's functional activities are outlined in a classic management paper by Gulick and Urwick (1937), in which they coined the acronym POSDCoRB, which stands for the following functions:

- Planning
- Organizing
- Staffing
- Directing
- Coordinating
- Reporting
- Budgeting

POSDCoRB functions underlie, in one form or another, all management behavior; however, they do not describe the work of a manager. They merely identify the objectives of a manager's work.

Henry Mintzberg (1973) suggested that because the functions fail to describe managerial behavior they are of little use. We believe this is too harsh a judgment, for if we do not know where we are going (that is, if we do not have objectives), how will we know when we get there? By studying POSDCoRB concepts, a person can gain an understanding of what good management attempts to accomplish.

A reasonable question to ask is, "Do all organizational levels engage in the same activities?" A short answer is "yes," but such an answer obscures many important differences, especially in terms of the skills employed (see figure 1.1). Senior managers tend to devote more time to planning than do other managers, and planning calls for a major use of conceptual skills. They also tend to devote more time to interacting with a variety of people, both internal and external, to the library. Such interaction calls for strong interpersonal relations skills. Finally, they typically engage in very little direct user service work, and thus they make limited use of the technical skills they once employed when they became librarians.

Mahoney, Jardee, and Carroll (1964) discuss the concept of time spent on various activities by "bottoms," "middles," and "tops." For bottoms, the emphasis is almost a mirror opposite of the tops: great emphasis on technical skills, a strong component of human-relations skills, and only limited use of conceptual skills. As always, middles are in

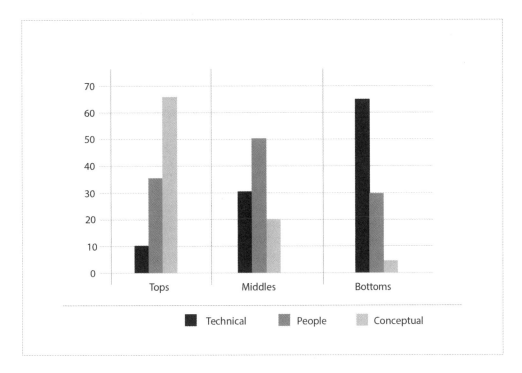

FIGURE 1.1 Organizational Skill Sets

between: less use of technical skills than bottoms but more than tops and a greater need for conceptual skills but less than for tops. You can envision these differences in terms of percentages. For bottoms, perhaps 60 to 70 percent of the emphasis is on technical skills, 20 to 30 percent on human relations, and the balance on conceptual abilities. Middles would perhaps be 20 to 30 percent technical, 10 to 50 percent human relations, and the balance conceptual. Conceptual abilities would be 40 to 50 percent for tops, with technical skills at 10 percent or less, and the balance involving human relations.

ORGANIZATIONAL SKILL SETS

Henry Mintzberg (1971, 1973, 1975) has had the greatest general influence in the area of how managers behave and how knowledge of behavior should change how management is taught. His critique of the functions approach led him to suggest that looking at the roles played would be more effective. He identified ten roles divided among three categories: interpersonal, informational, and decisional. Under interpersonal are three roles: figurehead, leader, and liaison. The informational category contains the roles of nerve center, disseminator, and spokesperson. Decisional activities include the roles of entrepreneur, disturbance handler, resource allocator, and negotiator. We suggest that there is a fourth role in the information category: politician. To some extent such a role is part of being a figurehead, leader, negotiator, and spokesperson. However, given the social and political changes that have occurred since Mintzberg carried out his research in the 1970s, the political role has become ever more important.

Without question, Mintzberg's work added substantially to our understanding of what managers actually do. For teaching and learning purposes, however, the approach does not work very well because the research on which he based his concept focused on top managers and, to a lesser extent, on middle managers, and it focused on observable activities rather than on the reasons for the activities. Also, it does not represent a full picture of a manager's work; as we noted, the role of politician is not clearly delineated. Because of these deficiencies, the classic "functions" approach is still the most useful method for newcomers to conceptualize managerial responsibilities. We will, at various points in later chapters, note how Mintzberg's ideas come into play.

As in many fields, there is a question of whether management is an art or a science. Our belief is that, despite elements of science, management is an art. Although a person can learn the basic concepts, principles, functions, techniques, and roles, each management situation is unique. Two situations may appear similar, but the individuals involved will be different. Even similar situations that involve the same personnel are unique. Thus, what worked yesterday may or may not work today. Your ability to read and anticipate the changes and make appropriate adjustments is the art of management.

There are a great many different approaches for thinking about and applying management concepts and ideas in an organization. They are far too numerous to address adequately in any one book. Here are, however, some very broad approaches that many textbooks that are written for those going into the for-profit world cover to a greater or lesser degree. They are:

- Scientific
- Administrative
- Behavioral
- Management science
- Systems
- Contingency
- Quality
- Composite

Table 1.1 provides an overview of these approaches and looks at some of the proponents. From a library management perspective, today's approach is a composite of the first seven approaches. In many ways the approach used by managers in any organization is a personal version of the composite style.

The scientific approach, which arose early in the Industrial Revolution, focuses on operational efficiency. Time and motion studies that identify the best way to do a task are the hallmark of this approach. A great book that applies this approach to the library is Richard Dougherty's (2008) *Streamlining Library Services: What We Do, How Much Time It Takes, What It Costs, and How We Can Do It Better.*

The administrative approach is reflected in almost every organization regardless of sector. This is the common foundation for almost all introductory management textbooks, including this one. Even when there is an emphasis on organizational leadership the basic management functions (planning, decision making, fiscal management, and the like) must take place.

The behavioral approach is reflected in a concern with employees (their existing skills, interpersonal relations, etc.) and the "social side" of the workplace. Team building draws on the ideas found in this style of management. As we will discuss in later chapters,

TABLE 1.1 Major Management Approaches

APPROACH	MAJOR CONCEPTS	MAJOR FIGURES
Scientific	Time management Efficiency	F. W. Taylor F. and L. Gilbreth H. Gantt
Administrative	Staff motivation Social interaction	H. Fayol, M. Weber L. Urwick, C. Barnard
Behavioral	Organizational structure Holistic organization	H. Munsterberg L. Gilbreth, E. Mayo
Management science	Operations research Mathematical modeling	H. A. Simon, R. Cyert and J. G. March
Systems	Interdependency System theory	L. von Bertalanffy R. L. Ackoff, P. M. Senge
Contingency theory	No universals Environmental setting	M. P. Follett, F. Luthans T. Burns and G. M. Stalker F. Emery and E. Trist
Quality	Customer satisfaction High quality	W. E. Deming, J. Juran
Composite	No single approach Multidimensional	P. Drucker, H. Mintzberg

teams are an important component in many libraries' operational practices. Organizational morale, as you may guess, is another element in the behavioral approach. A book related to libraries and the behavioral approach is Peter Hernon, Joan Giesecke, and Camila Alire's *Academic Librarians as Emotionally Intelligent Leaders* (Westport, CT: Libraries Unlimited, 2007).

Management science focuses on organizational decision making in an effort to make that process as rational as possible. There is an emphasis on mathematical modeling, risk management, and simulations of alternative outcomes. This approach is probably the least drawn upon by libraries. It takes time and effort to do properly and the level of risk for the majority of library decisions is generally modest. It might be beneficial when thinking about starting a new service for a new segment of the service population, locating a new branch, or remodeling, renovating, or building a new physical facility.

A systems approach views everything as interlinked and any change will have some impact elsewhere in the system. Perhaps the most significant aspect of this approach is that the organization's external environment will affect how the organization should go about its activities. For libraries, the environmental focus is central. The external environment is the determining factor in what type of library it is—academic, public, school, or special. Further, a library's primary purpose is to serve the needs of a specific service population. Understanding the current and changing needs of that population is critical to successful operations. (We explore the environmental factor in more depth in the next chapter.)

Contingency theory's primary tenet is there are no universals for managerial practice. This approach does not disregard the basic functions; rather, it acknowledges that their application will vary. It suggests that no two managerial situations are identical, no matter how similar they appear. In a way, the approach is a reflection of the notion that managing things is very much easier than managing people. People are unpredictable, are in a constant state of change, have good days and bad days, have good moods or bad moods, which makes managing them a challenging activity. Essentially, the approach says, "What worked yesterday may not work the same way today." For libraries, situational awareness internally and externally plays a surprisingly large role in managerial activities. Quality concerns are an obvious part of library operations. Poor quality services will, in time, have a negative effect on library support. There are many useful ideas in contingency theory that can help you achieve the best quality possible given the available resources.

The above are the major approaches to management; however, there is a veritable alphabet soup of spinoffs and various combinations with other labels. There are some that are "flashes in the pan" offered by one consultant or another, while others are a little more long-lasting. The point to keep in mind is they draw on elements from the approaches described above. We are not suggesting such ideas do not have their merits; they frequently spotlight an aspect of organizational activity that requires more attention. However, they are rarely *the* factor in organizational success. The real secrets to success lie in understanding the fundamentals and applying them thoughtfully.

YOU AS A FUTURE MANAGER

Earlier we mentioned that many library school students do not see themselves ever becoming managers. However, the fact is that you, more often than not, will quickly find yourself being a "manager." In today's tight economic conditions, libraries face staffing shortages and other financial concerns that result in such things as vacant positions going unfilled and new positions being impossible to secure. These in turn often mean newcomers are asked early on to assume some managerial duties. You are better served, as are those you supervise, if you have already thought about what to do when called upon to assume some supervisory duties before it actually happens.

Today's effective managers employ the full range of options in the management tool kit, choosing which to use at any given time depending on the circumstances—a mix of the contingency and composite approaches. Almost everyone has a preferred managerial style; good managers are flexible and make changes when necessary. Doing so is the art of management—drawing on the basics, developing the skills to assess situations quickly and accurately, and having a finely-honed set of people skills.

If you accept the idea that management is an art, it goes without saying that there is a need to develop a personal style. Furthermore, in moving from one management role to another, slight variations will emerge in that style. Individuals do not respond to everyone in the same way. A management style must change as situations, the organizational culture, and the persons involved change. A corollary of the statement that management is an art is that there is no such thing as a "correct" style. Many of us have had the opportunity to observe two persons of differing personalities and styles effectively manage the

▍▍▍ CHECK THESE OUT

The following list includes some of the most influential publications on managerial practice and thought. They are well worth perusing and it is helpful to spend some time thinking about what they have to say. They are some of the cornerstones for today's approaches to managing organizations.

Ackoff, Russell L., C. West Churchman, and Leonard Arnoff. 1957. *Introduction to Operations Research*. New York: Wiley.

Barnard, Chester. 1938. *Functions of the Executive*. Cambridge, MA: Harvard University Press.

Burns, Thomas, and George M. Stalker. 1961. *The Management of Innovation*. London: Tavistock.

Cyert, Richard M., and James G. March. 1963. *A Behavioral Theory of the Firm.* Englewood Cliffs, NJ: Prentice-Hall.

Deming, W. Edwards. 2000. *The New Economics for Industry, Government, Education*. 2nd ed. Cambridge, MA: MIT Press.

Emery, Fred, and Eric Trist. 1965. "Causal Texture of Organizational Environments." *Human Relations* 18, no. 1: 21–31.

Fayol, Henri. 1962. *Administration Industrielle et Generale*. Paris: Dunnod.

Follett, Mary Parker. 1941. *Dynamic Administration*. London: Pitman.

Gantt, Henry. 1916. *Work, Wages, and Profits.* 2nd ed. New York: Engineering Magazine Co.

——. 1919. *Organizing for Work.* New York: Harcourt, Brace, and Howe.

Gilbreth, Lillian. 1914. *Psychology of Management*. New York: Sturgis and Walton.

Gulick, Luther, and Lyndall Urwick. 1937. *Papers on the Science of Administration*. New York: Institute of Public Administration, Columbia University.

Juran, Joseph. 1995. *Managerial Breakthrough*. New York: McGraw-Hill.

Luthans, Fred. 1973. "Contingency Theory of Management: A Path Out of the Jungle." *Business Horizons* 16, no. 3: 62–72.

Mayo, Elton. 1933. *The Human Problems of an Industrial Civilization*. Salem, NH: Ayer.

Mintzberg, Henry. 1973. *The Nature of Managerial Work*. Englewood Cliffs, NJ: Prentice Hall.

Munsterberg, Hugo. 1913. *Psychology and Industrial Efficiency*. New York: Houghton Mifflin.

Senge, Peter. 1990. *The Fifth Discipline*. New York: Random House.

Simon, Herbert. 1947. *Administrative Behavior*. New York: Macmillan.

Taylor, Fredrick. 1947. *Principles of Scientific Management*. New York: Harper.

Urwick, Lyndall. 1943. *Elements of Business Administration*. New York: Harper and Bros.

von Bertalanffy, Ludwig. 1950. "Theory of Open Systems in Physics and Biology." *Science* 3, no. 1: 23–29.

Weber, Max. 1947. *The Theory of Social and Economic Organizations*. Translated by A. M. Henderson and Talcott H. Parsons. New York: Free Press of Glencoe.

same organization. Such an experience is the clearest demonstration that a variety of management styles can be effective in the same work situation.

You might well start the thinking process by assessing your personal strengths and weaknesses. Here are some sample questions to consider:

- What are the positive work experiences that I've had?
- What was it about those experiences that made them good?
- What were my worst work experiences? What made them so?
- What type of direction or supervision do I like?
- What type of directions am I comfortable giving?
- Can I, and how do I, tell someone that he or she has done a good or a bad job?
- What management approaches do I find most comfortable?

As you develop answers to such questions, you are drafting your own management style.

One of our professional mottos is "Everyone must get their hands dirty from time to time." This means that when a major task comes up, the entire staff does the work—from the top down. Having the entire organization shelf reading, shifting materials in the stacks, or doing whatever else needs to be done results in everyone feeling like part of a team and that there will be mutual support when needed.

FOR FURTHER THOUGHT

Regularly scanning recent issues of general and library-specific management journals is one easy method to keep current with trends and new approaches. On the general side we like the *Harvard Business Review, Public Administration Review,* and *MIT Sloan Management Review.* On the library side we like *Bottom Line, Library Management, Library Leadership and Management, Journal of Library Administration,* and *Evidence Based Library and Information Practice.*

PUBLIC AND NONPROFIT SECTORS

If you even briefly scanned the books listed in the sidebar suggesting resources about the major approaches to management, you probably noticed they all are focused on the for-profit organization. That might cause you to think, "Wait a minute, this is all about organizations making money. Libraries are different; how can any of this apply?" This is a good question to ask. The answer is, "they do when it is modified to fit the sector(s)."

What "sectors" are we talking about? Looking broadly at organizations, the common approach is to place an organization into one of three categories: private/for-profit, nonprofit, and public. There is some cross-over as a public sector organization may have non-profit status—libraries generally have dual status. We explore the non-profit status in the chapter on legal concerns (having such status is a function of Internal Revenue Service regulations). Do sector differences really matter? Yes, they do indeed. As we will discuss in the next chapter, an organization's environment and sector more or less determines how it goes about its business. Even libraries in for-profit organizations are nonprofit in the sense that they are not expected to directly increase the "bottom line." Libraries are, to use a common for-profit label, "cost centers" rather than revenue centers.

One of the major sector differences is how the organization determines success. There is one common success measure that all for-profit organizations share—profit. The other two sectors lack such a common measure, which means there are challenges in assessing

👥 AUTHORS' AND ADVISORY BOARD EXPERIENCE

The authors employed different management styles; however, each was successful in its own way.

Evans's preferred method was a mix of management by objectives, maximum delegation, and trust in those with whom he worked. That was the starting point in each new work relationship and remained so for as long as the individuals were successful. When there were problems, he adjusted the style to better match the situation.

Greenwell tends to take a participatory, team-based approach. She likes multiple perspectives and input on a situation. This approach is motivating for the team, and it typically produces educated decisions. Like Evans, she puts trust in colleagues through frequent delegation—as long as that continues to work.

Patricia Layzell-Ward identified her management style as situational, having worked in different types of information and library settings, small and large, and in three different countries. All had their own cultures and understanding each culture and how the parent organization operated was a major challenge. Each work setting was different and to be "successful" it was essential to quickly understand the challenges and how people responded to the setting. Moving between situations means that the manager needs to be a good listener and quickly adapt to changing circumstances. Without this it is difficult for team members to adapt to each other.

Joseph Mika's preferred administrative style is based on contingency theory, and he refers to it as "situational." He has been a library administrator, library consultant, and active in library and information science (LIS) programs for over forty years, and he has also been influenced by education in management courses from business schools, LIS classes, and U.S. Army programs. Over the years what developed was a participative management style that considers the individual who is being managed and that determines actions taken. As he put it, "my style was influenced by the U.S. Army, which had an approach much like that of Follett—get results through people—but over time the approach mellowed to get results *with* people."

performance, even among libraries of the same type. It can also make accountability more complex. The closest thing to a common measure of success is providing a social good or value, an underlying purpose of organizations in the two sectors.

Being in the public sector affects the library's mission, goals, and how it goes about planning (it requires more external input and direction setting). The number of stakeholders is considerably larger than for organizations in the other sectors. Perhaps fiscal management is the most distinct difference. Partisan politics become important. Hiring and firing are also very different. Even the nature of ethics plays out in a somewhat different way. We will explore these differences in later chapters.

Political "winds" play a surprisingly large role in managerial decisions for organizations in the public sector and to a lesser extent for the non-profits. Public sector operating funds are taxpayers' money and clearly the political winds matter in the budgeting process. Non-profits have less impact to think about; however, political attitudes regarding donations and grants can cause concerns.

You must be aware of such differences when reading about research done in the profit sector. This also applies to library literature, at least in the early days of a "new" approach.

Time is the true test for any new idea or method, not the volume of literature it generates. We are *not* suggesting you should ignore such ideas, rather, we suggest you take a hard look at where the idea has been implemented and why. Table 1.2 provides an overview of the some of the most important sector differences.

TABLE 1.2 Profit and Nonprofit Differences

	PRIVATE/ PROFIT	PUBLIC/NONPROFIT
Purpose	Maximum income	Social good
Ownership	Limited	Very broad/society
Stakeholders	Limited	Very broad
Governance	Internal	External control
Funding	Sales/sell shares	Taxes, donations/grants
Operational freedom	Almost unlimited	Highly circumscribed
Setting a "price"	Great freedom	Very limited freedom
Decision making	Great freedom	Highly circumscribed
Planning	Internal	Internal/high external input

🔒 KEY POINTS TO REMEMBER

- Managing is a pervasive activity, and it has been part of humankind's environment for as long as people have lived together.
- Thinking you will never become a "manager" as a librarian is counterproductive, as almost all of us do manage to some degree and much sooner than expected.
- Learning about management concepts and practices does not ensure success, but that knowledge can assist in avoiding mistakes that hurt everyone involved.
- Studying the major approaches to management and some of the major thinkers is part of the learning process for successful managers.
- Understanding the options available as well as understanding yourself is important in developing your own style.
- Locking into a single style is not wise, as different people require different approaches.
- Being flexible is one of the cornerstones to being a successful manager.

REFERENCES

Birkinshaw, Julian. 2010. "Rethinking Management." *MIT Sloan Management Review* 51, no. 4: 14–15.

Cohen, Don, and Laurence Prusak. 2001. *In Good Company: How Social Capital Makes Organizations Work.* Cambridge, MA: Harvard Business School Press.

Dougherty, Richard M. 2008. *Streamlining Library Services: What We Do, How Much Time It Takes, What It Costs, and How We Can Do It Better.* Lanham, MD: Scarecrow Press.

Faulkner, Autumn. 2016. "Teaching a New Dog Old Tricks: Supervising Veteran Staff as an Early Career Librarian." *Library Leadership and Management* 31, no. 1: 1-15. https://journals.tdl.org/llm/index.php/llm/issue/view/378.

Follett, Mary Parker. 1941. *Dynamic Administration.* London: Pitman.

Gulick, Luther, and Lyndall Urwick. 1937. *Papers on the Science of Administration.* New York: Institute of Public Administration, Columbia University.

Holley, Robert P. 2015. "Education and Training for Library Management." *Journal of Library Administration* 55, no. 7: 595-603.

Katopol. Patricia. 2016. "Putting Up Road Blocks on Your Path Toward Management." *Library Leadership and Management* 30, no. 4: 1-5. https://journals.tdl.org/llm/index.php/llm/issue/view/377.

Koizumi, Masanori, and Michael M. Widdersheim. 2016. "Surpassing the Business Model: A Public Sphere Approach to Public Library Management." *Library Review* 65, nos.6/7: 404-19.

Mahoney, Thomas, Thomas Jardee, and Stephen Carroll. 1964. "The Job(s) of Management." *Industrial Management* 4, no. 2: 97-110.

Mintzberg, Henry. 1971. "Managerial Work: Analysis from Observation." *Management Science* 18, no. 2: B97-B110.

_____. 1973. *The Nature of Managerial Work.* Englewood Cliffs, NJ: Prentice Hall.

_____. 1975. "The Manager's Job: Folklore and Fact." *Harvard Business Review* 53, no. 5: 49-61.

Perry, James L., and Robert K. Christensen. 2015. *Handbook of Public Administration.* 3rd ed. New York: Wiley.

Venner, Mary Ann. 2017. Mentoring Librarians for Management Roles in Academic Libraries. https://www.informedlibrarian.com/guestForum.cfm?FILE=gf1710.htm.

Wren, Daniel. 1979. *The Evolution of Management Thought.* 2nd ed. New York: Wiley.

CHAPTER 2

Organizational Issues

Environment scanning is not only a tool for business. Every organization, whether it is a for-profit or a nonprofit, needs to be aware of its environment if it wants to be competitive—and you must be competitive if you are going to survive.

Patricia Katopol, 2014

Organizational survival depends upon satisfactorily executing a plan and achieving a set of conscious or subconscious, predetermined objectives amidst calculated chaos and controlled disorder.

Michael Meeks, 2015

Each organization has its own unique culture, created over time through the shared attitudes, values, beliefs, perceptions, and customs of its members.

Jill Mierke and Vicki Williamson, 2017

Successful managers operate on the basis of the precept "adaptability is essential for survival," even if they are not aware of it. It is a precept that has a very long history—billions of years when you think of the geological and biological record. To adapt effectively managers must understand their current operating environment as well as ponder possible changes in that environment.

Organizations have a life and, like people, change over time. They are created and affected by outside factors, have a life span, and, often, eventually die. Someone suggested there are no more than 63 organizations still in existence that were established before the fifteenth century—most of which are religious organizations or universities. Organizations die because of several factors, one of which is a failure to adjust to a changing environment. A *Harvard Business Review* (2016) article reporting on recent research noted in a study of 29,688 publicly traded companies in existence between 1960 and 2009 that the life span of firms has been decreasing. The article went on to note that the researchers suggested that firms that don't monitor or understand the rapidly changing digital environment were the least likely to survive.

Organizations face challenges over which they have little control. However, just like us, they can develop plans for how to address potential challenges. Such planning may well reduce the negative consequences and, in some circumstances, even benefit organizations by anticipating these events. (We explore planning in some depth in chapter 7.)

There are two broad organizational categories—formal (voluntary and involuntary membership) and informal. Beyond these broad types there are variations, such as formal for-profit, formal non-profit, open/public membership, and restricted/private member-ship. Libraries fall into what Eleanor Glor (2008) labeled public service organizations (PSO), which are agencies that work directly with the public.

Like people, organizations grow and change, and so do their goals. Those goals may change over time to such an extent that the founders would have difficulty recognizing "their" organization. Goals expand and contract as a result of successes and failures as well as from changes in the environment. In time, an organization can change so much that some individuals leave because their personal goals or values no longer match the organization's goals.

FORMAL ORGANIZATIONS

Chester Barnard (1956), whom we mentioned in chapter 1, studied how organizations develop, function, and change through time. Human organizations, according to Barnard, consist of five basic elements: size, interdependence, input, throughput, and output. Organizations vary in *size* from one as large as the U.S. federal government to one as small as two people. Sometimes people forget that two- and three-person operations, such as small school and public libraries, are, in fact, organizations. As such, they share most of the same organizational issues as large ones.

Interdependence means there is a recognition of shared common goals as well as an understanding that by working together it will be easier to achieve these goals. Disagreement and tension will inevitably arise over how to achieve the goals, but the value of the shared benefits maintains organizational cohesion.

Established goals require a list of the *inputs* to achieve them, such as people, materials, money, and information. After acquiring the resources, the organization uses the resources (*throughput*) effectively to achieve the desired results. The end product of that processing is the *output*. Output can be as tangible as an automobile or as intangible as the answer to a reference question.

As an organization becomes more complex, its goals and objectives may conflict with one another, with other organizations, and even with some of its staff. Handling such conflicts becomes a normal fact of managerial life.

One major source of organizational conflict is competition for resources. No matter how "well off" others may think an organization is, within the organization there is a finite pool of resources to distribute. During any given period, some resources may be more available than others. In the 1950s, libraries worried about material resources, physical facilities, and funds to support intellectual freedom. During the 1960s, the big resource problem was personnel. In the 1970s and 1980s, it was financial support. In the 1990s, libraries faced the burden of having adequate funding for information communication technology (ICT) equipment and electronic resources. In the first two decades of this century, libraries became concerned about competitors such as Google, a very difficult economic environment, and the public's view about the value of library services. While the specifics vary, the conflict over resources remains a constant. We explore this type of competition in several later chapters, especially in chapter 17, "Managing Money."

Whatever the source, managers must have a tolerance for conflict. Methods of dealing with conflict situations range from using personal judgment to negotiation. Management writers have long addressed conflict control. They look at a series of interpersonal and interorganizational interactions that constantly occur:

- Individuals interact with the environment.
- Individuals interact with one another.
- Individuals interact with organizations.
- Organizations interact with other organizations.
- Organizations interact with the environment.

In the past, managers had a tendency to focus on internal issues, such as improving operations to achieve organizational goals more efficiently and effectively. That focus usually meant looking at technology and equipment, people, tasks, and structure from within the organization rather than looking at the external environment. Today, if their organizations are to succeed, managers must devote significant time to studying what is taking place in the world around them.

PUBLIC AND NONPROFIT SECTOR ORGANIZATIONS

Both public and nonprofit status carries several implications for managers, and libraries fall into one or both of these sectors. There are several important differences between the two. One such implication that we did not mention in chapter 1 is the need for transparency in almost all organizational processes. This almost always means significant project planning to secure stakeholder input.

What was once a sharp line dividing for-profit and nonprofit organizations has been blurring since the late 1990s. There is also a blurring of the line between donation-based and partially publicly funded nonprofits.

One factor driving the changes in both sectors is collaboration. Certainly, there has always been some useful and productive cooperation and collaboration among various PSOs on a voluntary basis. What is different today is that a large number of funding sources for nonprofits are more or less forcing cooperative ventures through funding preferences for collaborative projects. One such example is IMLS (the Institute of Museum and Library Services), which indicates in its "Grant Eligibility" that "ineligible organizations may still be able to participate in grant programs through partnerships with eligible organizations" (https://www.imls.gov/grants/available/national-leadership-grants-libraries). Many of the IMLS grants are for consortia or statewide activities. Single institutions can apply, and some do succeed; however, limited funds often mean collaborative projects have a definite edge in the process. Such joint efforts over time begin to blur the organizational difference. Stretching limited funds through partnerships is important; however, when the organization's real goal is just to secure extra funding, some strange partnerships can come into being.

Another feature of today's PSOs, regardless of type, is growing "commercialization." Almost all donation-based organizations face the issue of expanding their support base (you can think of this as increasing market share, a for-profit concept) as well as retaining their major donors to preserve customer loyalty. Publicly funded organizations, which include most libraries, are under pressure to "recover costs" for various services. To take a standard library service example—photocopy service—setting the cost of copies is very much like how for-profit organizations set their product prices (materials, labor, and equipment costs plus what the market will bear).

Faruggia Gianfranco (2007) summed up the changing world of nonprofits in a literature review:

Does all this sound like mission-driven stewardship or brazen commercialization for the sake of the nonprofit industry? . . . [T]he literature seems to offer very strong indications that the sector is more of an industry. . . . How can the sector possibly return to . . . the world in which community-oriented philanthropy in the pursuit of enlightened self-interest is no longer as compelling as ensuring short-term returns to stockholders and gaining market share? (p. 10)

He offers no answer to the last question beyond suggesting there should be broad-based community discussion of the issues.

With the exception of special libraries in the for-profit sector (such as law and corporate libraries), most libraries depend, to a greater or lesser degree, on tax funds derived from a government jurisdiction (community, county, state, or national) to cover operating expenses. Government funding always means that political issues are important factors in decisions about when, where, and if to spend money. A library manager who fails to recognize this fact will find herself or himself getting fewer and fewer dollars.

Politics (not partisan politics but the politics of decision making and organizational politics) and the political process are part of maintaining publicly funded libraries. The word "politics" has many definitions and connotations, most of which cover the following: the acquisition and maintenance of power, competition and conflict over scarce resources, allocation of resources, and determination of who gets what, when, why, and how. With the exception of the first point, libraries constantly find themselves involved in these "political" areas. Taxpayer "revolts," a global trading environment, and varying economies demonstrate that politics can dramatically affect funding for library operations and underscore the need to constantly monitor the world around us.

Most libraries (with the exception of a few private libraries) are a part of a larger organization. As part of a larger organization, you must also be aware of what the "whole" does as well as recognize that the whole will have a say in what the library does.

Beverly Lynch (1974, p. 127) described four very important factors to consider when studying the library environment:

- the nature of the environment itself
- the relationship among the libraries within a set of organizations
- the characteristics of the exchanges that take place among libraries
- the impact that the environment has upon the libraries' internal structure and operations

ENVIRONMENT AND THE ORGANIZATION

Libraries have a tripartite environment. As mentioned earlier, few libraries exist as independent entities; rather, they are part of a larger organization—a city, a university, a school district, or a corporation. First, there is the internal library environment, over which managers have or should have reasonably good control. Second, there is the parent organizational environment, over which librarians may have some, if slight, influence. Third, there is the environment beyond the parent institution, over which almost no one has control. All three environments require monitoring if the library is to be successful.

Some years ago, F. Emery and E. L. Trist (1965) identified four basic types of organizational environments regardless of type of organization: *placid-randomized, placid-clustered, disturbed-reactive,* and *turbulent.* Although Emery and Trist were not concerned with

 **TRY THIS**

What are the characteristics of library services that affect the management function? Try to identify six characteristics, drawing on this text and on your experience as a customer.

libraries, their four types of environments can be applied to library environments.

A *placid-randomized* environment is one in which the organization assumes that both the goals and the dangers are basically unchanging. (A danger is something that would adversely affect the viability of the organization.) Organizational goals are long-term and seldom need adjustment. Such organizations assume that changes or dangers to their well-being occur randomly and that here is little or no predictability as to when changes or dangers will be encountered. In such an environment, the organization collects information to meet long-term goals, and these goals are considered predictable. In the past, large research libraries and archives were typical examples of organizations that operated in a placid-randomized environment. Today, and for the foreseeable future, it seems unlikely that many libraries will be operating in a placid environment.

Many libraries operate in a *placid-clustered* environment, which is where goals are primarily long-term. but the organization must quickly adjust its goals when external factors warrant. In this environment, the organization assumes that dangers, and to some extent opportunities, will arise in clusters. Furthermore, the organization assumes that it will need to expend some effort in identifying and collecting information about the clusters. A library example from collection management is when the collection is relatively unchanging, but time, energy, and money are directed toward identifying changes in the parent (a new degree program or subject emphasis, for example) or external environment (changes in exchange rates or information delivery systems). Most educational institutions and public libraries operate in this type of environment. They set long-term goals and rarely change those goals, although they may change short-term objectives. However, they do recognize that dangers exist, such as changing public attitudes about the value of social services generally and library services specifically. Once the questioning starts, it generally expands in scope (a phenomenon known as "clustering") and does not disappear quickly. Also, new service opportunities arise as new technologies become available. These opportunities may counteract some or all of the dangers (competition, for example) arising from the new technologies.

Disturbed-reactive environments are those in which there are active organizational competitors. Two examples of library competitors are the Google Books Library Project for academic libraries and handheld reading devices to accommodate e-books for public libraries. In the disturbed-reactive environment, having prompt, accurate information about what the competitors are doing—and, when possible, what they are planning to do—is important. One label for this type of information is "competitive intelligence." Jan Davis (2008) noted the importance of competitive intelligence for clients of special libraries: "The conference theme, Energize, Explore, Evolve, was exemplified by the popularity of the competitive intelligence (CI) sessions. Indeed, law librarians were energized and ready to explore their evolving role as CI professionals with law firms" (p. 14). For libraries there are two aspects of CI. First, it can assist the library's clients in learning about what their competitors are doing. Second, it can gather information that may assist the library itself to become ever more competitive.

|||||| **CHECK THIS OUT**

Monice Kaczonowski in 2008 published an article on competitive intelligence in a library context. "Uniting in Competitive Intelligence" (*AALL Spectrum* 12, no. 5: 26–28, 2008).

Jan Schwarz (2007) also defined the concept: "Competitive intelligence (CI) has been perceived as an activity primarily concerned with analyzing the competitors of an organization and as an activity that considers the environment of that organization" (p. 55). For special libraries, CI has been used to assess what the parent organization's competitors are doing or may do. This type of CI is something in which for-profit organizations are interested in order to keep or increase their market share. All libraries can identify some useful techniques in CI to assist in effectively dealing with their competitors.

Although an organization in a disturbed-reactive environment has long-term goals, it revises its goals in light of information received about competitors' activities. Special libraries like business and industrial libraries operate in such an environment. Here, four or five years may represent a significant time span for long-term goals.

Finally, there is the *turbulent* environment. Not only do competitors exist but also the level of competition necessitates focused efforts in order to survive. As a result of knowing what others are doing or planning to do, an organization may make a radical change in its basic purposes. Anyone who reads the business section of a newspaper encounters examples of organizations that made successful basic goal changes and those that failed because they did not change. On a slightly less extreme level, libraries serving research and development teams experience occasional abrupt shifts in service emphasis. Thus, the organizational environment is also an information environment, and the nature of the environment affects the nature of library activities.

It is as Konstantinos Karyotakis and Vassillis Moustakis (2016) noted: "In the public sector, value can be created by social outcome, services or trust. Increased efficiency, improved quality, user satisfaction, greater usage of services, greater equity (fairness) in service provision or greater choice or variety, constitute facets of value creation in services" (p. 49). Although they were not writing about libraries, their list of how to increase value in the public sector fits the library context.

Managers must develop methods to assist in effectively handling a changing environment. The external environment has several major dimensions: sociocultural, technological, political, legal, economic, and institutional. In addition, there exist many sub-variables of the major dimensions that the manager must also consider, including dimensions on local, regional, national, and international levels. Other sub-variables, such as customers, suppliers, competitors, and sources of funding, become factors in developing an effective service organization. Information and communication technologies are a major issue in today's environments.

Governmental change (such as election outcomes) can produce policies and regulations that affect, for example, the management of staff. Political change can also introduce the possibility of additional funding if governments can be persuaded of the benefits of investing in library services. Managers working in countries that have volatile exchange rates should keep a close watch on economic developments that may benefit—or limit—their spending power. These are just some of the reasons why managers need to scan the

SOMETHING TO PONDER

In terms of libraries, compare the differences and similarities between Emery and Trist's concepts and those of Burns and Stalker.

environment for developments that may affect their services, seek opportunities and benefits, and watch for threats and impending problems.

Burns and Stalker (1961) identified two organizational systems that help match the organizational structure to the environment: "mechanistic" and "organic." Mechanistic systems emphasize specialization and a hierarchical organizational structure. This approach creates a stable organization that tends to change slowly, which is most suitable for placid environments. Organic systems typically emphasize work groups and a flat structure. Such systems work well in turbulent environments. Based on their research, Burns and Stalker suggested that some combination of mechanistic and organic systems was most effective in the disturbed environment. Lawrence and Lorsch (1967) further extended this work by looking at the relationship between departmental and/or unit values and goals and the environment. They found that organizations operating in changing environments had highly differentiated units and made use of committees, task forces, and a flat structure to achieve intra-unit coordination.

There are several ways to apply the concepts of Burns and Stalker to today's organizations. Martin Harris (2006) drew upon their concepts in a paper exploring innovation and organizational structure. His finding suggested that a "bureaucratic" structure may not have as negative an impact as some writers with a "post-bureaucratic organizational" view have contended. Ingrid Bonn (2005) explored methods for improving strategic thinking and relationships between environmental issues and organizations. The concepts of Burns and Stalker played a significant role in her analysis.

||||| CHECK THIS OUT

A good article, if brief, on organizations and their environments is Walter McFarland's 2015 article "Mastering Change Management" (*The Public Manager* 44, no. 1: 23–24, 2015).

Another good article that explores the reasons for examining the environment of a public organization is by Rhys Andrews, George Boyne, and Richard Walker "Strategy Content and Organizational Performance" (*Public Administration Review* 66, no. 1: 52–63, 2006).

ENVIRONMENTAL SCANNING

Sun-Tzu's *The Art of War* explores some concepts that can be useful for managers. Perhaps one of the most useful concepts, and which is related to this chapter's topics, comes from its first chapter:

"The art of war is of vital importance to the State. It is a matter of life and death, a road either to safety or to ruin. Hence it is a subject of inquiry which can on no account be neglected." (https://www.goodreads.com/work/quotes/3200649)

By substituting two words, we have the focus of this section: "Environment is a matter of life and death."

Environmental scanning is a structured process for gathering information about activities, trends, relationships, competitors, potential dangers, and any other factors in the environment that can impact the organization. The data collected can inform a variety of management activities, but they are essential in planning and decision making. Other library activities that may benefit include fiscal and collection management. With a formalized scanning process in place, you can avoid some pitfalls or being blindsided. Lacking such a process, the chances for long-term viability decline (Albright 2004). In today's rapidly changing world, monitoring the environment is important for any organization. (See the 2016 *Harvard Business Review* article we cited earlier in the chapter.)

Most libraries should examine some basic environmental factors on a regular basis. These are some of the common variables:

- **Customers**—user behavior and needs are the foundation upon which one should build information services.
- **Competitors/market**—libraries face competition from each other as well as from other information services.
- **Funding sources**—funding is crucial for effective library services, and knowing what factors are affecting the source(s) is the key to successful planning.
- **Suppliers**—two key categories of suppliers are firms that provide information materials services (jobbers and publishers, for example) and those that handle library and information service technologies. Factors impacting such firms will impact the library and end users and vice versa.
- **Labor issues**—an important ongoing concern is the availability of qualified people for positions in libraries, both professional and support staff.
- **Legal and regulatory factors**—legal, regulatory, and legislative factors impact managerial actions in many ways, from facilities to staffing. A worldwide example of a legal concern for libraries is copyright.
- **Economic trends**—economic factors affect information services in two primary ways: what you can buy with available funds and how much money is available to spend.
- **Technology**—technology is a critical variable for information services, as we will discuss in some depth in chapter 19, "Managing Technology ."
- **Political changes and trends**—any library that derives a significant portion of its operating funds from public sources must monitor political trends. Thinking about the potential implications of a changing scene is useful when developing short-term and medium-term plans.
- **Sociocultural factors**—by sociocultural factors, we mean the values, attitudes, demographics, historic context, and customs of the society in which the organization operates. All of the factors have obvious implications for libraries.

> ▎▎▎▎ **CHECK THESE OUT**
>
> You will find an excellent detailed discussion of environmental scanning in John D. Stoffel's *Strategic Issues Management: A Comprehensive Guide to Environmental Scanning* (Tarrytown, NY: Elsevier Science, 1994).
>
> An old example of a full scanning project in a library environment is Ray Lester and Judith Waters' *Environmental Scanning and Business Strategy* (Library and Information Research Report 75, London, British Library, 1989). While the data is clearly out of date, the methodology of conducting such studies is still sound.
>
> James Castiglione's 2008 article, "Environmental Scanning: An Essential Tool for Twenty-First Century Librarianship" is an excellent article about the process and libraries (*Library Review* 57, no. 7: 528–36, 2008).
>
> An example of a library scan is from the Association of College and Research Libraries. ACRL Research Planning and Review Committee's *Environmental Scan 2017* (Chicago: American Library Association, www.ala.org/acrl/sites/ala.org.acrl/files/content/publications/whitepapers/EnvironmentalScan2017.pdf). This scan is conducted every other year and is well worth reviewing for those interested in academic libraries.

FORECASTING

Forecasting is one method for looking at societal changes and thinking about what future implications such changes may have. Jack Malgeri (2010) defined forecasting as "the ability to develop and maintain a forward-looking perspective and to anticipate emerging opportunities and problems by continually scanning the environment for trends and new developments" (p. 39). There is a saying about forecasts: "The only certainty is the forecast will be wrong." While this holds true more often than not, a forecast does not have to be 100 percent accurate to be useful. If nothing else, forecasting requires managers to consider possible changes in the environment and to think about how to respond if change does occur. Being proactive is almost always better than being reactive. In essence, scanning and forecasting provide highly valuable data for planning and many other library processes.

Normally, forecasting focuses on factors that are critical to the organization. Some factors may be controllable to an extent, while others are beyond the organization's control (such as population, birthrate, and high school graduation rate which are of importance to libraries). Often, the data needed for forecasting are already available in the library; other data will be available from the parent organization or obtainable from government agencies. Forecasts can be qualitative or quantitative in character.

Like all methods intended to anticipate future events, environmental scanning and forecasting success is a function of what you look at and how you interpret what you see. Wayne Stewart, Ruth May, and Arvind Kalia (2008) noted that "Because environmental issues are often ambiguous and require interpretation for issue diagnosis, perceptions are critical in guiding decision making" (p. 86). Their main point is that the more ambiguous the situation, the more time and effort you should put into data gathering in order to reduce as much ambiguity as possible.

John Castiglione (2008) made a strong case for libraries to engage in efforts that help identify future trends, whether it is called scanning, forecasting, futuring, or some other term: "Libraries of every type and size are facing similar resource constraints and

SOMETHING TO PONDER

Think about the future and then list four changes that are most likely to impact a service of your choice. Rate those changes as most likely, possible, or probable in terms of one year, five years, and ten years. How difficult was it to identify the potential changes? How satisfied are you with your predictions? Persuade a colleague to do the exercise and then compare results.

competitive pressures from corporate entities—external to the library—that are vying to provide service directly to stakeholders that libraries have traditionally served. . . . [O]ur professional associations need to understand and monitor—on a global basis—the shifting competitive landscape" (p. 528). We agree that our associations ought to assist in the scanning process and are perhaps best able to do so on a global basis. However, only the individual library can economically assess the future local trends and how those trends may impact the library's services.

ORGANIZATIONAL CULTURE

Organizations, like societies, have a culture as part of their internal environment, which each member learns, or should learn, in order to be an effective member. That culture plays a significant role in how the organization operates. Unless someone acts in a manner contrary to the cultural norm, it is common for staff members to be unaware of the culture's influence on their actions—"learning" the culture is seldom a formalized process.

Organizational culture and the external environment may at first glance appear unrelated. However, they are related in that the external environment influences the internal organizational culture. To be effective, environmental scanning and assessing the implications of changes in the environment must be a complex activity. Some staff member is expected to do it. If the organizational culture is such that everyone understands the importance of scanning and can assist in the process, the activity will be even more beneficial for the library.

Just what is "organizational culture?" Edgar Schein (1992) described organizational culture (OC) as having three major components—artifacts, shared values, and shared assumptions. Artifacts are those things that you can observe or hear as the staff goes about their work (behaviors or comments, for example). Such staff actions reflect the underlying shared values and assumptions that exist within the organization. Thomas

CHECK THIS OUT

A good book that addresses the issues of perceptions regarding what to look for when engaging in scanning activities, as well as how to assess potential issues, is Bob Johansen's *Get There Early: Sensing the Future to Compete in the Present* (San Francisco: Berrett-Koehler, 2007).

Kell and Gregory Carrott (2005) noted, "Corporate culture, like personal character, is an amorphous quality that exerts a powerful influence" (p. 22). They further noted both the positive and negative aspects of organizational culture. Although we acknowledge that the concept is somewhat amorphous, some elements are generally agreed upon. One such element is that members of the organization (consciously or not) share a set of values, assumptions, and expectations regarding what the organization is "about," how things should be done, and what is important, such as environmental scanning, and what is acceptable. Staff members act on these views even though the culture is rarely articulated, much less recorded. You learn it, as you learn social culture, through observation and through making mistakes. Although it is an internal environment, it changes as the result of changes in the external environment. Managers who ignore this internal environment do so at their peril—understanding the culture can make all the difference when it comes time for the organization to make adjustments because of external factors.

One key element in an organization's culture is the view of top leadership, which sets the tone for the rest of the staff. Supervisors and middle managers further set the tone in their areas of responsibility based on what they perceive to be top management views. Jason Pett (2016) noted that "a healthy culture starts with clarity and transparency at the top" (p. 70). In the same article, Sandy Pundmann commented, "The hallmark of an unhealthy culture is the 'no bad news' approach" (p.70). There are other factors as well, as Sarah Rutherford (2001) noted: "An organization's culture is also heavily influenced by its past and its environment" (p. 374). According to Geoffrey Bloor and Patrick Dawson (1994), organizational culture arises from interactions among these elements:

- Operating and cultural systems (dynamic or ongoing interaction).
- Historical factors (founders' vision, for example).
- Societal context (external to organization).
- External organizational environment (competition).
- Professional external environment (association values, and practices).

▥ CHECK THESE OUT

A sound article that reflects the "anthropological" approach to organizational culture in a library setting, is Jason Martin's "Symbols, Sagas, Rites, and Rituals: An Overview of Organizational Culture in Libraries" (*College and Research Libraries News* 73, no. 6: 348–349, 2012).

An article that explores the various "disciplines" that come into play in OC is Katarzyna Lukasik, Paula Bajdor, Iwetta Budzik-Nowodzinska, and Katarzyna Brendzel-Skowera's "Interdisciplinary Paradigms of Organizational Culture. (*European Scientific Journal* 12, no. 13: 199–208, 2016).

Another article that illustrates the interwoven nature of organizational culture and processes is Faith Oguz's "Organizational Influences in Technology Adoption Decisions: A Case Study of Digital Libraries" (*College and Research Libraries* 77, no. 3: 314–34, 2016).

Two older but excellent articles about library organizational culture are William Sannwald's (2000) "Understanding Organizational Culture" (*Public Libraries* 14, no. 1: 8–13) and Ronald Patkus and Brendan Rapple's (2000) "Changing the Culture of Libraries" (*Public Libraries* 14, no. 4: 197–204).

👥 ADVISORY BOARD EXPERIENCE

Holland Christie worked underneath a supervisor who employed the "no bad news" approach; staff sensed that any criticism would be unwelcome, and they bit their tongues accordingly. Unfortunately, ignoring issues and problems didn't make them have less of an impact, and morale suffered. It wasn't until a new supervisor was hired that things improved, and changes were made based on staff recommendations that would never have been heard under the previous supervisor.

Joseph Mika has been fortunate to work in five different states and cities. He has enjoyed each location, while often hearing others complain about the same environment. What made the difference for him was his approach. Because he was the new professional, rather than expecting others to adapt to him, he adapted to the environment, by adopting the business, academic, and cultural norms of the institution and the city in which he lived. Having grown up in Pittsburgh, Pennsylvania, there were certainly adjustments to be made as he worked and lived in the Midwest, New England, and the South over the course of his career.

Ryan Olson (2002) noted that "descriptions of cultural variables within OC literature often utilizes the language of cultural anthropology, with researchers detailing rites, rituals, celebrations, artifacts and symbols of OC" (p. 472).

PEOPLE FRIENDLY ORGANIZATIONS

As long as you remain fully aware of the ramifications inherent in managing organizations and people and try to maintain a balance between the needs of the two, people control the organization. When the balance tips in favor of activities, people are no longer in control. An organizational threat to individual freedom and dignity cannot exist in a balanced situation. Saul Gellerman (1973) summed up the situation with the following:

> Thus we return to the dilemma that organizations have always faced, and always will, as long as they are comprised of individuals. The organization exists, thrives, and survives by harnessing the talents of individuals. Its problem is to do so without hobbling those talents or turning them against itself. This perpetual balancing act is the responsibility of management, especially those members of management in the lower echelons, whose influence upon employees is most direct. (p. 13)

Very few people deny that every workplace has a few anti-people elements; nevertheless, when someone threatens the entire organizational structure, many others rush to the defense of the status quo. If, however, you direct some of their attention toward correcting the anti-people elements and developing a balance between people and things, then almost everyone in an organization will help with the process.

🚹 KEY POINTS TO REMEMBER

- Organizations—formal and informal—are pervasive and play a key role in our working and personal lives.
- Objectives evolve or change over the lifetime of the organization.
- Organizations try to be self-sustaining, changing objectives in response to a changing environment.
- Most libraries operate as public nonprofit organizations (which entails public funding and scrutiny).
- How organizations operate and survive is in large part determined by their highly complex environments.
- Library managers must recognize the need to assess three environments—one external and two internal (internal to the service itself and to the internal environment of its parent organization).
- Managers who fail to monitor, assess, and adjust to changing environments (a process known as environmental scanning) risk failure for themselves and their organizations.
- Organizational culture plays a major role in an organization's internal environment.
- Understanding the organizational culture is essential for everyone on the staff.

REFERENCES

Albright, Kendra. 2004. "Environmental Scanning: Radar for Success." *Information Management Journal* 38, no. 3: 38–42, 45.

Barnard, Chester. 1956. *Organization and Management*. Cambridge, MA: Harvard University Press.

Bloor, Geoffrey, and Patrick Dawson. 1994. "Understanding Professional Culture in the Organizational Context." *Organization Studies* 15, no. 2: 241–75.

Bonn, Ingrid. 2005. "Improving Strategic Thinking: A Multilevel Approach." *Leadership and Organization Development Journal* 26, no. 5: 336–54.

Burns, Tom, and G. M. Stalker. 1961. *Management of Innovation*. London: Tavistock.

Castiglione, John. 2008. "Environmental Scanning: An Essential Tool for Twenty-First Century Librarianship." *Library Review* 57, no. 7: 528–36.

Davis, Jan. 2008. "Competitive Intelligence at AALL's 2008 Annual Conference." *Searcher* 16, no. 10: 14–15.

Emery, Fred, and Eric Trist. 1965. "Causal Texture of Organizational Environments." *Human Relations* 18, no. 1: 21–31.

Gellerman, Saul. 1973. *Management of Human Resources*. Hinsdale, IL: Dryden Press.

Gianfranco, Faruggia. 2007. "How is the Nonprofit Sector Changing?" *Futures Research Quarterly* 23, no. 1: 5–16.

Glor, Eleanor D. 2008. "Identifying Organizational Patterns: Normative and Empirical Criteria for Organizational Redesign." *Journal of Public Affairs Education* 14, no. 3: 311–33.

Harris, Martin. 2006. "Technology, Innovation, and Post-Bureaucracy: The Case of the British Library." *Journal of Organizational Change Management* 19, no. 1: 80–92.

Harvard Business Review. 2016. "Strategy: The Scary Truth about Corporate Survival." 94, no. 12: 24–25.

Kell, Thomas, and Gregory Carrott. 2005. "Culture Matters Most." *Harvard Business Review* 83, no. 5: 22.

Katopol, Patricia. 2014. "Managing Change with Environmental Scanning." *Library Leadership and Management* 29, no. 1: 1–7.

Karyotakis, Konstaninos, and Vassills Moustakis. 2016. "Organizational Factors, Organizational Culture, Job Satisfaction, and Entrepreneurial Orientation on Public Administration." *European Journal of Applied Economics* 13, no. 1: 47-59.

Lawrence, Paul, and Jay Lorsch. 1967. *Organization and Environment*. Homewood, IL: Irwin.

Lynch, Beverly. 1974. "The Academic Library and Its Environment." *College and Research Libraries* 35, no. 2: 127.

Malgeri, Jack. 2010. "Organizational Foresight and Stewardship." *The Public Manager* 39, no. 4: 39-42.

Meeks, Michael D. 2015. "Strategic Management and The Disparate Duties of the CEO." *Academy of Strategic Management Journal* 14, no. 2: 93-116.

Mierke, Jill, and Vicki Williamson. 2017. "A Framework for Achieving Organizational Culture Change." *Library Leadership and Management* 31, no. 2: 1-16.

Olson, Ryan. 2002. "Organizational Culture: Putting the Organizational Culture Concept to Work." *The Behavioral Analyst Today* 3, no. 4: 471-81.

Pett, Jason and Sandy Pundmann. 2016. "Care and Feeding of the Company's Culture: Two Experts Discuss Internal Audit's Role in Ensuring A Healthy Organizational Culture." *Internal Audit* 73, no. 3: 70-71.

Rutherford, Sarah. 2001. "Organizational Cultures, Women Managers, and Exclusion." *Women in Management Review* 16, nos. 7/8: 371-82.

Schein, Edgar. 1992. *Organizational Culture and Leadership*. 2nd ed. San Francisco: Jossey Bass.

Schwarz, Jan Oliver. 2007. "Competitive Intelligence: A Field for Futurists?" *Futures Research Quarterly* 21, no.1: 55-65.

Stewart, Wayne H., Ruth C. May, and Arvind Kalia. 2008. "Environmental Perceptions and Scanning in the United States and India." *Entrepreneurship Theory and Practice* 32, no. 1: 83-106.

CHAPTER 3

Legal Issues

District Library Agreement: An attorney for the participating municipalities draws up a District Library Agreement based on decisions made by the District Library Planning Committee and agreed to by all of the participating municipalities. This agreement is signed by the participating municipalities and approved by all current public library board within the district. All participating municipalities adopt resolutions to establish the district library.

Michigan District Library Law, 2017

While sales to public libraries are exempt from the sales tax, sales by public libraries are generally not exempt from the sales tax. Most public library sales, including sales of photocopies and computer printout charges, are subject to the Wisconsin sales tax and any county and stadium sales taxes.

Wisconsin Department of Public Instruction: Division for Libraries and Technology, 2017

Sec. 18881. Authorized services; adult literacy instructional program; coordinated literacy and pre-literacy and pre-literacy services to families; collaboration with nonprofit and other local organizations.

California State Library, 2017

§ 4509. Library records. Library records, which contain names or other personally identifying details regarding the users of public, free association, school, college and university libraries and library systems of this state, including but not limited to records related to the circulation of library materials, computer database searches, interlibrary loan transactions, reference queries, requests for photocopies of library materials, title reserve requests, or the use of audio-visual materials, films or records, shall be confidential and shall not be disclosed except that such records may be disclosed to the extent necessary for the proper operation of such library and shall be disclosed upon request or consent of the user or pursuant to subpoena, court order or where otherwise required by statute.

New York State Library, 2017

Libraries in the United States would not be what they are if not for a host of laws and regulations. There are federal, state, county, and municipal legislative bodies that create laws and regulations that affect what libraries do and how they go about their business. Some of those "rules" apply to any organization while many others are library-specific. Our opening quotations are but a very small sample of the library-specific laws that exist. More importantly, those laws and their specificity vary from locale to locale. Some legal matters will be addressed in later chapters within specific contexts, such as the hiring process and financial matters (chapters 13 and 17). Our best advice is: when in doubt, seek legal counsel (usually a law firm hired by the parent organization). Doing so may cost some money up front, but it saves money in the long run by heading off any major legal issue that may result from not seeking such advice. None of the material in this chapter is intended to be, nor should it be, regarded as legal advice.

There are a few federal regulatory agencies and laws that are frequently cited in library work. One example of a general federal regulatory body that can have an impact on library operations is OSHA (Occupational Safety and Health Administration). One of the areas where OSHA impacts library operations is in terms of ergonomic standards for computer-based activities. Needless to say, copyright laws are long-standing issues for libraries. The laws for print, media, and digital rights have further complicated what was already a complex issue when it was just a print and media world. For research libraries there can be issues related to copyright laws in other countries.

A more library-specific federal law in terms of library operations is CIPA, the Children's Internet Protection Act (https://www.untangle.com/wp-content/uploads/pdf/ UntanglingCIPA.pdf). This law, from one perspective, has First Amendment implications in terms of adult access to internet information in public libraries. Some children's advocates raised similar concerns during the legislative debates and during the early stages of CIPA implementation. We'll discuss CIPA later in this chapter.

ESTABLISHING A LIBRARY

As stated earlier, all libraries or their parent organizations have a legal basis. Few librarians have the experience of starting a new library. There are some very rare occasions when an unincorporated community incorporates and decides one of the amenities it will provide is a public library or when a new school district is established. Perhaps the most common occurrences are the creation of a library, school, or water districts.

As our opening quotation from Michigan suggests, library districts are complicated from a legal and operational perspective. They cross jurisdictional lines which means, more often than not, the libraries involved have "parent" organizations with different priorities (who funds what, and what services are priorities, for example). The following sidebar provides an example of a complex library district just in terms of the jurisdictions involved.

Consortia and other collaborative arrangements are standard elements today for most libraries. Such activities are also based in law. Consortia composed of public and private institutions usually must have some type of authorization in order for the public institutions to expand funds outside their political jurisdiction. Some cooperative ventures cross state lines. An example of a law allowing cross-state library cooperation is New York State's Interstate Library Compact.

> Because the desire for the services provided by the libraries transcends governmental boundaries and can most effectively be satisfied by giving such services to communities and people regardless of jurisdictional lines, it is the policy of the States party to this compact to cooperate and share their responsibilities; to authorize cooperation and sharing with respect to those types of library facilities and services which can be more economically or efficiently developed and maintained on a cooperative basis, and to au-

TRY THIS

Choose a state and investigate what laws it has that relate to libraries. If you have access to the Nexis Uni (formerly LexisNexis Academic) database, the search will be quick and informative.

thorize cooperation and sharing among localities, states and others in providing joint or cooperative library services in areas where the distribution of population or of existing and potential library resources make the provision of library service on an interstate basis the most effective way of providing adequate and efficient service . . . .

Article IV. Interstate Library Districts, Governing Board

(a)   An interstate library district which establishes, maintains or operates any facilities or services in its own right shall have a governing board which shall direct the affairs of the district and act for it in all matters relating to its business. Each participating public library agency in the district shall be represented on the governing board which shall be organized and conduct its business in accordance with provision therefore in the library agreement. But in no event shall a governing board meet less often than twice a year.

(b)   Any private library agency or agencies party to a library agreement establishing an interstate library district may be represented on or advise with the governing board of the district in such manner as the library agreement may provide. (NY CLS Unconsol Ch 111-B § 1 [2004])

The forgoing is a very small sampling of the many laws that have bearing on how library managers carry out library operations. All states have such laws that affect funding, cooperative activities, how and if fines are imposed, and where any such money goes—whether it is retained by the library or the parent institution.

LIBRARIES, USERS, SAFETY, AND THE LAW

Part of a library manager's responsibility, regardless at what level of management—senior, middle, or frontline—is to be a good steward of the resources and people involved in library services and activities. One aspect of that stewardship relates to safety. There are times when resources and people's safety conflict.

We cover the topic of managing physical facilities in chapter 20; however, we need to mention the issue here. When resources and people's safety issues collide, naturally people take precedence. This can mean substantial loss of collection resources even when there is no direct threat to people. One example is the fire code-mandated ceiling sprinkler systems. In the case of fire, such systems are invaluable; however, such systems can spring leaks—it often seems as if the system that's about to leak waits until the weekend when the library is closed and has forty-eight hours to drip or spray on the collection. It is surprising how much damage can be done in just a few hours and how costly the cleanup

👥 AUTHORS' EXPERIENCE

Evans lives in a community that is part of a library district—the Flagstaff City-Coconino County Public Library System. As the name suggests, there are two major components in the system. However, there are three other incorporated communities with libraries that are "affiliates." There are also three branches, beyond one located in Flagstaff. One is in a community located on a Navajo reservation (which can therefore involve the Navajo Nation government) and another branch located in the Grand Canyon National Park (federal jurisdiction). You can imagine the complexities that might arise from having such diverse jurisdictions trying to work together.

and recovery turn out to be. (Mold forms quickly in wet materials, creating yet another hazard for staff, users, and materials.) A 2017 example of a sprinkler break took place in the Phoenix Central Public Library building. The estimate to resolve the problems caused by the break was $10 million dollars (*Arizona Republic*, p.17a). There are ways to avoid such problems and still comply with fire codes, but they almost always cost more than the funds that are available.

Another fire code challenge involves the placement of emergency exits around the library. All emergency exits are seldom under the visual control of staffed service points; if they are, staffing costs are higher than average. Again, the manager has to balance costs, safety, and preservation of collection and equipment resources.

Health and injury issues

We discuss risk assessment in depth in chapter 20 because it is key to avoiding many health and safety dangers and OSHA site visits. OSHA rules and regulations present a set of issues for managers. "Congress created the OSHA to ensure safe and healthful working conditions for working men and women by setting and enforcing standards and by providing training, outreach, education, and assistance" (www.osha.gov/about.html). The agency's responsibilities cover almost all aspects of workplace health and safety concerns. It also makes an effort to inform workers of their rights. Many, if not the majority, of OSHA library site visits arise from employee calls. Workplaces such as libraries are rarely in the top fifty or so of hazardous work environments. Even so, library managers must have an awareness of OSHA rules and regulations because OSHA issues arise from time to time. The U.S. Department of Labor periodically issues *Nonfatal Occupational Injuries and Illnesses Requiring Days Away from Work* (www.bls.gov/news.release/osh2.nr0.htm) where you can review lost library work days.

Libraries need to have the proper equipment and furniture for staff to prevent injury. However, just having physical items is not enough; there also needs to be training in their proper use. Although a workstation may have all the necessary ergonomic features, this does not mean the person working there will use them properly; therefore, training is a part of the library's due diligence. We are not aware of a library that was fined by OSHA for health or safety issues, but we do know of cases where the agency set a time frame for correcting reported problem(s) with the possibility of a fine for failure to meet the deadline.

Another challenge, in older buildings, is asbestos and the environmental health problems it causes. Asbestos was a common fireproofing and insulating component used in older buildings. Left undisturbed, it poses little health risk. However, older libraries are modified from time to time to meet the needs of new technology, which disturbs the asbestos. This creates the potential for health problems. Removing hazardous materials is costly and requires trained personnel to conduct clean-up operations. Senior library managers should know if their buildings contain any hazardous material—not just in construction but also in the products used in operational activities. Something as innocuous as installing new carpet can lead to health concerns for some members of staff or the public because fumes from the adhesive used with the carpeting can cause allergic reactions. Not knowing or thinking about such issues ahead of time can lead to a visit from OSHA inspectors.

Disruptive user behavior

User behavior, and to some extent staff behavior, can create unsafe situations, over which you as manager will have only modest control. Certainly, given daily contact with staff members, you have ample opportunities to observe any changes among them that have the potential to be disruptive. For the general public, however, you have to rely on proper policies and staff training to keep the inevitable problems to a minimum. There are two common user behavior concerns: situations when a person is upset about some library issue and situations when issues arise between users. Both types of challenging situations will occur from time to time. Being prepared is the key to keeping the situation to its lowest possible level in terms of disruption and to resolving it quickly.

Most libraries address disruptive behavior through policies and staff guidelines. You might think that school libraries are low on the scale for disruptive behavior. They are certainly lower than libraries open to the general public, but their managers do have to think about how to handle potential problems. In times when a kindergarten student can bring a loaded gun to school and discharge it (https://www.thedailybeast.com/6-year-old -brings-gun-to-school), you know that there is serious potential for unacceptable behavior, even in an elementary school library. Middle and high schools have increasing levels of concern about confrontations among students in the library (involving drugs, bullying, or weapons, for example).

Libraries open to the public have the greatest number of incidents. Sarah Farrugia (2002) stated, "Public libraries are more susceptible to patron violence than academic and other special libraries, as their open door allows anyone to use the building. This can sometimes invite trouble from asocial citizens who can cause disruption and uneasiness amongst staff and patrons and even lead to acts of extreme violence" (p. 309). It is disconcerting when this behavior comes from a fellow staff member; however, with a colleague you have a baseline for judging what is wrong. With the public, there is almost no basis for knowing what is wrong and what to expect, unless it involves one of the regular visitors.

The following list presents some of the most common unacceptable behaviors that library staff will encounter:

- drug and alcohol use
- drug and alcohol sales
- verbal abuse toward staff by a user
- verbal abuse among users
- assault on staff
- assault among users

- gang activity
- indecent exposure
- users viewing or printing pornographic material
- trespassing
- arson (especially in book return boxes)
- theft (especially of computer equipment)
- disorderly or menacing conduct

We noted earlier that successful handling of any of the above behaviors, as well as others not listed, depends on having sound legal policies in place and having staff trained in what to and what not to do when a circumstance arises. It is *essential* to work with legal counsel when developing appropriate policies. Additionally, legal counsel will be aware of community and state laws, as well as court decisions, that will affect these policies.

If the library posts reasonable rules regarding access, hours, and behavior, it may, without too much legal concern, remove anyone violating those rules. The two key considerations are reasonable rules and posting. The rules *must* reflect existing laws and policies and should be reviewed by legal counsel. Both conditions must be met for removal from the library to be legal. Repeat offenders can face legal action, if the library wishes to press charges or pursue other sanctions.

In 2006, *American Libraries* reported on problems with the "reasonableness" of library access and behavior polices. In one instance, the Dallas Public Library's plan to ban persons "emitting odors (including bodily odors or perfumes) which interfere with services by other users or work staff" was challenged (*American Libraries* 2006c, p. 11). Homeless advocates questioned the fairness of such a rule. In Massachusetts, the ACLU filed a lawsuit over a rule that limited a homeless person to checking out only two books at any one time when other users could have at least ten items (*American Libraries* 2006b). These two incidents illustrate the fact that written rules need to be reviewed by legal counsel.

Another type of disruptive situation occurs when a user becomes verbally abusive. Anyone who has worked in public services for any length of time will have experienced

---

||||| **CHECK THESE OUT**

An excellent book to consult on handling problem behaviors of all types in libraries is Mark Willis's *Dealing with Difficult People in the Library*, 2nd edition (Chicago: American Library Association, 2012). It addresses just about every type of "difficult person" category you can think of in a library setting.

Jan Thenell's *The Library's Crisis Communications Planner: A PR Guide for Handling Every Emergency* (Chicago: American Library Association, 2004) provides practical guidance for managing a situation if a complaint explodes beyond the library.

Two other good resources for handling difficult people are Karen Mannering's *Dealing with Difficult People* (London: Hodder Education, 2008) and Susan Benjamin's *Perfect Phrases for Dealing with Difficult People: Hundreds of Ready-to-Use Phrases for Handling Conflict, Confrontations, and Challenging Personalities,* special edition (New York: McGraw-Hill, 2015).

✋ **HELPING THE HOMELESS**

San Francisco Public Library System administrators thought that the homeless library user situation at their central library was extreme enough that they devoted a full-time (FTE) librarian salary to hire a full-time social worker who was housed in the central library. This was after library staff complained repeatedly that they were not adequately trained to handle such a pervasive social issue. This led to a much better work environment for the library employees, and it also led to the library social worker collaborating with other city and county agencies to help homeless library users.

such abuse over some library issue. How much verbal abuse must you tolerate? F. J. DeRosa (1980) commented:

> People in all areas of public service, and librarians in particular, seem resigned to the opinion that abuse from their public is inescapable and there is not much they can do about it. Much of this misconception is due to the fact that many people do not realize the point when disruptive behavior becomes antisocial behavior and when antisocial behavior becomes criminal behavior. (p. 35)

You cannot avoid some verbal abuse if you work in public services, but certainly there are limits to what you have to endure. Libraries should work with legal counsel to establish legally sound guidelines for when "enough is enough," although this does not guarantee that there will be no lawsuits from angry users.

We know that dealing with irate people is neither comfortable nor easy. It is something you get better at with training. Having an opportunity to practice conflict-management skills in a workshop environment is useful for frontline staff as well as supervisors and senior staff. Knowing what conflict-management skills are and using them are two very different things. Staff members who work shifts that have minimal staffing should be the first to receive training and practice; they have fewer backup resources available when disruptive behaviors arise. Sometimes, no matter how carefully handled the circumstance was, the person will go to the media or to an attorney. This happens occasionally and having proper policies in place and posted and staff trained in conflict control as well as strong administrative support will help keep the fallout as minimal as possible.

TORT LAW AND LIABILITY

In writing about public sector mangers' liability, Stephanie Newbold (2015) wrote "More so than at any other time, reviewing courts are increasing public administrators' liability when they violate or undermine the individual or constitutional rights of citizens or when the government fails to provide essential services for which they are to perform" (p. 616). What is liability, what is involved, and what does it mean? Liability is

> a comprehensive legal term that describes the condition of being actually or potentially subject to a legal obligation. . . . Primary liability is an obligation for which a person is directly responsible; it is distinguished from secondary liability which is the responsi-

bility of another if the party directly responsible fails or refuses to satisfy his or her obligation. (The Free Dictionary, http://legal-dictionary.thefreedictionary.com/liability)

Are libraries susceptible to being held liable for an action or failure to act? Sometimes the answer is yes, and sometimes it is no. In the past, tax-supported libraries had some form of governmental immunity from law suits and liability. Today many states have greatly reduced the available immunity.

One of the most common concerns for library liability is personal injury, which is governed by tort law. Tort law addresses injuries—physical or mental—resulting from negligence or from intentional acts. Libraries have been involved in litigation arising from both causes. For libraries, it is the negligence category that is most significant.

Broadly speaking, there are three interrelated issues related to negligence regardless whether the resulting injury is mental or physical in nature. Negligence requires the existence of three conditions:

- The cause of the injury is a person, not an act of God.
- The person causing the injury has a responsibility and duty to the injured party.
- The duty is one of warning or one of action.

An example of possible library negligence would be if staff fails to put out signs warning of slippery entryway floors on a rainy or snowy day and a person falls and injures himself or herself.

Within the concept of personal injury law in the United States and England is a subsection that involves premises, such as the library's property. Premises include everything associated with a building—sidewalks, grounds, parking lot, and lighting, for example. The courts have divided the "controller" of the premises' duties into three broad categories: those involving invitees (users and staff in public areas), those involving licensees (users and staff in nonpublic areas, such as technical services and administrative offices), and those involving trespassers. There is a descending order of duty to the categories, from invitees down to trespassers. Beyond these basic categories, there are special duties to children and to persons who are mentally or physically challenged.

One all too common situation for libraries regarding potential liability is the presence of unattended children and occasionally mentally challenged individuals. Dealing with "latchkey children" has been a major challenge for public and academic libraries. Some parents tell their child to go to the library (which is considered a safe place) after school and wait to be picked up. A few parents even bring children to the library and leave them unsupervised while the parents attend to other business outside of the library. There is a question of just how much liability a library has for looking after unsupervised children. Can the parent(s) hold the library and its staff liable for an injury or health problem that occurs when the child is alone in the library?

Whatever steps the library takes to control such a problem, a first step is absolutely necessary to prevent even greater problems: have clear policies and a plan of action that have been reviewed by the library's or parent institution's legal counsel. Some of the options that exist in various jurisdictions are to:

- Offer special programs designed for unattended children
- Have libraries bar children without parental supervision

- Have policies requiring staff to call child welfare services or police to pick up any unattended child at closing time
- Have policies allowing staff to contact police or security when a child is left unattended for a specified period of time during normal school hours.

Libraries need to make it clear that they assume no child care responsibilities. Policies need to be posted on the website and in prominent locations, especially at public entrances, and provided to parents when a child is given a library card.

MALPRACTICE AND LIBRARIANS

The issue of malpractice is complex because the librarian is almost always an employee and as such the library or government jurisdiction is the legal party with the duty (*respondent superior*). Is malpractice truly a library issue? Over the years the matter has remained an open question. Paul Healey (2008), who holds both a JD and an MLS, wrote: "Reliance on the librarian such that liability would result is just not reasonable" (p. 76). His point was that both tort and contract laws rely on reasonable expectations. Essentially, it is unreasonable to expect a librarian to be an expert on a topic (the basis for a malpractice suit) such as the subject of a reference question. It is reasonable to assume a librarian is expert in locating information about the topic but not for the correctness of that information.

LIBRARY SERVICES AND THE LAW

Many of the services libraries provide are circumscribed by a variety of laws. Accessibility to facilities and collections, what users may do with the resources available, and who has access to materials are but a few of the issues involved.

Access to library resources must comply with ADA (Americans with Disabilities Act), as we noted earlier. Title III of the act states that it is a violation to discriminate "on the basis of disability in the full and equal enjoyment of the goods, services, facilities, privileges, advantages, or accommodations of any place of public accommodation" (42 U.S.C. § 12182[a] 2000). Access includes such physical factors as wheelchair ramps where needed from the front entrance to elsewhere in the building, drinking fountain height, restroom accommodations, and the aisle width in publicly accessible stacks. Many libraries built long before the act was passed faced substantial remodeling and renovation costs to become compliant. Most libraries have addressed the physical access issues; however, modifications to ADA or new legislation may bring about new requirements and costs. For example, ADA requirements changed in 2004 when new guidelines were issued (69 Fed. Reg. 44,084, et seq., July 23, 2004, http://blog.librarylaw.com/librarylaw/disability _access/).

On the service side, there are compliance concerns. For example, what percentages of your library's collections are accessible to the visually impaired users? Does the collection access meet the "full and equal" provision of ADA? Large-print books are one way to meet this need; however, only a small fraction of books may be available in that format.

Online resources and other types of media also need to be taken into account. Diane Murley (2008) provided some sound advice regarding improving accessibility for websites. Solutions are available, but you must think about the issues on an ongoing basis. We know from firsthand experience that failure to address these issues for one user leads to lack of access for that user (and likely others), potentially resulting in a lawsuit.

As mentioned earlier, an example of legislation that circumscribes what resources a library may make available to users is CIPA (the Children's Internet Protection Act). CIPA primarily impacts school and public libraries and to a lesser extent any library hoping to get federal funds for internet access. CIPA is the outcome of an earlier effort to protect children from offensive internet material that was ruled unconstitutional on First Amendment grounds. The issue was resolved by using access to federal funding; according to CIPA, a library wishing to secure federal E-Rate funding must employ filtering software on its computers.

In between children and adults are young adults. What about CIPA's impact on them? Barbara A. Jansen (2010) wrote, "The landscape of Web 2.0 offers various viewpoints, original information from many sources, and a means to express ideas and share results with a wide audience" (p. 49). Jansen also noted, "In addition to blocking access to educationally valuable resources as described above, restricting access to social media sites in schools also calls into question the erosion of the principle of intellectual freedom for youth" (p. 48).

Many libraries have meeting rooms that the public can book for events. How those spaces may be used is often a question of what the law allows. For example, in Colorado Springs (*American Libraries* 2005), the Rampart Library District had a board-approved policy that stated if the rooms were used by religious or political groups, their meetings must provide a balanced view. Early in 2005, a religious group asked to use a room, and the request was turned down because it would be a religious service. Shortly after the denial, the library received notice that a lawsuit was being filed by Liberty Counsel (a religious rights defense organization located in Florida) against the library district for denying use of the room for a religious service. The Rampart District decided to modify its use policy because it did not have the funds to engage in a legal battle. Liberty Counsel has filed at least seven such suits since 2000. It won some for the same reason that Rampart conceded—lack of funds to engage in a legal battle. More recent (2015) example suits filed against libraries by the organization are available on the following sites: www .indyweek.com/indyweek/in-the-case-of-right-wing-nut-jobs-v-wake-county-the-rwnjs -may-have-a-point/Content?oid=4424498 and www.eagletribune.com/news/christian-group -files-lawsuit-against-lawrence-public-library/article_82ce7fde-3ee3-53eb-bf58-31cd 31d2d1a7.html.

Another example took several years to resolve (2004–2007). It started in 2004 when the Antioch branch of the Contra Costa County (Orinda, California) Library system rejected a room request from the Faith Center Church Evangelistic Ministries. The denial led to a lawsuit. The denial was based on the library board's policy that stated that rooms cannot be used for religious services, based on separation of church and state grounds. Library staff stated the denial was made because the group indicated it would hold prayer services as part of the program. The group had distributed flyers throughout the area inviting people to attend a worship service at the library. Interestingly enough, the U.S. Department of Justice took the position that Contra Costa County had to allow the group to use the library room for the service, a somewhat strange twist on the separation of church and state concept (*American Libraries* 2006a). Contra Costa County persisted because it viewed this more than a matter of library room use. It had no problem with the group using the space for any other purpose than a religious service. Each side appealed the case, and each side won and lost in the lower courts. On the first day of the 2007–2008 term, the U.S. Supreme Court refused to hear the appeal of the Ninth Circuit Court of

Appeals ruling that the library and county had acted properly. (Note: the ruling applies only to those libraries in the Ninth Circuit Court's jurisdiction.) *American Libraries* (2007) reported that the religious group said it would revisit the case in lower courts using a new set of arguments.

USER PRIVACY

Just because there is a legal basis for confidentiality (see our opening quotation from the New York State Library) does not mean that decisions regarding confidentiality are always simple for library staff to make. Librarians must release information when there is a court order or subpoena. It is not uncommon for law enforcement officers to request such information without the proper documentation and to present the request as a means of speeding up an investigation. Once again, having a policy in place for handling such requests is important. The ALA website "Implementation of Privacy Policies and Procedures" is a good starting points for policy formulation (www.ala.org/advocacy/privacy/toolkit/implementation).

There are three broad categories of user information libraries must consider in terms of confidentiality: data collected from a person upon becoming a registered user, data about what a person uses (items checked out, online services, document delivery services, for example), and user data collected by library vendors as a result of a person accessing their services. Law enforcement officers are rarely concerned about the first category; however, other people may want that information and can and have presented their requests in seemingly innocent terms (someone trying to locate a family member who "just needs the address," for example). A library should have good control over the data in the first category. Just how to control data in the other two categories is less clear. A staff member receiving such a request should politely, but firmly, refuse to comply and immediately report the request to the supervisor and otherwise follow the library's confidentiality policy.

Libraries with online circulation systems are in a good position to ensure collection usage data confidentiality, as these systems are able to break the link between the borrower and the items upon return, as well as any associated fees. If the circulation system requires that the name of a borrower appear on a book card or some other traceable record, the staff should render the name illegible as part of the discharging process. Beyond circulation records, there may well be other data to consider, such as specific times reserved to use library computers and usage of document delivery services.

One type of usage data that the library has little control over is database usage. Angela Maycock (2010) noted, "Privacy, one of the foundations of intellectual freedom, is a compelling concern for school librarians. We live in an era when more and more personal information is available online" (p. 68). Many library database vendors, like almost all commercial web organizations, collect data about people using their services. Trina Magi (2010) stated the issue well: "The Web 2.0 environment . . . poses new challenges for librarians in their commitment to protect user privacy as vendors of online databases incorporate personalization features into their search-retrieval interfaces, thereby collecting personally identifiable user information not subject to library oversight" (p. 254). Most of the major online library product vendors have a prominently placed button on their opening search page that allows users to personalize their search; some examples are EBSCO's "My EBSCO*host*," and Emerald's "Your Profile."

What might vendors collect and do with such data? Many vendors also offer the option for e-mailing the requested file(s) to the person. That alone provides a vendor with two pieces of marketable information: what the person may be interested in and a means of contacting the person. The personalized profile can generate more marketable data.

Is what others do regarding use of library services a concern for libraries and the issue of confidentiality? What can libraries do about vendor data collection activities? Should users be told that vendors are collecting personal information when they use a database? Do users care? We do not have these answers; however, we do believe that libraries ought to have a serious discussion of the matter and develop a policy regarding how to address a complaint from a user who objects to personal information being collected.

After 9/11, there was a change regarding access to library records at least by federal law enforcement officers. The USA PATRIOT Act authorized warrantless searches and required that the library not communicate to anyone that such a search occurred or was underway. What data might law enforcement officials obtain from library records that they might more easily access elsewhere? Karl Gruben (2006) wrote, "In actuality, the Department of Justice does not have as much interest in what Johnny is reading as it does in what he is looking at or e-mailing or Instant Messaging on the Internet, particularly since there is suspicion that the 9/11 hijackers communicated through Internet terminals in public libraries" (p. 303).

Section 215 of the act allows the government to secure secret warrants to obtain "business records"—this includes library records and records from library database vendors for named individuals. The act also authorizes the issuance of National Security Letters (NSLs), which do not require a judge's review, and which require organizations to secretly provide information. At least one library has been on the receiving end of such a letter.

CONTRACTS AND LICENSES

People sign contracts every day. Probably several thousand car rental agreements (they are contracts) are made every few hours. If people had time to read the agreement and understand it, there would probably be many fewer cars rented every hour. Hasty signing usually has no adverse consequences until something as simple as a scratch or a chip comes up. Then you learn just what was in the agreement.

Organizations cannot afford a hasty contract signing. Even when attorneys have put in days, weeks, or months of work and all the people involved thought they understood the terms, interpretation problems can and do arise. This in turn often results in lawsuits being filed. As we noted earlier regarding lawsuits over meeting rooms, many times a library simply has no money for fighting a lawsuit, be it for something it wants or needs to defend.

What is the difference between a contract and a license? They are certainly related; however, there are differences, and understanding the differences can help the library avoid legal entanglements. A contract is a "voluntary, deliberate, and legally enforceable (binding) agreement between two or more competent parties. . . . Each party to a contract acquires rights and duties relative to the rights and duties of the other parties" (*Business Dictionary*, www.businessdictionary.com/definition/contract.html). A license is a "revocable written (formal) or implied agreement by an authority or proprietor (the licensor) not to assert his or her right (for a specific period and under specified conditions) to prevent another party (the licensee) from engaging in certain activity that is normally forbidden (such as selling liquor or making copies of a copyrighted work)" (*Business Dictionary*, www.businessdictionary.com/definition/license.html). Essentially, a license gives one the privilege to use something under certain conditions.

Typical library licensing agreements outline the library's (lessee's) responsibilities for such things as security, customer service, payment and delivery, limitations and warranties, termination, indemnification, and assignment. All of these factors can affect allowable use of a product or service. Although adding attorney fees to the cost of creating user-oriented services or collections is unappealing, the fact is that most of the vendors will negotiate changes, and librarians should demand changes, based on attorney input, that benefit or at least do not place unreasonable demands on the library and its end users.

Compliance is a key issue, and the library must do what it can to ensure compliance with contracts and licenses. Some database licensing agreements contain language that places responsibility on the library (or subscriber) to monitor what users do with material after they leave the premises. Such clauses are beyond any library's control, and librarians should insist that they be deleted from the agreement. This may require the assistance of legal counsel.

COPYRIGHT

Copyright is the most widely discussed legal issue in the profession's literature. It has been bedeviling librarians for a very long time. The term "copyright" comes from the law's original purpose—to protect against unauthorized copying and sale of a printed work. Over time, the concept became more complex, going far beyond copying someone else's work and selling it. Today it is thought of as protecting "intellectual property" (IP)—a concept that relates to almost all formats that individuals and organizations produce. The complexity is a result of the variety of materials covered, and each new technology is viewed as a potential threat to the copyright holder's rights.

Adding yet more complexity is the fact that most countries have copyright laws based on their own varying definitions of coverage terms and so forth. For the better part of eighty years there has been an international effort to "harmonize" the laws. Today, the major international body trying to bring some standardization to the field is the World Intellectual Property Organization (WIPO). Its website states, "The World Intellectual Property Organization (WIPO) is a specialized agency of the United Nations. It is dedicated to developing a balanced and accessible international intellectual property (IP) system, which rewards creativity, stimulates innovation and contributes to economic development while safeguarding the public interest" (www.wipo.int/about-ip/en/).

IP is divided into two categories: industrial property, which includes inventions (patents), trademarks, industrial designs, and geographic indications of source; and copyright, which includes literary and artistic works such as novels, poems and plays, films, musical works, artistic works such as drawings, paintings, photographs and sculptures, and architectural designs. Rights related to copyright include those of performing artists in their performances.

Fair use and performance are probably the two areas that create the greatest headaches for libraries, especially those supporting educational programs. Although the concept of fair use appears in the current law, just what constitutes fair use is not defined. There are guidelines, but even they leave ample room for interpretation or misinterpretation. Users often ask librarians to help them understand what is and is not fair use. There are long books about copyright and libraries, such as Kenneth D. Crews's *Copyright Law for Librarians and Educators: Creative Strategies and Practical Solutions* (4th ed., Chicago: American Library Association, 2018) and Carol Simpson's *Copyright for Schools: A Practical Guide* (5th ed., Santa Barbara, CA: Linworth Publishing, 2010). Even they cannot provide more than guidance. The only safe answer is, "It depends."

Almost all libraries provide photocopy services. There are regulations regarding posting proper signage related to photocopying and copyright. Failure to have such signs could put the library in jeopardy of becoming a defendant in an alleged copyright violation lawsuit.

Interlibrary loan (ILL) has been a staple service for a very long time. There are copyright ground rules for how often a library may borrow articles from a single journal title before it risks a lawsuit or having to pay a fee for each item because of using ILL instead of subscribing to the title. Some online database vendors' licenses do not allow for the use of its materials for ILL purposes unless the library can negotiate that the clause be dropped.

The Digital Millennium Copyright Act of 1998 (DMCA) updated U.S. copyright law in terms of digital formats and technology, as well as to conform to the 1996 WIPO treaties. The 1978 copyright law is still in force but dramatically changed as a result of amendments and the DMCA. One aspect of the DMCA that is important to libraries is "Title II: Online Service Provider Liability." It is important because the DMCA defines "online service provider" (OSP) very broadly, and libraries that offer electronic resources or internet access could be considered OSPs. The law creates some "safe harbors" for specified OSP activities. When an activity is within the safe harbor, the OSP qualifies for an exemption from liability. You should read the most current material available about this title (www.copyright.gov/legislation/dmca.pdf), as it is complex, and legal interpretation of it is likely to evolve.

Distance education activities are also addressed in Title IV. The Registrar of Copyrights (the director of the U.S. Copyright Office) provided Congress with a report on how to promote distance education through digital technologies (www.copyright.gov/docs/regstat52599.html). Part of the report addresses the value of having licenses available for use of copyrighted works in distance education programs.

DOCUMENTATION

No matter the incident or the event, we have three strong words of advice when dealing with any issue: document, document, document. This is something the head of any library, her or his management team, or any library manager must never forget. Documentation is essential in building or defending a case. You might like to think that not all actions would require this, but it is better to be on the safe side and document. Documentation can range from e-mail transactions to something written on paper—anything that records what transpired. When in doubt, check with your parent organization's attorney.

Army - write up bad behavior to show later in EVALS. Promotions etc.

🚹 KEY POINTS TO REMEMBER

- A variety of legal issues constrain a library's freedom of action, from establishing the organization to specifying who, how, and what users and staff may do.
- It is important to get legal counsel involved early in any potential legal issue.
- Have counsel review polices regarding access and services.
- Training staff about policies, such as those on user access and handling difficult users, is a key step in avoiding liability issues.
- Professional malpractice lawsuits are unlikely to impact library services, at least in the near term. Liability and negligence lawsuits, however, are a different matter, and libraries and some staff have been sued.
- Keeping up with current developments in the field is something you ought to do; however, following legal developments that impact the field is critical to avoid potential stressful and costly legal action.
- Document, document, document!

REFERENCES

American Libraries. 2005. "Colorado Gets Meeting-Room Religion." *American Libraries* 36, no. 9: 28–29.

――――. 2006a. "DOJ Supports Prayer Meets." *American Libraries* 37, no. 2: 18–19.

――――. 2006b. "Homeless Residents Sue Over Borrowing Limits." *American Libraries* 37, no. 7: 18.

――――. 2006c. "Stir Raised by Dallas Body Odor Rule." *American Libraries* 37, no. 2: 11.

――――. 2007. "Supreme Court Won't Hear Meeting Room Appeal." *American Libraries* 38, no. 10: 18.

Arizona Republic. 2017. "Three Fired in Probe of Library Flooding." October 28: 1a–17a.

California State Library. 2017. *California Library Laws—2017*. https://www.library.ca.gov/publications/2017CaliforniaLibraryLaws.pdf.

DeRosa, Frank J. 1980. "The Disruptive Patron." *Library and Archival Security* 3, no. 3/4: 29–37.

Farrugia, Sarah. 2002. "A Dangerous Occupation? Violence in Public Libraries." *New Library World* 103, no. 9: 309–19.

Gruben, Karl T. 2006. "What Is Johnny Doing in the Library? Libraries, the U.S.A. PATRIOT Act, and Its Amendments." *St. Thomas Law Review* 19, no. 2: 297–328.

Healey, Paul D. 2008. *Professional Liability Issues for Librarians and Information Professionals*. New York: Neal-Schuman.

Jansen, Barbara A. 2010. "Internet Filtering 2.0: Checking Intellectual Freedom and Participative Practices at the Schoolhouse Door." *Knowledge Quest* 39, no. 1: 46–53.

Magi, Trina. 2010. "A Content Analysis of Library Vendor Policies: Do They Meet Our Standards?" *College and Research Libraries* 71, no. 3: 254–72.

Maycock, Angela. 2010. "Choose Privacy Week and School Libraries." *Knowledge Quest* 39, no. 1: 68–72.

Michigan District Library Law. 2017. "Establishing a District Library." www.michigan.gov/documents/mde/LM_Michigan_District_Library_Law_329703_7.pdf.

Murley, Diane. 2008. "Web Site Accessibility." *Law Library Journal* 100, no. 2: 401–06.

New York State Library. 2017. "Library Records." www.nysl.nysed.gov/libdev/excerpts/statutes.htm.

Newbold, Stephanie P. 2015. "Understanding Your Liability as a Public Administrator." In *Handbook of Public Administration* ed. by James L. Perry and Robert K. Christensen. New York: Wiley.

Wisconsin Department of Public Instruction: Division for Libraries and Technology. 2017. "Sales Tax." https://dpi.wi.gov/pld/legislation-funding/sales-tax.

 Leadership

To continue to be relevant, libraries will need to make dramatic changes, and for this to happen, leadership of a different kind is needed.

Deanna Marcum, 2016

Assuming and then succeeding in a leadership role in an academic library, regardless of one's formal position in the organizational structure, requires the right balance of two disparate types of skills.

Diane Klare, 2017

Transactional leaders use rewards and/or sanctions linked to effort and results to try to obtain better performance, and whether this leadership strategy is applicable to public organizations is a controversial issue.

Christian B. Jacobson and Lotte B. Andersen, 2017

L eadership is a widely discussed topic in all the organizational sectors. However, it is of particular importance in the public and non-profit sectors. From the library perspective, it is of great significance, as our opening quotation from Deanna Marcum suggests. Melisa Mallon (2017) further emphasized its importance when she wrote: "Whether it is articulated or not, library deans, managers, subject liaisons, technicians, and library student employees should ideally share a common goal to contribute to the success of both their library and their university. Successful leadership isn't top down; rather, a strong organization sees everyone (at all levels) working in conjunction to fulfill the mission of the organization" (p. 90). She also made the point that leadership development is a key ingredient for employee engagement and increased productivity.

Some of the literature on leadership can leave you with the impression that it is "good" and that management is "bad." Many of the writers do not say that directly; rather, they give that impression by listing traits and activities that contrast the two roles. Bennis and Goldsmith (2003) have a section that illustrates this duality in the first chapter of their book *Learning to Lead*. (Warren Bennis is considered one of the leading scholars and researchers in the field of leadership.) Table 4.1 summarizes some differences between leaders and managers (note it is a composite of a variety of a number of lists). These are stark differences, but they are not that clear-cut, and Bennis and Goldsmith's extended discussion makes it clear that effective managers and leaders in organizations carry out both roles. Such lists are often taken out of context and presented as either-or behaviors. A typical pattern is to become a manager early in your career and then develop your leadership skills while still managing.

TABLE 4.1 Characteristics of Managers Compared to Leaders

MANAGER	LEADER
Administers	Innovates
Is a copy	Is original
Maintains	Develops
Accepts reality	Investigates reality
Systems/structure focus	People focus
Relies on control	Inspires trust
Short-term view	Long-range view
Asks how and when	Asks what and why
Eye on bottom line	Eye on the horizon
Imitates	Originates
Accepts status quo	Challenges status quo
Classic good solider	Own person
Does things right	Does the right thing

Abraham Zaleznik leaves you in no doubt about his view of the differences. His 1992 article "Managers and Leaders: Are They Different?" was viewed a classic when *Harvard Business Review* reprinted it in 2010. In the article, Zaleznik (2010) stated: "But just as managerial culture differs from the entrepreneurial culture that develops when leaders appear in organizations, managers and leaders are very different kinds of people. They differ in motivation, personal history, and in how they think and act" (p. 16). We don't fully agree with Zaleznik's position—yes, it can be true, but the differences are not always as clear-cut as he would make them. Gary Yukl, another major researcher in the field, held that both skills are necessary in order to have a successful organization: "To be effective, a leader must influence people to carry out requests, support proposals, and implement decisions. In large organizations, the effectiveness of most managers depends on influence over superiors and peers as well as influence over subordinates" (Yukl 2009, p. 207). We would suggest that his statement applies to any size organization, not just large ones, as well as to every administrator.

We agree that leadership can bring about good things for an individual, workplace colleagues, and the organization. However, as Barbara Kellerman stated (2004), leadership

---

:bulb: **TRY THIS**

It is difficult to define "leadership." Think of someone whom you consider is a successful leader. Now try to identify the qualities that make her or him a successful leader.

can be good or bad. Kellerman related a story about giving a speech in which she said that Hitler was a bad leader and immediately someone in the audience shouted—"ethically he was bad, but he was a good leader. There is a difference." Indeed, there is; leadership outcomes are not always good.

WHAT IS LEADERSHIP?

Leadership is about convincing people that there is an organizational vision that is exciting, realistic, and doable. It is about inspiring people and getting them committed to the organization. It is about giving them confidence so that they can achieve the organizational goals and about coaching and mentoring them in their career development activities. Leadership isn't easy to define, and some writers have compared it with love, saying leadership is easier to recognize than to define.

The changes taking place in the public sector have prompted research into leadership in the library sector. Pors and Johannsen (2003) carried out a comprehensive survey into leadership and management in Danish libraries, one aspect of which focused on leadership roles. They analyzed the data in relation to the new public management and value-based management. They found that the library leaders perceive their future roles as being oriented toward people and values.

Mullins and Linehan (2006a) carried out a wider investigation into leadership, examining the views of thirty top-level public librarians from Ireland, Britain, and the east coast of the United States. One finding explored senior library leaders' perceptions of leadership: whether they distinguished classic leadership from management and administrative practices, both conceptually and in their daily work. They found that in all three countries leadership and management were confused and that leadership is a scarce quality (Mullins and Linehan 2006a). A second finding was that there was no universal behavior, even within national boundaries, for effective leadership, but two-thirds of the respondents prioritized the implementation of vision as being the most essential element of library leadership (Mullins and Linehan 2006b).

The perceptions of the senior public library leaders indicated that they supported the centrality of leadership for optimal strategic and operational practices in librarianship. However, it is a challenge to identify and consider the leadership skills and personal attributes needed for success (Mullins and Linehan 2005a). Taken together, the findings of this transnational study appear to indicate that there is a need for leadership development programs to be provided for those at middle management levels in the three countries in order to ensure the health of public libraries at a time of major changes in their operating environments.

So what do leaders do? The most important aspect of library leadership is to drive the library forward. The driving force is a vision that sets the direction for the library and one that motivates staff and supporters alike. A leader is also a planner, working with the staff to turn the vision into reality by preparing concrete plans for implementing the vision and for their area of authority and accountability and in accordance with organizational policies.

A manager operates on authority, receiving policy guidelines from above, but a leader derives the power as a policy maker both from their superiors and from their subordinates as a result of gaining the trust of their subordinates by formulating policy with them. After consultation and taking advice, the leader has to be the ultimate decision maker.

A leader is more effective if she or he is an expert in the field in which she or he operates. Being an expert facilitates communication with staff. Expertise also generates trust in the person's judgments regarding professional practice. Leaders also share knowledge and skills willingly and in a manner that suggests an equal relationship, not a superior-subordinate relationship. This is an effective means of building a collaborative workplace.

Increasingly a leader has to be a role model. A leader sets the tone and pace for the group, particularly in ethical behavior. Sometimes a staff member emulates a leader's methods of working, attitudes, and, occasionally, even style of dress. The leader is the ultimate arbitrator and mediator. When the staff has respect for and trust in their leader, they bring some of the tricky problems to the leader for resolution.

Library managers and leaders are the library's spokespeople to outsiders. Although other people may be capable of assuming this role, the staff "knows" that the leader will not only present the library's position but also do everything possible to protect their interests.

Leaders know they can be scapegoated for almost any problem and accept this as they accept the accountability that accompanies their position. The phrase "the buck stops here," used by President Harry Truman, still holds now in terms of leadership accountability.

Moving into a leadership role tests any individual. Think about the descriptions of the two roles (manager and leader) listed in table 4.1 and you'll see that they are, in some ways, diametrically opposed. From having the responsibility for ensuring the smooth operation of part of an organization and focusing on the bottom line, leaders take a wider, forward-looking perspective. Public sector leaders, and to some degree those in such roles in non-profits, have a challenge that was outlined in Patrick Ibarra's 2016 article. That challenge is that "leaders in government often suffer from inertia, where past solutions are

👥 ADVISORY BOARD EXPERIENCE

Joseph Mika successfully used assessment tools in his management and leadership courses and workshops. He is partial to a self-survey set of instruments by Teleometrics International, namely, the Blake and Mouton's Managerial and Leadership Style Grids, and particularly the Styles of Management Inventory (SMI), which identifies the individual's management style and indicates areas to be changed. Teleometrics also offers a Management Appraisal Survey designed to be taken by coworkers and can be used by a manager to measure employee assessment against her or his own SMI; a Styles of Leadership Survey (SLS) that ascertains the individual's leadership style and suggests its effects on staff; and a Leadership Appraisal Survey that provides the leader with his or her associates' assessments of his or her leadership behavior as identified in the SLS (available at www.teleometrics.com/programs/leadership_style_grid_blake _and_mouton.html).

He is also fond of using Taylor Hartman's *The People Code* (New York: Scribner, 2007; formerly titled *The Color Code*), which utilizes a very simple questionnaire (forty-five total questions) called The Hartman Personality Profile. This is a straightforward assessment tool that helps managers and leaders in classifying their personality and behavior (categorized as the colors Red, Blue, White, and Yellow) and aids in improving relationships with others—including coworkers and family members.

resynthesized to fix today's problems . . . . Indeed, playing safe is no longer smart." (Ibarra, p. 24). Taking some carefully assessed risk is necessary in today's rapidly changing world.

Diane Klare's quotation at the beginning of this chapter suggests there are two broad categories of skills a leader must have—soft and technical. The soft category relates to people skills. Technical skills are developed through training and experience. All of the opening quotations at the beginning of this chapter imply leadership can be learned, something that was not always believed. In the following section, we explore some of the standard approaches and theories regarding leadership.

LEADERSHIP THEORIES

The literature of leadership in general is extensive and ranges from research-based theories to gurus' philosophies. All have value in outlining what it takes to become a leader. The writings that form the theoretical base can be grouped into seven traditional approaches that draw from a number of disciplines, including psychology, management, sociology, and political science.

The trait approach was followed by most writers from the early twentieth century until the late 1950s. It assumes that a person is born either a leader or a follower. However, as is the case with so many other personality trait studies (for example, of the creative person, the successful writer, or the famous singer), the list of traits became very long, general in character, and sometimes contradictory. Hernon, Powell, and Young (2003) likewise produced an interesting list as a result of their contemporary research into the "qualities" or traits of library directors.

The behavioral approach was influenced by a classic paper in which Lewin, Lippitt, and White (1939) reported an experiment that examined three leadership styles: autocratic, democratic, and laissez-faire. Likely motivated by world events in the 1940s, researchers moved on to examine how people act when operating as leaders. One outcome was the development of a questionnaire at Ohio State University in the late 1950s that is still used today in leadership surveys—the Leader Behavior Description Questionnaire (LBDQ). Originally it was a two-factor instrument measuring task-oriented and people-oriented behavior. Efforts to develop a more complex format have met with limited success.

In the 1960s, the focus shifted from personality traits and behavior to the environment in which leadership exists—the situational approach. Researchers began to study such factors as the interactions between the manager (leader) and the staff (followers), the organization's needs at any given time, the type of work that the organization performs, and/or the group's values, ethics, experiences, and so forth. Both experience and research

---

‖‖‖‖ CHECK THIS OUT

A good article that discusses situational leadership in a library context is Rick L. Fought and Mitsunori Misawa's "Effective Leadership in Academic Health Sciences Libraries: A Qualitative Phenomenological Study" (*Journal of Library Administration* 56, no. 8: 974–89, 2016).

studies indicate that the operating environment is an important factor in the success or failure of a leader, but it is not the sole issue.

Perhaps the best situational model is Fiedler's (1978) contingency theory. Believing that there was no single best way to lead, his model contains three main variables: leader-member relationship, task structure, and leader's power position. Each variable has two subcomponents: good or bad relationships, structured or unstructured tasks, and strong or weak power positions. Two other factors indicate whether the leader was or is relationship- or task-oriented. Research suggests that task-oriented leaders generally do better in situations that have good relationships, structured tasks, and either a weak or a strong power position. When relationships are good, the task unstructured, and the power position strong, they do equally well. The other situation in which task-oriented leaders perform well is in poor to moderate relationships, unstructured tasks, and a strong power position. Relationship-oriented leaders tend to do better in all the other situations.

In terms of libraries, the leader's power position in relation to outside agencies may be low because the library is normally part of a larger organization. So, when the library needs strong leadership in its relationship with other agencies and organizations, there may be a problem; the staff often fail to remember this constraint when assessing their leader's success with outside groups. Within the library, an individual has a clearly defined position of power resulting from the hierarchical structure that is typical of most libraries. Again, the more structured the work environment, the less room there is for maneuvering in order to obtain a desired result for the group.

Transformational leadership emerged in the 1970s from the work of James McGregor Burns (1978), who blended the trait and behavioral concepts. A key element is influence, with both the leader and followers influencing one another. Burns distinguished two interrelated types of influence: transforming and transactional. Both charismatic and transformational leaders have vision, self-confidence, and the ability to arouse strong follower support, but transformational leaders possess two other factors—intellectual stimulation and individual consideration. Transactional leadership takes place when there is an exchange of valued "things" between leaders and followers, such as economic rewards and support.

▌▌▌▌ CHECK THIS OUT

Jason Martin's 2017 article described the impact of transformational leadership in libraries in "Personal Relationships and Professional Results: The Positive Impact of Transformational Leaders on Academic Librarians" (*Journal of Academic Librarianship* 43, no. 3: 108–15, 2017).

One approach that has been adopted in a number of libraries is servant-leadership, developed by Robert Greenleaf (1977). He considered that people who are viewed as great leaders first feel the need to serve, followed by making a conscious choice to lead. Greenleaf felt that servant-leaders are more likely to be trusted, to use initiative, to be thoughtful listeners, to have an active imagination, to feel empathy, to be persuasive, to have foresight, and to become a builders of communities.

In 2016, Schwarz, Newman, Cooper, and Eva explored how servant-leadership affected public service motivation, or PSM (see chapter 16). One of their findings was that "servant-leaders are able to mobilize 'subsidiary actors' who would like to become servant-leaders themselves and are able to induce higher levels of PSM, thus increasing their job performance" (p. 1035).

Adaptive leadership thinks about today and what is likely to happen in the near future, and this is important for libraries. Fulmer (2000), writing about adaptive organizations, describes the volatile and complex landscape in which organizations operate in the twenty-first century—and libraries form part of that landscape. There will be increasing need to anticipate the nature and speed of change that will take place in the social, political, economic, and technological systems within which libraries operate and to determine how they can best adapt to change. Melding the situational, transformational, and servant-leadership approaches could create adaptive leadership, but it will call for smart footwork.

▌▌▌ CHECK THIS OUT

Joe Heaply's essay "Servant-Leadership in Public Libraries" (journals.iupui.edu/index
.php/IndianaLibraries/article/down) provides an example of the application of the
servant concept in a library setting.

EMOTIONAL INTELLIGENCE

Two concepts have been described by Goleman (1995, 2006)—emotional intelligence (EI), which creates awareness of our own feelings and those of others, and social intelligence, which explores our relationships with others. Understanding these concepts is important to developing the behavior patterns essential for working effectively with staff, colleagues in the wider organization, the ultimate boss, and the community served.

Perhaps the most widely used definition of EI appeared in 1990 (Mayer and Salovey 1990). EI is "the ability to monitor one's own and others' emotions, to discriminate among them, and to use the information to guide one's thinking and actions" (p. 189). This definition is fairly broad and encompasses most of the elements various authors and researchers include in their work regardless of the label they use for the concept. It is also one of the first efforts at defining the concept.

There are two primary models of what constitutes EI—mental ability and mixed (Zeidner, Matthews, and Roberts 2004). The *mental ability* approach is led by John Mayer, while Daniel Goleman has led the popularized *mixed* approach. Mayer and Salovey divided EI into four broad areas—accurately perceiving emotions, using emotions to assist in thinking, understanding emotional meanings, and managing emotions. Meanwhile, Goleman and his followers employ a five-category approach—identifying one's emotional states and the links among emotion, thought, and action; managing one's emotions; entering emotional states related to the drive to achieve and succeed; reading, sensitivity to, and influencing others' emotions; and entering into and sustaining satisfactory interpersonal relationships. Both approaches clearly relate to the earlier definition—knowing your own and others' emotions, understanding those emotions, and employing that information in a positive manner.

You can see the potential value of understanding workplace emotions, especially one's own, along with the ability to control and use those feelings in a positive manner. Being able to effectively and positively influence others based on an understanding of their emotions is a major plus. Both models provide guidance for developing such abilities. Emotionally intelligent leaders usually have a greater sense of well-being, stronger relationships, high morale employees, and overall greater success.

▦ CHECK THESE OUT

Goleman, Daniel. 2004. "What Makes a Leader?" *Harvard Business Review* 82 (1 January): 82–91. (Goleman's seminal paper on emotional intelligence)

Hernon, Peter, Joan Giesecke, and Camila Alire. 2007. *Academic Librarians as Emotionally Intelligent Leaders.* Westport, CT: Libraries Unlimited.

McKee, Annie, Richard E. Boyatzis, and Frances Johnston. *Becoming a Resonant Leader: Develop Your Emotional Intelligence, Renew Your Relationships, Sustain Your Effectiveness.* Boston, MA: Harvard Business Press, 2008.

Mills, John. 2006. "Affect, Emotional Intelligence and Librarian–User Interaction." *Library Review* 55, no. 9: 587–97.

Richer, Lisa. 2006. "Emotional Intelligence at Work: An Interview with Daniel Goleman." *Public Libraries* 45, no. 1: 24–28.

DEVELOPING LEADERSHIP SKILLS

Given the broad range of functions, what should a person do to become a leader? First, check back to the characteristics of a leader presented in table 4.1. Consider whether you possess the attributes and skills and can achieve a healthy work-life balance—and then think about your motivation. Getting honest feedback from a mentor and colleagues can help a prospective leader identify his or her strengths and weakness. This is one way to evaluate your self-assessment. There are many instruments you can use in the assessment process.

The assessment results are meaningful only to the degree that the process is undertaken with the goal of gaining self-understanding. What follows is but a sampling of what a person can find searching online for "leadership assessment." One starting point for online leadership assessment sites is the Leadership Learning Community's website (www.leadershiplearning.org/). This site also supplies links to other sites that have assessment instruments. Another resource is R. E. Brown and Associates' site (http://rebrown.com/). One of the resources offered is a forty-question instrument that assesses both managerial and leadership behaviors. The firm recommends that the manager-leadership scale be used in conjunction with two other instruments it offers. The goal of the assessments is to create a personal development program that the firm also offers.

Strengths Finder (https://www.gallupstrengthscenter.com) is an online personal strengths assessment sometimes used in leadership programs. The assessment evaluates an individual's predisposition to thirty-four "talent themes" (based on interviews from the Gallup Organization) such as achiever, activator, adaptable, analytical, arranger, and so forth. While there have been some criticisms of the instrument, it can be helpful for self-assessment. (It could potentially serve as a strong team-building activity to learn where each team member's strengths and common characteristics lie, as well as areas that may be lacking among the team.)

The Learning Center offers a thirty-point Leadership Assessment—Personal Satisfaction Survey (www.learningcenter.net/library/leadership.shtml). Some of the areas covered include "making and communicating decisions promptly," "involving others in planning actions," and "believing in and providing training that teaches leadership, teamwork, and technical skills." One responds on a five-point scale from very satisfied to very dissatisfied with a "neutral" midpoint.

Having secured information from the self-assessment activity, you can make decisions about what areas to concentrate on in your development program—assuming you still wish to be a leader. (Even if you find you have no desire to become a leader, it is still worthwhile to work on those areas identified for improvement, as some individuals find leadership "thrust upon them" or becomes leaders "by default.") As is so often the case, Warren Bennis provides some sage advice about how to start a self-assessment process (Bennis and Goldsmith 2003). He suggests there are four key areas to think about—self-motivation, taking responsibility, having self-confidence in the ability to learn, and thinking about your experiences. He, like almost every other writer on the topic of leadership, believes a key factor in long-term success is a commitment to lifelong learning.

Leaders keep up-to-date with changes in approaches to management and leadership issues, and, of course, information and communications technologies. By maintaining currency in professional practice and issues, leaders help staff with their informal learning.

One-on-one learning can take several forms; however, we will cover three of the most common—coaching, mentoring, and modeling. Coaching, mentoring, and modeling are interrelated to some degree. A coach is often modeling while engaged in coaching and thus has an influence beyond the one-on-one coaching activity. A mentor can be, and often is, both a model and a coach. As Frederic Hudson (1999) says, coaching is not about advising, nor is it about fixing things or solving problems. Rather, it is about establishing a trust relationship with the goal of improving or developing a skill or ability. Likewise, mentoring is also about trust and respect. Modeling is not directed at a particular individual but rather demonstrates a behavior, value, or similar trait that others can copy. Nevertheless, only a person who is trusted or respected is likely to have his or her actions and values modeled by others.

Coaching ought to play an ongoing role in the management of any library as a normal part of the control process and/or performance appraisal program. However, the type of coaching of interest here is not the "corrective" type, but, rather, it is developmental in character. As such, the coach may not necessarily be a member of the organization. Many of the firms that offer leadership development programs make available one-on-one coaching services. (Coaching at the senior level in both for- and not-for-profit sectors has become a small growth industry.)

Coaching for "success" is what the leader's goal should be. Most people have a desire to succeed, and activities directed toward improving (becoming faster, easier, etc.) success are welcomed, especially when the source is trusted and/or respected. Building and striving for ever-greater success means coaching is not a one-time event. The process should be a "philosophy" rather than a job for the leader.

Because coaching as well as mentoring is one-on-one, it should be clear that the one-size-fits-all approach is not very effective. Tailoring the approach to the individual being coached is what works best, but it calls for the coach to have a high degree of "people sensitivity." Working on developing or improving one's "people sense" is a worthwhile activity. One area where it should be clear that a different approach would be more appropriate is when the work group's members come from a range of generations. A tailored approach also requires the coach to keep in mind that the coaching process in itself will not change the person being coached. What coaching can and should do is motivate the person being coached to want to change (to undertake a personal "transformation").

A 2016 article about the impact of leadership training by Seidle, Fernandez, and Perry concluded:

> The empirical analysis attempted to answer the question of whether a leadership training and development intervention that combines four popular methods can be effective at improving both individual leader performance and organizational effectiveness. On that question the findings are fairly clear. A combination of coaching, classroom instruction, multisource feedback, and experiential training has a decided impact. (p. 611)

E-LEADERSHIP

Technology-mediated environments require some adjustments in leadership behavior. We believe the underlying leadership basics remain valid, but there are changes in emphasis. Leadership in an e-environment calls for meeting the challenges posed by several paradoxes (some new and some old ones in new guises), accepting greater ambiguity, and understanding peoples' complex behavior. Deanna Marcum's (2016) opening quotation is from her essay about library leadership in the digital age and is well worth reading.

Pulley and Sessa (2001) described five sets of paradoxes and complex challenges that face e-organizations and their leaders:

- swift and mindful
- individual and community
- top-down and grassroots
- details and big picture
- flexible and steady

These paradoxes will exist, to some degree, for all organizations, regardless of size or profit orientation.

Is it possible to make *swift and mindful* decisions, responses, and so forth, in today's e-environment? While it may be possible, it also becomes increasingly challenging. E-mail, cell phones, instant messaging, texting, and the like make it possible to communicate quickly and, in some cases, to places not possible in the past. The communications technologies also make it more difficult to get away from work pressures. Senders of messages know their message will arrive in a matter of seconds, and they very often have the expectation or hope of getting back a quick response whatever the time zone or location of the recipient. A recognized problem with quick responses is regret—"I hit 'send' too quickly."

Rapid decisions usually require drawing on past experiences with little or no opportunity to assess the current situation to determine to what degree the current environment matches the past environment(s) of decision making. They also depend on quick and easy access to current management information. Collecting, locating, and using additional data or information is not very compatible with speedy decision making. Unless there are well-designed and robust information systems in place, technology's speed and capabilities may drive a behavior that may not always be beneficial in the e-world.

In terms of the *individual and community* paradox, there may be greater freedom and autonomy when communicating with each other and the "outside" world as an outcome of information and communication technology (ICT). E-mail and the cell phone have generally replaced the landline telephone. As noted earlier, while technology facilitates *individual* autonomy and connectivity, it can also lead to a sense of isolation. Virtual teams and individuals working from home or elsewhere may not have the same opportunities to meet face-to-face and build the same *community* as those who are in the traditional workplace. Certainly, almost all the research on employee motivation and job satisfaction in the twentieth century shows that social interaction in the workplace was an important issue. Dependency on face-to-face communication and meeting at the water cooler will change significantly as the boomers retire.

The *top-down and grassroots* paradox has existed for a great many years. What makes it more important today is the impact of technology and the relatively recent changes in management practices. Empowering staff and the flattening of the organizational structure have been occurring for some years, driven largely by economic conditions and technological developments. Both empowering and flattening (grassroots) means staff have a much greater influence on operations than in the past. Technology makes it possible for any or all "voices" to speak to an issue, invited or not. Those voices can be heard both within and outside the library. It is the unthinking leader who does not recognize the potential impact of one or more voices being heard by the outside world. Another factor favoring grassroots is the fact that change is occurring so rapidly that it is almost impossible for one person (the leader) to absorb it all; thus, input from the frontline people becomes very valuable. Leaders must grapple with the task of maintaining control and accountability while engaging in collaborative activities and empowering behavior.

The *details and big picture* paradox is also not a new phenomenon. Leader-managers have had to address this issue for a long time. Some individuals are prone to see only details (they can't see the forest for the trees) while others can't seem to get beyond the big picture. Either of these single perspectives will cause issues in the workplace.

You ought to maintain some focus on the overall direction (*big picture*) of the library, its progress toward achieving desired goals, while keeping a sharp eye out for factors (*details*) that may indicate some adjustments are needed. One goal should be to ensure that all staff members understand the importance of both details and long-term goals and know to share their observations when they notice something out of the ordinary. Many staff members may have access to the information, but if no one has the responsibility for monitoring changes, critical information may fall through the cracks.

Pulley and Sessa's final paradox is *flexible and steady*. Again, this is not a new paradox for organizations. What have changed are its pervasive implications for all types of organizations. In the past, there were a number of organizational types—including a great many research libraries—that operated in what you might call a "placid" environment (limited threats, little change; think about the discussion regarding Emery and Trist in chapter 1) and only a few in a "turbulent" environment (many threats and high level of change). Today most organizations must be aware of changing circumstances and recognize there may be serious threats. In the past, stability, as long as it did not endanger long-term viability, was highly desired, as it allowed for a clear focus and momentum toward well-established goals. For most of today's organizations, the requirement for flexibility and the associated changes make it difficult to discern how much, if any, progress is taking place.

For today's leader, a major challenge is keeping everyone focused on long-term directions while responding to a rapidly changing environment.

Paradoxes like these, along with other challenges, make it less and less likely a successful organization will be led by a "Great Person" or "Lone Ranger." The "I am the boss, and I am in control" leadership style is probably a thing of the past. Yes, there are almost always one or more senior persons with ultimate accountability for the organization's success or failure. However, in many organizations, there is a growing use of multiple leaders and managers to share most of the responsibility.

A real challenge is when the leader has some followers interacting with her or him face-to-face and others primarily through technology. Often the e-group members believe (or sense) that the face-to-face group, because of the collocation with the leader, has greater influence than they do. Naturally, this can influence their attitudes and morale in a somewhat negative way. The leader with such groups must work especially hard to create a balance between them.

Avolio and Kahai (2003, p. 333) summarized what they saw as the major issues for e-leadership:

- Leaders and followers have more access to information, which changes their interactions.
- Leadership is migrating to lower organizational levels and through the boundaries of the organization.
- Leadership creates and exists in networks that cross traditional organizational and community boundaries.
- Followers know more at an earlier point in the decision making process, and this potentially affects the credibility and influence of leaders.
- Unethical leaders with limited resources can now negatively impact a much broader audience.
- The amount of time the most senior leaders can have with their followers has decreased.

We would add, although it could be subsumed under the first point, that written communication and trust have become increasingly important in the virtual workplace.

E-TEAM ISSUES

There are two broad categories of e-teams—internal and external (multi-organizational)—with which libraries deal. A major difference in both is that a leader seldom has as much control over basic issues, especially in the case of external teams. The primary reason for using virtual teams is to overcome time and/or geographical issues.

Cascio and Shurygailo (2003) suggest a four-cell matrix for thinking about variation issues with virtual teams. One axis is for either a single or a multiple leader situation, and the other axis represents either single or multiple locations. The least complex situation is the single leader/single location variation. We would suggest that this is the place to start any migration to virtual teams or telecommuters, as it gives everyone a chance to work out problems and issues. One can then follow up with more complex arrangements.

Internal library teams, especially those created for a special project, usually consist of people from several departments who often engage in the team activities along with some or all of their "normal" duties. This creates the multiple leader-manager and, most commonly, the one location situation, although, where there are branch operations, it could be a multiple location situation. We mentioned earlier some of the problems that can arise from cross-departmental teams when "normal" duties exist alongside team responsibilities. While the use of technology makes it easier to shift work activities to "off hours," it cannot reduce the pressure of performance expectations for team members with additional duties.

When leading a virtual team tasked to handle a project, whether an internal or external team, there are several significant areas to address if the team is to succeed. In the case of a multi-organizational team, such as one working on a nationwide 24/7 reference service, the challenges are more complex than for the internal team. Based on our experience, the first key activity is to ensure that senior leaders are committed to the project and are willing to devote the necessary resources to see it through. Senior leaders must work out several important details, such as selecting one person to be the liaison or contact point between the team and the senior leaders. Establishing reporting and communication responsibilities should also be done before the team is created. A significant amount of time should go into discussing team mileposts, timelines, assessments, and the types of skills and abilities team members need to bring to the table. The last item regarding skills and abilities is very important to selecting a staff person based on his or her capability of making a contribution to team activities rather than one based on local politics or personal feelings. Without such discussions it is almost inevitable that the team will have performance problems; the project could be delayed, and a growing sense of frustration will occur among the libraries.

We have noted from time to time in earlier chapters, and will do so in later chapters, that some libraries are unionized. Most public libraries operate under some type of public employee/civil service system. Both unions and civil service contracts and regulations can limit your leadership options. You may have a wonderful vision—the correct one—of what direction the library should move in. As one of our Advisory Board members commented, changing library direction can be akin to steering a mega tanker in a new direction rather than turning a row boat. Contract provisions and civil service regulations will slow your progress. It can be done, but not quickly—take your time, actively engage in advocacy, be political, and think both tactically and strategically. If you do so, you will likely succeed; just know it may take longer than you'd like.

Note that in the remaining chapters we will employ the terms manager-leader, leader-manager, managerial leader, leader, and manager interchangeably. In part we do so to provide some variation, but more importantly, to emphasize the fact that to be effective in today's work environment you need to be both a leader and a manager.

🛈 KEY POINTS TO REMEMBER

- The most successful people in organizations are both leaders and managers.
- Leaders can be found at every level in a library.
- Leadership is difficult to define but easier to recognize.
- There are significant differences between managing and leading.
- Seven traditional approaches to leadership can be identified.
- Leadership functions are enduring.

- It is never too soon to start learning how to be a leader.
- Leaders need to have many different skills.
- Communication, political, and team-building skills are very important.
- Appropriate structures are needed for employee-centered services.

REFERENCES

Avolio, Bruce, and Surinder Kahai. 2003. "Adding 'E' to E-leadership: How It May Impact Your Leadership." *Organizational Dynamics* 31, no. 4: 325–38.

Bennis, Warren, and Joan Goldsmith. 2003. *Learning to Lead: A Workbook on Becoming a Leader.* New York: Basic Books.

Burns, James McGregor. 1978. *Leadership.* New York: Harper Collins.

Cascio, Wayne, and Stan Shurygailo. 2003. "E-leadership and Virtual Teams." *Organizational Dynamics* 31, no. 4: 362–76.

Fiedler, Fred E. 1978. "The Contingency Model and the Dynamics of the Leadership Process." In *Advances in Experimental Social Psychology*, edited by L. Berkowitz, 60–112. New York: Academic Press.

Fulmer, William E. 2000. *Shaping the Adaptive Organization: Landscapes, Learning, and Leadership in Volatile Times.* New York: AMACOM.

Goleman, Daniel. 1995. *Emotional Intelligence.* New York: Bantam Books.

_____. 2006. *Social Intelligence: The New Science of Human Relationships.* New York: Bantam Books.

Greenleaf, Robert K. 1977. *Servant Leadership: A Journey into the Nature of Legitimate Power and Greatness.* New York: Paulist Press.

Hernon, Peter, Ronald Powell, and Arthur Young. 2003. *The Next Library Leadership: Attributes of Academic and Public Library Directors.* Westport, CT: Libraries Unlimited.

Hudson, Frederic. 1999. *The Handbook of Coaching.* San Francisco: Jossey-Bass.

Ibarra, Patrick. 2016. "Cultivate Creative Leadership. Realize Extraordinary Results." *Public Management* 98, no. 11: 24, 26.

Kellerman, Barbara. 2004. *Bad Leadership: What It Is, How It Happens, Why It Happens.* Cambridge, MA: Harvard Business School Press.

Klare, Diane. 2017. "The Accidental Director: Critical Skills in Academic Library Leadership." *Library Leadership and Management* 31, no. 2: 1–11.

Jacobson, Christian B., and Lotte B. Andersen. 2017. "Leading Public Service Organizations: How to Obtain High Employee Self-Efficiency and Organizational Performance." *Public Management Review* 19, no. 2: 253–73.

Lewin, Kurt, Ronald Lippitt, and Ralph White. 1939. "Patterns of Aggressive Behavior in Experimentally Created Social Climates." *Journal of Social Psychology* 10: 271–99.

Mallon, Melissa. 2017. "Leadership Development." *Public Services Quarterly* 13, no. 2: 90–97.

Marcum, Deanna. 2016. "Library Leadership for the Digital Age." *Information Services and Use* 36, nos. 1–2: 105–11.

Mayer, John, and Peter Salovey. 1990. "Emotional Intelligence." *Imagination, Cognition, and Personality* 9, no. 3: 185–211.

Mullins, John, and Margaret Linehan. 2005. "The Central Role of Leaders in Public Libraries." *Library Management* 26, nos. 6/7: 386–96.

_____. 2006a. "Are Public Libraries Led or Managed?" *Library Review* 55, no. 4: 237–48.

_____. 2006b. "Desired Qualities of Public Library Leaders." *Leadership and Organizational Development Journal* 27, no. 2: 133–43.

Pors, Niels Ole, and Carl Gustav Johannsen. 2003. "Library Directors under Cross Pressure between New Public Management and Value-Based Management." *Library Management* 24, nos. 1/2: 51-60.

Pulley, Mary Lynn, and Valerie Sessa. 2001. "E-leadership: Tackling Complex Challenges." *Industrial and Commercial Training* 33, no. 6: 225-30.

Schwarz, Gary, Alexander Newman, Brian Cooper, and Nathan Eva. 2016. "Servant-Leadership and Followers Job Performance: The Mediating Effect of Public Service Motivation." *Public Administration* 94, no. 4: 1025-41.

Seidle, Brett, Sergio Fernandez, and James L. Perry. 2016. "Do Leadership Training and Development Make a Difference in the Public Sector?" *Public Administration Review* 76, no. 4: 603-13.

Yukl, Gary. 2009. "Power and the Interpersonal Influence of Leaders." In *Power and Interdependence in Organizations*, edited by Dean Tjosvold and Barbara Wisse, 207-23. Cambridge: Cambridge University Press.

Zaleznik, Abraham. 2010. "Managers and Leaders: Are They Different?" Reprint of 1992 article in *Leadership Insights: 15 Unique Perspectives on Effective Leadership* (*Harvard Business Review*). Cambridge, MA: Harvard Business School Publishing.

Zeidner, Moshe, Gerald Matthews, and Richard Roberts. 2004. "Emotional Intelligence in the Workplace: A Critical Review." *Applied Psychology* 53, no. 3: 371-99.

CHAPTER 5

Ethics

Ethics and genuine professional success march together in the enterprise called *public service.*

Carol W. Lewis and Stuart C. Gilman, 2012

Professional ethics are the principles of conduct that guide and govern behavior.

Lilli Luo, 2016

With a plethora of digital resources literally at our fingertips, as well those of our teachers and students, we continue to face other, older problems, such as the violation of intellectual property rights.

Barbara Fiehn, 2016

Some professional associations have included case studies on their websites with a view to assisting members in their ethical decision-making.

Stuart Ferguson, Clare Thornley, and Forbes Gibb, 2016

E thical behavior is important for any organization; however, it is critical for public and non-profit organizations, especially in today's world. In that the U.S. trust of government is low in the United States, there is variation in the level of trust by agency. Interestingly, libraries are among the most highly trusted publicly-supported organizations. To maintain such trust ethical actions are essential. Any hint of unethical behavior reduces the level of the trust.

Ethics, organizational values, and organizational social responsibility are interrelated yet different concepts that apply to all organizations, including libraries. ALA has demonstrated interest in all three for a great many years. There is the code of ethics, standards of service, and the work of the Social Responsibilities Round Table (SRRT; www.ala.org/srrt/) as examples. Such efforts are fine in the abstract, but what matters is how they are implemented on the service floor. Managers and supervisors set the tone at the practical level (known as managerial ethics).

Some people believe that "managerial ethics" is an oxymoron. Management ethics deal with right and wrong actions and decisions. The difference between social responsibility and management ethics is that the focus of the former is on organizational action and activities while the latter focuses on personal actions. Although the definition appears clear-cut, it is seldom so in practice.

A study published in the 1980s indicated that frontline supervisors (41 percent), middle managers (26 percent), and top managers (20 percent) all believed they had to

/ 63 /

> ▕▏▕▏ **CHECK THIS OUT**
>
> An interesting article about the mangers role in maintaining an ethical workplace is Donovan A. McFarlane and George Alexakis's "Sustaining an Ethical Culture: A Systems Approach" (*Journal of Ethics and Entrepreneurship* 6, no. 2: 143–58, 2016).

compromise personal principles in order to conform to organizational expectations (Schmidt and Posner 1982). A more recent study (*The Economist* 2016) reported that 9 percent of the employees surveyed "said they had been pressured by managers to undertake a task that compromised their ethical beliefs" (p. 70). It is important to note this study focused on the personal beliefs not professional codes of conduct. However, as we will cover later, it is difficult to keep personal and professional values separated.

A key to keeping ethical conflict to a minimum is for senior managerial leaders to behave in clearly ethical ways and to recognize that conflicts may exist in the minds of subordinates. A very simple example of how such a conflict could arise would be in a library with a policy that the collection should contain all points of view on subjects. Do the collection developers face a possible conflict between personal values and organizational expectations? The answer is often yes, depending on the subject and on an individual's religious, political, and other beliefs. We look at such issues in more depth later in this chapter.

Library staff members make dozens of decisions every day, some of which have ethical implications whether recognized as such or not. The public services area is where the majority of such occur (see Luo 2016 for examples); however, even "backroom" decision may have some ethical elements. For example, decisions regarding what subject headings to use for an item can either increase or decrease its accessibility. Personal values and beliefs can influence decisions that should be based on professional values. It can happen without our awareness.

Jean Peer (2008) made the following point:

> Ethics is about choices. As a system of principles determining right or wrong conduct, ethics defines the parameters of those choices. . . . Indeed, ethics relates to "custom," the word deriving from ethos, the way things are done. . . . In the years before publicly-funded libraries, librarians had no transcendent obligation to the local community, to the larger society, to their profession, or to the values it embodied. (pp. 1–2)

Her book, *Library Ethics*, provides a detailed look at our professional values and the ethics that do, or should, underlie how libraries operate. So, ethics is about choices. Staff members make their choices about what is the important outcome—users, library, and funders for example—generally without thinking about ethics.

What are some of the personal approaches to what is ethical, especially when there are options (as is almost always the case)? There are several approaches and bases for making choices. Making ethical choices is more complex than you might think. For starters, you have a lifetime's worth of personal values and beliefs' regarding what is right and what is wrong. You developed these views starting when you were a child and as such they are probably deeply held. Some of these values probably arise from the religious environment in which you were raised. Others may be the product of groups you identify with, such as political and social. Further, you more than likely rationalized any incongruities into a very personal value system. To that mix, as a librarian you must add a set of professional values (derived from professional codes of ethics and value statements). Table 5.1 provides a list of some of the most common approaches to making ethical choices.

There are challenges for any of these approaches, as table 5.2 suggests.

TABLE 5.1 Common Organization Approaches to Ethical Decision Making

APPROACH	CENTRAL CONCEPT
Common Good	Ethical decision is based on balancing individual and social good
Contextualism	Ethical decision depends on circumstances
Cost-Benefit	Ethical decision is the one that generates greatest benefit for the least cost
Kantian	Ethical decisions are based on people as the ends not the means
Moral Obligation	Ethical choices are based on the social good
Moral Rights	Ethical choices respect social rights
Theological	Ethical choices follow religious beliefs of rights and wrong
Utilitarian	Ethical choices produce the greatest good for the greatest number of people

TABLE 5.2 Interpretation Challenges

APPROACH	CHALLENGES FOR MAKING ETHICAL CHOICES
Common Good	What is the 'common" good and who decides what that is?
Contextualism	Situational decisions can cause at least an appearance of being inconsistent and a reduction of trust.
Cost-Benefit	Who defines the benefit and should money alone drive choice?
Kantian	For libraries, people are both the means and the ends.
Moral Obligation	Moral obligations vary among groups. Which group is to carry the most weight?
Moral Rights	Moral rights are variable and make it difficult to prioritize which rights prevail.
Theological	In pluralistic societies, religious-based choices can generate high levels of distrust.
Utilitarian	Difficult to always determine what is the greatest good and greatest number; also, can this work in a pluralistic society?

As you can see from the above, there are a number of approaches to making ethical decisions and/or taking action, and the preceding are only some of the most common methods. Adding in a set of professional values can lead to personal dilemmas. Few of us knew of the existence of ALA's Code of Ethics when we entered library school, much less what its contents were. It is also very likely that few people seeking or accepting a position in the public sector thought about potential ethical dilemmas that might arise as a result of personal values and the agency's values and obligations. We tend to think of discussions about professional ethics, in the classroom, as interesting and easy to implement. The real world with its pressure of doing all the work as quickly as possible and making ethical decisions, can be very different.

👁 FOR FURTHER THOUGHT

Locate a copy of the code of ethics or statement of values from a professional area you are interested in. (Try the ALA Code: www.ala.org/advocacy/sites/ala.org.advocacy/files/content/proethics/codeofethics/Code%20of%20Ethics%20of%20the%20American%20Library%20Association.pdf) Does the document provide practical guidance that you can act on as a managerial leader? What do you consider to be the most difficult ethical or moral dilemma that you are likely to encounter today?

ETHICS DO MATTER

Ethics do matter and, as we noted earlier, they are a critical component of public and non-profit sector organizations. Librarians have been concerned with professional values and ethics for more than 100 years. ALA published its first code of ethics in 1938, although there was discussion of professional values, responsibilities, and ethical behavior for librarians starting in the early twentieth century. The latest revision of the code occurred in 2008. The code touches on collections, services, access, intellectual freedom, intellectual property, personal and professional values, and personal interests and user needs. It is a mix of social responsibility (organizational values) and personal behavior (ethics). It is up to each library to implement the guidelines. Other library professional associations, such as the Medical Library Association and Special Libraries Association, have their own codes of ethics.

Earlier we noted that managerial leaders can help staff members behave ethically by modeling such behavior. One reason ethics matter is that managerial leaders can also, perhaps unknowingly, cause staff to behave unethically. There is no doubt that people are motivated, in large part, by their personal values. Some people have very, very strong value systems (religious or political, for example) and believe it is their responsibility to convince others that their values are the correct values. If such a person is the senior managerial leader of a library, what are the chances that staff members would act in ways that went against the leader's articulated values? Would they have the moral courage to at least quietly follow the ALA ethical guidelines, such as adding items to the collection that they know are contrary to the director's beliefs? According to Tepper (2010), "A compelling body of empirical research evidence suggests that it is disturbingly easy for authority figures to put their direct reports in positions where unethical choices are preferred over ethical choices" (p. 592). Some of the empirical studies that support Tepper's point are Thomas Blass's (2000) *Obedience to Authority: Current Perspectives on the Milgram Paradigm*, and Kerry Patterson, Joseph Grenny, David Maxfield, Ron McMillan, and Al Switzer's (2008) *Influencer: The Power to Change Anything.*

Wotruba, Chonko, and Lee (2001) made the further point that "the ethical climate of an organization is a composite of formal and informal policies of that organization as well as the individual ethical values of its managers. In this context, an ethics code as a formal policy would be one building block of the organization's ethical climate, representing a statement of corporate ethical values" (p. 60). We suggest that the ALA Code of Ethics be discussed with each new library employee as part of his or her orientation program. This approach serves to emphasize for the new employee, as well as for existing staff, that ethics do matter and to clarify just what those ethical values are.

Dave Anderson (2011) wrote about a very common ethical issue—"little white lies." He suggested, "White lies are like the gateway drug to bigger offenses. . . . And in a business world that is already unstable, it's not a risk you should be willing to take" (p. 22). Most of us do tell white lies from time to time. On a personal level, we say we "have a prior engagement" when we don't want to attend an event. At work, we say "I'm sorry, but I cannot do that" when the fact is that we could but wish to avoid the issue. He also suggested there are four little words we often use that are a tip-off that we are being less than ethical in our work activities: "just tell them that. . . . Any sentence that begins with that phrase is usually followed by a lie" (p. 22). Sometimes there is good reason for asking a staff member to say that you are in a meeting and will get back to the person quickly. At other times it is avoidance. Certainly not all avoidance is unethical, but sometimes it is.

Sometimes professionals find that a conflict arises between a code developed by their professional association and an instruction issued by their manager. Such issues can occur in terms of access to certain services or information. Divided views of ethical behavior are probably the greatest challenge that managerial leaders encounter and resolve. Certainly, there are other challenges of greater importance (budget cuts and staffing challenges, for example); however, unlike most other major challenges, the ethical challenge is in the decision maker's hands.

STANDARDS, VALUES, AND CODES

There are a variety of library standards, guidelines, statements, and codes promulgated by ALA and other professional organizations that in some way touch on professional ethics, values, and behavior. We cover standards and guidelines in other chapters in this book. You can check out the wide range of ALA standards and guidelines at www.ala.org/tools/guidelines/standardsguidelines. An interesting document on the ALA list is the Association of College and Research Libraries' (ACRL) *Standards for Libraries in Higher Education* (adopted in 2011 and revised in 2018, www.ala.org/acrl/standards/standardslibraries). What makes this document particularly interesting is that it includes a mix of both operational standards (institutional effectiveness) and professional behaviors (professional values).

A good example of library values is ALA's Freedom to Read Statement (www.ala.org/advocacy/intfreedom/freedomreadstatement). Its seven propositions cover many of the long-held values of librarians, publishers, and booksellers. The fact that both for-profit and nonprofit organizations put forward these values carries greater weight in society than if just one organization did so. This does not, however, mean there are not challenges to carrying out these values. Likewise, ALA's Library Bills of Rights (www.ala.org/advocacy/intfreedom/librarybill) is a statement of values that has ethical implications, for example, "Libraries that make exhibit spaces and meeting rooms available to the public they serve should make such facilities available on an equitable basis, regardless of the beliefs or affiliations of individuals or groups requesting their use." There have been a variety of legal cases related to room use. Some cases involve public libraries and the notion of separation of church and state while others involve maintaining balance in views on controversial topics (see chapter 3 for other examples).

It is likely you will have more than one occasion during your career when both the Freedom to Read Statement and the Library Bill of Rights will come in handy. They may not solve your ethical dilemma, but they will provide serious food for thought about what choice to make.

ALA CODE OF ETHICS

Turning to ALA's Code of Ethics, we will cover the first seven points of the code. The final point, professional development, is a function of your career motivation and desires rather than an ethical concern. (We explore career development in chapter 22.) Some people might say that privacy (point III) and intellectual property (point IV) are matters of law rather than ethics. Both certainly are matters of law. However, unless you take the strictest approach to the law, there are times when there are grey areas and when ethical choices come into play.

Most national professional associations have such codes. However, in order to be truly effective, some sanctions must be attached to violations. Failure to include sanctions turns a code of ethics into a set of guidelines. Because ALA's Code contains no sanctions for violations of the Code, it is thus a guideline at best. Does that fact make it less stressful to a make an ethical choice? Because there is no risk of sanctions there is less stress, but there can be other types of constraints that influence choices, for example, colleagues' opinions.

Access

Point I of the code relates primarily to access to library services and programs, while the final clause addresses personal conduct with users. One outcome of this is seen almost daily across the country as people line up to use internet access in public libraries, many of whom cannot afford access. As more and more agencies at all levels of government require some or all interaction take place online, the pressure on libraries to maintain and expand such access increases. This places a burden on already tight budgets and forces the library staff and governing boards to make hard choices. Some of those decisions will be ethical in nature.

As a friend of the authors once said, "So many ethical choices are so d—— relative." Point I of the code provides an example of the relativity issues. There is a little word in that section that is loaded: "equitable." Just what that means is open to wide-ranging debate. If you look up "equitable" in a thesaurus, the first synonym usually listed is "fair." Equitable and equal are not synonymous, although some people would argue they are. More often than not what is viewed as equitable or equal depends on your point of view. The reality is that it is impossible for a library to provide equal service to its entire service community—the funding simply does not exist to do that. That would require that a user group of 100 would receive the same amount of support as a group of 1,000. Educational libraries, in particular, face the question of equitable and equal support each year when it comes to allocating funds for teaching departments' collection development. Would it be equitable to allocate as much funding to an honors program as to a subject area? Would it be equitable to spend less? As you might expect, those little words, *equitable, equal,* and *fair,* can generate debates about choices that have to be made.

Intellectual freedom

Intellectual freedom (IF, point II) is a long-standing concern for librarians. It has been a centerpiece in legal actions between members of the service community and libraries. You have undoubtedly read about and discussed this concern in one or more of your LIS classes. IF and censorship are interrelated, but IF is much broader in scope than censorship and is tied to the First Amendment of the U.S. Constitution. This is not the place to explore the complexities of IF, but we will briefly look at censorship and ethics.

In today's world of tight library budgets and lean (and at times almost skeletal) staffing, it is common for librarians to have some collection management responsibilities in addition to several other significant library obligations. Should you find yourself in this situation, you will find yourself stretched for time and energy to do everything as well as you would like. Any extra work, such as a committee assignment or presentation, is an added burden. Suppose you are reviewing possible additions to the collection and see an item that could be useful in the collection. You also know from reading the current literature that the item has caused a number of libraries problems with complaints and, in at least one case, a lawsuit. Challenges are time-consuming, stressful, and frustrating regardless of their outcome.

What should you do? To top things off, you are scheduled to have your annual performance review in a few weeks, and there are a couple of small projects you want to get finished in order to accomplish the goals you and your supervisor set a year ago. You can avoid the potential work from dealing with a challenge by not ordering the item. Is that ethical professional behavior? You can always justify not adding the item on the grounds of a limited budget and/or because some better item might be available later. Who will know you made the choice not to add the item for personal reasons? It is easy to say you would never do such a thing when sitting in a classroom and is quite a different matter when you are in the real work world.

As much as the profession might wish otherwise, librarian self-censorship is a very real issue. Debra Lau Whelan (2009) in writing about self-censorship, stated:

> It's a dirty secret that no one in the profession wants to talk about or admit practicing. Yet everyone knows some librarians bypass good books—those with literary merit or that fill a need in their collections. The reasons range from a book's sexual content and gay themes to its language and violence—and it happens in more public and K–12 libraries than you think. (p. 27)

The issue is long-standing and goes beyond the topics Whelan mentioned.

Some in the profession have been willing to raise the issue, and there is evidence of self-censorship in the literature. Perhaps the first book on the topic was Marjorie

Fiske's 1959 *Book Selection and Censorship.* Her work was commissioned by the California Library Association in response to heavy pressure from individuals and groups to remove anything that could be considered communistic or socialistic. In her report, she noted librarians often waffle or weasel-worded their views about avoiding adding "potentially objectionable" items to the collection. Fiske illustrated the problem by quoting a librarian in her study: "We haven't been censoring but we have been 'conservative.' After all, this is a conservative community and that is how parents want it to be" (p. 62). You almost always have one or more rational reasons to justify your negative decision regarding an item. The question is, is the decision ethical?

Privacy

We explored the technical and legal aspects of privacy and confidentiality (point III) in chapter 3. There is an ethical side to the topic as well. Some questions to ponder include whether or not you or the library has an ethical obligation to (1) inform users that "personalization" of library database sites can provide the vendor with more personal and marketable information than the user might like and (2) inform database vendors that they must comply with library privacy and ALA confidentiality policies, if they wish to retain your library's business—and enforce this policy. You can review ALA's Policy on Confidentiality of Library Records at www.ala.org/advocacy/intfreedom/statementspols/otherpolicies/policyconfidentiality. Some of the other standards and guidelines also contain recommendations regarding user confidentiality.

Another potential issue that is likely to arise in some corporate library settings is that some firms view material in their library as proprietary, even if the material is from the open literature. Such situations will call for yet another recalibration of traditional professional ethics. One of the members of our Advisory Board for the last edition commented on the differences in the appropriate professional ethics in the special library environment and the academic world. She stated that the issue of individual borrower confidentiality required resetting when she moved from an academic library environment to a special library, where the expectation was the library shared information with staff about who had what items when asked.

There are times when the sections of the code can present you with the dilemma of choosing between competing ethical areas. One example is between privacy (point III) and intellectual property (IP; point IV). Over the years IP laws have become ever broader in scope and more restrictive of what you may freely use without permission (i.e., fair use).

Assume you are assisting a student with a class report or term paper. The student wants to find an online image to include in the project and has asked for help. After some time, the two of you find something the student likes, copy it, and save the web address for the image. Just before closing the page you notice the image is copyrighted. You decide to take the opportunity to briefly talk about copyright and permissions, indicating that using the desired image would require such permission. As you see the student's eyes glazing over, you wonder if the student will ask for permission.

You know that there is widespread belief that everything on the web is free to use as a person wants. Furthermore, you know that the recognition that permission might be required is almost nonexistent. So, what should you do? Ignore the matter, because no one will know the difference and chances of the copyright holder finding out and tracking the use of the image to a library IP is almost nil? (Do remember that in the United States any organization allowing internet access is considered to be an internet service provider [ISP] and may have some liability for a proven infringement if a user accessed the material through that ISP.) Do you have an obligation to follow up with the student regarding getting permission? Do you have a responsibility to check with the student's instructor about the project and image usage? Do you have any obligation to the copyright holder? You face some difficult choices, and the code will provide only a little guidance.

Is this hypothetical example an unlikely occurrence? Probably not, at least based on a 2017 literature review about undergraduate student ethics regarding online materials, which stated; "The literature testifies to the rapid expansion of unethical information practices among undergraduates, whether or not these phenomena reached epidemic levels" (Al-Nuaimi, Al-Aufi, and Bouzazza 2017 p. 392). Looking at the two relevant sections of the code, you see they are in conflict in this situation. So, where do you go for guidance? You could check websites such as ALA's Copyright Advisory Network (www .librarycopyright.net/resources/). Probably your best option is to go to your mentor, if you have one, or to a trusted experienced colleague for advice and just to talk out the options and issues.

 **TRY THIS**

You can probably think of similar situations. List four and outline the potential ethical challenges for each. Share your thoughts with some classmates. Do they agree with your assessments?

Coworkers

Point V covers ethical coworker behavior. We mentioned earlier in the chapter an added consideration for managerial leaders—their impact on subordinates regarding ethical behavior. Aline D. Masuda (2011), in summarizing earlier findings on the topic by Raskin, Novacek, and Hogan (1991), noted that "individuals with an unhealthy self-concept are likely to use power-seeking strategies to regulate self-esteem. Because these individuals' source of esteem is power, they would not mind violating moral values" (p. 6). Her point, as well as ours, is that there are individuals who, especially in an organizational setting, can engage in unethical behavior as a means of securing increased power or authority. They may also influence others to behave in a similar manner. It is something to keep in mind as you begin to think about seeking a more influential position.

Self-interest

Self-interest at the expense of the library or its service community is the subject of point VI. Just what constitutes self-interest is sometimes a matter of debate. One argument has to do with accepting or rejecting vendor gifts. Some individuals believe vendor gifts, be they boxes of candy or meals, are nothing but bribes. They think accepting such gifts harms the library and its service community because the cost of the gift will be incorporated into the price of the vendors' products. In one sense they are right; vendors do factor in all their

---

‖‖ **CHECK THIS OUT**

A good article that provides eight ethical situations to think about is Helen R. Adams's "Reflections on Ethics in Practice" (*Knowledge Quest* 37, no. 3: 66–69, 2009). The situations depicted in the article are set in a school library media environment; however, it is easy to see how each one could occur in any type of library.

---

costs when setting a price. You can refuse vendor gifts, but your prices will not be lowered because of that fact. From the vendors' perspective, the holiday gift is simply a marketing tool and a small means of saying thank you for your business. They do not believe it changes your mind about the company, and they understand your judgments will be based on the firm's performance. Furthermore, the dollar amounts are so small, even in aggregate, that they would not reduce the price of the product. Vendors view meals at a meeting or when vendor representatives visit the library and offer to take one or more staff to lunch as market research. They know that few, if any, individuals are going to make a business decision based on getting, or not getting, even the most elegant lunch or dinner. We do not believe this is a serious ethical issue for librarians, although some people do.

There are much more serious ethical self-interest concerns. Suppose you are assigned to work with a contractor on one of what will be several library renovation projects. Near the end of the project you say to the contractor, "I have enjoyed working with you on this project. I hope we can do so again in the near future. I have a question for you. I have a small remodeling project at home. Could you recommend any contractors I might contact who are reputable?" Is that question ethical under the circumstances? How would the library or its users be harmed if the contractor did undertake the project? Would you be obligating the library to giving the contractor one or more of the remaining library projects?

Perhaps a more common issue is using library funds or services for personal interest. The authors know of several instances when collection development funds and income from the sale of duplicate items were directed toward acquiring items outside the library's collecting scope and directly related to a librarian's research or hobby interest. Certainly, the funds go to acquisition of items that go into the collection, but does that make it ethical? What if the person claims the purchase is to begin a new collecting area for the library? As a staff member not involved in the activity, do you have an obligation to report any behavior that you believe to be unethical to the governing board or to the office of the CEO of the parent organization—assuming you are certain of the facts? If you don't do so, are you behaving ethically?

Many years ago, Douglas J. Foskett (1962) wrote *The Creed of a Librarian: No Politics, No Religion, No Morals*. In it, he made the case for professional practice that is neutral, noting that "the librarian ought virtually to vanish as an individual person, except in so far as his personality sheds light on the working of the library. . . . He must put himself in the reader's shoes" (p. 10). This is what point VII of the code identifies as ethical professional practice.

It is a simple-sounding goal, but one that is very difficult to put into practice day in and day out. We mentioned one challenge earlier in this chapter—choosing not to select a certain item in order to avoid a possible challenge. The same set of questions we listed then applies to almost any item—you don't like the author's style, the author's philosophy, religion, politics, and so on. This can come up in your service activities as well. One

---

||||| CHECK THIS OUT

Our opening quotation for this chapter is from a book we highly recommend—Carol W. Lewis and Stuart G. Gilman's *The Ethics Challenge in Public Service: A Problem-Solving Guide* 3rd edition (San Francisco: Jossey-Bass, 2012). The "public service" refers to public sector organizations rather than to library public services. It will be a great help in resolving some of the ethical dilemmas you may face from time to time. It is also useful in staff development activities.

---

frequently encountered situation is that of homeless individuals in the library. Some libraries even have policies regarding body odor (for example, see the 2006 *American Libraries* article "Stir Raised by Dallas Body Odor Rule." Is such a policy equitable?).

We conclude with two quotations that reflect the challenges involved in professional practice:

> It is evident that the professional ethics and principles of an organization may often conflict with societal and personal ethics. In fact, professional ethics and principles often have internal conflicts. These conflicts are interwoven into professional responsibilities of information science professionals. (Jefferson and Contreras 2005, p. 66)

Woodward, Davis, and Hodis (2007), in paraphrasing Trevino and Youngblood (1990), wrote:

> Individuals throughout life's experience will struggle with feelings about what is right and what is wrong. More adept individuals at ethical reasoning are more likely to make judgments based on principles they choose as opposed to those gained through peer pressure and other outside influences. Individuals with higher levels of moral development are less likely to engage in unethical behavior. (p. 195)

🔒 KEY POINTS TO REMEMBER

- Ethical behavior is a matter of choices.
- Organizational ethics rest on three types of philosophical theories—utilitarian, Kantian, and social contract.
- Ethical professional behavior is your responsibility.
- Library professional codes of ethics have no sanction powers, so there is generally no danger of facing penalties should you chose to ignore the code(s). There is just your conscience to guide you.
- ALA's Code of Ethics addresses just about all aspects of library activities that you carry out on a regular, if not daily, basis.
- As a leader-manager you have the extra responsibility of not placing those who report to you in awkward ethical positions by your actions or suggestions, for example, "just tell them that _____."
- There will be times when the ethical choice will not be clear-cut and will be difficult to make.

REFERENCES

Al-Nuaimi, Mariam, Ali Al-Aufi, and Abdelmajid Bouzazza. 2017. "The Effects of Sociocultural Factors on Information Ethics of Undergraduate Students: A Literature Review." *Library Review* 66, nos. 6/7: 378–98.

American Libraries. 2006. "Stir Raised by Dallas Body Odor Rule." *American Libraries* 37, no. 2: 11.

Anderson, Dave. 2011. "Leadership and Little White Lies." *Public Management* 93, no. 10: 22.

Blass, Thomas. 2000. *Obedience to Authority: Current Perspectives on the Milgram Paradigm*. Mahwah, NJ: Lawrence Erlbaum Associates.

Economist. 2016. "Religion, Ethics and the Workplace: Cross the boss." 418, no. 8981: 70.

Ferguson, Stuart, Clare Thornley, and Forbes Gibb. 2016. "Beyond Codes of Ethics: How Library and Information Professionals Navigate Ethical Dilemmas in a Complex and Dynamic Information Environment." *International Journal of Information Management* 36, no. 4: 543–56.

Fiehn, Barbara. 2016. "Just Because You Can Doesn't Mean You Should." *Knowledge Quest* 45, no. 2: 34–40.

Fiske, Marjorie. 1959. *Book Selection and Censorship*. Berkeley: University of California Press.

Foskett, Douglas J. 1962. *The Creed of a Librarian: No Politics, No Religion, No Morals*. Library Association Occasional Papers No. 3. London: Library Association.

Jefferson, Renée N., and Sylvia Contreras. 2005. "Ethical Perspectives of Library and Information Science Graduate Students in the United States." *New Library World* 106, nos. 1208/1209: 58–66.

Lewis, Carol W., and Stuart C. Gilman. 2012. *The Ethics Challenge in Public Service: A Problem-Solving Guide*. 3rd edition. San Francisco: Jossey-Bass.

Luo, Lilli. 2016 "Ethical Issues in Reference: An In-Depth View from the Librarian's Perspective." *Reference and User Services Quarterly* 55, no. 3: 189–98.

Masuda, Aline D. 2011. "Power Motives and Core Self-Evaluation as Correlates of Managerial Morality." *Academic Leadership: The Online Journal* 9, no. 1. https://scholars.fhsu.edu/cgi/viewcontent.cgi?article =1621&context=alj.

Patterson, Kerry, Joseph Grenny, David Maxfield, Ron McMillan, and Al Switzer. 2008. *Influencer: The Power to Change Anything*. New York: McGraw-Hill.

Peer, Jean. 2008. *Library Ethics*. Westport, CT: Libraries Unlimited.

Raskin, Robert, Jill Novacek, and Robert Hogan. 1991. "Narcissism, Self-Esteem and Defensive Self Enhancement." *Journal of Personality* 59, no. 1: 19–38.

Schmidt, Warren H., and Barry Z. Posner. 1982. *Managerial Values and Expectations*. New York: American Management Association.

Tepper, Bennett J. 2010. "When Managers Pressure Employees to Behave Badly: Toward a Comprehensive Response." *Business Horizons* 53, no. 6: 591–98.

Trevino, Linda K., and Stuart A. Youngblood. 1990. "Bad Apples in Bad Barrels: A Casual Analysis of Ethical Decision-Making Behavior." *Journal of Applied Psychology* 75, no. 4: 378–85.

Whelan, Debra Lau. 2009. "A Dirty Little Secret: Self-Censorship Is Rampant and Lethal." *School Library Journal* 55, no. 2: 26–30.

Woodward, Belle, Diane C. Davis, and Flavia A. Hodis. 2007. "The Relationship between Ethical Decision Making and Ethical Reasoning in Information Technology Students." *Journal of Information Systems Education* 18, no. 2: 193–202.

Wotruba, Thomas R., Lawrence B. Chonko, and Terry W. Lee. 2001. "The Impact of Ethics Code Familiarity on Manager Behavior." *Journal of Business Ethics* 33, no. 1: 59–69.

PART II

Managerial Functions

CHAPTER 6

Accountability, Authority, Power, and Delegation

> Accountability in public administration has historically grounded in vertical power structures and chains of hierarchy, with one official reporting, liable, or answerable to a superior who can enforce sanctions for non-performance.
>
> **Charles Conteh, 2016**

> Much has been said about accountability as an end—although what the end actually entails might be disputed, depending on one's choice of perspective.
>
> **E. Madalina Busuioc and Martin Lodge, 2016**

> Almost anything is possible in attaining positions of power. You can get yourself into a high-power position even under the most unlikely circumstances if you have the requisite skill.
>
> **Jeffrey Pfeffer, 2009**

Accountability, authority, delegation, duty, power, and responsibility—these are all words that affect managerial leadership in complex ways. While they are unmistakably interrelated, they are also different. Authority and power are a clearly interrelated pair, as are duty and responsibility. In a sense, accountability draws on elements of the other two pairs. In the public and nonprofit sectors, these words carry great weight in part because such organizations depend on allocations of tax monies and donations to fulfill public missions. Although the base factor is the money, the matter is much broader than that. In the previous chapter, we discussed the notion that under ALA guidelines services should be "equitable" and that there are differing views as to just what that word means. As our opening quotation from Busuioc and Lodge suggests, what is equitable and accountable is often a matter of one's perspective. Sometimes people overlook the fact that once you gain power and authority, you are accountable for its use.

All managerial activities involve elements of power, authority, accountability, responsibility, and influence. Understanding the differences among the concepts is important to becoming an effective manager. Having this understanding can make work relationships more efficient and pleasant and much less stressful.

The terms power, authority, and influence are often used interchangeably; however, they are very different concepts. Power is the ability to do something, authority is the right to do something, and influence (something charismatic leaders employ) is the ability to use words or actions to cause others to change their behavior.

There is another term that, like power and accountability, has gained popularity in recent years, especially within public and nonprofit organizations: transparency. In the past 20+ years it has taken on something of a "magical" process that fosters accountability. Transparency, in this context, is about the organization sharing information with its stakeholders. The greater the level of information sharing, the greater the organizational transparency, and generally the higher trust stakeholders have in the organization's operations. James L. Perry and Robert K. Christiansen (2015) noted that to be effective transparency depends upon two qualities—institutional relationships and information shared.

Maintaining high quality relationships with all stakeholders is a goal for all organizations. When it comes to public and nonprofit organizations it can be a matter of survival; poor relationships translate into distrust and little or no belief in accountability. Perceptions matter when it comes to stakeholders and, at best, poor relationships cloud perceptions.

A component in the character of the perception is the timeliness and quality of what information the organization choses to share. There are matters that cannot be shared; personnel matters are typically confidential as is most of library users' information. Some contract information may be restricted. Governing bodies may impose other restrictions on what may and may not be shared. The more timely and complete the sharing is the more transparency people perceive. The more a library involves the service population in its planning and decision making processes the greater the level of trust the population has in its operations and goals.

POWER

We begin with power because it is the foundation upon which all the other concepts in this chapter rest. Defining power is a challenge for management scholars. Dean Tjosvold and Barbara Wisse (2009) commented on the challenges to achieve an acceptable definition: "power is such a pervasive phenomenon and involves many important issues, including moral ones, that agreeing on a definition of power has proved difficult; imposing a definition is impossible. Indeed, even holding a discussion about it is a challenge. Some researchers seem to assume that defining power is too obvious even to specify; others just give up" (p. 2). Tjosvold and Wisse go on to list six "assumptions" about power that create this difficulty:

1. Power as the potential to influence another's actions. . . .
2. Power as the potential to overcome resistance. . . .
3. Power as the potential to affect outcomes. . . .
4. Power as the potential to bring about desired change. . . .
5. Power as actual influence. . . .
6. Power as actually overcoming resistance. . . . (p. 3)

While defining power may be a challenge, the managerial importance of power in part comes from the sanctions available to the person holding power. A manager's sanctions include the ability to give, promise, and withdraw (or threaten to withdraw) rewards; inflict (or threaten to inflict) punishment; and fire (or threaten to fire) subordinates. These sanctions are common to all organizations and form the basis of power. From a positive perspective, power involves the right to give such things as praise, rewards, and public recognition. For example, good managers use power to achieve plans and goals while knowing that the less negative sanctions come into play the more effective the work environment will be. All library managers are in turn influenced by the power exercised by their supervisors as well as by outside bodies such as governing boards.

A frequently overlooked aspect of power is its subjective nature. Opinions differ as to how much power a position or person should have. There is also a reciprocal aspect of power that is unrecognized at times. That is, staff can also employ sanctions, particularly when they believe abuses of managerial power exist. The weakness of subordinate sanctions is that, to be effective, they require the cooperation of most of the staff. While many libraries are a government unit and employees are therefore generally forbidden to strike, this sanction does exist. Groups outside the organization can also contribute to staff sanctions. Unions, professional associations, and special interest groups can bring pressure to bear on an institution and its administrators. The existence of independent bodies, therefore, acts as a strong sanction against blatantly prejudicial managerial actions.

To some degree, all sanctions act as psychological whips simply because they exist, and they impact workplace behaviors of both employees and employers. When it becomes necessary to apply a sanction, it is in a very real sense an admission of failure. No matter who imposed the sanctions, it is a managerial failure.

Reviewing the literature on the nature of managerial power suggests there are five basic types:

- Reward power derives from staff members seeing the supervisor as entailed to grant rewards (raises or promotions, for example).
- Coercive power, as the name suggests, is the staff's knowledge that the supervisor is able to impose sanctions when necessary (transfers or demotions, for example).
- Referent power arises from a person's desire to be associated with a manager and her or his power.
- Legitimate power, as the label suggests, comes from the staff understanding the manager as some level of "authorized" power granted by a higher manager.
- Expert power comes about from staff recognizing the manager's competency in the activities supervised.

Most managerial power is a combination of these categories, usually with one or two of them being dominant. When a manager has strong expert and referent power, there is seldom a question in the staff's mind about the manager's right to power. When expert power is weak, there is usually a significant question about legitimate power. When an individual becomes a senior manager, there is generally a testing period during which staff wait to see how much expert knowledge the person possesses. Should they find the person lacking, a power struggle may result.

John Kotter (1977, pp. 135–36) identified six characteristics of managers who use power successfully for the good of the organization and its employees:

- Effective managers are sensitive to the source of their power and are careful to keep their actions consistent with people's expectations.
- Good managers understand—at least intuitively—the five bases of power and recognize which to draw on in specific situations and with different people.

- Effective managers recognize that all bases of power have merit in certain circumstances.
- Successful managers have career goals that allow them to develop and use power.
- Effective managers temper power with maturity and self-control.
- Successful managers know that power is necessary to get things done.

INFLUENCE

The dividing line between power and influence is blurry. Influence implies persuasion and can be exercised by using words, actions, or personality. Within a library, a person can be influential but not hold a position of power—or may hold a position of power but have little influence. The more influence you have within the workplace and the wider organization, the more likely it is that the library will benefit. In fact, from a library perspective the best type of manager (at any level) has strong influential skills. Managers who understand organizational politics can identify those who have influence within the library, the user community, and the profession.

Respect is a factor in gaining influence. You gain respect when you are straightforward; for example, discussing an issue with a peer prior to raising it at an organization wide meeting or issuing an instruction within the library. Over time this ensures that you are seen as open and trustworthy. Developing good listening skills, understanding how to work effectively in committees, and thinking strategically all help you gain influence.

AUTHORITY

Authority is a necessary part of organizational life; it is the right to give orders and to expect proper compliance. Max Weber, in his *Theory of Social and Economic Organization* (1947), suggested that there are three types of authority: (1) traditional, (2) charismatic, and (3) legal. Traditional authority is found in monarchies, where it gains a level of legitimacy through the concept of "divine right." Charismatic authority is moral authority gained through an individual's special abilities, vision, or sense of destiny. Gandhi, Mohammed, and Castro are examples of charismatic individuals. This type of authority seldom passes on to others. Legal authority is a function of the position held by a person; it resides in the office rather than in a person. Legal authority derives from laws established by legislative bodies to govern the ways in which a society agrees to function.

⦚⦚⦚ CHECK THESE OUT

One of the classic works on the nature and role of power in organizations is Jeffrey Pfeffer's *Managing with Power: Politics and Influence in Organizations* (Cambridge, MA: Harvard Business School Press, 1992). A more recent book is *Power and Interdependence in Organizations*, edited by Dean Tjosvold and Barbara Wisse (Cambridge, England: Cambridge University Press, 2009).

All organizations, including libraries, must address the distribution of power and authority within the organization. R. V. Presthus (1962) provided a full definition in an excellent article on authority and organizational structure:

> Authority, power, and influence are usually interlaced in operating situations. However, the definitions attempt to focus on the conception of organizing as a system in which interpersonal relations are structured in terms of the prescribed authority of the actors. (p. 123)

In a library environment, a manager's authority consists of rights such as those related to making decisions, assigning work to subordinates, reviewing their work, and recommending their retention or release on the basis of performance.

Authority is made legitimate in part by the process of socialization. While socialization is basic to the legitimization process, other factors are equally important for individuals to accept authority. There must be a constant validation process. A position may carry an accepted amount of authority, but the office holder must demonstrate an ability to retain that office and exercise its authority, usually through technical or professional skills and/or knowledge. Presthus calls this legitimation by expertise. Whenever subordinates begin to doubt a supervisor's ability or knowledge, that person loses authority and may resort to the use of sanctions. In so doing, the supervisor is admitting to a loss of authority by using whatever power is available. While wielding power may enforce conformity, that conformity will last for only a limited time.

Formal role and rank is another way to legitimate authority. For instance, if your position in the library is above mine, then you probably have more authority than I do. In large archives and libraries, small amounts of authority are held in a number of positions, but each level in the structure has some authority. As Presthus pointed out, both expertise and formal role methods of establishing the right to authority lead to conflict at the higher levels, where the office holder cannot be expert in all the fields in which authority has to be exercised.

Leadership that depends on personal qualities apart from technical expertise represents another method of legitimating authority. Presthus labeled this as legitimation by rapport, and it seems to have an element of Weber's ideas about charismatic authority. For many individuals, their real basis of authority lies not in position or professional skill but in an ability to work with people. Some can hold a great deal of authority in an institution solely on the basis of being "a real person with a genuine interest in people." Individuals of this type hold their positions because of the affection and loyalty that their subordinates and superiors have for them. They also have to demonstrate an understanding of the area managed, or they will not be able to retain authority for very long.

Authority is an active process that is both subjective and reciprocal. It flows in two directions: downward, through an organizational structure of positions, and upward, from staff to individuals holding superior positions. The bases for validating authority are traditional acceptance of authority, expertise, position, rank, and personal characteristics.

DELEGATION AND ORGANIZATIONAL STRUCTURE

Delegation is the process of creating a structure for handling the duties and activities of a library. Perhaps there was a time when the structure, once established, could be ignored.

That is certainly not so in today's rapidly changing environments. Today's organizations, especially libraries, must be agile in how they structure their work activities as well as their goals.

In all but the smallest organization, there will be some degree of structuring of duties and responsibilities. Even "flat" organizational structures have some degree of a hierarchy—not everyone is "in charge." An organization's formal structure (its authority and reporting "lines") is often visualized in the form of an organization diagram known as an org chart. Keep in mind the org chart reflects the formal structure; often there is an equally important structure based on influence which may reflect a different structure. The org chart is also a representation of delegation of duties and responsibilities and reporting lines.

There are a variety of ways to structure or assign duties in an organization. Table 6.1 provides an overview of some of the most common approaches for doing so. There is no "best" approach to structuring and, as suggested by the table, libraries can and do make use of multiple approaches at the same time.

There is a common issue related to delegation: risk. When you delegate a duty or task, you expect the person accepting it will handle the matter effectively. Risk comes into play in several ways. One obvious risk is the person will be unsuccessful. A related risk is that you may have delegated the issue, but you will retain some accountability for the failure. You can never completely delegate responsibility or accountability for activities under your supervision. Another risk, related to the foregoing, is that some managers delegate a task but do not provide the necessary authority for the person to whom they have delegated to be successful. A very important aspect of successful delegation is workplace trust, as well as a sound understanding of the staff's skills sets and capabilities.

TABLE 6.1 Common Methods for Structuring an Organization

METHOD	MAIN CONCEPT	LIMITATION
Functional *technical services, public services, administration*	There are three primary functions	Little flexibility in a changing world
Customer *adult, children's services*	Personalized focus	Less focus on the basics
Territorial *branches*	Convenience/speed of service	Duplication of basic functions
Product *database staff*	High quality service by expert staff	Coordination a challenge
Usage *copying services*	Maximize use of limited resources	Less customer focus
Matrix *collection management*	Flexibility in use of staff skill sets	Multiple supervisors
Teams *short- and long-term efforts*	Better productivity/moral, greater staff independence	Accountability issues

DUTY AND RESPONSIBILITY

Although similar, "duty" and "responsibility" are not identical, especially in terms of the workplace. As we will discuss in chapter 13, job descriptions (JDs) outline the duties and tasks of particular position (assignment) the person holding the position is expected to carry out. Many such JDs have a final item on the list reading something like "and other duties as assigned." When you accept a position listing tasks to perform, you take on (voluntary assumption) the responsibility to carry out those duties. Thus, duties are assigned and are responsibilities that you assume.

Responsibility and accountability are related yet different. You are responsible for doing your work, whereas accountability is being answerable for what you actually do. Thus, accountability is important in the process of enforcing responsibility.

When you accept a task or duty, you also accept responsibility, more often than not, without giving much thought to that fact. Someone unwilling to accept responsibility usually refuses the task. Everyone has worked at some time with an individual who did not accept responsibility for his or her work and performed just well enough to keep from being fired. No amount of talking or delegating responsibility will change such a person's attitude. Acceptance must come from within. Responsibility is a person's obligation to himself or herself to perform given tasks.

ACCOUNTABILITY

accountable for our actions

As Fernando Filgueiras (2016) stated about accountability in organizational sectors, "Accountability has been a central theme in contemporary democratic theory. It is a concept particular to political theory of liberal States, as it posits distinction between the public and the private" (p. 193). The concept has become a key element in public and nonprofit organizational operations. Despite its importance, as commented on by Phillip J. Jones (2000) and as we found seventeen plus years later, it is not a topic widely written about in library literature. It is perhaps so assumed to be necessary that there is no need to explore the concept. However, the fact is, as Jones noted, "Regardless of the library's internal organization, the director's superior(s) will almost always hold him or her solely accountable for the workings of the library" (p. 135).

👥 ADVISORY BOARD EXPERIENCE

Joseph Mika was informed early in his career, while serving in the U.S. Army Reserve, about the difference between responsibility and accountability. As a young unit commander, he made members of the unit responsible for specific tasks. Their failure was noted by his superior, who informed Mika that he could make individual soldiers responsible but that he never relinquished his accountability or responsibility. Similarly, a library director may provide a librarian with the responsibility for collection development, but the director never surrenders accountability or responsibility for library purchases or for the collection development budget.

When you think about delegation and its shared nature, is it no wonder that account-ability can be very contentious. People frequently believe they are held accountable while others are not. This is especially true when the person held most directly accountable for a problem is often the one lowest in the structure and with the least authority. This belief can and does affect work relationships. A manager needs to believe that everyone in the organization is accountable—and that this is in fact true. Power does not stand alone; it comes with responsibility and accountability. Every staff member has some; they just have to recognize it and deal effectively with it.

There are times when accountability seems not to be in play (such as in the case of the Deepwater Horizon or BP oil spill, where all the parties point the finger of blame at one another). This is never the case for libraries, which are almost always part of a larger orga-nization and, as such, are always accountable to one or more bodies for how they handle their operations. For example, public libraries often have boards of trustees; academic libraries have faculty governance "library committees." Such structures can lead to ques-tions about who has the power, authority, responsibility, and accountability for what. Ultimately, libraries are accountable to the patrons and citizens that they serve. Account-ability, authority, and power are interrelated yet different. The process of accountability includes three basic factors: legal, legislative, and administrative. The first two are, for the most part, extra-institutional. Administrative accountability is basically internal, although it can be external.

Legal accountability relates to laws about actions both taken and not taken. Most frequently, failures involve national laws or orders concerning such matters as equal employment, affirmative action requirements, and access to services.

Lawmaking bodies enforce legislative accountability in two main ways: through the courts and through hearings. Hearings are the most common approach. Investigative hear-ings, budgetary hearings, and legislative hearings are some of the types you will frequently encounter. Lawmaking bodies also have the ability to reduce or increase an agency's authority and appropriations. Libraries in the public sector are especially vulnerable to such control.

Legislative control operates within limits. No legislative body has the time to oversee all operational details of all the agencies accountable to it. Because details are left to the agencies, interpretations of what a legislative order means and what can be done vary. Usually, the legislative body's primary interest arises only during budget hearings, or

👥 AUTHORS' EXPERIENCE

Evans had only positive experiences with his oversight groups. They were instrumental in securing important library objectives. One such experience was at a university where libraries had an outside group known as "overseers." Evans's overseers were key to gaining approval for the library to switch to the Library of Congress Classification (to be an effective member of cooperative projects) from the local classification system that had a 150-year history. The objections to the switch were worldwide, not just on the campus. The overseers spent a substantial amount of time and effort looking at the pros and cons of such a move before supporting the library's position that the switch was essential to the library's future.

when an agency makes a request, or when it receives a number of complaints about the agency.

Although legislative bodies require accountability, a library director usually discovers that there is a wide range of activities not determined by legislative mandates. For example, rarely does the legislative body look at who is hired for a vacant position (although it may impose a time frame for when a position may be filled), what items should added to a collection (it may get involved when there is a challenge about a collection item), and what vendors the library may use (it may have some rules about how the contract selection takes place). These examples illustrate the sometimes-complex processes of being accountable and having the authority to act.

Administrative accountability is common to all libraries. For government-associated libraries, the matter is somewhat more complex than it is for private institutions. Political factors enter the picture. Frequently there are doubts as to where real accountability lies, especially when legislative and administrative units clash over an issue in which political gain seems to be the dominant factor.

GOVERNANCE

Obviously, authority, power, and accountability are factors in the governance of libraries. There are few libraries, with the exception of those in the for-profit sector, that do not have some type of board or committee that has some oversight of their activities (either advisory of governing in character). For example, most academic libraries have some type of advisory "library committee" composed of a mix of campus stakeholders. Public libraries generally have a board of trustees (either advisory or governing), and school libraries have governing school boards that take an interest in their operations. Boards almost always have legally based oversight responsibilities. Although most academic "library committees" are advisory in character and appointed or elected, there are times when the question arises of just how "advisory" advisory really is.

Charlotte Gellert (2011) identified the key point about oversight bodies when she quoted from the section of the *Georgia State Library Handbook* about trustees: "Trustees represent citizen control and governance of the library as specified by state law. The library director represents the administration and management of the library" (p. 14). Words such as "control," "governance," "administration," and "management" can be viewed differently depending on perspective. This, as you can imagine, has implications for the accountability process.

Achieving the proper balance between the board and the library director regarding these terms is a delicate matter, calling for skill and goodwill on everyone's part. Nanci Milone Hill (2008) highlighted the balancing issue when she opened her article regarding boards and library directors with, "The relationship between library boards and library directors is a fragile one, yet it need not be. Education and understanding of each other's unique roles and responsibilities can help smooth the path to a more fruitful relationship" (p. 26).

David C. Miller (2011), a long-time library trustee and a member of ALA's National Advocacy Honor Roll, wrote a short article about some of the "unique roles" mentioned in the Hill (2008) essay. He said, "To avoid micromanaging, library boards of trustees need to remain focused on the big picture and let the staff deal with details that make up the big picture" (p. 18). Table 6.2 presents some examples of the big picture and the details that Miller made reference to in his article.

TABLE 6.2 Division of Roles and Responsibilities

TRUSTEE AREAS	STAFF AREAS
When to seek additional funds for the library	When to pay invoices for services received
How to allocate funds to services, such as collection development	What items to buy for the collections
When to seek a new physical facility	How to lay out service points within the library
When to set official policies	When to draft proposed policies
What the average salary percentage increases are	Which employees get salary increases and how much they get within the set percentages
Whom to hire as a director	Whom to hire for other library positions

SOURCE: Based on Miller, 2011.

Given the delicate balance among (and at times the differing views of) the definitions of concepts such as accountability, authority, control, management and administration, and power, it is not surprising that there are occasional head-to-head battles between trustees or committees and directors. Mary Wilkins Jordan (2008) wrote, "I'm sure the members of my board were actually human and not demons from hell, but at the time I was not so positive" (p. 270).

There are times when differences of opinion lead to a director resigning or to the board dismissing the director. You will occasionally see a "news note" about such events in the professional journals. One such instance that gained national attention (*American Libraries* 2007) was when the Boston Public Library Trustees voted not to renew the director's employment contract. Some people outside Boston viewed the decision as a political firing (Robinson 2007).

Certainly, conflicts, some very serious, do arise; however, they are very much the exception. The vast majority of relationships between directors and boards or committees are highly positive. Such bodies can be among the most effective advocates for the library. The starting point for developing effective relationships is for all involved to review and understand any existing laws, regulations, and polices that relate to the functions and

---

▓▓▓ CHECK THESE OUT

Howell, Donna W. 2004. "The Politics of Public Library Boards." *Rural Libraries* 24, no. 1: 15–24.

Moore, Mary Y. 2010. *The Successful Library Trustee Handbook.* 2nd ed. Chicago: American Library Association.

Reed, Sally Gardner, and Jillian Kalonick. 2010. *The Complete Library Trustee Handbook.* New York: Neal-Schuman.

responsibilities of the parties. Keeping everyone informed is another key to maintaining positive relationships. Having a few early sessions devoted to developing clear understandings regarding who is accountable for what is also beneficial.

Issues of accountability, authority, delegation, duty, power, and responsibility can spark major disagreements. The good news is that in libraries, they seldom rise to major confrontations. However, even the most apparently minor situation has the potential to escalate.

🔒 KEY POINTS TO REMEMBER

- Power is not as powerful as many people think. There are very real limits in terms of workplace power.
- Authority is not identical to power, although the concepts are interrelated.
- You are always accountable and responsible for your use of power and authority.
- Senior management does not hold all the power or even all the authority.
- Staff have the power and ability to withhold recognition of the skills of the manager as well as to withhold knowledge from the manager, which effectively reduces the manager's power and authority.
- Staff have the power to control the level and quality of their work, which places a control on the manager's actions.
- Managers can delegate activities and duties to others; however, they always retain responsibility and accountability for how the work was performed.
- Libraries almost always have some type of oversight group (for example, trustees or a committee) in addition to the parent organization.
- Senior managers must devote considerable time and effort to developing and maintaining solid working relationships with oversight groups.
- Organizations are structured in different ways, and there is a visible and an invisible structure.
- Everyone is accountable to someone (librarian to director; director to board; board to city; city to taxpayers, etc.).

REFERENCES

American Libraries. 2007. "Boston Board Ousts Director Margolis." *American Libraries* 38, no. 11: 21–22.

Busuioc, E. Madalina and Martin Lodge. 2016. "The Reputational Basis for Public Accountability." *Governance* 29, no. 2: 247–63.

Conteh, Charles. 2016. "Rethinking Accountability in Complex and Horizontal Network Delivery Systems." *Canadian Public Administration* 59, no. 2: 224–44.

Filgueiras, Fernando. 2016. "Transparency and Accountability: Principles and Rules for the Construction of Publicity." *Journal of Public Affairs* 16, no. 2: 192–202.

Gellert, Charlotte. 2011. "The Roles of Library Trustees, Directors and Friends." *Georgia Library Quarterly* 48, no. 4: 14.

Hill, Nanci Milone. 2008. "Whose Job Is It? The Relationship between Trustees and Directors." *Public Libraries* 47, no. 5: 26–27.

Jones, Phillip J. 2000. "Individual Accountability and Individual Authority." *Library Administration and Management* 14, no. 3: 135–45.

Jordan, Mary Wilkins. 2008. "Buyer Beware." *Public Libraries* 47, no. 3: 27-28.

Kotter, John P. 1977. "Power, Dependence and Effective Management." *Harvard Business Review* 55, no. 4: 135-36.

Miller, David C. 2011. "Avoid Micromanaging." *Library Administrator's Digest* 46, no. 3: 18.

Perry, James L., and Robert K. Christiansen. 2015. *Handbook of Public Administration.* San Francisco: Jossey-Bass.

———. 2010. *Power: Why Some People Have It and Others Don't.* New York: HarperCollins.

Pfeffer, Jeffery. 2009. "Understanding Power in Organizations." In *Power and Interdependence in Organization,* edited by Dean Tjosvold and Barbara Wisse. Cambridge, England: Cambridge University Press.

Presthus, R. V. 1962. "Authority in Organizations." In *Concepts and Issues in Administrative Behavior,* edited by S. Mailick and E. H. VanNess. Englewood Cliffs, NJ: Prentice-Hall.

Robinson, Charles W. 2007. "Politics in Boston." *Library Administrator's Digest* 42, no. 10: 77-78.

Tjosvold, Dean, and Barbara Wisse. 2009. *Power and Interdependence in Organizations.* Cambridge, England: Cambridge University Press.

Weber, Max. 1947. *Theory of Social and Economic Organization.* Translated by A. M. Henderson and T. Parsons; edited by T. Parsons. New York: Free Press.

CHAPTER 7

Vision, Mission, and Planning

Most libraries reside in the complex ecosystem that is the non-profit sector where interrelated organizations interact with each other, the public and public sector to deliver services within legally defined parameters. Mission statements are the core of non-profit operations, defining roles, service targets and partnerships.

Linda R. Wadas, 2017

We often hear strategic planning described as boring, exclusive, and sometimes even out of our control. . . . But with so much change in libraries happening so quickly, we feel it is critical that all library staff understand the drivers of change, help shape organizational decisions, and feel ownership of what is put into operation.

Aaron L. Brenner, Robin Kear, and Eve Wider, 2017

Indeed, the SWOT analysis is the precursor of strategic planning and decision-making tool, helping to identify and assess the internal (strengths and weakness) and external (opportunities and threats) forces...

Y. Srinivasa Rao, 2017

Almost everyone understands the importance of planning, both personally and organizationally. However, before creating any plan you need to know what it is you want to achieve. Like Alice in *Alice in Wonderland*, if you don't know where you want to go, any direction is fine. From an organizational perspective, an Alice approach will not do, at least not in the long run. Organizational vision and mission statements provide the broad long-term directions and purposes as well as the framework for planning how to reach those purposes. As Ronald Jantz (2017) wrote, "A vision describes a future preferred state of an organization and the corresponding statement, communicated throughout, is a critical factor in the future success of the organization" (p. 234). Our opening quotation by Wadas spells out the value of a mission statement that forms the foundation for planning and action.

We all plan, and some of us are better at it than others; the same is true for organizations. In part, the difference in effectiveness is how well and how far into the future you look and how flexible you are in adjusting plans to changing circumstances. In today's rapidly changing world, library managers are challenged on every front—technology, demographics, funding, and so forth. Navigating the library through a highly uncertain world requires many skills and a great deal of thinking and planning. John M. Bryson (2017), a major researcher and writer on the planning process for public and nonprofit

make a tentative plan

sector organizations, noted that "the environments of public and nonprofit organizations have become not only increasingly uncertain in recent years but also more tightly inter-connected; thus, changes anywhere in the system reverberate unpredictably—and often chaotically and dangerously—throughout society" (p. 1). A lack of sound planning only amplifies the uncertainty and dangers for such organizations, especially for libraries. In terms of strategic planning, Michael Allison and Jude Kaye (2015) suggested that, from the public and nonprofit perspective, "because organizational aspirations and broad strategic directions don't often change fundamentally in the period of a few years, purposes and strategy are less subject to short-term shifts in the environment" (p. 2). Essentially, their point is that long-term planning is worthwhile even in the face of rapid change. Planning enables libraries to better adjust and adapt to changing environments.

Plans are like charts that set forth where you are and where you want to go. They do not ensure that you will not run aground, but they do help you avoid some of the reefs, assuming the plans are thoughtfully developed. Plans allow you to check on your progress toward defined goals. They assist in coordinating activities designed to achieve an outcome. Planning is forward-looking and should force you to look to the future. Plans indicate to people, both inside and outside the organization, what the organization hopes to achieve.

▐▐▐▐ A POINT OF REFLECTION

Think about an organization in which you have worked. Were you aware of its mission and/or vision statement? If so, how well did these match up with actual day-to-day activities? Was there any evidence of planning? If so, how was it made evident to you? Was the plan made available to all staff? Was planning long- or short-term in character? Was the staff involved in developing the plan?

 ## MISSION STATEMENTS

We begin with mission statements rather than vision statements because they are more constrained in terms of scope, at least in the public and nonprofit sectors. Our opening quotation from Linda Wadas touches on a major limiting issue (legally defined parameters). Almost all libraries are a sub-units of larger organizations, and as such, the purposes of the parent body place limits on sub-unit purposes. Even solely nonprofit organizations have legal constrictions on their purposes—articles of incorporation. Such documents try to allow for some flexibility in purposes, an acknowledgement of a changing environment; however, they can impede a shifting purpose. For example, a library's foundation (always in a nonprofit library organization) may be empowered to raise money for the endowment but is not allowed to raise money for a capital project due to the articles of incorporation.

A mission statement is the library's long-term strategy: What do we want to accomplish? Where do we want the library to go? For a strategy to be useful there must be congruity between the library's capabilities, its operating environment, and its parent organization. In most cases, the strategic activities of libraries occur within a larger organization or system, which sets the parameters for thinking and planning.

There should be a dynamic interaction between assessing the organizational environment and reviewing the mission and vision statements. Although the mission and vision statements should have a long-term perspective, you must revisit them periodically. We addressed the basics of environmental scanning in chapter 2. In the analysis and monitoring of the environment, it is important to focus on the degree of congruence between the mission and vision statements and the environmental factors.

Most mission statements are relatively short and general in character, but not so generic that they could apply to almost any organization in the same field. Such statements vary in character; some are only a few hundred words long, while others may contain several paragraphs. As you would expect, the longer statements contain greater detail. Striking the correct balance between conciseness and detail can be a challenge. V. Kasturi Rangan (2004) provides sound advice for achieving a good balance. He states, "Most non-profits have broad, inspiring mission statements—and they should. But they also need a systematic method that connects their callings to their programs" (p. 112).

Valentinov and Larsen (2011) maintain that nonprofit managers, who are aware of the need for broad mission statements in order to maximize support from interested individuals and other stakeholders, take risks each time they broaden the statement: "Non-profit managers are motivated to keep non-profit missions sufficiently broad to make them legitimate; yet excessive mission breadth may be perceived as vagueness that would provide disincentives for the potential stakeholders to support" (p. 20). It is a true challenge to create a mission statement that is sufficiently broad, succinct, and memorable, yet not vague.

In his 2009 article "Missions, Mantras, and Meaning," Peter Gow noted an all too common problem with mission—and, we would add, vision— statements: "Assembled by committees from a parts kit of hoary clichés and trendy buzzwords, many of today's school mission statements are so general and so alike that they fail to differentiate themselves and the schools they represent, reducing even most noble aspirations to banalities" (p. 25). While his focus was private schools, libraries also face falling into banality; avoiding banality is not simple.

Fred David (1989) provided some insights into how to address the challenge of being short, general, and yet specific. He suggested thinking in terms of answering a series of questions. We modified his questions to better fit the library context:

- What is our primary service community?
- What are our key programs and services?
- Who are our competitors within the service area?
- What are our key technologies?
- What are our basic values and aspirations, and what are the philosophical priorities of our activities?
- What is our fiscal operating base?
- What are our major strengths and weaknesses?
- What is our operating philosophy regarding staff?

VISION STATEMENTS

In chapter 4, we indicated that one of the characteristics of an effective managerial leader was to have a vision for the library and the ability to communicate that vision. A vision statement should be concise while providing clear guidance for the more detailed thinking and planning that must follow. A good vision statement is articulate, compelling, exciting, and challenging. It paints a broad picture of how the library will or should operate at some point in the future. It should be appealing to the staff, the service community, and all other stakeholders. Burt Nanus (1992) drew up a list of questions to ask about a vision statement (pp. 28–29). His view is that for a statement to be useful the answer to all of these questions should be "yes":

- Does the statement reflect the organization and its environment?
- Does it set forth a clear purpose?
- Is it forward-looking?
- Is it likely to inspire and motivate the staff?
- Is it challenging and ambitious but attainable?
- Will it require the staff to perform at high levels?
- Can it be easily understood?
- Does it communicate what is special about the services and programs that the organization hopes to achieve?

One of the challenges for those new to writing mission and vision statements is determining the difference, if any, between them. Piet Levy (2011) provides one of the clearest distinctions: "A mission statement basically says who we are as a company and the vision statement says what we want to be in the future" (p. 10). Vision statement should go far beyond the near future.

Top managerial leaders propose a great many questions regarding the future to staff and stakeholders. They know some, if not many, of those ideas are rather unlikely, but also know that proposing them can generate thoughts and ideas that may lead to a new vision of the library's future. The more managerial leaders can involve others in planning and other operational matters, the better the organization's health will be.

▥ CHECK THIS OUT

A good article that explores the issues of vision and leadership is Ronald C. Jantz's "Vision, Innovation, and Leadership in Research Libraries" (*Library and Information Science Research* 39, no. 3: 234–41, 2017).

VALUE STATEMENTS

Related to a vision statement is a value statement. For a library, the preparation of a value statement can be a useful exercise when done with the staff. A value statement expresses the operational priorities and values of the library. Although this might appear to be an unnecessary activity, it can often lead to some surprising staff input regarding operational values (or at least assumptions about what is "valued"). While there may be general agreement that service to the user is a top priority, there are often strongly differing views about how that goal translates into behavior and services. It is also likely that the discussion will raise ethical concerns. A value statement, while not essential for planning or for operational success, can be beneficial as long as the values are represented "on the floor and not just the wall."

PLANNING PROCESS

Twenty-first-century managerial leaders must devote more time and thought to handling risk, uncertainty, and doubt than in the past. While planning looks to the future, there is great uncertainty as to what will actually happen. This means more risk and doubt. Nohria and Stewart (2006) suggested three variables should be considered: risk, uncertainty, and doubt. These are distinct yet interrelated factors that may disrupt plans.

Risk is something you can calculate to some degree. Uncertainty is incalculable. With risk and uncertainty, there is the underlying assumption that you know what you want, if not how to achieve it. "Doubt comes into play when there is no right outcome, when one must choose between two evils, or when good outcomes have bad side effects. . . . How does one choose between valued objectives, for example, safety versus liberty, scientific discovery versus the sanctity of human life, individual versus group?" (Nohria and Stewart 2006, p. 40). Although libraries do not face making such weighty plans or choosing between such complex issues, they still have to consider risk, uncertainty, and, at times, doubt.

Miles and Snow (1978) outlined four ways that organizations go about handling risk and uncertainty. There are the "defenders"—those who stick with what they do best and operate on the assumption that keeping to the narrow, well-trodden path will minimize risk and uncertainty. Such behavior, in the past, often worked well, especially for long-established organizations, such as libraries and archives. Today, this is a much higher risk strategy. "Analyzers" are inclined to take on a moderate amount of risk and uncertainty. Their approach is to watch and analyze what others are doing and imitate what appears to be working ("Let's not be on the bleeding edge of the IT curve"). "Prospectors" see opportunities in risk taking and uncertainty. They want to be leading the way. Their plans do not devote much time to "what if;" essentially, they pay little attention to risk calculation. As a consequence, they experience a higher rate of failed plans. When they succeed, they create tremendous results, often forcing competitors out or causing major shifts in how similar organizations operate. Finally, there are the "reactors." These organizations are passive and change direction only when there is a crisis. This is probably the riskiest of all options. Effective planning requires time and careful thought—which are generally in short supply during a crisis. Although there is no way to avoid risk, uncertainty, and doubt in the planning process, some techniques will make them less intimidating and problematic.

SWOT ANALYSIS

Another source to assist in your planning and handling risk and doubt is SWOT (strengths, weaknesses, opportunities, and threats) analysis. It can stimulate thinking by considering the implications of environmental data and organizational capabilities. Although the process is time-consuming, especially when done as a group endeavor, it can produce useful ideas. The process may also feed into the writing or revision of the mission and vision statements as well as the strategic planning process. Further, it will help you identify what went right, went wrong, or changed since the last major planning effort. Two of the SWOT elements are outward-looking (opportunities and threats), and two are inward in character (strengths and weaknesses). Such factors as staff skills, competencies, programs, service-community relations, and fiscal base can be either strengths or a weaknesses. When conducting a SWOT analysis, consider whether a factor will help, hinder, or enhance the accomplishment of your strategy or plan. Opportunities and threats are anything that would hinder your plan.

Despite its widespread use, SWOT is not without its critics (see Armstrong 2004, Hill and Westerbrook 1997, and Valentin 2005). Everett and Duval (2010, pp. 525–26) listed seven common concerns related to SWOT usage:

- It yields banal or misleading results.
- It has a weak theoretical basis.
- It implies the organization factors can be "neatly" categorized as positive or negative.
- It encourages "superficial scanning and impromptu categorization."
- It promotes list building as opposed to thoughtful consideration.
- It does not look at tradeoffs among factors.
- It promotes muddled conceptualizations, particularly between accomplishments and strengths.

We would add that it is not really a forward-looking activity. Typically, it asks us to identify what our challenges are and what our strengths are in the current situation. SWOT forces thinking about the current situation and, when properly implemented, assists in thinking about changes for the future.

⦚ CHECK THIS OUT

An example of a library SWOT analysis is Joe Fernandez's "A SWOT Analysis for Social Media in Libraries" (*Online* 33, no. 5: 35–37, 2009).

TYPES OF PLANS

There are three broad categories of plans. *Strategic plans* are long-term (most often three to five years) and generally are initiated by senior managers, although the actual planning process may involve most, if not all, of the staff. *Tactical plans* are mid-term in length (six months to three years) and are geared toward achieving the strategic plans. Middle managers and supervisors are the people who initiate work on tactical plans. *Operational plans* are short-term (one day to one year) and are intended to guide staff in their day-to-day activities; these plans obviously need to be clearly linked to the tactical and strategic plans. Such plans are generated by individuals, teams, supervisors, and middle managers. In an ideal world, all plans arise from and are linked to the organization's strategic plan.

There are a variety of sub-plans within tactical and operational categories. Table 7.1 provides an overview of the typical sub-sets.

Goals

An organizational goal can be defined as the target accomplishment that will aid in the achievement of a mission and vision. Most goals have a mid-term to long-term time frame.

TABLE 7.1 Sub-Tactical and Operational Plans

PLAN	PURPOSE	TIMEFRAME	LIMITATIONS
Budget	Effective use of available funds	12 months the norm	Overemphasis on cost and control
Goals	Achievement of long-term purpose	2–5 years	Can limit flexibility in changing situations
Objectives	Assist in goal achievement	1–4 years	Some, but limited flexibility
Policies	Guidance in decision making	Indefinite	Can be rules rather than guides
Procedures	Establish proper initiative work methods	Indefinite	Can dampen staff development
Programs	Combine the above for the accomplishment of a special purpose	Indefinite	Often retained long after need is gone
Projects	Handling one-time activity	12–18 months	Time sensitivity

A library might divide its goals into the three broad categories suggested by Heather Johnson (1994, p. 9): "service goals, resource management goals, and administrative/directional goals."

Objectives

To illustrate objectives and their connection to goals, we use an example based on an academic library environment. The example is a slightly more complex approach than what some libraries employ in that it starts by establishing strategic goals and then sub-goals and objectives. One strategic goal might be to "prepare an information literate student." A sub-goal might be to "provide effective and sustainable instruction to 100 percent of a larger and more diverse student body and curricula by 2021." The sub-goal has three related objectives:

- Develop electronic tools and web tutorials as alternatives to face-to-face instruction by creating two or more modules each year.
- Provide faculty and student mentors with tools and methods to integrate information literacy in 60 percent of classes by 2020.
- Remodel and increase the capacity of the library instruction classroom by 2019. Capacity will be increased by 20–25 percent.

A useful concept when developing goals and objectives is the SMARTER technique—specific, measurable, acceptable, realistic, time-framed, extending, and rewarding. An example of a SMARTER goal for an archive is, "By 2021, 80 percent of the archival electronic records will be accessioned within ten working days." The statement is specific and measurable, and it specifies two time frames. Because it is an example, there is no way to know if it is acceptable, realistic, extending, or rewarding. If staff were involved in writing the goal, it is reasonably safe to assume there is some degree of staff agreement that it is both acceptable and realistic. It is unlikely that an organization would waste time formulating goals that do not, in some manner, stretch its capabilities. Just how rewarding its achievement may be is difficult to say; however, for libraries the achievement of a goal that serves the parent body will often translate into greater support in the future.

Once you establish the goals and objectives, it becomes relatively easy to identify appropriate activities, policies, and procedures as well as the resources required to achieve the desired results.

Policies

Policies are statements that guide staff thinking in decision making and handling work processes. Policies set the limits within which you may act. There are several types of policies: originated, appealed, implied, and imposed. Libraries must deal with all four types. Originated policy is the ideal. It is created because the library anticipates a situation will occur that requires it. A danger for originated policy is structuring it so tightly that it becomes a rule rather than a guide.

Appealed policies arise when a situation occurs and there is no policy for how to resolve it. Lacking a policy, staff will create their own when the need comes up, although they are often unaware that they are doing so. When several people do this, several somewhat different "policies" come to exist. Appealed policies most commonly cause problems when a user becomes unhappy after experiencing variations in an assumed "policy." Often the frontline staff appeal to their supervisor to sort out the differences. If the supervisor believes the issue is too important to resolve, the problem moves up the hierarchy. When this happens, time passes, and differences of opinion become entrenched, making it more difficult to resolve the matter.

Implied policy is the most dangerous type for user relations. Such policy arises from staff or user perception of what a policy actually intends. Senior managers usually assume that staff members understand and employ policies as originally intended. At the operational level, however, people may well be acting on the basis of what they believe is the intent of a policy.

Imposed policy comes from outside agencies and groups. Some imposed policies for libraries come from the parent organization (examples are personnel, promotion, retirement, and budget policies).

Procedures

Procedures are guides to actions. They provide a chronological sequence or linear steps that staff use to carry out the activities necessary to achieve a specific policy, objective, or outcome. Procedure planning consists of a number of elements, including keeping procedures to a minimum. Long lists of procedures that detail every action stifle initiative and individuality and induce staff boredom.

Programs

The term "program" is usually applied to a complex undertaking that involves several types of plans. Programs consist of policies, procedures, rules, job allocations, resource requirements, sources of resources, and other elements necessary to carry out a combination of objectives. Not every program includes all types of plans, but anything labeled as a program should outline actions to take (when, where, and by whom).

Projects

Projects, which we cover is some detail in chapter 8, are usually one-time activities that must be completed within a fixed period of time. As such, they place a heavy emphasis on careful planning of each activity and often have what staff members consider impossibly tight schedules for completion of each associated task.

STRATEGIC PLANNING

Three important concepts need clarification to underscore their interrelated character as well as their differences: strategy, strategic planning, and strategic management. A strategy identifies and sets the overall direction of an organization. Strategic planning is the process of creating action steps designed to achieve the strategy. Strategic management involves all the staff in formulating and implementing activities intended to move toward the desired outcome of the strategy and strategic plan.

Think of the planning process structure as starting with an environmental scan that provides the basic material for thinking about and formulating the strategy. Three key elements in strategic plans are the mission, vision, and value statements. All these factors are the context for developing a strategy and designing an action plan. Once the strategic

👥 FROM THE ADVISORY BOARD

Joseph Mika has been involved in approximately 100 strategic plans (as consultant, facilitator, and library school director). His preferred approach to vision and mission uses minimal, meaningful statements. He interprets vision as an all-encompassing statement that needs to be brief and to the point. Vision examples include "Anchored in Excellence . . . Unlimited Horizons" (for a library with a waterfront); "World-Class Education in the Real World" (a university); "Treasured Past—Vibrant Future" (a library that prides itself on its community ties); and "Inspiration through Information." Mission examples are "The XXX Library provides information, resources, and quality service" and "The mission of the XXX Library is to enrich our community with unlimited opportunities for learning and discovery through excellence in services, resources, and cultural programs." He likes it when the mission and/or vision statements can easily fit on the staff's business cards; the cards serve as a reminder for the staff and as a public relations tool when given to community members or visitors.

plan is set, work begins on identifying a set of goals and objectives. With the goals and objectives in place, it is relatively easy to determine what tasks are necessary to address them.

Carter McNamara (2001) suggested there are five models of strategic plans: basic, issues-based, alignment, scenario, and organic (https://managementhelp.org/strategic planning/models.htm). Basic is what most people think of as strategic planning. Issues-based is a more detailed methodology; one of its components involves the use of SWOT analysis and similar techniques to assess various elements in the environment. Alignment is a further fine-tuning with a focus on internal organizational issues. Scenario plans (to be covered later) develop alternative future possibilities (which help deal with the uncertainty factor). McNamara's organic plan is similar to what many people label "rolling" plans: "on an ongoing basis, e.g., once every quarter, dialogue about the processes needed to arrive at the vision." We touch on rolling planning in later chapters. Realistically, the ideal strategic plan incorporates all of these approaches. As you might expect, it is a highly labor-intensive and time-consuming process.

⦀⦀ CHECK THESE OUT

Two articles about library strategic planning worth the reading time are:

Saunders, Laura. 2016. "Room for Improvement: Priorities in Academic Libraries' Strategic Plans." *Journal of Library Administration* 56, no. 1: 1–16.

Buck, William. 2016. "Organizational Integration, Strategic Planning, and Staff Assessment in Publicly Funded Libraries." *Public Services Quarterly* 12, no. 4: 277–89.

SCENARIO PLANNING

Scenario planning differs from strategic planning in that it develops alternative future possibilities. David Axson (2011) defined the concept as "a way of understanding the forces at work today, such as demographics, globalization, technological change, and environmental sustainability, which will shape the future" (p. 22). Balfe and Tretheway (2010) observed, "Scenario analysis is not about predicting the future or identifying a 'most likely' scenario. Rather, it is about developing several plausible outcomes, monitoring them, and trying to influence the one(s) that are most desirable" (p. 31).

There is consensus that scenarios must be relevant, challenging, and plausible if they are to be an effective managerial tool. To create an effective tool, you need to take a number of steps. The obvious starting point is to define the question(s) you want to answer, which should be specific rather than broad in character. With the questions in mind, set a time frame for your future—five, eight, and ten years are most common. The further out you place the end time, the less plausible the scenario. As with any plan, you must identify the stakeholders that may be affected by outcomes. One of the biggest challenges is to identify those drivers of change that could or will affect the outcomes. Next you need to assess the factors—are they totally uncertain or somewhat predictable? In addition, you have to prioritize the factors—most to least significant—and consider their possible interactions. One aspect of the power of scenarios is that they tell a story which people can understand and remember. Finally, you and others, must assess the plausibility of each scenario.

O'Connor and Au (2009) wrote about the application of scenarios in an academic library setting. The library generated three scenarios—"Learning Hub," "Meeting Place," and "Wal-Mart." The final "preferred scenario" contained nine elements—everywhere, outreach, social space, digital lives, sustainable, research involvement, avatar librarians, print value, and integral value. The authors concluded by stating that "the images were being turned into the path of reality. The aim was to achieve this scenario in three years' time. . . . [F]ive working groups who were charged with creating the actions and accountabilities . . . focused on Learning and Teaching, Research Enhancement, Collection Re-design, Physical Space, and Communication and Promotion" (p. 63). Typically, once a scenario is developed, a reaction would be predicted: if *this*, then the library would *that*, or *this* would impact the library in *that* way. The next step would be to determine how would we forecast that scenario or predict that it was coming. And once it happened, what would we do? And what do we need to do today in order to prepare for such a scenario?

||||| CHECK THIS OUT

For details and insights into scenario planning in the library setting, see Steve O'Connor and Peter Sidorko's *Imagine Your Library's Future: Scenario Planning for Libraries and Information Organizations* (Oxford: Chandos Publishing, 2010).

A 2010 library-oriented scenario article by Ludwig, Giesecke, and Walton describes the use of the process in health sciences libraries. In this case, the planning was for the Association of Academic Health Sciences Libraries. The authors concluded their article with the following thought:

> Libraries face a real dilemma: how to guide the library through an uncertain, changing environment while agreeing to follow some sort of action plan. Managers have tried numerous techniques including strategic, long-range, and short-range planning, crisis management, reengineering, redesigning, and total quality management. . . . We have no oracle to tell us what kind of world will result from the interplay of forces impacting our libraries, but it is possible to envisage plausible futures. (p. 34)

WHO SHOULD PLAN?

Our opening quotation from Brenner, Kear, and Wider (2017) provides the basic answer to this question. Certainly, every staff member as well as volunteers plan their daily activities. Supervisors and middle managers develop operational plans; if they are wise, they involve their staff in that process.

When it comes to tactical and strategic planning, the "who" becomes increasingly important. In the not too distant past, these types of planning were viewed as a solely senior management prerogative, perhaps with some assistance from an outside consultant. Woolridge, Schmid, and Floyd (2008), in writing about middle managers' perspectives on the strategy process, identified when this began to change: "The recognition in the research literature of middle management's relevance to strategy formulation began in the 1970s. Up to that point, conceptualization of management generally, and strategy in particular, assumed a top-down analytical process that separated decision making from action" (p. 1193). Today there is general agreement that effective long-term planning should to some degree involve people in many, if not most, staffing categories, in planning activities.

▌▌▌▌ **CHECK THESE OUT**

John M. Bryson's *Strategic Planning for Public and Nonprofit Organizations,* 5th ed. (Hoboken, NJ: Wiley, 2017) provides a good planning model for libraries. Elizabeth Stephan's "Strategic Planning on the Fast Track" (*Library Leadership and Management* 24, no. 4: 189–198, 2010) presents an example of the Bryson model in a library setting. The latter includes examples of mission, value, and vision statements.

Despite the positive outcome of such an approach, there is also general agreement that engaging a lot of staff can present challenges. The more staff involved in the process, the higher the productivity "costs" will be. Good planning takes a substantial amount of time, and that time comes out of normal work time. The people involved will either spend less time performing their job description duties or put in overtime. Then there is the morale factor. Those not involved may resent that they were not among "the chosen few." Others may resent having to pick up at least some of the duties of those who are selected. Mantere and Vaara (2008) summed up the challenges: "Participation is a key issue in strategy research and practice. While there is no consensus on the degree to which organizational members should participate in strategy formulation, most scholars agree that lack of participation easily leads to poorly developed strategies, dissatisfaction among those excluded, and consequential difficulties in implementation" (p. 341). Reading this article is well worth the time and effort.

Regardless of the challenges, we firmly believe staff participation is essential for successful library planning. Melanie Schlosser's 2011 article discusses staff participation and makes the point that "the process aims to create a long-term plan for the organization while fostering a more collaborative, innovative culture" (p. 152). The planning process is more informed due to staff insights and expertise and it creates buy-in for the plan implementation if staff are directly involved in determining how they will achieve the vision.

VALUE OF PLANNING

Almost everyone agrees that planning is important and that good plans are useful. That said, a growing body of literature raises serious questions about strategic planning. Questions about what characterizes meaningful long-range planning are also being raised. Kaplan and Norton (2006) began their article on implementing strategy by saying, "Strategic dreams often turn into nightmares if companies start engaging in extensive and distracting restructuring. It's far more effective to choose a design that works reasonably well, rather than develop a strategic system to tune the structure to the strategy" (p. 100). They also note that, because of changing circumstances, it is rare to achieve all the stated goals and that adding restructuring to the plan creates more obstacles to that achievement. Markins and Steele (2006) were direct in their article:

> Is strategic planning completely useless? . . . In the fall of 2005, Markins Associates . . . surveyed senior executives from 156 large companies worldwide. . . . We asked these executives how their companies developed long range plans and how effectively they thought their planning drove strategic decisions. The results [indicated] . . . that timing and structure of strategic planning are obstacles to good decision-making. . . . No won-

der only 11% of the executives are highly satisfied that strategic planning is worth the effort. (pp. 76, 78, 81)

Many of the negative views about strategic planning arose from Henry Mintzberg's article "Crafting Strategy" in the July–August 1987 issue of *Harvard Business Review*. In that article, he took exception to the presumed rationality and detachment of strategic planning. Given his stature as a management thinker, the article had a more profound impact than he probably intended. He did not believe strategic planning is a worthless activity. In 2008, Richard Whittington and Ludovic Cailluet edited a themed issue of *Long Range Planning* (41, no. 3) titled "The Craft of Strategy." The purpose was to "recall Mintzberg's classic study in formal strategy making and the plurality of forms such strategy activity can take in different contexts" (p. 241). The Whittington and Cailluet issue makes it clear that, done properly, strategic planning is valuable. The effort is worth the time and resources for the library within a changing environment.

❶ KEY POINTS TO REMEMBER

- Planning aids in achieving goals by measuring progress, coordinating activities, addressing the future, and coping with uncertainty.
- Effective planning requires time and careful thought.
- Planning is forward-looking and entails elements of risk, uncertainty, and doubt.
- Planning considers three time frames: long-term (strategy), mid-term (tactical), and short-term (operational).
- There are five major models for long-term strategic planning: basic, issue-based, alignment, scenario, and organic.
- Strategic plans build on mission, vision, and value statements.
- A mission statement sets overall organizational purpose (i.e., why we exist).
- A vision statement sets forth the long-term direction or goals.
- A value statement sets forth how the library expects to operate (its service philosophy).
- Environmental scanning and SWOT analysis are key tools for effective long-term planning.
- Creating SMARTER goals and objectives is important to achieving the desired outcome(s) of any long-term plan.
- Plans come in several varieties: strategies, goals, objectives, policies, procedures, rules, programs, and budgets.
- Effective planning draws on input from all affected and interested parties.
- Successful project management requires careful and detailed planning.
- Staff involvement is a key element in achieving a successful strategic plan.

REFERENCES

Allison, Michael, and Jude Kaye. 2015. *Strategic Planning for Nonprofit Organizations: A Practical Guide for Dynamic Times*. 3rd ed. Hoboken, NJ: Wiley.

Armstrong, J. Scott. 2004. "Don't Do SWOT: A Note on Marketing Planning." ManyWorlds.com. August 8. https://www.ukessays.com/essays/marketing/business-life-cycle-characteristics-and-strategies -marketing-essay.php.

Axson, David A. J. 2011. "Scenario Planning: Navigating through Today's Uncertain World." *Journal of Accountancy* 211, no. 3: 22–27.

Balfe, Bruce E., and Barton G. Tretheway. 2010. "Scenario Planning Power for Unsettled Times." *Association News* 6, no. 2: 31–35.

Brenner, Aaron L., Robin Kear, and Eve Wider. 2017. "Reinvigorating Strategic Planning: An Inclusive, Collaborative Process." *College and Research Library News* 78, no. 1: 28–31.

Bryson, John M. 2017. *Strategic Planning for Public and Nonprofit Organizations.* 5th ed. Hoboken, NJ: Wiley.

David, Fred R. 1989. "How Companies Define Their Mission." *Long Range Planning* 22, no. 1: 90–97.

Everett, Robert F., and Catherine Rich Duval. 2010. "Some Considerations for the Use of Strategic Planning Models." *Northeast Decision Sciences Institute Proceedings* March: 525–30.

Gow, Peter. 2009. "Missions, Mantras, and Meaning." *Independent Schools* 69, no. 1: 24–30.

Hill, Terry, and Roy Westerbrook. 1997. "SWOT Analysis: It's Time for a Product Recall." *Long Range Planning* 30, no. 1: 46–52.

Jantz, Ronald C. 2017. "Vision, Innovation, and Leadership in Research Libraries." *Library and Information Science Research* 39, no. 3: 234–41.

Johnson, Heather. 1994. "Strategic Planning for Modern Libraries." *Library Management* 15, no. 1: 7–18.

Kaplan, Robert S., and David P. Norton. 2006. "How to Implement a New Strategy without Disrupting Your Organization." *Harvard Business Review* 84, no. 3: 100–109.

Levy, Piet. 2011. "Mission vs. Vision." *Marketing News* 45, no. 2: 10.

Ludwig, Logan, Joan Giesecke, and Linda Walton. 2010. "Scenario Planning: A Tool for Health Sciences Libraries." *Health Information and Libraries Journal* 27, no. 1: 28–36.

Mantere, Saku, and Eero Vaara. 2008. "On the Problem of Participation in Strategy: A Critical Discursive Perspective." *Organization Science* 19, no. 2: 341–58.

Markins, Michael, and Richard Steele. 2006. "Stop Making Plans; Start Making Decisions." *Harvard Business Review* 84, no. 1: 76–84.

McNamara, Carter. 2001. "Basic Overview of Various Strategic Planning Models." https://managementhelp .org/strategicplanning/models.htm.

Miles, Raymond, and Charles C. Snow. 1978. *Organizational Strategy, Structure, and Process.* New York: McGraw-Hill.

Mintzberg, Henry. 1987. "Crafting Strategy." *Harvard Business Review,* July–August: 66–74.

Nanus, Burt. 1992. *Visionary Leadership.* San Francisco: Jossey-Bass.

Nohria, Nitin, and Thomas A. Stewart. 2006. "Risk, Uncertainty, and Doubt." *Harvard Business Review* 84, no. 2: 39–40.

O'Connor, Steve, and Lai-chong Au. 2009. "Steering a Future through Scenarios: Into the Academic Library of the Future." *Journal of Academic Librarianship* 35, no. 1: 57–64.

Rangan, V. Kasturi. 2004. "Lofty Missions, Down-to-Earth Plans." *Harvard Business Review* 82, no. 3: 112–19.

Rao, Y. Srinivasa. 2017. "C5 Model for the Consortium Management: SWOT Analysis." *Library Management* 38, nos. 4/5: 248–62.

Schlosser, Melanie. 2011. "OSUL 2013: Fostering Organizational Change through a Grassroots Planning Process." *College and Research Libraries* 72, no. 2: 152–65.

Valentin, Erhard K. 2005. "Away with SWOT Analysis: Use Defensive/Offensive Evaluation Instead." *Journal of Applied Business Research* 21, no. 2: 91–104.

Valentinov, Vladislav, and Karin Larsen. 2011. "The Meaning of Non-Profit Mission Breadth." *Social Sciences Journal* 48, no. 1: 29–38.

Wadas, Linda R. 2017. "Mission Statements in Academic Libraries: A Discourse Analysis." *Library Management* 38, nos. 2/3: 108–16.

Woolridge, Bill, Torsten Schmid, and Steven W. Floyd. 2008. "The Middle Management Perspective on Strategy Process." *Journal of Management* 34, no. 6: 1190–21.

CHAPTER 8

Assessment, Quality Control, and Operations

Assessment by definition focuses on evidence of impact on undergraduate learning, on the effectiveness of faculty and students as teachers and learners, and on the campus as a learning environment.

Anne Liebst and David Feinmark, 2016

Evidence-based practice consists of a systematic and structured process for identifying, appraising, and applying evidence in making decisions in professional practice.

Faye Miller, Helen Partridge, Christine Bruce, Christine Yates, and Alisa Howlett, 2017

By using Project Outcome surveys, libraries are tracking their impact across time; improving and expanding programs and services to meet community needs; supporting new and deepening existing partnerships; and increasing library championships.

Samantha Lopez, 2017

People engage in "assessment" every day, although few think of it as assessment (determining likes and dislikes, for example). Making judgments is natural and, at the most basic level, essential to survival. We form views everywhere we go, including the workplace, so is it any wonder that those who support and/or use a library have opinions about the quality and value received? In the case of organizational assessment, it goes beyond just having an opinion—assessment must take place.

Performance quality is a significant issue for libraries; they ought to always be looking at what they are doing and how they are performing their services. In difficult economic times, libraries must redouble their focus on quality, effectiveness, and efficiency. As Richard Dougherty (2008) suggested, maintaining the status quo is, and probably will be, a major challenge for many U.S. libraries. Assessment, quality control, and operations management activities are tools you can use to stretch limited funds and to gather value data and facts to support your requests for funding and/or support.

In chapter 6, we discussed accountability; here we look at its link to assessment. The concepts are interrelated; both can, and at times do, look at what libraries have done and currently do. Both can, and at times do, lead to significant changes in what, how, when, and where we carry out library activities. Both can be conducted internally and externally. One useful way to differentiate the two concepts is that accountability is usually performed by someone from the outside, while assessment is something we do, or should do, ourselves. The goal in both cases is to improve the quality of our operations, services, and programs.

ASSESSMENT AND ACCOUNTABILITY

Assessment, outcomes, and quality almost always play a role in the accountability process. Libraries are attempting to address the accountability challenge through new and more purposeful assessments that go beyond quantifying inputs and outputs. Stakeholders want evidence of value for monies provided. The call for increased accountability and value is partially driven by economic pressures, especially for those in the public and nonprofit sectors. Increased accountability is also driven by political or ideological perspectives such as the government is wasting tax dollars, or an agency can be perceived as liberal thus requiring more oversight or restrictions.

Many libraries are moving toward more user-centered assessments that measure how a library affects its users. In higher education, for example, for the regional accreditation process, libraries are called on to provide evidence of their contribution to the teaching and learning mission of the parent institution.

Ultimately library stakeholders demand value for their support (funding and volunteer activities, for example). The concept of organizational value has several facets. There are some implied values (for example, that collection size is an indicator of quality). In the past, input data was taken as the primary measure of quality or value. One of the replacement measures is outcomes (derived value); essentially, what was the result of the inputs. A third measure of value is monetary in character (cost-benefit and return on investment, or social return on investment in the case of public and nonprofit sector organizations).

Certainly, two of the key reasons for conducting assessment are to address accountability issues and to support budget requests. However, there are several other reasons that are at least equally important. Libraries have stakeholders in addition to those who provide the operating funds. Two obvious stakeholder groups are users and staff. Another group is the general community, members of which either directly or indirectly support the library. One group that is sometimes overlooked is other libraries, especially members of consortia to which the library belongs. All of these groups have an interest in the library's performance.

Catherine Haras (2010) wrote about efforts to assess the outcomes of an academic library information literacy program. Although assessment is important for accreditation, it is also valuable in terms of planning, assigning resources, improving services, and the like. In her discussion of starting an assessment effort, Haras noted that

---

||||| CHECK THIS OUT

A sound article that explores the value of some input data is William H. Walters's "Beyond Use Statistics: Recall, Precision, and Relevance in the Assessment and Management of Academic Libraries" (*Journal of Librarianship and Information Science* 48, no. 4: 340–52, 2016).

The library involved all campus stakeholders early in the process, including students, faculty, and administration. To this end, we used measures that were by turns home-grown and standardized, direct and indirect, and qualitative and quantitative, on the basis of type, need, and stakeholder. (p. 92)

Haras makes three important points. First, assessment is, or should be, ongoing. Second, getting and keeping stakeholders involved in the process helps ensure that they buy into the results. And third, you should always keep an eye open for potential new stakeholders.

Users are why libraries exist, which is why involving them in your assessment program will pay dividends. People take a keen interest in the quality of service they receive from any organization. Generally, people have four criteria by which they judge service. They expect to get what they want, when they want it, at a cost that is acceptable, and delivered in a way that meets their expectations. Organizations that provide services work hard to ensure that consumers' criteria are met in order to retain user loyalty. This is as important for libraries as it is for supermarkets. You probably have been on the receiving end of poor service more than once in your life; thus you can understand how easy it is to walk away and become an ex-customer. Libraries need to keep all existing users and also expand that pool. Assessment data can help in both of these efforts.

Today's libraries operate in an environment filled with competitors. One way that libraries attempt to meet this challenge is by providing a rich collection of online resources available 24/7. Very few libraries can provide such access on their own. Libraries are increasingly dependent on consortia to achieve some "economy of scale" in terms of database costs. Many libraries are members of several such groups, and the other members of those groups are at least indirect stakeholders in your library. How is that possible? Most database vendor pricing models are based either on the number of participating libraries or on the total number of users in the group of libraries taking part in the deal. As those numbers increase, the cost per library usually declines. That means that if your library runs into serious assessment or accountability issues and must pull out of a deal, the remaining libraries may face increased costs.

There are times when libraries, especially special libraries, have to address some form of the request or requirement: "Prove the worth of your library." The statement may not be that sharp (perhaps "What benefits are we getting from the library?"), but however stated, the message is the same: "We want evidence of the return on investment (ROI) from our funding your library." When you face the "prove it" question for the first time, you may well feel as though you and your library are under fire and may not be sure what to do next. There are resources available to assist you in answering the question. This is especially true if you have been engaging in assessment and evaluation activities on an ongoing basis. All you need do is to pull the data together in a thoughtful manner and present it. Virginia Cairns's (2006) article provides many useful ideas for generating an effective answer.

||||| **CHECK THIS OUT**

J. Stephen Town edited a themed issue of the journal *Library Management* on performance management and library management in 2012 (*Library Management* 33, nos. 6/7: 339–444, 2012).

Cairns (2006) put this issue succinctly, principally for the special library environment:

> Much of what librarians do are considered "soft" costs and difficult to quantify in the current business climate that stresses hard numbers, return on investment, and cost-benefit to the organization. Since the majority of special library funding is dependent on budget allocations from executive administration, the development of sound strategies for demonstrating the worth of our services becomes crucial to our continued success. (p. 1)

Since the mid-1990s, public libraries have worked on demonstrating their ROI. Almost all studies of the public library's value to its community, in terms of dollars and cents, have shown positive ROIs. Studies done by independent agencies are particularly useful to illustrate the dollar value of a library or library system.

Related to assessment and proving one's worth is a relatively new approach: the evidence-based practice. The concept is not really new; using research results to improve practice has probably been around since research activities started. What is new is the philosophy that almost all practice should be based on research evidence and provide approaches to speed the implementation of research results. EBP (evidence-based practice) has developed a library and information science following, albeit a small one. (The journal *Evidence Based Library and Information Practice* is available at https://journals.library.ualberta.ca/eblip/index.php/EBLIP.) Both the Medical Library and Special Libraries Associations promote the development and implementation of EBP.

Doug Suarez (2010) wrote a good article about how you might engage in assessing research studies and reports for useful evidence for practice. As he stated in his closing sentence, "By employing an assessment framework such as the one offered here, and by combining its use with personal work experience and common sense, librarians will be able to judge the inherent value of published library research and to use it as evidence for practice" (p. 84).

WHAT IS QUALITY?

Just how to define and how to measure library quality (value) has been debated over the years. Some critics argue that library "performance" and "quality" are elusive concepts that are difficult, or even impossible, to measure. Critics are correct that both are difficult to measure but are wrong about the possibility of doing so. We can count most of our library activities (outputs), but those numbers fail to tell us anything about quality or very much about performance. Here's a short exercise to do; ask yourself the following questions:

1. What do the terms "performance," "quality," "effectiveness," "impact," and "outcomes" mean to you? Can you define them? How do they differ from other measures you can think of? Can you come up with lucid definitions of the terms "goals," "needs," and "satisfaction?" Do these definitions reflect your philosophy of the library?
2. Where does the demand for the measures originate? From policy makers, funding agencies, the parent organization, users, nonusers, ex-users, or staff?

3. What is the purpose behind the request for measures? Is it to continue or discontinue a service, improve practices or processes, add or drop specific service strategies, allocate resources among competing services, accept or reject a service approach or theory, justify existing activities, or justify a new activity? Or is it a public relations exercise?

4. What other information is needed to achieve measures? Assessment of costs, efficiency, professional opinion, policy makers or users' opinions; comparison with standards or with similar services?

5. Before you measure, ask: Have you specified what you want to measure and why you want to measure it? Have you designed the investigation; ascertained what sources to use, decided what method to use and designed a sample, decided how to analyze the data and information, and how to present the findings? Have you calculated the cost of this exercise in terms of visible and invisible costs (e.g., staff time, including your own)?

6. Who will do the measuring? Are you making the best use of available resources? Would it be cost-effective to bring in outside assistance? Do you have the skills required? Could there be a benefit in terms of staff development for the project? Have you discussed the exercise with stakeholders and obtained feedback?

7. After you measure, ask: Have you collected all the data and information required? Is it in a suitable form and reliable and valid for the purpose? Is it sufficient to base decisions on? Is other data or information needed? In the course of collecting information or data has the problem area been altered? Are your objectives still relevant and feasible? Have the outcomes been reviewed with the staff? What is their response?

8. What action is now required? Returning to the purpose of the investigation, do you need to institute change or need no change, deploy resources, communicate the outcomes, and determine to whom to communicate them? Who should carry out this action? How and when should this be done? how will you assess the effect of the action taken?

One way to interpret quality is to break the concept down into small components. This gives you both a better basis for selecting the best assessment technique(s) and reduces debates on how to interpret the data generated. These are some components of quality:

- reliability (consistency in performance)
- currency (age of resources to provide service)
- accessibility (ease of use—both services and facility)

IIIII CHECK THIS OUT

For an in-depth look at measuring quality, see Eddie Halpin, Carolyn Rankin, Elizabeth L. Chapman, and Christopher Walker's "Measuring the Value of Public Libraries in the Digital Age: What the Power People Need to Know" (*Journal of Librarianship and Information Science* 47, no. 1: 30–42, 2015).

- courtesy and responsiveness (adjusting style to user, friendly service)
- speed (response time)
- service variety (broad-based, user-focused)

You can probably think of additional components. Breaking quality into components helps focus on the significant quality issues for your library and reduces interpretations of what you mean by quality. You can use the same approach to break down effectiveness.

ASSESSMENT TOOLS

Selecting which data collection approach to adopt depends to a great extent on the reason for the assessment. For example, is it intended to:

- meet the requirements of an external body (government or accreditation, for example);
- examine how well the library meets one or more professional standards;
- examine performance in a holistic way;
- examine the efficiency of service delivery
- gather the users' views of the service;
- be an ongoing data gathering exercise.

You have to stay well informed about the current objectives, policies, and procedures of the agencies that take an interest in library operations. The data or information collected for addressing outside interests also forms part of the internal management information system.

Standards

In a sense, professional standards are not directly linked to assessment activities, and they do not carry the same weight as funding authorities or accreditation agencies. Nevertheless, they can be useful yardsticks for looking at your operations and services. While voluntary, standards can generate some broad-based quality levels across library types. There are professional association standards, such as the Association of College and Research Libraries' (ACRL) *Standards for Libraries in Higher Education* (www.ala.org/acrl/standards/standards libraries) and the American Association of School Librarians' (AASL) *Standards for the 21st-Century Learner* (https://standards.aasl.org/wp-content/uploads/2017/11/AASL-Standards -Framework-for-Learners-pamphlet.pdf).

The National Information Standards Organization (NISO) Z39 information standards (which relate to library, vendor, and publisher activities) are intended to make work more efficient. An example is Z39.9, which is the International Standard Serial Number standard that helps publishers, vendors, and libraries handle serials more efficiently. OCLC's development and support of the Dublin Core Metadata Initiative (DCMI) is another example of an organization helping to create a standard, in this case for handling e-materials.

Standards, especially from professional groups such as ALA, have a way of changing over time and occasionally shifting back and forth between an emphasis on general and specific factors as new versions appear. Two examples of changing versions make this point. In 2010, Pat Franklin and Claire Gatrell Stephens wrote about some concerns with the earlier version of the AASL *Standards for the 21st-Century Learner.* Franklin and Stephens (2010) reported that "many school librarians thought they were vague" and that many others "had trouble visualizing how the program would be applied in their school and work with state standards" (p. 36). Keep this in mind when thinking about doing any standards assessment project—competing standards can pose a challenge for libraries.

Some standards, such as the ones from AASL and ACRL, do look at a library holistically. Depending on the overall focus of the standards—qualitative or quantitative—you may or may not have a total picture of service quality. Libraries, by their nature, provide many services that are intangible. Thomas Shaughnessy (1987) identified three points that help to explain "service intangibility." First, services are often performances or processes rather than products, and unspecified (unarticulated) user expectations are the typical criteria by which a service is evaluated. Second, most services are heterogeneous. Performance varies by staff member, from user to user, and from day to day even when the same individuals are involved. Staffing varies during long service hours, so uniform staff service quality becomes more difficult to assess. Third, judgments of quality involve evaluations of the delivery process and are linked to consumer expectations, not just outcomes. There are several commercial survey instruments that help libraries gather data and present quality evidence. Some libraries develop their own surveys to compile a more locally oriented data set while recognizing they may lose some cross-institutional comparability. Whichever approach a library uses, it is important to understand data collected are only one element in a true assessment of the overall performance.

LibQUAL+®

LibQUAL+® is the most widely used commercial instrument both in the United States and throughout the world. LibQUAL+® (www.libqual.org/), which grew out of interest in the for-profit system ServQual, takes the form of an annual survey completed by subscribing libraries in a number of countries. The instrument measures user perceptions and expectations of library service quality in three dimensions: Affect of Service, Information Control, and Library as Place. Users are asked for their judgments on three scales for each question: the desired level of service they would like to receive, the minimum they are willing to accept, and the actual level of service they perceive to have been provided.

Few libraries participate in the survey every year. In 2017, eighty libraries participated in the survey. The survey is not inexpensive—it cost $3,200 to participate in 2017 and 2018. Each year ARL creates norm tables based on that year's responses, so a library can compare its data with a broader base. The participating libraries receive both a summary of their data and the raw data so that they can engage in further analysis. Libraries that repeat the survey can also measure change over time and assess the success of adjustments they have made. This form of benchmarking against local and national institutions helps a library gain deep insights into its service quality.

Some libraries use another service , similar to LIBQUAL+®, for assessment purposes— Counting Opinions (www.countingopinions.com/). The organization intends to provide "comprehensive, cost-effective, real-time solutions designed for libraries, in support of customer insight, operational improvements and advocacy efforts." Its list of customers includes both academic and public libraries. Two of the company's products are LibSat

---

||||| **CHECK THIS OUT**

An interesting article about interrupting LibQUAL+® data is Prathiba Natesan and Xing Aerts's article "Can Library Users Distinguish between Minimum, Perceived, and Desired Levels of Service Quality? Validating LIBQUAL+® Using Multi-Trait Multimethod Analysis" (*Library and Information Science Research* 38, no. 1: 30–38, 2016).

("the means to measure customer satisfaction") and LibPAS (library performance assessment).

Benchmarking

To some degree, LibQUAL+® offers a limited form of benchmarking; however, the benchmarking technique is generally a stand-alone process. Benchmarking, at least in U.S. libraries, is a relatively recent phenomenon that has become more popular as jurisdictions and parent organizations have become increasingly concerned about operating costs. Benchmarking is a tool for either internal or external comparisons.

The goal of benchmarking is to provide data that can help managers answer the following questions:

- How well are we doing compared to others?
- How good do we want to be?
- Who is doing the best?
- How do the best do it?
- How can our organization adapt what the best do?
- How can we be better than the best?

There are four basic types of benchmarking—internal, competitive, industry, and best-in-class. As the label suggests, *internal benchmarking* looks at internal practices within an organization. An example is what it costs to create a purchase order in various departments across a campus. A *competitive benchmarking* project might collect data on the cost of creating purchase orders in various departments in a number of institutions. *Industry benchmarking* would collect data from all or a representative sample of organizations within an industry. *Best-in-class benchmarking* collects information across industries, essentially seeking the most effective practices.

Internal benchmarking may also vary between vertical and horizontal projects. A vertical project seeks to quantify the costs, workloads, and productivity of a defined functional area, for example, handling accounts payable. A horizontal study analyzes the cost and productivity of a single process that crosses two or more functional areas; an example is database searching in acquisitions, cataloging, and document delivery.

The National Association of College and University Business Officers (NACUBO) has been conducting benchmarking studies of various areas in academic institutions, including libraries, since the mid-1990s. These are large-scale efforts involving various member institutions in the United States and Canada (https://www.nacubo.org/Research/2009/NACUBO-Benchmarking-Tool). The Urban Libraries Council has occasionally joined with the International City/County Management Association and several other city and county management organizations to develop benchmarks for public library technology access. The goal is to provide public libraries with information about technology practices in order to create more effective policies regarding access.

Six Sigma

Based on the statistical tools and techniques of quality management developed by Joseph M. Juran (1995), the Six Sigma approach adopted by Motorola in the 1980s has been implemented in some U.S. public libraries. It is both a philosophy and a technique designed to eliminate waste and improve performance. Using statistical analysis, it aims to bring down defects in processes and services to near zero. At the same time, it fosters a culture that focuses on creating value for the user and eliminating any redundant processes. Thomsett (2005) wrote an introductory book about the technique that can be applied to libraries. Brett and Queen (2005) described the application of Lean Six Sigma to streamline a records management service. Improving library self-service using Six Sigma has been reported by Kumi and Morrow (2006).

Sarah Murphy (2009) provides one example of an academic library employing the Lean Six Sigma method. She discussed the applicability of the concept to one service element at the Ohio State University (OSU) libraries. Library service is a fleeting event and presents challenges as to when and how often to assess such transactions. As Murphy (2009) stated, "Services are both intangible and heterogeneous, inviting variability in processes as customers and providers contribute to the inputs and outputs of the service product" (p. 216). The focus of her project was the OSU libraries' process for managing and answering users' e-mail questions. Murphy concluded her article with this statement:

> Libraries can customize and borrow a number of quality management systems and tools from the business community to both assess their service process and continuously improve their operations. By adopting an approach like Lean Six Sigma, a library can respond better to changing customer needs and desires by creating an infrastructure that supports, nurtures, and sustains a culture of assessment and change. (p. 224)

Balanced Scorecard

The balanced scorecard was developed by Robert Kaplan and David Norton as an approach to strategic management based on a measurement system. It provides feedback on the internal operations and the external outcomes to assist organizations to continuously improve strategic performance (Kaplan and Norton 2006). The approach views the organization from four perspectives for which metrics are developed and data are collected and analyzed. The perspectives are the learning and growth perspective, the business process perspective, the customer perspective, and the financial perspective (www.balancedscorecard.org/).

Alfred Willis (2004) published an article based on interviews with two key University of Virginia library administrators who were lead figures in using the balanced scorecard at the library. Jim Self, in responding to a question regarding the value of the technique,

> ||||| **CHECK THIS OUT**
>
> Marta de la Mano and Claire Creaser published the thoughtful article "The Impact of
> the Balanced Scorecard in Libraries: From Performance Measurement to Strategic
> Management" *(Journal of Librarianship and Information Science 48, no. 2: 191–208, 2014)*.

said that "It can focus the library. It makes the library as an organization decide what
is important. It can be used to improve organizational performance. It broadens our
perspective in a structured way, and gives us a more balanced view of our work" (Willis
2004, p. 66). Lynda White's response to the question was that "Our balanced scorecard is
so user-oriented, it fits really well with what we value. Many of our metrics focus on the
results for our users whether or not they are technically in the user perspective" (Willis
2004, p. 66). Tom Bielavitz's 2010 article provides a detailed assessment of the method in
the library context. He concluded that, "The example illustrates that the balanced scorecard can serve as a typical systems planning model to evaluate and assess an academic
library's learning outcomes" (p. 45).

LOCAL DATA COLLECTION

Libraries' service communities' views regarding library quality are essential to understand
for several reasons. Obviously, those views play, or should play, a key role in making adjustments in programs and services. Perhaps even more important is the impact those views
may have on library funding levels and funding authorities. Such views, whether positive or
negative, can and do impact library usage levels, which will in turn influence library support.

Individual and group interviews and mailed or telephone surveys have a long history
of library use for gathering service community data. To a large extent the assessment tools
discussed earlier have superseded these methodologies. A more recent technique for more
targeted local information is focus groups.

Focus groups are intended to elicit information about individuals' thoughts and
views about some topic or issue. The technique involves a small group of individuals. The
researcher serves as moderator, listener, observer, and, ultimately, analyst. As the name
suggests, the topic under discussion is narrow and focused (an example would be the
usefulness of the library's web presence). To have some assurance of valid results, at least
three groups should make up the sample. In general, the usefulness and validity of the
collected data depend on the groups' comfort in sharing views that may not be popular. A
moderator or researcher must have some skill in assessing an individual's comfort level as
well as the group's and make the environment as nonthreatening as possible.

Comparing focus groups to other approaches, you will find focus groups are an
economical method for identifying group norms. They are not that useful for gathering
data about attitudes and behaviors—interviews and surveys are better for this type of
information. One special aspect of focus groups is that they extend public participation in
assessment and planning activities.

Assessment is *not* a one and done process; it must be ongoing if it is to be effective. Maurini Strub and Samantha McClellan (2016) made a strong case for creating an
organizational culture of assessment. They noted, "As libraries respond to a changing

> ||||| **CHECK THESE OUT**
>
> For more details about the focus group methodology and its values and limitations, see Richard A. Krueger and Mary Anne Casey's *Focus Groups: A Practical Guide for Applied Research*, 5th ed. (Thousand Oaks, CA: Sage, 2015) and Thomas L. Greenbaum's *The Handbook for Focus Group Research*, 2nd rev. ed. (Thousand Oaks, CA: Sage, 2002).
>
> A useful bibliography on the use of focus groups for art and humanities and social science research (including librarianship) is Graham R. Walden's *Focus Groups Volume 1: A Selective Annotated Bibliography* (Lanham, MD: Scarecrow Press, 2008).

environment by establishing assessment programs, building buy-in is critical for creating the culture of assessment needed to establish and sustain such programs" (p. 11). Their article provides details on how to achieve such buy-in and sustainability. Ray Laura Henry (2016) discussed another important factor in both assessment and library management in general—documentation. Solid documentation helps provide evidence rather than anecdotal information and establishes a paper trail for administrative purposes. He wrote, "Successfully integrating regular documentation efforts across libraries' workflows (not just library systems projects) can support assessment, transparency, and marketing efforts by providing quantitative and qualitative measures that might not otherwise be captured effectively" (p. 181). As we have noted, a useful managerial leadership mantra is "document, document, document."

Because assessment is both important and complex, it is wise to have at least one person on the staff who becomes the assessment guru. This person should be key in planning, or assist in planning, any assessment program as well as in suggesting additional activities that would help the library prove its worth to whoever asks.

QUALITY CONTROL

Quality performance and assessment go hand-in-hand. Chances of achieving quality performance in the absence of on-going monitoring and assessing are almost nil. The monitoring and controlling process has four components: establishing reasonable performance expectations, assessing actual performance, comparing performance against expectations, and correcting any deviations.

In terms of performance expectations, the key issue is the basis of their establishment—historical, comparative, engineered, or subjective. Historical data on past performance are useful if the performance elements remain constant. They may serve well as the initial standard until more current data is available. Their limitation lies in the fact there is no assurance that past efforts were efficient or effective. "We've always done it this way" does not always translate to the best, or only, way.

Another approach is to compare the same activities in a number of like organizations Benchmarking is one approach to this activity. However, because no two institutions are totally identical, implementing even the best practices of others will require thoughtful assessment to account for local capabilities and conditions.

"Engineered standards" is another label for "scientific management." Engineered standards use hard data collected from work analysis. Basing expectations on sound analytic data is a reasonable method for creating achievable performance goals based on local circumstances. However, there are some areas where work analysis is not very useful—think of reference service or storytelling. Such areas are almost impossible to directly measure in an objective manner. An attempt to measure some aspect of these issues can be made through questionnaires and surveys, but these are at best indirect. The questions asked would reflect subjective assessments about what is important. Having subjective standards is better than not having any standards but recognize them for what they are.

There are a variety of work analysis techniques. Table 8.1 provides an overview of some of the most common methods.

Work sampling is a component of any work-analysis project and requires an understanding of basic statistics. The process consists of two parts: establishing realistic workloads to use as standards and comparing them to the staff's performance. Not all work-analysis techniques relate directly to establishing standards. They may help improve the work flow so that standards can be set, aid visualization of the interrelated nature of a set of activities to improve coordination or establish that the present system is the best method. *Block diagrams* are the most elementary form of work analysis, providing a simple overview of the relationships among various units or activities and identifying possible problem areas. The *flow diagram* introduces a finer level of analysis, as it gives a graphic

TABLE 8.1 Common Work Analysis/Control Techniques

TOOL	PURPOSE/VALUE
Sampling	To create a small data set that will produce reliable information without looking at the total population
Cost accounting	To assist in managing allocated funds to work activities for efficiency and effectiveness
Block diagrams	To review and assess work relationships (units, activities for example)
Form analysis	To assess the utility of forms and other paperwork (often retained too long)
Decision flow charts	To visualize and evaluate decision making processes
Queuing theory	To assess and improve waiting times (people and things)
Game theory	To assist in allocating scare resources
Project management chart	To assist in planning and managing projects and Visualize the relationships between activities and time

For a comprehensive resource about the above and many other quality and performance control methods in the context of libraries, see Richard M. Dougherty's *Streamlining Library Services: What We Do, How Much Time It Takes, What It Costs, and How We Can Do It Better* (Lanham, MD: Scarecrow Press, 2008).

> ||||| **CHECK THIS OUT**
>
> A standard text for project management is the classic *Project Management: A Systems Approach to Planning, Scheduling, and Controlling*, 12th ed., by Harold Kerzner (Hoboken, NJ: Wiley. 2017).

view of both the work area and the movement of personnel or materials within that area—for example, a scale drawing of the facility with all activities clearly identified. The *decision flow chart* analyzes work flows in which numerous decisions occur.

Form analysis studies paper forms, electronic forms, and files that seem to multiply rapidly. Too often they remain in use because "we've always done it that way." *Queuing theory* deals with waiting lines and provides models for operations. You can apply the concept to people or things, and it is especially effective in determining the optimum number of service points. *Game theory* is useful when allocating resources among competing demands. *Cost accounting* is the process of comparing costs (expenses) with results (products or services). The purpose is to ascertain the actual cost of a single product or service (processing a document or answering a telephone inquiry, for example). When done properly, cost accounting is a powerful tool for preparing a budget, determining staffing needs, planning new services, or arranging new service locations. Quality control and business process management might require additional assistance to analyze library operations. Consultants can provide a service for a fee but there are additional options such as working with an affiliated library, a local business professor, a library vendor, or colleagues who can provide guidance for examining processes, workflows, and quality.

PROJECT MANAGEMENT

Project management does not require that you develop new managerial leadership skills. However, it does require you use those skills in a different manner. Your assessment and control skills become very important in your daily work. Your leadership skills need special attention and honing your time management skills become critical.

Timeliness is always important in organizational activities; it becomes the core of successful project outcomes. Most library projects are constrained by some time factor—even "standard," but infrequent, projects (weeding or shifting a collection, for example) carry a limited time frame for completing the effort. One of the most common time constraints for library projects involves funding. Applying for and securing a grant for a project carries with it a time frame for accomplishing the work—grant funds do expire.

Library projects, more often than not, involve a series of interlinked activities and frequently the participation of a number of individuals who have to perform their regular duties while working on projects (which often fall under the job description of "other duties as assigned"). Multiple interlinked activities, people with other duties, and a fixed time period for completion may suggest why you need to recalibrate you managerial leadership skills if you become the designated project team leader. Some skeptics suggest the title should be "project team dictator." Although that may sound harsh, it does contain more than a few grains of truth. The role does require a strong directive approach, a substantial amount of diplomacy as well as tact, and less participative decision making than might be your preferred managerial style.

Determining the best sequence of activities, some of which may need to operate concurrently, is often a challenge, even for experienced project leaders. The good news is there are software programs that make project planning and control easier. One product of such programs is the project management chart we noted above.

🔒 KEY POINTS TO REMEMBER

- Determining the effectiveness and efficiency of library services is essential in today's world.
- Those who provide library funding demand proof of value for monies given.
- Libraries should gather assessment data on outcomes rather than just statistics about inputs and outputs.
- Tools such as LibQUAL+® assist in assessing quality service.
- A sound assessment program includes monitoring and controlling library operations, in part through the use of work analysis techniques.
- The key components of successful library projects are planning, scheduling, and monitoring and control.
- Research and sampling will lead you to choose one or more of the assessment, quality, and operational control tools that will work best for you and your library.

REFERENCES

Bielavitz, Tom. 2010. "The Balanced Scorecard: A Systematic Model for Evaluation and Assessment of Learning Outcomes." *Evidence Based Library and Information Practice* 5, no. 2: 35-46.

Brett, Charles, and Patrick Queen. 2005. "Streamlining Enterprise Records Management with Lean Six Sigma." *Information Management Journal* 39, no. 6: 58, 60-62.

Cairns, Virginia L. 2006. "Demonstrating Your Worth to Administration." *Tennessee Libraries* 56, no. 2: 1-11. www.tnla.org/displaycommon.cfm?an=1&subarticlenbr=38.

Dougherty, Richard M. 2008. *Streamlining Library Services: What We Do, How Much Time It Takes, What It Costs, and How We Can Do It Better*. Lanham, MD. Scarecrow Press.

Franklin, Pat, and Claire Gatrell Stephens. 2010. "Learning for Life: Applying the AASL Standards." *School Library Monthly* 26, no. 5: 36-37.

Haras, Catherine. 2010. "Listening to the Customer." *Library Leadership and Management* 24, no. 2: 91-94.

Henry, Ray Laura. 2016. "Creating a Culture of Documentation." *Journal of Academic Librarianship* 42, no. 3: 181-83.

Juran, Joseph M. 1995. *Managerial Breakthrough*. New York: McGraw-Hill.

Kaplan, Robert S., and David P. Norton. 2006. "The Balanced Scorecard: Measures That Drive Performance." *Harvard Business Review* 83, no. 7: 172, 174-80.

Kumi, Susan, and John Morrow. 2006. "Improving Self-Service the Six Sigma Way at Newcastle University Library." *Program* 40, no. 2: 123-36.

Liebst, Anne, and David Feinmark. 2016. "Tools of Academic Library Assessment: User Survey." *Journal of Library Administration* 56, no. 6: 748-55.

Lopez, Samantha. 2017. "Project Outcome Results in Action." *Public Libraries* 56, no. 6: 22-28.

Miller, Faye, Helen Partridge, Christine Bruce, Christine Yates, and Alisa Howlett. 2017. "How Academic Librarians Experience Evidence-Based Practice: A Ground Theory Model." *Library and Information Science Research* 39, no. 2: 124-30.

Murphy, Sarah Anne. 2009. "Leveraging Lean Six Sigma to Culture, Nurture, And Sustain Assessment and Change in the Academic Library Environment." *College and Research Libraries* 70, no. 3: 215-225.

Shaughnessy, Thomas W. 1987. "Search for Quality." *Journal of Library Administration* 8, no. 1: 5-10.

Strub, Maurini, and Samantha McClellan. 2016. "Getting to a Culture of Assessment: Antecedents to Change Readiness." *Kentucky Libraries* 80, no. 4: 5-12.

Suarez, Doug. 2010. "Evaluating Qualitative Research Studies for Evidence Based Library and Information Practice." *Evidence Based Library and Information Practice* 5, no. 2: 75-85.

Thomsett, Michael C. 2005. *Getting Started in Six Sigma*. Hoboken, NJ: Wiley.

Willis, Alfred. 2004. "Using the Balanced Scorecard at the University of Virginia Library." *Library Administration and Management* 18, no. 2: 64-67.

CHAPTER 9

Decision Making

Professional and managerial decisions in libraries range from those involving resources, personnel, facilities, and technology to governance, users, and competition.

Mark Winston, 2015

Senior government executives make many difficult decisions, typically defined in the literature as those that are very complex–requiring lots of information, fraught with uncertainty or ambiguity, and involving hard trade-offs among conflicting values and interests.

Steven Kelman, Ronald Sanders, and Gayatri Pandit, 2016

The very nature of decision making relies on degrees of uncertainty. While decision makers may wish to seek rational solutions, uncertainty makes absolute rationality impossible.

Cheryl Stenstrom, 2015

Everyone makes dozens of easy decisions every day-what to wear, where to go, etc., in their personal lives with little thought that they are making choices. When it comes to more complex decisions, such as whether or not to take a job offer, some people are much better than others at deciding quickly. As choices become more complex, so does the uncertainty. For some individuals, the greater the uncertainty the more reluctant they are to choose an option.

Napoleon is reputed to have said, "Nothing is more difficult and therefore more precious than the ability to decide." Whether he said this or not does not change the fact that the sentiment is accurate. A significant factor in your career is how well you handle decision making and problem solving. We each develop a personal style of decision making and problem solving that's a result of our life experiences. An obvious difference between personal and workplace decision making is the number of people impacted by the quality of your decisions.

In a broad sense, decision making underlies all managerial action. Before you develop a plan, you must make a decision about the plan's goal(s). Libraries cannot hire someone without making a decision about the required and desired skills and abilities of the successful candidate. Managers monitor employees based on decisions made about acceptable and unacceptable performance. The list could go on and on, but the point is that decision making is a part of daily work life. Staff members, no matter what their level, do make some decisions.

Henry Mintzberg (1976) described some of the complexities of decision making and elaborated on its dynamic factors:

> Decision-making processes are stopped by interruptions, delayed and speeded up by timing factors, and forced to branch and cycle. These processes are, therefore, dynamic ones of importance. Yet it is the dynamic factors that the ordered sequential techniques of analysis (problem-solving) are least able to handle. Thus, despite their important analysis, the dynamic factors go virtually without mention in the literature of management science. (p. 55)

DECISION MAKING ENVIRONMENT

Two of our opening quotations note that decision making carries some risk. Every decision has some element of unpredictability, uncertainty, and, yes, risk. Thus, you have to assume not all of your decisions will turn out as you had hoped— resulting in what some people would call "mistakes"—and such thinking adds to the complexity of decision making.

Throughout life we each develop a "risk tolerance" based on past risk taking and outcomes. Thinking about risk taking, ambiguity, and conflict tolerance levels as a continuum helps you assess personal and workplace comfort levels with making decisions. At one end of the scale is "flight," at the opposite end is "fight," with a midpoint of "flow."

Individuals at the flight end avoid risk, confrontation, and change as much as they can. We all face times where flight is undoubtedly the best action. However, you should not become like Linus from the *Peanuts* cartoon in which he said, "This is a distinct philosophy of mine. No problem is so big or complicated that it can't be run away from."

In the organizational setting a typical flight behavior is procrastination. How often have you heard, "We are still waiting for a decision?" Although it is not always the case, all too frequently the wait is in fact caused by decision avoidance in action. "Needing additional information" can also be an avoidance mechanism. Occasionally a decision making situation will pass without a decision being made; however, this rarely occurs in an organization. More often than not, any decision is better than no decision.

Fight-inclined individuals see opportunities and challenges in change and decision making. They have confidence in their skills, accept occasional mistakes as unfortunate but natural outcomes, and are quick to move on when mistakes happen. Risk taking

---

:bulb: **TRY THIS**

Examine your decision styles by answering the following questions:

- How comfortable are you with uncertainty?
- How much risk do you usually take?
- Do you think and assess options or "just decide"?
- When there is a deadline, do you wait as long as possible to make a decision or do so well in advance?
- When confronted with a "people versus thing" decision, which do you favor?
- When making a decision, do you seek advice frequently or only when necessary?
- How often do you regret a decision?

and ambiguity are not things about which they worry. Working for such people can be rewarding and exciting as well as frustrating and unsettling. At its most extreme—the "gut" decision—the results can be spectacular—either smashing successes or resounding failures.

Most people are somewhere in between the extremes of flight and fight. They move toward one end or the other based on recent experiences. They also tend to shift along the continuum more frequently than do individuals at the extremes. Essentially, they flow with events. They assess risk, have a concern about ambiguity, know that mistakes are inevitable, and do their best to balance all the factors.

(MDMP)

TYPES OF DECISIONS

One common approach to thinking about decision making environments is in terms of contexts—routine/simple, intricate/complicated, convoluted/complex, and turbulent/chaotic. The first context is one with repetitive events and patterns, clear causes and effects, and almost total "knowns." The second environment requires careful analysis as the causes and effects are not clear; however, you can, with effort, identify most of them. The third environment is full of unknowns and unpredictability, with many potential and competing options. The final environment, such as a disaster or emergency, is characterized by high tension, pressure to quickly decide, and little sense of what the causes and effects may be for a given choice.

Some management writers suggest there are only two types of decision making— programmed and non-programmed. Programmed decisions are routine and occur on a regular basis (making a reference desk schedule, selecting items for the collection, determining who prepares an annual report, and determining who may use or check out a particular item are examples). Such decisions are the stuff of a day in the library. People rarely think of them as decisions; they are low risk, the outcomes are highly predictable, and few people have trouble making them.

Non-programmed decisions are another matter. They occur infrequently, their risks are high, their outcomes are uncertain, and the decision environment is often unstructured. They often have wide implications for the organization. They are also relatively uncommon at lower levels of an organization (probably the most common situation for staff to confront a non-programmed decision is during low staffing periods on nights and weekends). Some examples of non-programmed library decisions concern remodeling or planning a new facility or purchasing a new integrated library system. On a personal and professional level, the decision whether to accept a new position or promotion is non-programmed.

You should not think of decision making as single event. The vast majority of decisions develop over time. Yes, there is the moment of choice, but generally there is a passage of time between knowing a decision is necessary and reaching the decision point. Even quick gut decisions draw upon some knowledge of the situation and the reason for making a choice. Research suggests that people who view decision making as a process rather than an event are more effective.

RATIONAL DECISION MAKING

Rational decision making as a concept has value and a place in the decision making process; however, it does have limitations. Herbert Simon (1976) noted that managers could never be 100 percent logical in their decision making because of what he called "bounded rationality." Constraints on rational decision making are numerous; some of the obvious ones are time, money, information, conflicting goals or objectives, complexity, and even intellectual capability.

Rational decision making rests on three basic assumptions. The first assumption is that the decision is, or can be, made if complete information is available; thus, there is no uncertainty or risk. (However, there is almost always some risk even with simple decisions.) The second assumption is that the decision maker will be free of bias or emotion and therefore logical. (Unfortunately, none of us is without biases and personal values.) The third assumption is that the decider knows the organization's future directions and thus the decision will be the best one possible. (Predicting the future with any degree of accuracy is unlikely; what is best for today may not be best tomorrow.)

One decision style might be called reflexive, gut, or reactive. Basically, these are just the opposite of the rational approach—quick decisions based on limited information and without looking for alternatives. Stewart Thomas (2006) suggested that "the contest between rationality and gut instinct pervades the research on decision making" (p. 12). Eric Bonabeau (2003) indicated that although increasing numbers of decision makers are doing so, it is not a good idea to "trust one's gut" when making key decisions. He described what he considers three major factors causing people to make decisions based on instinct rather than on fact and assessment. First, as decisions become more complex, so do the number of alternatives that potentially can address them; developing and accessing more and more possibilities takes precious time. Second, as we all know, the volume of information grows faster than we are fully capable of processing. Finally, and perhaps most significantly, the time frame for making decisions keeps shrinking.

PROBLEM SOLVING AND RATIONAL DECISION MAKING

Problem solving is the first step in almost any decision making situation. You need to know the purpose for the decision. In essence, it helps you identify the desired outcome. Nooraie (2008) noted that "managers are faced with a multitude of problems every day. In order to solve the problems, they have to make decisions. To make too many decisions, too fast, about too many strange and unfamiliar problems introduces a new element into management" (p. 641). The ways individuals go about solving the multitude of problems is highly varied.

The most commonly used model consists of six steps. First, start by defining the situation requiring a decision (a problem, opportunity, or challenge). Second, determine the objective(s) that the decision must address. Third, gather information about the issue, and generate as many alternatives as possible—even those that might initially seem foolish. Fourth, evaluate each of the alternatives in terms of the decision objectives, and consider what the possible consequences or outcomes might be if you implement each alternative. Fifth, carefully consider how the alternative would be implemented (by using people, time, or resources, for example). Sixth, implement and monitor the "best" alternative.

Charles Kepner and Benjamin Tregoe, perhaps the best-known scholars focused on organizational problem solving, identified seven factors in analyzing and solving problems (Kepner and Tregoe 1965). The following is a summary of their approach to problem analysis:

1. Assume that a standard exists against which to compare real performance. For most libraries, this statement usually reads, "There should be a standard of performance against which one can compare real performance." A decision making or problem-solving situation arises when there is a difference between the actual and the desired results.

2. Determine whether a deviation from the standards has occurred, and if so, determine the degree of deviation. Once managers establish standards, it becomes possible to monitor if and how much deviation occurs. Without a standard, managers may only have a sense that deviation exists, and staff members may or may not agree. (Thus, standards save time and conflict.)

3. Locate the point of deviation in the sequence of activities or in the situation. Frequently, it is more difficult to establish such a point than it might seem, especially when the deviation appears only in the finished product. The deviation may have entered the system at the very beginning, come into the system with the material itself, entered with a person somewhere during the processing sequence, or intruded into the presentation of the final product. The important thing is to correctly identify the source of deviation; failing to do this is a common problem with intuitive problem solving. Failure to identify the source correctly can create additional problems in terms of staff morale and trust.

4. Ascertain what distinguishes the affected group from the unaffected group. What constitutes the deviation? Once the manager carefully reviews what distinguishes the affected group from the unaffected group, the problem is almost solved.

5. Look for a change in the system. The change may be minor, or it may be in a related system; however, some type of change is causing the problematic deviation. The only exception to this rule is when one is testing a new system.

6. Analyze all possible causes that can be deduced from the relevant system changes. First, identify all changes in the system. Then examine each change to determine if it could be the cause of the problem or if it is, in fact, the actual problem.

7. Select the cause that most exactly explains the facts, correct that point in the system, and test the system to see whether deviation continues to occur. If the deviation disappears, the proposed solution was correct; if not, continue to search for other potential causes. Managers ignore this step too often, which usually results in even more problems.

Clearly, not every decision involves a problem, except under the broadest definition. For example, selecting a method for providing selective dissemination of information to users is a problem only in the sense that there may be several reasonable alternatives. A decision about how to handle a specific complaint from a user, on the other hand, may indeed be a problem situation. Even a manager's values and beliefs influence the problem she or he chooses to work on. Guth and Tagiuri's (1965) research showed that managers who are primarily motivated by economic values prefer to make decisions about practical matters. Managers with a theoretical orientation prefer to work on long-term issues, such as planning and strategy. Individuals who put a higher value on politics tend to focus on competitive issues and on those that will likely be career enhancing.

Types of solutions

Once a problem is identified, managers have options for solving it. Five of the more common methods are interim, adaptive, corrective, preventive, and contingency.

Interim solutions buy you time while you search for the cause of the problem. They will also give you more time to implement long-term solutions. All too often, interim solutions have a way of becoming permanent or at least becoming long-term bandages.

Adaptive solutions do not really solve the problem, but they allow the organization to continue to function somewhat normally. If an interim solution is a bandage, an adaptive solution is a plaster cast. It is often chosen in the hope that, with the application of a few cosmetic changes, the problem will take care of itself. Most job situations, unlike broken bones, do not heal themselves. More often than not, someone who glosses over a problem will find it coming back as a larger problem later.

Corrective solutions resolve the problem. Such solutions require time, effort, and careful analysis of the problem. Resolution is the ideal. If a system is to be healthy, the corrective solution is the one to seek.

Preventive solutions go back to Kepner and Tregoe's (1965) idea of exploring decisions for adverse consequences. In this way, you solve not only the problem at hand but also potential problems arising from the planned solution. This method takes even longer than finding a corrective solution, but it could repay its costs by allowing you more time in the future to devote to other management functions.

Contingency solutions simply involve the establishment of standby or emergency procedures to help offset the effects of a serious problem. Libraries typically have contingency plans for disasters such as fires, earthquakes, and floods. Unfortunately, some

👥 AUTHORS' EXPERIENCE

One challenge, when it comes to decisions, is not to quickly think of a couple of options and then pick one. There are times when this is a good approach, such as with many programmed decisions. However, even when making a first-time programmed decision, some extra time and thought may well be beneficial.

When Evans teaches management courses, he always uses case study reports as a course component. As part of the discussion of what he considers an ideal report, he uses a PowerPoint slide depicting a perplexed individual standing in front of a coffee vending machine. (What could be more simple/programmed than buying a cup of coffee?) The perplexity arises from the fact that the machine, dispensing only caffeinated coffee, offers twenty-four choices, from plain black to two creams with one artificial sweetener. If you added a decaffeinated option, the possibilities rise into the forties.

Evans's point is: don't assume three or four options are all you ought to consider, especially in the workplace. As Hammond, Keeney, and Raiffa (2011) suggested, bad decisions come about in part when "the alternatives were not clearly defined" (p. 1).

Typically, even with the discussion about the fact that many options exist, the first student reports rarely contain more than eight or ten possibilities. After the class discussion of the first case, students see, from one another, that twenty or more possibilities exist. By the end of the case studies almost every report contains twenty to thirty options.

|||||| **CHECK THESE OUT**

An interesting article that explores the differences between rational and gut decision making is H. Frank Cervone's "Systematic vs. Intuitive Decision Making and the Pareto Principle" (*OCLC Systems and Services: International Digital Library* 31, no. 3: 108–11, 2015).

managers do not make time to prepare such contingency plans. The issue is not if a disaster will strike, but only a question of when. While a disaster plan will not forestall a disaster, it will help keep the damage to a minimum.

Decision limitations

The discussion above may leave you with the sense that decision making as a process is more or less straightforward and, with enough effort, it is relatively risk free and the best choice will be clear. Rational decision making may be an ideal model for making organizational decisions; however, it does not do away with risk, nor is the "best" choice always the one taken. This is especially true for public and nonprofit organizations. As Cheryl Stenstrom (2015) noted, "But hard data does not always provide the complete picture" (p. 646). If nothing else, chance is always a potential wild card.

Some decisions, especially those of an ethical nature, often have little data associated with the potential choices. Mark Winston (2015) opened his essay on ethical decision making by stating, "While often presented as the simplistic choice between right and wrong, ethical decision making can be far more complicated. Increased understanding of why individuals engage in unethical behavior reveals that ethical decision making is not necessarily intuitive" (p. 48). Just thinking back to the chapter on ethics and the variety of approaches to making ethical choices should make it clear why there is less data to consider when faced with the ethical choice.

You can list a host of options, collect and analyze data, ponder the various outcomes of each choice, and yet not be able to select the "best" one. Why? Denise Koufogiannakis (2015) suggests why this may occur: "Academic librarians have different levels of control over their decisions. An individual librarian sometimes makes decisions independently but also makes decisions as part of a group, and often the final decision making power lies with someone else" (p. 110). Another component in the answer to why you may not always be able to select the "best" option, especially for public organizations, are the political winds tied to funding and support that shift in unpredictable ways. From a library perspective, another factor is the available resources often restrict your choices; on more than a few occasions libraries have had to make sub-optimal choices due to resource considerations.

GROUP DECISION MAKING AND ACCOUNTABILITY

Up to this point we have primarily addressed individual decision making. Although much of the discussion thus far also applies to group decision making, there are some special group process issues. If anything, group decision making is even more complex than individual decision making.

Because most decision making situations involve risk and unpredictability, we make the wrong decisions from time to time. People who are afraid of making a mistake try to avoid making decisions in hopes of avoiding accountability for decisions that go wrong. From an organizational point of view, decision making normally calls for clear-cut accountability on someone's part. Accountability is one reason that committee decision making is somewhat problematic.

Problems like the one reflected in the sidebar below occur in most organizations from time to time. Certainly, they occur most often when the organization makes extensive use of committees. However, you will also encounter situations in which the only decision maker involved doesn't remember how, when, or whether he or she made the decision. Unfortunately, the issue of ultimate accountability does not disappear.

Ana Shetach (2009) noted that, in team environments, "decision-making and decision implementation are the heart of all team management activity, at all levels of organizational life. . . . A cardinal dilemma regarding efficient implementation is, therefore, how to verify in advance that a decision one is about to take, is a good one, in terms of quality and applicability" (pp. 7–8). While there are aids for assessing potential decisions, you can never be totally confident that your ultimate choice is in fact a good one. When it comes to group decisions, the uncertainly is even greater.

One important aspect of group decision-making involving committees and teams is how the group views the process. Is it searching for the best outcome, or is it making a case? While this aspect also affects individuals, it becomes critical in the group setting.

 SOMETHING TO PONDER

Some years ago, the *Los Angeles Times* published a news story about a controversial committee decision. The University of California, like many U.S. academic institutions, employs numerous committees; some have decision making authority. In the situation in question, there was concern regarding what high school courses would count toward meeting the university's English language entrance requirement. The university established a system-wide committee to make a decision about which high school courses would satisfy the freshman entrance requirements. Eventually, the university sent letters to California high schools announcing that journalism, speech, and drama courses would no longer be acceptable. Not surprisingly, there were objections to the decision, especially from high school journalism teachers. In an attempt to learn when and how the decision came about, a *Los Angeles Times* reporter interviewed the committee members who presumably made the decision as well as university officials, all of whom could not remember making such a decision. The reporter concluded the article by saying, "the result: a circle of accused, bemused, and slightly embarrassed designated decision makers in search of an important decision that no one says he made. And yet a decision was made. Minutes of a June 3 committee meeting of the statewide Academic Senate say so!" (Speich 1976, p. 34).

Have you ever had such an experience when being a member of a committee? How do you achieve accountability in group decision making situations?

When a group considers its purpose is to advocate for a case, there is often competition to see if a personal view can prevail. This type of atmosphere does not lend itself to sound decision making. Strong personal views and hidden agendas can get in the way of meaningful and open exchanges while limiting the number of alternatives that are developed and considered.

Another issue is that vigorous debate about positions or alternatives can generate conflict. Here the fight, flight, and flow scale can come into play. In a group setting, it is likely that two, if not all three, of these behaviors will be present and thus will impact the group process and the quality of the decision reached. Conflict, in and of itself, is not a problem. It can be beneficial when it is cognitive rather than emotional in character. The challenge is to achieve the highest possible level of cognitive conflict and the lowest level of emotional conflict. One way to achieve this is by carefully framing the decision goals for the group. Another technique is to monitor the group—when emotions are running high, call a time-out.

Groups can easily fall into the trap of "groupthink." Two factors frequently play a role in groupthink. Perhaps the most common factor is the desire to get or keep things moving. This desire often results in a hasty decision made without much effort and without assessing multiple options. The second common factor is the desire to be a team player; this too, can reduce options and very likely will limit critical assessment or thoughtful idea generation.

An interesting article about impasses in team decision making is Bob Frisch's 2008 article "When Teams Can't Decide." Although his focus was senior management teams, his points apply to most kinds of team and committee settings. "Reaching collective decisions based on individual preferences is an imperfect science. Majority wishes can clash when a group of three or more people attempt to set priorities among three or more items" (p. 122). What can happen is a "voting paradox." The paradox arises even with apparently simple yes/no voting—there is always the third option—to abstain.

Consider this example of a three-person team of librarians—Al, Betty, and Carol—charged with selecting one of three online databases—DB-1, DB-2, or DB-3. They decide they should each list their first, second, and third choices. The results could be a voting paradox (see table 9.1) because three different people can have three different preferences. Any outside person (supervisor, department head, or director, for example) who breaks the impasse will offend two-thirds of the committee, no matter what selection is taken, thus proving that the boss is always wrong, at least in terms of voting paradoxes.

Libraries increasingly are part of another group that makes decisions—a consortium. While all the elements and issues covered thus far are in play with this type of situation, some other matters complicate the matter. First and foremost, unlike internal group decisions, in consortial decision making there is rarely a single person in charge of the

TABLE 9.1 Voting Paradoxes

	1ST CHOICE	2ND CHOICE	3RD CHOICE
Al	DB-1	DB-2	DB-3
Betty	DB-2	DB-3	DB-1
Carol	DB-3	DB-1	DB-2

decision. Thus, accountability is very vague at best. Also, for a library concerned about a decision, the choices for action are limited—accept and hope, pull out of the group, or fight to reverse the decision and, perhaps, risk breaking up the group.

Generally, within consortia decisions become a matter in which the "four Cs" play important roles; concessions and consensus are the keys to a resolution. Another "C" for such decision making is consideration—you may not always get what you would like—if the group is to succeed. A final "C," often the most significant, refers to coalitions. In many ways, coalitions assist in moving matters forward, as they normally reduce the number of variables in play within a large group.

A major challenge for consortia is determining what is best. The number of bests is substantially greater in a consortial environment than for a single library. There are the bests for each institution, the bests for coalitions, and, of course, the bests for the group as a whole.

Building trust is always a factor in group decision making, but it becomes a significant challenge for consortial members because they spend less time together than internal groups. Time is a key factor in creating trust, and it is limited in consortial situations. A related factor is that, more often than not, institutional representatives at such meetings are senior, if not the most senior, managers. Generally, such people are not used to having their views openly challenged, which may happen in a consortial setting. Time together, trust, concessions, and consensus are the key elements for successful consortial decision making.

DECISION AIDS

Many techniques exist to aid the decision maker in selecting the best alternative. Some of these techniques are quantitative in nature; other methods are qualitative. Qualitative techniques are useful in assessing those elements that are value oriented. Almost all decision making has some value elements, but those that relate to customer service and/or involve ethical situations can benefit from qualitative techniques. "Thing" decisions benefit most from quantitative methods.

Quantitative methods

Libraries face ever-increasing pressure to be accountable. One very valuable tool to demonstrate accountability is hard data. Information about increased usage, number of reference questions answered, and number of documents delivered is useful in making decisions. Without question, evidence-based decisions informed with hard data carry greater credibility than those that are anecdotally based. An integrated library system (ILS) can provide a wealth of data, but without a plan for how to use the information, the data can be overwhelming. As Caroline Cummins (2006) stated, "making sense of the data lurking in the ILS is crucial" (p. 14). Hiller and Self (2004) defined data as "records of observations, facts, or information collected for reference or analysis" (p. 129). ILSs are capable of providing an ocean of data; the good news is that most vendors offer packages that make it possible for the decision maker to organize and analyze the data.

Another approach to help demonstrate accountability is through data mining, sometimes labeled "bibliomining" in a library context (Nicholson 2006). A short definition of data mining is the identification of new, useful patterns and trends in large quantities of data through the use of statistical and mathematical techniques. A common use of the methodology is pattern recognition/description and prediction. Koontz and Jue (2004) describe a form of data mining from the Public Library Geographic Database. They identify several possible "questions" that one might address using the database, such as the relationships among collection usage, community demographics, and the number or percentage of U.S. public libraries that serve areas with more than a 25 percent poverty level. Their article has some exercises for exploring the potential of the database and the concept of data mining.

Other useful quantitative aids include linear programming, simulation modeling, queuing theory, decision trees, matrix algebra, and linear mathematical equations—all forms of operational research techniques. To use linear programming, the circumstances must meet several conditions. First, there must be a definite objective, and the manager must be able to express the objective in a quantifiable way, for example, cost, time, or quantity. Second, the variables that will affect the outcome must have a linear relationship. Third, restrictions on variables must be present (otherwise, this approach would not be necessary). Linear programming is very mechanical; most library processes do not have a linear relationship. Even in the circulation of items in the collection—the most obvious place to apply the technique—there are enough variations in terms of work to make the application of quantifiable methods difficult.

Simulation model techniques attempt to carry out a solution in a controlled environment. The researcher or decision maker creates a model representing some aspects of the real-world situation and subjects the model to various changes, one at a time, to determine what might happen. The simulation model attempts to trace changes in activities as variables come into play. It tries to quantify the behavioral and non-logical attributes of a situation. The Monte Carlo technique is a simulation model in which the goal is to control chance. Random sampling helps to simulate natural events and to establish the probability of each of several outcomes. This type of simulation assists in answering a variety of questions: What are the chances of an event actually happening? Which of the alternative decisions appears to be best? What are the probabilities of a breakdown in a given unit or in a class of equipment? In the case of libraries, the use of this method can assist in decisions related to technology, new services, and changes in service.

Queuing theory deals with the length of time it takes to render a service or to process something. For instance, how long must staff, customers, and equipment remain idle because of an inefficient physical arrangement? Combining queuing theory and the Monte Carlo approach, a manager can determine expected arrival rates in a facility and the anticipated delay that an arrival will generate. This approach could be quite valuable in a heavily used customer area (for example, an academic library's course reserve service or a public library's reference unit) in determining staffing patterns in a way that will meet demands most efficiently.

A technique that any library manager can use is a decision tree, which presents a graphical representation of different alternative decisions. It helps the manager understand the consequences of implementing different decisions. Successful use of decision trees depends on the careful analysis of the situation and the examination of a variety of options.

An example of how a decision tree might apply to a library situation is the problem of how to increase access to a growing volume of serial publications in an environment of limited funding. A library might consider four broad options:

1. Subscribe to all the desired journals in hard copy
2. Expand traditional interlibrary loan and document delivery services
3. Subscribe to online databases and drop paper-based titles in the online resources
4. Subscribe to an on-demand document delivery service for access to necessary articles with users ordering directly (for which they might be asked to pay service fee)

Each option has consequences in terms of staffing, equipment, budget, customer satisfaction, and, perhaps, cost of services passed on to customers. By developing a decision tree and/or decision matrix (which incorporates the concept of probability of an event happening), the decision makers are provided with a picture of the outcomes.

Qualitative methods

Because of the inability to validate ethical (value) judgments objectively, managers must ask a very basic question concerning the values employed: whose standard of correctness (ethical approaches) should be used? The steps that we outlined earlier can help bring this process to a more conscious level and perhaps improve the quality of the decisions being made.

Consider the issue of whether to charge "outside" users a fee for accessing library online databases. (We are assuming the library knows that its license agreements would not preclude this if the fees are shared with the vendor.) An unlikely approach would be simply "to decide" to impose a fee. A more likely approach would be to attempt to use the quantitative methods previously outlined. Such an approach would help identify the major variables and assist in weighing the alternatives. But neither approach will resolve the ethical (conflicts that will arise; and the ethical considerations often determine the final disposition of a matter. Thus, the hypothetical manager may have determined demands on the library's resources by outsiders, the cost of providing the service, and an equitable fee (based on demand and cost). However, the basic question of deciding whether to charge a fee remains unanswered. Some of the qualitative questions to answer are: Would creation of a service fee hurt the library's relations with its users? Would it hurt the public relations of the institution of which the library is a part? Would continuing free service lead to greater support of the institution and the library? Would a service fee be contrary to public welfare? To whom is the library (if publicly supported) obligated to provide free service and under what circumstances? Every answer involves a value judgment.

🔢 KEY POINTS TO REMEMBER

- Careers are made or broken by the quality of decisions made.
- Decision outcomes are rarely completely certain or risk-free.
- Decisions are either programmed or non-programmed.
- Programmed decision making takes place daily at all levels of the organization.
- Non-programmed decisions carry the greatest uncertainty and risk.
- Understanding decision making and problem-solving processes is a managerial asset.
- Rational decision making, despite its limitations, is a useful tool.

- Decision making carries with it accountability.
- Group and team decision making is more complex than individual decision making.
- Consortial decisions involve the four Cs: concessions, consensus, consideration, and coalitions.
- Decision aids are both quantitative and qualitative in character.

REFERENCES

Bonabeau, Eric. 2003. "Don't Trust Your Gut." *Harvard Business Review* 81, no. 5: 116–23.

Cummins, Caroline. 2006. "Below the Surface." *Library Journal* (Net Connect Supplement), Winter: 12–14.

Frisch, Bob. 2008. "When Teams Can't Decide." *Harvard Business Review* 86, no. 11: 121–26.

Guth, William, and Rento Tagiuri. 1965. "Personal Values and Corporate Strategy." *Harvard Business Review* 37 (September–October): 123–32.

Hammond, John S., Ralph L. Keeney, and Howard Raiffa. 2011. "The Hidden Traps in Decision-Making." In *Harvard Business Review on Making Smart Decisions*, 1–27. Cambridge, MA: Harvard Business Review Press.

Hiller, Steve, and James Self. 2004. "From Measurement to Management: Using Data Wisely for Planning and Decision-Making." *Library Trends* 53, no. 1: 129–55.

Kelman, Steven, Ronald Sanders, and Gayatri Pandit. 2016. "'I Won't Back Down?': Complexity and Courage in Government Executive Decision Making." *Public Administration Review* 76, no. 3: 465–71.

Kepner, Charles H., and Benjamin B. Tregoe. 1965. *The Rational Manager*. New York: McGraw-Hill.

Koontz, Christie, and Dean K. Jue. 2004. "Customer Data 24/7 Aids Library Planning and Decision-Making." *Florida Libraries* 47, no. 1: 17–19.

Koufogiannakis, Denise. 2015. "Determinants of Evidence Used in Academic Librarian Decision Making." *College and Research Libraries* 76, no. 1: 100–14.

Mintzberg, Henry. 1976. "Planning on the Left Side and Managing ON THE Right." *Harvard Business Review* 54, no. 4: 49–58.

Nicholson, Scott. 2006. "Proof in the Pattern." *Library Journal* 131 (Supplement January): 2–4, 6.

Nooraie, Mahmood. 2008. "Decision Magnitude of Impact and Strategic Decision-Making Process Output." *Management Decisions* 46, no. 4: 640–55.

Shetach, Ana. 2009. "The Revised Decision-Square Model (RDSM): A Tool for Effective Decision Implementation in Teams." *Team Performance Management* 15, nos. 1/2: 2–17.

Simon, Herbert. 1976. *Administrative Behavior*. 3rd ed. New York: Free Press.

Speich, Daniel. 1976. "English Ruling: UC Decisions Sometimes Just Seem to Happen." *Los Angeles Times*, November 14 (pt. 1): 34.

Stenstrom, Cheryl. 2015. "Decision-Making Experiences of Public Library CEOs: A Study Exploring the Roles of Interpersonal Influence and Evidence in Everyday Practice." *Library Management* 36, nos. 8/9: 644–52.

Thomas, Stewart. 2006. "Did You Ever Have to Up Your Mind?" *Harvard Business Review* 84, no. 1: 12.

Winston, Mark. 2015. "The Complexity of Ethical Decision Making." *Journal of Information Ethics* 24, no. 1: 48–64.

CHAPTER 10

Change Management

Evolution, change and adaptation have become a natural part of academic research libraries for decades but in more recent times have been characterized by the pace of that change and the disruptive and transformational technologies that are, in part, facilitating them.

Donna McRostie, 2016

Change, transformation, the reassessment of services and professional capabilities are key concepts in the language of academic libraries today.

Heli Kaatrakoski and Johanna Lahikainen 2016

O ur opening quotations make the point that change is part of a library's environment. It certainly is, but it is not truly a new phenomenon. What is relatively new is the pace of change. The fact is, we live in a universe where change is inevitable, constant, and unavoidable. Since that is a given, people and organizations change no matter what they might prefer. The challenge is to address change in a productive and timely manner. Some years ago, Karen Brown and Kate Marek (2005) in discussing change in libraries, commented, "The tendency to rely on what is most familiar, even when it may become a hindrance, is also common in organizations and professions" (p. 69). Staying static is often the worst choice in a changing environment.

People handle change in different ways. Some fear it, and others embrace it. In our personal lives, we more often than not accept change when we have some control over its pace. When it comes to the workplace, we tend to resist change and cling to the status quo, partially because it is imposed on us and we have very little control over it.

The literature on change management primarily focuses on the for-profit sector. Although the basics of handling a change process are the same across sectors, public sector organizations in particular have a more complex situation when trying to change. When you ask people about their first thoughts when they hear the words "government agency," a very common response is some variation of bureaucracy. People have something of a love-hate relationship with both the reality and concept of public organizations. They expect flexibility while wanting stability—a rather difficult feat for any organization in a changing environment. Another fact that adds to the complexity is that public agencies have a heterogeneous "service population," and what may please one segment may not please some other segments. Public organizations can and do change, albeit slowly because there should be conscious plans about what to change and by how much. Even libraries face these added complexities, at least when it comes to services.

Change and innovation are tightly linked for organizations. To implement innovative ideas or practices the staff must make changes. There are times when developments in the

environment (in a turbulent environment, for example) call for change that can be some-
times radical in nature. The two concepts are drivers of one another many times. Tomalee
Doan and Mary Lee Kennedy (2009) noted in their article "Innovation, Creativity, and
Meaning":

> Librarians today have come to view change as the means of accomplishing significant
> goals, recognizing that our organizations must keep pace with user needs, acknowledg-
> ing that we do indeed have information competitors and that we are part of organiza-
> tions and therefore must align with larger objectives than our own. It is essential to
> innovate in order to continue to be meaningful. (p. 349)

Managing change is central to organizational viability, and innovation may be especially important to long-term well-being. To manage change well and to be innovative,
you must understand the change process and the techniques that help staff accept and
embrace change.

NATURE OF CHANGE

"There is nothing more difficult to take in hand, more perilous to conduct, or more uncertain in its success than to take the lead in the introduction of a new order of things" (Machiavelli 1952, p. 52). Organizational change takes place across a continuum from incremental
to radical. A "new order of things" may be required when there are crisis conditions in the
organization's environment. On the other hand, every day there are small changes both externally and internally. Staff members deal with change on a daily basis without realizing it.
The vast majority of the changes are so small as to be almost unnoticeable.

Leslie Szamosi and Linda Duxbury (2002, p. 186) discussed change as a continuum—
incremental to radical. They defined radical change as something that:

- interrupts the status quo
- happens quickly or abruptly
- is fundamental and all encompassing
- brings something that is dramatically different from what used to be

Radical change is difficult for any staff, even those who are accustomed to change and
are generally positive about its value. Clearly a change that has the features Szamosi and
Duxbury outlined is much more than an "adjustment." Nevertheless, organizations with
staff who have positive attitudes about change are better positioned to successfully navigate what will be turbulent times than those that do not have such staff.

At the opposite end of the continuum, incremental change may not be the best
approach either. Michael W. McLaughlin (2011) identified two potential flaws beginning
with the tortoise, or incremental, approach. He suggests that "many people respond negatively to incremental change. . . . When stakes are low, some people cling to entrenched
positions until forced to change. . . . Second, starting small is often an invitation to push
issues that really matter to the back burner" (p. 12).

Kate Hawker and Melissa Garcia (2010) made a case for a tortoise approach: "One of
the great misconceptions about making incremental change is that doing nothing translates into passivity. This is not true. While an organization may 'wait' to take a specific

SOMETHING TO PONDER

Some academic and public libraries, at least the larger ones, tend to be bureaucratic in structure, and some are unionized. Both issues restrict a library's ability to respond with any kind of flexibility to external changes. Bureaucracies are, after all, designed for permanence. This is their strength, as well as an ironic weakness. Civil service rules and union contracts further tie the hands of managers who want to respond creatively to environmental changes or to simply streamline or improve operations. Recent budget shortfalls have shaken things up for some libraries, and they have been forced to change. This is another dimension of change. It is one thing to change because it will improve the way you do business. It is quite another when change is dictated by outside forces. How can managers put a positive spin on a budget cut that will mean decreased pay and increased workload?

action until the right pieces are in place, progress should be a constant. If you relentlessly nudge many projects forward by small amounts, significant achievements can occur quickly" (p. 27). They go on to describe how their organization made slow but steady progress by following five practices (p. 28):

- Be self-aware—know when the organization is ready to change.
- Have good information—gather data aggressively.
- Be nimble—don't be unwilling to adjust if there are problems.
- Develop goals and budgets from the bottom up.
- Exert pressure from the top to create incentives for staff to change.

Hawker and Garcia describe something near the middle of the change continuum. Essentially, it is a state of constant small changes being made that all lead toward larger change goals. They indicated that they drew on the Chinese saying, "The sage does not attempt anything very big and thus achieves great things." Seeking the middle ground is often the best approach to change. In today's environment you may find that something similar to their approach—almost constant change—is what you will have to engage in.

CHANGE PROCESS MODELS

There are two widely discussed models for planned change: Lewin's model and Kotter's model. Kurt Lewin's (1951) change model was one of the first models and it is certainly the one most commonly thought of when it comes to discussing the change process and management. His force-field analysis has become a classic model for thinking about organizational change.

How change occurs is a factor in how staff will react to a proposed change. Imposed change mandated by outside agencies presents significant challenges for managerial leaders as they have less control over how to convey the need to change. Recently, libraries have undergone many imposed changes as a result of the economic downturn. Static or reduced funding has often led to less hiring or hiring freezes, reduced service hours, and

> ▥ **CHECK THIS OUT**
>
> A good example of the effective use of Kotter's methodology in a library is in Timothy A. Hackman's article "Leading Change in Action: Reorganizing an Academic Library Department Using Kotter's Eight Stage Change Model" (*Library Leadership and Management* 31, no. 2: 1–27, 2017).

fewer programs— all of which mean change for the staff. Mandated changes almost always present you with the challenge of broader based and stronger resistance to the proposed or required change. Oreg and Sverdlik (2011) emphasized the importance of understanding the different types of change, stating:

> An important factor that distinguishes between the various types of change . . . is the amount of discretion that individuals have in adopting change. Whereas some changes are voluntary, others are imposed, and whereas reactions to any change are influenced by how the individual feels about the notion of change, reactions to imposed (vs. voluntary) change are also influenced by how the individual feels about the imposition. (p. 338)

Lewin (1951) developed his three-step model (unfreezing, changing, and refreezing) from his force-field analysis concept. The concept involves a person, unit, or organization and how he, she, or it must overcome the status quo or the state of equilibrium in order to change. He suggested that two sets of forces are at work to maintain the equilibrium: driving forces and restraining forces. For changes to occur, the driving forces must be greater than the restraining forces.

"Unfreezing" is a process for creating a readiness to acquire or learn new behaviors. This means assisting staff in recognizing the ineffectiveness of the current behavior in terms of the area of the planned change. It also means pointing out how the change will benefit the staff and the organization (for example, a task will take less time, a task will be less stressful, the organization will stay viable). Unfreezing staff may be a time-consuming process, and without their active participation it will be difficult. Not only do people need to adjust to change but also, in many cases, the organizational culture needs to adjust as well. Without successfully completing this process, you are not likely to achieve long-lasting change.

"Changing" is the period when the staff begins to work with the new behavior pattern. More often than not, there will be a testing period while staff members make up their minds about a new situation. You should be watchful during the changing period, as staff may begin to slip back into the old pattern. You should be even more supportive than usual during this period.

"Refreezing" takes place when the staff internalize the change and it becomes part of the organizational culture. Rewards for implementing the new pattern are a key factor in achieving refreezing.

John Kotter (1990) expanded Lewin's three-phase model by breaking down Lewin's steps into eight smaller components. During the unfreezing process he suggested that managers should establish a sense of urgency, create a "guiding" coalition, develop a vision and strategy for the change, and finally communicate the change vision. (All of these processes are more difficult when the changes are being imposed.)

SOMETHING TO PONDER

Think about successful and unsuccessful changes you have experienced in an organization. What factors can you identify that led to either the success or the failure? Did managers employ elements of the change models?

His components for the change phase are: empower staff for action, generate some short-term "wins," and consolidate gains (that is, don't declare victory too soon). The only difference between Lewin's refreezing stage and Kotter's "anchoring" stage is that Kotter points out that it may take years for change(s) to be anchored and become a part of the organizational culture.

Research into organizational change has shown that almost 70 percent of change efforts fail to achieve all or most of their objectives. That figure may at first glance seem surprising and almost unbelievable; however, when you think about it, how many times do you read about failures as compared to announcements of success? Few of us like to announce a failed effort. Also, remember that the statistic covers "all or most" of the objectives; therefore, a partial success counts as a failure. Regardless of what the count of failures should or should not include, why is total success difficult to achieve?

One significant factor is the traditional way managers are taught to think about change. Recent research suggests that long-standing models may no longer be fully sufficient for managing change. The sense is that, at best, managers have an understanding of how to address complicated change as opposed to radical change.

Another approach is "emergent change." The essential point in the emergent model is that you should not think of change as a linear process through time. Rather, you should think of it in terms of being an open-ended process in which unexpected turns and events are normal. Thinking this way, advocates believe, allows you to cope more effectively with complexity and uncertainty (for details, see Burnes 2004; Bamford and Forrester 2003). Another aspect of the emergent change concept is the need to have staff members who are open to learning.

Moran and Brightman (2001) defined change management as "the process of continually renewing the organization's direction, structure, and capabilities to serve the ever-changing needs of external and internal customers" (p. 111). Brown and Marek (2005), reporting on focus group sessions with librarians regarding organizational change, suggested librarians are well aware of the need to manage change: "It is particularly interesting to note that the study's participants spoke consistently in positive terms about successful change mechanisms" (p. 73). It takes little thought to understand how McWilliam and Ward-Griffin's (2006) quote applies to libraries: "Declining resources and organizational restructuring distract attention from efforts to develop more client-centered, empowering partnership approaches to health and social services" (p. 119).

RESISTANCE TO CHANGE

While resistance to change is inevitable, there is no definitive means of knowing who will resist and how strong that resistance will be. Some people seem to thrive on change, and some prefer never to change. Occasionally, people switch reactions, creating an unexpected

> ▶ **TIP**
>
> **Basic Steps for Addressing Resistance to Change**
>
> - Develop a plan.
> - Communicate the need to change and communicate the plan.
> - Build trust from existing trust.
> - Identify potential benefits.
> - Openly acknowledge any potential drawbacks.
> - Empower people by securing their input and modifications to the plan.
> - Provide active encouragement, training, and resources to ensure success.

challenge. Knowing exactly what circumstances and what types of change will trigger acceptance or resistance is difficult.

What are some of the issues in resistance? When faced with a greater than incremental change, people normally go through a four-stage process: denial, resistance, exploration, and commitment. Denial may take the form of "It will not impact me" or "Why is this necessary?" or "This is unnecessary." When confronted with change, some people will actively resist, some will unknowingly resist, and a few will move on to the next stage on their own. Exploration is the first phase of actively accepting the need to change and starting to look at how it will impact personal activities. The final phase is actively working toward making the process a success.

A few people resist change based on some type of fear. One obvious fear relates to job or wage security: "What will happen to my job?" Change generally brings uncertainty that goes well beyond an individual's job. The status quo is known and is, to a greater or lesser degree, comfortable. "What will happen to my work relationships?" is a common issue. Possible loss of control regarding one's status, power, and future prospects may play a role for some people.

Change often calls for new duties that may require learning new skills. Learning anxiety is a very real issue for many people ("Can I learn what is required?" "Will I look incompetent in front of my peers?"). The anxiety can lead to serious resistance when something like a new software package is introduced.

Kegan and Lahey (2001) describe a form of resistance that is frequently unrecognized because it occurs with people who appear to be committed to change: "Many people are unwittingly applying productive energy toward a hidden *competing commitment*" (p. 85, emphasis in original). One example Kegan and Lahey give is a project manager who is "dragging his feet" on a project because of a stronger and unrecognized competing commitment (avoidance)—the fear that the next project will be beyond his capabilities. Kegan and Lahey acknowledge that overcoming such hidden commitments is difficult because "it challenges the very psychological foundation upon which people function" (p. 86). Their article is well worth reading before you undertake a major change.

Lack of information and poor communication are other causes of resistance. The more you explain the exact nature of change and listen to staff concerns, the less likely the staff are to actively resist. Open and honest communication is a key component to achieving a successful change. People who understand the change and its necessity are more accepting than those who do not understand.

Related to that understanding is the sense of having a say about the change. Managers must realize that some valid resistance develops when people identify flaws in the proposed change. Pointing out potential or perceived problem areas is not always a method for passively resisting or delaying a change. It may identify an important but over-looked problem.

John Kotter and Leonard Schlesinger (1979) provided four realistic suggestions for managing resistance to change. In fact, the four points are good management tools for almost any purpose:

- education plus communication
- participation plus involvement
- facilitation plus support
- negotiation and agreement

You can never predict with 100 percent accuracy who will or will not resist a change, because a host of variables interact with one another. Over the years, researchers interested in change management have studied dozens of variables. Table 10.1 lists nine of the most common variables. Not only does each variable manifest itself differently over time and according to the nature of a proposed change, but each variable also interacts with one or more of the other variables. When you consider the range of possibilities created from just the nine variables (there are many others as well) you can understand why you can never be 100 percent certain about how much and from whom resistance is likely to arise.

One of the best means for overcoming resistance to change is creating an environment in which people become more accepting of change and its steps. There are at least six broad long-term processes for creating such an environment: generating an acceptance that change is necessary and positive, building a willingness and ability to change, cultivating a support structure for change, providing necessary resources for change, creating an organizational culture that assists staff in changing, and rewarding efforts to change. These are some of the steps you can take to carry out the processes:

- Offer coaching and training in the change process and its value.
- Form teams of diverse staff members to assist in planning change.
- Have frequent meetings to discuss and think about potential changes.
- Encourage staff to talk to users about their perceptions of service enhancements.
- Emphasize the importance of thinking about the changing external environment and what, if any, implications it might have for the library
- Listen to and reward staff suggestions for change, even if the suggestions are not implemented and/or the rewards are modest.

TABLE 10.1 Common Resistance-to-Change Variables

PERSONAL	WORK SITUATION
Tenure in position	Organizational position (level)
Disposition to resist	Tenure in position
Ambivalence to change	Employment status (full, part-time)

IMPLEMENTING CHANGE

Organizational development (OD) is a method for generating both individual and organizational changes. Over the years the focus has shifted in emphasis from its initial concern with creating a "mechanistic" (scientific management) method of managing organizations to today's need to manage change. OD's primary focus is on people who are or will be undergoing an organizational change process. Some of the most frequent uses of OD are assisting with mergers, managing conflict, and revitalizing organizations.

Karen Holloway (2004) outlined twelve elements of OD as applied to libraries. The people elements are: letting the people doing the work make as many of the decisions related to their activities as possible; focusing on user community needs and wants; having a focus on group or team dynamics and organizational culture; improving collaborative work efforts and processes; and understanding and accepting shared responsibility and accountability. The organizational elements are: creating trust through the organization; focusing on being an agile organization; constantly looking to improve processes; thinking in terms of improvements in "service" for both internal and external customers; employing evidenced-based data in decision-making; generating performance-based managerial tools; and linking all activities to mission, vision, values, and organizational goals.

In looking at these elements, you can probably see how you might employ OD for managing change, innovation, team building, and many other activities. One reason that OD has lasted as long as it has is its flexibility. How one organization makes use of OD is often very different from what you will see in another OD-oriented entity.

Change is likely to generate some amount of conflict, if at a low level, even when there is a sound OD program in place. David Payne (2010) suggested that some conflict can be beneficial for an organization:

> A recently overheard criticism of a work colleague was surprising—"she makes her employees too comfortable." This appeared to fly in the face of much that librarians have been taught about management, such as fostering team spirit, encouraging openness, and making employees feel valued. In this case, however, the issue was that the manager's employees were not growing. . . . They were not being taken outside their comfort zone; they are never challenged. (p. 6)

He went on to review the value of conflict within the organization and how to manage it for the organization's benefit. Another good resource about this topic in relation to libraries is Jane McGrun Kathman and Michael D. Kathman's 1990 article "Conflict Management in Academic Libraries" (*Journal of Academic Librarianship* 16, no. 3).

STRESS AND THE ORGANIZATION

No Shit!!!

Workplace stress is very common. It arises from many causes. It seems clear that organizational change is one of the leading causes of stress for many employees. One question is whether workplace stress is always a bad thing. The answer: not always.

Excessive stress, personal or organizational, can undermine health and thereby adversely affect work productivity; however, "less agreement exists regarding the effects of stress on organizational effectiveness" (Zaccaro and Riley 1987, p. 1). Some management researchers, such as James Quick (1992), suggest that organizational and staff stress is not necessarily bad. J. E. McGrath (1976) showed that in the workplace there is an inverted-U relationship between stress and performance. That is, when there is little or no stress, staff are in a state of boredom where performance and productivity are low as well. As stress increases, so does performance up to a point (after which it falls). Using a scale of 0 to 100 to indicate the level of stress, when stress is somewhere near the midpoint, performance begins to fall off and drop back to a low point, indicating boredom. The issue for managers is to find the right level and type of stress to achieve maximum performance and not go beyond that point.

For many people, the response to too much stress is physiological, often taking the form of illness. Stress contributes to mental illness, alcoholism, and drug and other substance abuse, as well as to other dysfunctional conditions that lead to poor job performance. It is also clear that stress is not just work-related. People can usually cope effectively when either personal or workplace stress is low, but problems develop when both are high. When coping strategies fail, burnout is often the result. Stress, distress, strain, and burnout are a continuum of a condition wherein

- on the whole, challenges are sources of happiness and productive responses;
- perceived imbalances between demands and resources are painful, but coping strategies restore the balance and reduce the pain;
- inappropriate coping strategies are out of control (i.e., are contributing to the problem); and the person's physical and mental resources are depleted (Bunge 1989, p. 94).

One of the challenges for you as a manager comes from the fact that what is stressful for one person may not be stressful for someone else. There is no way to know what will or will not be stressful for any staff member, nor is there a single cure for resolving the stress once you identify it. Some methods of coping can be taught, such as relaxation, meditation, and biofeedback. While these techniques are individualized and require no organizational support, some organizations do offer training courses to interested staff.

David Fisher (1990) claimed, based on critical analysis of stress and burnout studies in the library profession published up to 1989, that there is no empirical evidence that stress and burnout are any higher in library services than in similar professions.

INNOVATION AND LIBRARIES

Is there a difference between creativity and innovation? The most straightforward answer is that creativity is the process of generating new ideas, while innovation is about implementing a new idea in an organization. Thus, it is possible to be "innovative" through the

---

||||| **CHECK THIS OUT**

A good comprehensive guide to change management in libraries is Susan Curzon's *Managing Change: A How-To-Do-It Manual for Librarians* (New York: Neal-Schuman, rev. ed., 2005).

introduction of a new idea for your organization even if the idea itself has existed for some time or has been used in other organizations.

Catherine Wang and Prevaiz Ahmed (2004) conducted a literature review and identified five areas of typical organizational innovativeness: product, market/service, process, behavioral, and strategic. In an academic library, an example of product innovation might be developing the concept of an electronic institutional repository for the parent institution. In terms of market/service innovation, it might be to offer faculty members office delivery of printed materials. From a process point of view, ceasing to check in serials (and we do know of at least one case of this) might qualify as innovative. A behavioral example might be greeting each person when she or he enters the library or archives and perhaps offering jelly beans or mints. A strategic innovation might be to shift from an institution-wide service focus to a tailored service focus—including staffing—aimed at a college, school, institute, and so forth.

Voelpel, Leibold, and Streb (2005) concluded that "recent academic and business evidence indicates that innovation is the key factor for companies' success and sustained fitness in a rapidly evolving, knowledge-networked economy" (p. 57). They described how 3M, known for its innovations, fosters innovative thinking and actions. Although libraries may not be able to set as clear a target for innovations as does 3M (30 percent of future sales should come from products that did not exist four years earlier), the principle is relevant to their situation—thinking about and acting innovatively. The idea that top management can foster, or not foster, innovative ideas is true. The point to remember is that you will demonstrate your support, or lack of support, for innovative ideas whether you are aware of that fact or not; your values and beliefs are the key to whether your unit or library is innovative.

You should give some thought to innovation as part of the change process. If you seek input from staff regarding how to change and let them know that "crazy ideas" are welcome, you will cultivate an environment where staff members see themselves as part of the process of making things better, where new approaches are encouraged, and where change is less frightening. Do you want to be on the incremental end of the continuum—adopting ideas that are successfully and widely used in other libraries? Do you want to move toward the center by using an idea that has a successful track record in other types of organizations but has not yet been tried in a library? Or do you want to be the innovator on the radical end of the change continuum by applying new knowledge to your unit or library? Only you can answer these questions.

▌▌▌ CHECK THESE OUT

A recent article about innovation issues in public sector organizations is Mahmoud Moussa, Adela McMurray, and Nuttawuth Muenjohn's "The Conceptual Framework of the Factors Influencing Innovation in Public Sector Organizations" (*Journal of Developing Area* 52, no. 3: 231–40, 2018).

A good article about innovation and libraries is Jennifer Rowley's "Should Your Library Have an Innovation Strategy?" (*Library Management* 32, nos. 4/5: 251–56, 2011).

A very informative resource on innovation and information services is Carmel Maguire, Edward J. Kazlauskas, and Anthony D. Weir's *Information Services for Innovative Organizations* (Bingley, England: Emerald Group Publishing Limited, 2010).

We suggested earlier that organizational culture plays a significant role in the success or failure of organizational change. Organizational culture influences creativity and innovation in at least two ways:

- through shared values and norms, people make judgments and assumptions about the acceptability of creative and innovative behavior within the organization
- through established forms of behavior and activity, especially as reflected in practices and procedures, lead people to develop perceptions about valued and non-valued behaviors and activities (Martins and Terblanche 2003, p. 68).

Other factors that encourage organizational innovation include the following:

- socialization regarding acceptable work behavior
- values related to acceptability of risk taking
- flexibility in actions and thinking
- freedom and encouragement to explore new ideas
- cooperative, empowered work teams
- support from management
- treatment of mistakes as opportunities for learning rather than punishment
- tolerance of conflict as natural and useful in developing new ideas
- open and honest communication

What can a small library do to encourage innovative thinking? The typical small public or school library is staffed by one or two professionals, with perhaps a few paraprofessionals or volunteers. Sometimes a person is the only staff. Certainly, this situation can encourage stagnation, because the stimulation of working with professional peers is missing. In such cases, resources about new ideas and their managerial applications is of the utmost importance.

It takes considerable mental stimulation to keep current with professional developments and to continue professional growth. You should try to keep up with the profession by reading journals and attending conferences to avoid settling into an unimaginative routine, even though finding the time for these activities can be difficult. Perhaps you could delegate one or two of your tasks to a coworker or a trusted volunteer to gain a few minutes for professional reading during work time.

Within a library (regardless of size), managers need to make special efforts to encourage innovation. Although micromanagement does provide a stable environment, it is not the best method for generating new ideas, independent thinking, and responsibility on the staff's part. The more they see they are considered to be part of decisions, planning, and so forth, the more willing they will be to explore and accept possible changes in their work environment.

You shape library services and programs based on user needs, or you should. Getting the users involved in planning changes and even for generating innovative ideas can pay dividends when you have time to do so. Sara D. Smith and Quinn Galbraith (2011) provided an example of user involvement when they described how a Student Advisory Board had an impact: "These groups have led to changes in their respective libraries.

... One of the most significant and innovative changes has been the creation of a music zone" (p. 395). The authors report that this innovation in a low-use area increased student use there by 20 percent. Users often think outside the library box when asked to be involved.

Here is a final thought about creativity and innovation. Perhaps we can take some comfort regarding the recent "Great Recession" from Steve Jobs (Gallo 2011, p. viii): "The good news is that recessions often act as catalysts for innovation. . . . History shows that the greatest innovations have been introduced in periods of severe economic stress. . . . Indeed stress, conflict, and necessity seem to be nature's way of saying, 'Find a new way.'" Libraries and you must find those "new ways" using your creative thinking.

❶ KEY POINTS TO REMEMBER

- Change is inevitable.
- Change is essential.
- Change is a managerial challenge.
- Change is either reactive or proactive.
- Change takes place along a continuum from incremental to radical.
- Change most often happens in terms of people, technology, structure, and/or strategy.
- Change generates resistance.
- Change process models assist but do not completely solve organizational issues.
- Change management is essential.
- Innovation can lead to uncertain outcomes, but those often are rewarding.
- Innovation and change are complex processes.
- Innovation is knowledge intensive.
- Innovative and new ways of staff thinking can be developed.
- Innovation can be controversial—what some might perceive as a benefit, others might consider a boondoggle.
- Innovation requires taking risks.
- Innovation and effective change flourish in flexible, open, learning-oriented, empowered organizations.

REFERENCES

Bamford, David, and Paul Forrester. 2003. "Managing Planned and Emergent Change Within an Operations Management Environment." *International Journal of Operations and Production Management* 23, no. 5/6: 546–64.

Brown, Karen, and Kate Marek. 2005. "Librarianship and Change: A Consideration of Weick's 'Drop Your Tools' Metaphor." *Library Administration and Management* 19, no. 2: 68–74.

Bunge, Charles. 1989. "Stress in the Library Workplace." *Library Trends* 38, no. 1: 93–102.

Burnes, Bernard. 2004. *Managing Change.* 4th ed. New York: Prentice-Hall.

Doan, Tomalee, and Mary Lee Kennedy. 2009. "Innovation, Creativity, and Meaning: Leading in the Information Age." *Journal of Business and Finance Librarianship* 14, no. 4: 348–58.

Fisher, David. 1990. "Are Librarians Burning Out?" *Journal of Librarianship* 22, no. 4: 216–35.

Gallo, Carmine. 2011. *The Innovation Secrets of Steve Jobs: Insanely Different Principles for Breakthrough Success.* New York: McGraw Hill.

Hawker, Kate, and Melissa Garcia. 2010. "Radical Change One Step at a Time." *Associations Now* 6, no. 11: 27–30.

Holloway, Karen. 2004. "The Significance of Organizational Development in Academic Research Libraries." *Library Trends* 53, no. 1: 5–16.

Kaatrakoski, Heli, and Johanna Lahikainen. 2016. "'What We Do Every Day Is Impossible:' Managing Change by Developing a Knotworking Culture in an Academic Library." *Journal of Academic Librarianship* 42, no. 5: 515–21.

Kathman, Jane McGrun, and Michael D. Kathman. 1990. "Conflict Management in Academic Libraries." *Journal of Academic Librarianship* 16, no. 3: 145–49.

Kegan, Robert, and Lisa Laskow Lahey. 2001. "The Real Reason People Won't Change." *Harvard Business Review* 79, no. 10: 85–92.

Kotter, John. 1990. *A Force for Change: How Leadership Differs from Management.* New York: Simon and Schuster.

Kotter, John, and Leonard Schlesinger. 1979. "Choosing Strategies for Change." *Harvard Business Review* 57, no. 2: 106–14.

Lewin, Kurt. 1951. *Field Theory in Social Sciences.* New York: Harper and Row.

Machiavelli, Niccolo. 1952. *The Prince.* New York: New American Library.

Martins, E. C., and F. Terblanche. 2003. "Building Organizational Culture That Stimulates Creativity and Innovation." *European Journal of Innovation Management* 6, no. 1: 64–74.

McGrath, Joseph E. 1976. "Stress and Behavior in Organizations." In *Handbook of Industrial and Organizational Psychology*, edited by Marvin D. Dunnette, 1351–95. Chicago: Rand McNally.

McLaughlin, Michael W. 2011. "The Trouble with Incremental Change." *The Conference Board Review* 48, no. 1: 12–13.

McRostie, Donna. 2016. "The Only Constant Is Change: Evolving the Library Support Model for Research at the University of Melbourne." *Library Management* 37, nos. 6/7: 363–72.

McWilliam, Carol L., and Catherine Ward-Griffin. 2006. "Implementing Organizational Change in Health and Social Services." *Journal of Organizational Change Management* 19, no. 2: 119–35.

Moran, John, and Baird Brightman. 2001. "Leading Organizational Change." *Career Development International* 6, no. 2: 111–19.

Oreg, Shaul, and Noga Sverdlik. 2011. "Ambivalence toward Imposed Change." *Journal of Applied Psychology* 96, no. 2: 337–49.

Payne, David. 2010. "Harnessing Conflict." *Library Leadership and Management* 24, no. 1: 6–11.

Quick, James. 1992. *Stress and Well-Being in the Workplace.* Washington, DC: American Psychological Association.

Smith, Sara D., and Quinn Galbraith. 2011. "Shopping Carts and Student Employees: How Student Committees Can Bring Innovative Ideas to Academic Libraries." *College and Research Libraries News* 72, no. 7: 395–97.

Szamosi, Leslie, and Linda Duxbury. 2002. "Development of a Measure to Assess Organizational Change." *Journal of Organizational Change Management* 15, no. 2: 184–201.

Voelpel, Sven C., Marius Leibold, and Christoph K. Streb. 2005. "The Innovation Meme: Managing Innovation Replicators for Organizational Fitness." *Journal of Change Management* 5, no. 1: 57–69.

Wang, Catherine, and Pervaiz Ahmed. 2004. "The Development and Validation of the Organizational Innovativeness Construct Using Confirmatory Factor Analysis." *European Journal of Innovation Management* 7, no. 4: 303–13.

Zaccaro, Stephen, and Ann Riley. 1987. "Stress, Coping, and Organizational Effectiveness." In *Occupational Stress and Organizational Effectiveness*, edited by Stephen Zaccaro and Ann Riley, 1–18. New York: Praeger.

CHAPTER 11

Communication

Effective communication, facilitated by the appropriate use of language, is a core aspect of ensuring that library clients successfully obtain information within physical and virtual library environments.

Michael Alexander Fauchelle, 2017

The foundation for communicating library value to senior leadership has been noted above in regard to alignment with the university's mission, strategic plan, and reaccreditation effort.

Scott Walter, 2018

An increasing number of researchers are using Web 2.0 applications to communicate with other researchers, collaborate with peers, publish and disseminate their research among scholarly community.

Ahmed Shehata, David Ellis, and Allen Edward Foster, 2017

Effective communicators are, first and foremost, effective listeners.

Judi Brownell, 2018

In the workplace, communication skills matter. It is something of a toss-up whether your decision making or your communication skills are more important to your long-term career success. Both are significant; but for a new manager, communication skills—or lack thereof—are probably most apparent. When a manager lacks communication skills, workplace colleagues quickly notice and begin to doubt other abilities.

We are increasingly dependent on technology for workplace communication, far more so than our opening quotation from Shehata, Ellis, and Foster suggests. It is now critical for organizational success regardless of sector. That dependence has an impact on how we engage in face-to-face interactions with both our work colleagues and our users. Years ago, David Berlo (1960) estimated that more than 70 percent of the average person's time was spent listening, speaking, reading, and writing. Since the introduction of social media, the total time probably is much greater today. It can be challenging to draw attention to organizational messages and other workplace communications. Knowing how to create attention-getting messages requires an understanding of the communication process.

During your career, three important communication skills will impact your progress—oral, written, and listening. The first two skills get more attention than does the last one. In many ways, it is listening that separates the great manager from the good manager, as suggested by the Brownell quotation. There is a significant difference between hearing and listening. To develop the skill of listening, you must practice.

Ralph Waldo Emerson supposedly said, "Communication is like a piece of driftwood in a sea of conflicting currents. Sometimes the shore will be littered with debris; sometimes it will be bare. The amount and direction of movement is neither aimless nor non-directional at all, but is a response to all the forces, winds, and tides or currents that come into play." The "currents and tides" can become obstacles to effective communication. Library communication activities should not be pieces of driftwood; rather, they should be targeted and appropriate for the intended.

Despite the attention, energy, and time devoted to the communication process, it sometimes ends in failure—if success means complete agreement on the intended and perceived meanings of the message. Certainly, more often than not the general sense of a message gets through, but not its precise meaning.

COMMUNICATION PROCESS

To understand the challenges in communication, it helps to have knowledge of the basic communication model and the issues associated with that model. When individuals understand the effects of their communication habits, they are more effective in getting their intentions across and having them understood.

At its simplest level, a message has a sender and a receiver. There may be times in our personal lives that communication is as simple as this—I say dinner is ready, and you come and sit down at the table. In the workplace, it is never this straightforward.

For the vast majority of our communication efforts, there is a five-step sequence—sender, encoding a message, sending the message, a recipient, and decoding. Think of yourself as the sender—you select the words and encode them to create a message. You pick a means for sending it (face-to-face, memo, e-mail, texting, etc.). The receiver(s) decode the message and gives it a meaning. That is a surprisingly complex process. A host of factors can interact at each step that can result in your intended meaning differing from the receiver's interpretation of the meaning.

There are a variety of factors (known as noise) that can lead to different intended and perceived meanings. Feedback is a critical element for achieving effective communication. In our simple statement, "dinner is ready," coming and sitting down is feedback. I know you heard and understood the message. Had you not done so, the feedback would let me know something failed. Feedback is an essential component in effective communication.

Some common workplace noise factors are sender and receiver stress levels, current work atmosphere, past experiences, cultural and social differences, and sender and receiver trust levels. Any one of these, as well as many other such factors, can create misunderstandings. Certainly, most messages are more or less understood, at least well enough to move forward. The more complex the message, the greater the danger of distortion.

There are semantic issues that further complicate our efforts to communicate effectively. These are three key factors that impact our word choices for encoding: words are not the thing they represent; words never cover everything about anything; we use words about words that are increasingly abstract. We learn the meaning of words through life experiences, which can distort intended meanings. When we encounter a new word, some of us look it up in a dictionary; many more of us just ignore it. Usually no great harm

> ► **TIP**
>
> Keep in mind that people from different cultures may have varying approaches to authority, which adds yet another noise factor. Some may feel it is inappropriate to question a statement made by someone whom they perceive is in an authority role, which affects meaning and how the message is understood. The extra time spent verifying messages results in better performance and better relations and, in the long run, saves the library time and money.

comes from not knowing a word's meaning, but sometimes it does. The more abstract the word, the greater the chances that some people will not understand the message. Using jargon increases the risk that a message will be misunderstood, unless you *know* the receiver will understand. See Michael Fauchelle's 2017 article, which explores noise factors in the library context.

An important part of the way we learn word meanings comes from our upbringing and attitudes about word choices. Depending on our cultural beliefs and past experiences, we may perceive a person who uses "fancy" words as untrustworthy or a show-off. Early learning experiences carry forward and color our interpretations of messages received.

Common words often have multiple meanings, and their intended meaning depends on their context. For example, a word commonly used in the workplace is "fair." According to *Webster's Third New International Dictionary,* that word has thirty-four meanings. Will your staff know just what you intend to convey when you use it—or for that matter when you use many other short, common words? Chances are they will not know which meaning you intend the first few times you use it. In time, with shared experiences, they will have a basis for knowing what you mean. Shared experiences are an important element in gaining better and better communication. Therefore, when you are new to a group, take more time and give deeper thought to what you wish to convey.

The emotional status or stress level of the individual is a common factor in how a person encodes or interprets a message. Staff members who are anxious or worried about something can be extra-sensitive to what they perceive as a hidden meaning in a statement. An effective communicator takes into consideration expectations and anxieties (especially if they are at a high level) when preparing any message.

The way in which you say something—the emphasis, lack of emphasis, omissions, and order of presentation (all are potential noise factors) can influence meaning. Only when you have had some experience working with the same people will the meanings conveyed by their word order, tone of voice, facial expressions, and other nonverbal characteristics become clear.

ORGANIZATIONAL COMMUNICATION

The organizational structure of the library can influence the way in which staff interpret messages. A large archive or library is a series of overlapping and interdependent units, each with its own immediate and long-range objectives and managers. Each manager has his or her preferred managerial style. Members in each unit first interpret messages in light of their shared experiences; only after they finish that assessment can they take a broader view.

Bartels and colleagues (2010) noted, "Insight into the existence of different identities within an organisation is critical to managing communication therein. Identifying with one's profession is not the same as identifying with the entire organisation; encouraging participation in decision making and supplying adequate information can contribute to making employees identify more strongly with the organisation as a whole" (p. 221). Too strong a professional identification in libraries can lead to tensions between librarians and the rest of the staff, which in turn hinder effective communication and cooperation. Work relationships, authority structure, and status also impact the communication process by influencing people's expectations regarding who should communicate with whom, about what, and in what way.

Judging how much communication is too much is a challenge for managers. In medium-sized and large libraries, a manager will never be able to satisfy everyone. Some people will want more, and others will want less. You should aim for the middle ground, look at the results, and then adjust with more or less information.

Time and feedback are necessary for effective communication on the job. Different organizational cultures produce their own accepted communication practices. Knowing when a written message is expected and whether it should be on paper or electronic, or when a phone message is sufficient, are some examples of the value that time and shared experiences bring to organizational communication.

Time is important in another way. You should always provide sufficient time for the staff to assimilate messages. This can be challenging given today's communication speed. Needless to say, timing is critical when change is necessary. There needs to be adequate time for feedback. But there are urgent situations when time is of the essence and feedback is not possible.

Conroy and Jones (1986) outlined the major purposes for managerial communication. It is a good list to keep in mind:

- To inform: convey both information and understanding.
- To gather information: collect input from others to help make decisions and solve problems.
- To motivate: change or reinforce behavior and prompt specific action.
- To instruct and/or train: enable another to carry out instructions, tasks, or procedures appropriately.
- To coach and/or discipline: encourage faster growth, prevent disciplinary action, help another learn how to do a specific task better, and improve attitudes or behavior.
- To counsel: help someone with a personal problem that affects work productivity or morale.
- To mentor: help another succeed, usually by imparting better understanding of organizational policies, practices, or politics.
- To build teams: help work groups establish interpersonal rapport, build esprit de corps, and develop cohesion.

There are times when the staff may interpret a message as manipulative, but there are ways you can counteract potential hostility. First, try to establish authenticity by building rapport with the staff and creating an atmosphere wherein the staff realizes that they can freely discuss problems without fear of reprisal or rebuke. Also, by shortening the time between work activities and their evaluation, you can improve trust. Job evaluation is less threatening when it involves the immediate situation rather than in a review of a person's annual performance. A third step is to involve the staff in all processes of the unit that are not sensitive or confidential and give each person an opportunity to see that each job is important to the unit's success.

WRITTEN AND ORAL COMMUNICATION

Deciding when to write or when to talk is a matter of fine judgment that requires a good understanding of organizational culture. You need to decide on the channel to use—face-to-face, paper memo, e-mail, text message, and so forth. Communication in the workplace is both informal and formal, and there are situations when one may be more appropriate than another.

Information and communication technologies (ICT) can either facilitate or act as barriers to communication. In the days when communications were paper-based and telephones lacked voice mail, a person handled an absentee's mail and phone calls. Today this does not always the case. It can be frustrating for someone contacting the library to use a specific phone extension or e-mail address and does not receive a reasonably prompt response.

There is also the question of work-life balance. Today's ICT work environment can carry over into personal time and personal messages may arrive at work. Getting the balance right and establishing an acceptable practice is challenging.

Written messages

Every letter and memo, whether electronic or paper, should be a "sales" letter in some sense. Persuasion results from fine directional hinting that isn't too strong. Writing a memo should take as much thought as other written messages. Some managers spend too little time on memos, which can cause misinterpretations. Robert Cialdini (2011) noted that "research shows that persuasion works by appealing to a limited set of deeply rooted human drives and needs, and does so in predictable ways" (p. 30). Taking a few moments to review some of the following questions can improve any written or oral communication:

- What am I trying to convey?
- With whom am I communicating?
- When is the best time to do this?
- Where is the best place?
- What is the best channel?
- Why am I communicating?

When you add to these questions the four elements of clarity, conciseness, advance preparation, and respect for the person receiving the message you're on the road to effective communication.

Online communication

Social media can be an organizational challenge. First, what are legitimate work uses? Second, what type, if any, of personal usage is permissible? Third, what should be archived, by whom, where, and for how long? Generating such guidelines may even require some legal advice. A particular challenge relates to the files of a departing staff member—who deletes them and when? Another challenge is monitoring the guidelines.

An internal staff intranet (such as Microsoft SharePoint or Google Drive) has benefits and potential pitfalls. It can provide quick access to basic organizational information. One concern is that perhaps not everyone has access. Sometimes part-time staff members are slow to get an account. This can lead to some people, perhaps people significant in terms of the message's content, failing to get the word. These are some advantages of intranets:

- They can be quickly updated.
- Managers can be sure that staff members have access to the most recent information.
- Internal details such as dates, times, and agendas for meetings can be broadcast quickly.
- General information such as the success of a staff member can be quickly disseminated.
- Internal discussion groups can be established.
- The volume of paper circulated can be greatly reduced—and a few trees saved!
- The work of office staff can be examined to see if it is possible to make their workloads more interesting.

These are some of the potential pitfalls:

- Not every staff member (part-time, volunteers, interns, etc.) may have equal access.
- There is a real danger of information overload.
- One person must have responsibility for managing the intranet or else chaos may reign and information will not be updated systematically or organized effectively.

The design and layout of the intranet needs care and attention so that it is visually attractive and easy to navigate and locate information. You can add links to useful external information sources that can make the work of staff easier. The aim of the intranet is to provide easy access to up-to-date information required by the library staff in their daily work. In a library where the staff work shifts, or where telecommuting makes it difficult to get everyone together, an intranet will ensure that they all have access to needed information.

Electronic messaging is both a great blessing and a headache. One of the blessings is the quick and easy communication we enjoy. One headache is the widespread expectation of a speedy response 24/7. Information overload can also become a problem. It can be difficult to keep up with e-mail. There can be a perceived sense of urgency about attending to e-mail. And, even with the best filters, there is the constant issue of spam messages.

Libraries make substantial use of social media to connect with their users to build a community. Rania Hussein and Salah Hassan (2017), in writing about users engagement with social media and libraries, noted, "It is expected that those who show more intensive and dedicated use of social media are the ones who already perceive these sites to be important and useful to them in their lives and thus they are also the ones who are most

---

||||| CHECK THESE OUT

Schimpf, Lynette. 2014. "Creating a Social Media Strategy at Your Library." *Florida Libraries* 57, no. 1: 13–16.

Solomon, Laura. 2016. *The Librarian's Nitty-Gritty Guide to Social Media.* Chicago: American Library Association.

Verishagen, Nina. 2018. *Social Media: The Academic Library Perspective.* Cambridge: Chandos Publishing.

Young, Scott W. H. 2017. *Using Social Media to Build Library Communities.* Lanham, MD: Rowman and Littlefield.

---

likely to continue using those platforms" (p. 1019). Getting library social media "right" (attracting, providing value, keeping current, etc.) is a challenge that libraries must meet.

LISTENING

As we stated earlier in the chapter, careful listening is one of the hallmarks of great managerial leaders. It is a skill you must work at developing despite the fact that most of us confuse hearing and listening. Effective listening is harder than most people realize.

A major challenge is that we can process what we hear about four times faster than most people speak. This leaves about three-quarters of our listening time free for our minds to wander, and they will unless we work at not letting that happen. Think back to your most recent class session. Did you think about the next class with a test scheduled? Were you thinking about something you wanted to tell a friend in the class? Perhaps you started wondering where the instructor came up with *that* idea. Did you doodle? Were you checking your phone? Our list could go on and on, but you get the point; all of those behaviors meant you were not actually listening. We all do such things all the time while we think we are listening.

In addition to having substantial amounts of time available for our minds to wander while listening, we also filter what we do hear. Communication process researchers identify three major types of filtering: leveling, sharpening, and assimilating. Leveling occurs when the recipient of a message omits certain elements of the original message, which essentially changes its meaning. For example, assume a children's librarian is told a vacant position will not be filled until the level of usage of children's library services increases. The department head, in a leveling situation, might report to the staff that the position was withdrawn because of a declining use by children. While part of the original content comes through the filtering process, the meaning has been changed through significant omissions.

Sharpening is a process in which a part of a message receives greater emphasis than the original message intended. Assume during a staff development review that a supervisor tells a staff member, "Your performance is excellent. If you continue at the present rate of development, you may be considered for a new position that we expect to have in the next year or so." What the staff member tells others is, "I have been chosen for the new position the department will get next year." In essence, the person emphasizes what she or he wants to hear and plays down, or filters out, the qualifying elements.

Assimilation retains the entire original message and adds elements to it, thereby expanding the original meaning. Suppose a university president told the university librarian, "I am talking with a potential donor who is interested in making a major contribution to the new library building fund. I expect we will have an answer soon." The university librarian reports to the staff that "the president is very supportive of a new library building—it is a priority. The president is working with a prospective donor at present and a new building will be started very soon, as soon as the donor makes the major contribution." All of the elements of the original message are present, but there are many added elements that change the meaning.

Some other common problems in "hearing" a message are assuming you already know the content, assuming the content is uninteresting or irrelevant, or thinking the topic is unimportant. Listening with such thoughts in mind almost ensures that the message's purpose is lost. Not only is the "extra" listening time wasted but so is the one-quarter of the time needed to take in the message. The best way to overcome this problem is to make a conscious effort to suspend judgment. From the outset, keep an open mind; the message may not be what you think it will be.

A related issue is assessing or criticizing the speaker's method of presentation. People who make presentations are particularly prone to criticizing others' presentations. When you do that, you cease listening to the content. How often do we hear, "Oh, it was a good talk, but she had a horrible PowerPoint presentation," or "there were too many pauses and asides"? The person making such comments had stopped listening and transferred his or her attention to the delivery of the message. Keeping an open mind helps, but the real issue is to stop focusing on the "how" and switch to the "what" is being said. Think, off and on, during a presentation, "Am I thinking about the "what" or the "how" of the message?" Failing to concentrate on the "what" erects barriers to effective communication.

Jumping to conclusions is something most people do, at least occasionally. Once you assume you know where the speaker is going with her or his talk, your listening tends to fall off, if not cease. Again, suspending judgment until the message is complete is an effective way to keep communication open. Another technique that helps slow conclusion-jumping is to consciously reflect on what is being said.

A less common but nonetheless significant barrier to effective listening is wanting only the "big picture" or general information. This can take the form of not wanting to waste time on particulars: "Spare me the details." Certainly, the big picture is essential, but often the details of how the speaker has arrived at the big picture are critical to understanding the message or situation. Thinking about how the details interconnect, and how the speaker is making the connections, helps to concentrate on the "what" of the message.

A related barrier is an overreaction to certain words or phrases (i.e., "hot buttons"). Each of us has a set of phrases and words we really do not like to hear. These phrases and words carry special meanings based on past experiences—when someone used them in a manner that caused us discomfort, harm, or emotional distress. Frequently, these are relatively common words and phrases that have no special meaning for other people. In the workplace we must be cautious about overreacting to any message, especially when we hear words or phrases from our personal hot button list. One step to take is to spend time thinking about the words and phrases that tend to upset us. Thinking about what those are and why they cause us discomfort helps us control our reactions. Another obvious step is to always wait before responding. An angry or confrontational response seldom leads to a discussion in which the people listen to one another. Rather, such a response, more often than not, leads to a situation of talking *at* one another. Thoughtful, unemotional responses are much more likely to lead to real communication.

NONVERBAL COMMUNICATION

It is useful to pay attention to nonverbal communication when talking with staff members. Not doing so can result in an unpleasant surprise. Some people appear attentive when their minds may be far, far away. There are nonverbal cues that suggest that listening is or is not occurring. If there is no feedback, a normal assumption is that the message was understood.

Body language and the other signs we give, often unconsciously, can aid or impede communication. Arms akimbo, running our hands through our hair, and other idiosyncrasies that we all possess can be very off-putting to someone who doesn't know us well. Face-to-face communication entails more than the words said and how they are said. Everyone in a conversation sends a variety of messages through nonverbals. Your emphasis, lack of tone, speed, and so forth are factors in nonverbal communication. Other elements in the process are facial expressions (frowns, smiles, eye contact, etc.); gestures (head nodding, hand movements, method of pointing, etc.); and body posture (arms and legs folded, angle of the body, etc.). You may also send intended or unintended messages by the color of your clothes, the way you arrange your office furniture, and seating arrangements for meetings. To add to the complexity of the process, cultural background plays a major role in nonverbal communication. Is it important to understand the nonverbal communication cues? In our opinion, absolutely! An estimated 60 percent of the real message comes from the nonverbal side of the communication process (Arthur 1995).

Trust in the workplace is essential for many reasons. We sometimes forget that people constantly judge our trustworthiness all the time, especially if they believe we misled them in the past. Christian L. Hart, Derek Fillmore, and James Griffith (2010) wrote about how people often judge another person's veracity:

> The cues that many people report using to detect deception in everyday situations are non-verbal behaviors, verbal cues, and paraverbal cues. Non-verbal cues are the movement of limbs, torso, head, and face that might yield some indication of lying or truthfulness. . . . [V]erbal cues of deception can be defined as the content of speech that may provide evidence of deception. . . . Paraverbal cues can be defined as those that accompany speech behavior such as voice pitch, response latencies, filled and unfilled pauses, message duration, speech errors, and repetitions. (pp. 176-77)

When working in a culturally diverse library or one that serves a diverse population, having a sound grasp of the nonverbal side of communication is very important. Even in what may seem to be a homogenous group, there are likely to be some unexpected interpretations of what you might think of as unimportant actions or gestures. If you come from a Western European background, your comfort zone for conversation is at least three feet away from the others—in fact, a wider distance is often preferred. People from Latin America or Asia prefer to be much closer (one foot on average). Learning what is or is not the comfort range of interpersonal space in a diverse group can take some time.

Eye contact also differs among in cultures. Most children with a Western European background learn early on to look directly at their parents. A common phrase is, "look me in the eye when I'm talking to you." English-language novels are filled with nasty

||||| **CHECK THESE OUT**

The following journal articles give you a starting point for further exploring nonverbal communication:

Collett, Peter. 2004. "Show and Tell: Think You Can See When Someone Is Lying?" *People Management* 10, no. 8: 34–35.

Page, Daniel. 2004. "The Importance of Nonverbal Communication in Library Service." *Library Mosaics* 15, no. 6: 11.

The following books provide in-depth information:

Lawton, Eunice. 2006. *Body Language and the First Line Manager.* Oxford: Chandos.

Pease, Allan, and Barbara Pease. 2017. *The Definitive Book of Body Language.* E-book. New York: Bantam Books.

Ribbens, Geoff, and Greg Whitear. 2007. *Body Language.* London: Hodder.

characters with "shifty eyes." For some Native American groups and Asian peoples, on the other hand, direct eye contact is thought to be impolite at best and rude at worst. Not understanding such differences can play havoc with work-related activities, in job interviews and continue throughout your working life, all the way to retirement. Devoting time to learning about, and gaining some understanding of, the variations within your work group can pay dividends.

A related problem is conveying disagreement, either verbally or nonverbally, before the speaker has finished. Doing so effectively cuts off further communication. Such a response conveys to the speaker the sense the listener has reached a conclusion without hearing everything. Even when you disagree with what is said, not showing those feelings or thoughts until after the speaker finishes will improve your chances of having a meaningful discussion about the topic or issue.

LEGITIMACY OF COMMUNICATION

Channels of communication run up, down, and across an organization. In cases of upward communication, tact and diplomacy are very important. Also, sensitive topics, such as disagreements with a supervisor's actions, probably should be discussed orally (with considerable supporting detail). Distinguish clearly between fact and opinion and be neither subservient nor argumentative.

Communication with senior management or the governing board requires careful handling. A manager who gives too many messages may look insecure. Giving too little often means the board or senior managers are not fully informed about what is happening—they may start to feel insecure. Seeing a problem coming down the track and failing to inform senior management is a managerial disaster waiting to happen. So, judge how much information should be passed upward, how frequently this should be done, and using which channel. Discover how much communication should take place in social settings. Two golden rules in upward communication—never be evasive, and keep senior management informed.

When you are planning on sending important information, especially if it is complex, it is wise to have at least one other person review the message. For significant messages to the user community, governing board, and senior managers of the parent organization, you really need to have more than one extra pair of eyes. Almost everyone has difficulty seeing errors in their written work—they know what they mean to say and that is what they often see. Spell checkers are helpful, but they do nothing in terms of catching a properly spelled word that is the wrong word. There are similar issues with grammatical software packages. Essentially, the rule is that someone—not just a software package—should review an important message before it is sent to the intended recipient(s).

In downward communication, diplomacy and tact are also the keys to success. Avoid carelessness in communications, as it indicates a lack of respect for the recipient. A manager who fails to give explanations for actions risks allowing the workers' imaginations to fill in the gaps. Managers should always encourage staff to ask questions and to

👥 ADVISORY BOARD EXPERIENCE

Joseph Mika was drafted back as director from faculty in a situation which had a number of administrative problems. He prepared the following "Mika Missives" and informed all staff that these would be the "rules" under which the administrative team would operate:

1. **STUDENTS ARE WHY WE ARE HERE.** Our focus, and reason for being, are the students of the Library and Information Science Program. CUSTOMER SERVICE is everyone's responsibility.
2. **THE GOLDEN RULE.** After students, the faculty, the library staff, and ourselves are customers—Internal Customers. Treat them like you would like to be treated. Their requests and needs are important too.
3. **LOYALTY**—to your job, the LISP, your coworkers, the University, the Library System, and to me—is required.
4. **IF YOU CAN'T SAY SOMETHING NICE,** don't say anything at all. Reserve your criticisms for me. I will not tolerate hearing your concerns secondhand.
5. **YOU ARE THE SOLUTION.** When you bring me a problem, bring me your suggestions for solutions. This goes for problems that we identify in each other's areas as well.
6. **REACCREDITATION** is important to the University, the Program, students, alumni, faculty, and you. We all MUST work toward ensuring we receive the full seven years reaccreditation.
7. **CONFIDENTIALITY** is Key! What we say among ourselves at meetings, what we learn about students, faculty, etc., stays among ourselves. WHAT IS SAID HERE STAYS HERE!
8. **THERE IS TIME FOR FUN.** I enjoy my job, and I like to have fun at it. I want us all to enjoy our jobs, have fun, and like what we do!
9. **CHANGE IS A GIVEN.** We don't do things because we have always done them that way—we'll do them better, smarter, and more effectively.
10. **DO YOUR JOB!** I work hard; I expect you to work hard too! I have my job to do; I don't want or expect to do your job too.

contribute ideas. If management encourages such behavior on all levels, the result is likely to be more buy-in and greater appreciation and loyalty throughout the library.

Although the classic functions of the manager are to make decisions and to give direction, the reality is that they occupy only a small proportion of managerial messages. In a library, a vast amount of communicating takes place among peers. This type of communication in a collective enterprise involves not only the formal structures but also the informal structures (status structure, friendship structure, prestige structure, etc.) of the library. All of these are in constant flux, contradicting the notion that all communication in an organization is downward.

There is a dark side to communication. Some individuals, for a variety of reasons, deliberately miscommunicate. We have encountered such instances in both our personal and work lives. Sometimes it is a matter of unconscious filtering. Misinterpreting a message happens for numerous reasons; however, there are occasions when it is deliberate and intended to cause problems for the organization. In the workplace, when you receive a message that seems unbelievable, be sure to check the legitimacy of the source.

🔒 KEY POINTS TO REMEMBER

- Effective and clear communication is vital in decision making, planning, organizing, staffing, and budgeting.
- Improved understanding leads to better working conditions, higher morale, and greater staff commitment.
- Supervisors have the responsibility to provide these benefits by ensuring that communications are as honest, clear, and open to discussion as possible.
- Avoid information overload, particularly in electronic formats, because it can create stress for staff members—and supervisors—and impede communication.
- Personality—for example, being outgoing or reserved—influences communication practices.
- Develop a sense of humor and learn how to lighten situations when this will aid the communication process.
- Learn how to use the various channels of communication efficiently and effectively, especially as new channels emerge.
- Observing the strengths and weaknesses of staff identifies training needs.
- All staff members, at all levels, need to have excellent communication skills if quality library service is to be provided.
- Adhere to these five key points for clear and effective communication:

  - Know what to communicate.
  - Know who needs to know what.
  - Know who should communicate with whom.
  - Know how to time messages.
  - Know how to listen and read nonverbal cues such as body language.

REFERENCES

Arthur, Diane. 1995. "Importance of Body Language." *HRFocus* 72 (June): 22–23.

Bartels, Jos, Oscar Peters, Menno de Jong, Ad Pruyn, and Marjolijn van der Molen. 2010. "Horizontal and Vertical Communication as Determinants of Professional and Organisational Identification." *Personnel Review* 39, no. 2: 210–26.

Berlo, David K. 1960. *The Process of Communication*. New York: Holt.

Brownell, Judi. 2018. *Listening: Attitudes, Principles, and Skills*. 6th ed. New York, NY: Routledge, Taylor and Francis Group.

Cialdini, Robert E. 2011. "Harnessing the Science of Persuasion." In *Harvard Business Review on Communicating Effectively*, pp. 29–51. Cambridge, MA: Harvard Business School Press.

Conroy, Barbara, and Barbara S. Jones. 1986. *Improving Communication in Libraries*. Phoenix, AZ: Oryx Press.

Fauchelle, Michael Alexander. 2017. "Libraries of Babel: Exploring Library Language and Its Suitability for The Community." *Library Review* 66, nos. 8/9: 612–27.

Hart, Christian L., Derek Fillmore, and James Griffith. 2010. "Deceptive Communication in the Workplace: An Examination of Beliefs about Verbal and Paraverbal Cues." *Individual Differences Research* 8, no. 3: 176–83.

Hussein, Rania, and Salah Hassan. 2017. "Customer Engagement on Social Media: How to Enhance Continuation of Use." *Online Information Review* 41, no. 7: 1006–28.

Shehata, Ahmed, David Ellis, and Allen Edward Foster. 2017. "Changing Styles of Informal Academic Communication in the Age of the Web: Orthodox, Moderate and Heterodox Responses." *Journal of Documentation* 73, no.5: 825–42.

Walter, Scott. 2018. "Communicating Value through Strategic Engagement: Promoting Awareness of the 'Value of Libraries' through Alignment Across Academic, Student, and Administrative Affairs." *Library Management* 39, nos. 3/4: 154–65.

CHAPTER 12

Advocacy and Marketing

There is still a lot of mystery about what constitutes a school library and how librarians can embed advocacy into their everyday practice.

Debra Kachel, 2017

Competition in the marketplace is increasing the demand for information, while the budgets for information centers are decreasing. The library and information sectors have to escalate their fight for every budget dollar, and some struggle to justify their very existence.

Marketing Library Services, **2018**

We know that social media is an important piece of our marketing plans, and we need to manage it well.

Jennifer E. Burke, 2017

Taking this broad view of marketing and outreach, it makes perfect sense for a library to create a well-considered, manageable marketing plan.

Julia Chance Gustafson, Zachary Sharrow, and Gwen Short, 2017

Combining advocacy, marketing, and associated activities (public relations and branding, for example) may seem to be creating strange bedfellows. They are different but interrelated—as suggested by Debra Kachel (2017), they are on a continuum. The continuum she proposed is: **public relations** (tells the story) ➝ **marketing** (sells the "product") ➝ **advocacy** (creates partnerships).

There is a related term that touches on the process—lobbying. In a sense, branding is the glue that binds the others together.

Libraries need to handle all these concepts effectively if they want to survive in an environment of limited resources. That need is suggested in this chapter's second opening quotation. Being in the public and nonprofit sectors makes the first three activities of vital importance as libraries face increasing competition and are confronted with more and more questions about their value. For-profits rarely engage in advocacy activities and their public relations efforts, while important, are generally modest. For public organizations, it is essential to tell the story, sell the services, and create partnerships that actively support the organization.

Advocacy is about gaining and supporting partners—at least for libraries. For years before the label "advocacy" became a common component in library operations, ALA was taking stances on social issues (advocating for a concern such as diversity, for example). However, the notion that libraries should be active self-advocates is relatively new. A definition of advocacy is "the action of advocating, pleading for, or supporting a cause, person, or purpose *International Dictionary of the English Language: Unabridged. (Third Edition,* 2 volumes (Springfield, MA: G. and C. Merriam Company, 1966, p. 32). Although the definition does not mention partnering you can see where it is implied—"pleading for, or supporting a cause."

Marketing is the process of making potential customers know you exist and what services you offer. This may appear straightforward and simple; however, doing it effectively is surprisingly complex. It requires a mix of information and persuasion. Striking the correct balance between the two elements is delicate. Today's competitive world of librarianship makes the persuasive side more and more important but going too far in that direction may be a turnoff for some people.

Public relations (PR) tells the stories—good, bad, and/or neutral stories as the situation requires. There is a slight stigma associated with PR—that it "spins" stories. This is almost always true, as the basic concern of PR is to present as positive a picture of an organization as possible. People talk about spinning when they object to the message and/ or the organization that sends it. Almost any PR message can be positive, negative, or neutral depending on a recipient's views about the issuing organization. The good news for libraries is, as we have noted from time to time, that they have very high trust levels within their service communities. Such trust generally results in library PR messages being viewed positively (no spin!).

We begin our discussion with marketing because it has generated the greatest volume of literature, both generally and within librarianship, compared to the other concepts we address in this chapter.

MARKETING

You can think of marketing as a social, as well as managerial, process, in that it is about communication between your library and the service community. It is, or should be, a two-way process of exchanging information between the library and its community—addressing what the community wants and what the library can provide. It is also a means for developing better relations between the library and its community. Good collection development librarians have been engaged in key marketing processes for years without thinking of it as "marketing." Marketing is finding out what your customers want and/or need and determining how to deliver those services.

Lisa Smith-Butler (2010) wrote, "As a new librarian many years ago, I found the concept of marketing a library to be anathema. I was certain that sensible and intelligent patrons immediately understood the value and the necessity of a library. Marketing, in my opinion, was a dirty word, something done by MBAs marketing a product. Now, fifteen years later, I think my younger self naïve" (pp. 7–8). She was not alone in her thinking at the time; perhaps newcomers to the field may hold similar beliefs. We firmly believe that in today's highly competitive information world, libraries must market themselves.

There is evidence that almost all libraries have a positive ROI; however, this fact is not widely known outside the profession. Marketing, advocacy, and sound public relations efforts can be effective tools in getting out the message that libraries do provide good returns on the funds invested in them.

In the past, libraries and archives saw little need to market their services. This was a perception issue rather than a lack of information on how to market libraries. Starting in the 1980s a number of texts on marketing appeared that focused on libraries (Cronin 1992;

Kies 1987; McNeal 1992; Rowley 2001; Savard 2000; Walters 1992; Weingand 1998; Wood and Young 1988).

There are four key reasons why you should consider developing a marketing program. First and foremost, almost all archives and libraries face either a decreasing resource base or stronger competition for existing resources while needing to provide an increasing range of services. Second, as a result, user convenience usually decreases—shorter service hours, fewer public service staff, and reductions in the number of locally owned information resources are some examples. Third, libraries frequently reach a smaller and smaller percentage of the total service population. (Although actual numbers of interactions and customers may increase over the previous year, but when the overall service population increases sharply there can be a drop in the percentage served.) Finally, all libraries face stiff competition as providers for transferring information from the creators or producers to the end consumer.

A sound marketing program provides the staff with market intelligence data that help them address these issues and develop a plan to increase both the number of customers and the percentage of total target population, or market share.

MARKETING PROCESS

Philip Kotler's strategic marketing process for not-for-profit organizations has three major elements: analysis, strategy, and implementation (Andreasen and Kotler 2008). Much of the process involves the steps of strategic planning. The steps are:

1. Generic product definition
2. Target group definition
3. Differential marketing analysis
4. Customer behavior analysis
5. Differential advantages analysis
6. Multiple marketing approaches
7. Integrated market planning
8. Continuous market feedback
9. Marketing audit

Generic product definition

A key to the long-term success of any organization is a realistic answer to the question, "What is our business?" Every organization produces at least one of the following: physical products (tangible), services (intangible), persons (press agents), the organization itself (political parties or professional organizations), or ideas (population control or human rights, for example). Often, the answer to the question is product-oriented rather than customer-oriented. When that happens, the outcome limits the organization's growth potential. Thinking about the organization in terms of the user tends to broaden the scope of possible activities. Rather than being in the railroad business, think in terms of transportation; similarly, soap becomes cleaning, movies become entertainment, and documents become information.

Target group definition

The generic or user-based product definition usually results in identifying a wide market. Looking at such a market can lead to the creation of a marketing program so broad that it fails to produce the desired results. Dividing the large market into smaller units usually produces more cost-effective marketing. A market segment comprises units with similar or related characteristics, units with common needs and wants, and units with similar responses to like motivations, and it accepts these needs at a reasonable price. For years, libraries have developed different services for different types of users (children/young adult/adult, undergraduate/graduate, literacy-skill learners, and English as a second language users, for example).

Market segmenting takes time and effort but pays off in a better response from a particular market segment. For example, for an academic library, what might its segments be? The most obvious segments are the faculty and students; however, even those groups are probably too large to fit our definition of market segment. There are likely to be more useful segments if you think in terms of subject interest or major. A segment might group doctoral students with faculty instead of with the broader category of graduate students. Another way to divide students would be into undeclared-major lower-division undergraduates, declared-major lower-division undergraduates, undeclared upper-division undergraduates, declared upper-division undergraduates, master's degree students, and doctoral-level students. The many ways to approach segmentation emphasize the need to think outside the box.

All types of libraries have equally diverse markets when you think carefully about the possibilities. The goal is to analyze the service population and divide it into small, homogenous units. There is never enough money to address all the potential marketing areas; however, having smaller homogenous segments helps you make decisions about where to expend the available marketing funds. Thinking about each segment and asking questions such as the following will help:

- What are the common needs and wants of this group?
- Which, if any, of those needs do we now serve?
- What do we know about the group's behavior patterns?
- How much benefit does the group currently receive from our services?
- What is the potential gain from meeting more of this group's needs and wants?
- What type of message is most effective for reaching this group?
- What do we know about the group's perceptions of the service?
- Compared to other market segments, how important is this group for the service?
- Who is our competition?

The answer to the last question should facilitate the ranking of the various market segments by the library. (These rankings will vary over time as the situation and the operating environment change.) Some of the other questions may indicate the need to collect more data before a final decision is reasonable. All of the answers will help determine which group(s) will be the target(s).

Differential marketing analysis

Different segments require different approaches and thus differentiated marketing. While most libraries have three basic product lines—collections, services, and programs—importance of each for a particular market segment will vary. Using for-profit terminology, each product line consists of several different, specific products. To take the example of a university library, specific collection products might be defined by dividing the collection into instructional, secondary research, and primary research materials. Services might be document delivery and online searching. Program products might be search methods, instruction, and dissertation format assistance. As you examine specific products, it becomes apparent how different packages would have greater or lesser interest to various market segments. For-profit organizations learned long ago that when serving more than one target population, differentiating products and communications about the products produces the maximum results. Thinking about the packages in terms of what costs and benefits a person accrues from using the package gives you two useful perspectives. First, it offers a complete picture of what the package consists of and the interrelationship between the component parts. Second, it gives you some sense of how the person perceives, or will perceive, the package. This latter element is very important because nonprofit organizations tend to believe that their services are vital.

Customer behavior analysis

For many years, collection development librarians knew that it was important to understand the service community's lifestyles, information needs, wants. Asking questions about what topics are of interest, product usage, when and where people use information, and when and where they would prefer to use it allows staff to structure services and programs more effectively. Such information is helpful in determining the most effective approaches to marketing existing services as well as in promoting new services. Focus groups can be a highly effective method for gathering answers to such questions.

A major issue for any organization, profit or nonprofit, is changing customer behavior and interests. Patrick Barwise and Sean Meehan (2010) asked the question, "How do managers ensure that their products and services are, and remain, relevant to customers?" (p. 63). They suggest the key to knowing this requires unsanitized information from frontline staff about what they hear and observe about users when it comes to the organization's products and services. Certainly, marketing data helps with this; however, marketing programs cost substantial amounts of money, especially for libraries. This means there may be several years between full market assessments, which increases the importance of frontline staff feedback.

Barwise and Meehan provided some important questions to ask regarding the quality of staff feedback; we have paraphrased the questions to better reflect the library environment:

- Can your middle managers accurately describe what the library promises its service community? (Start with mission, values, vision, and goals.)
- Can senior and middle managers identify the four or five major issues that most undermine the trust and satisfaction of users regarding the library's services?
- Are the services designed for targeted segments the best options for them? Now, next year, in two years? If not, what can be done with the existing services to better fit user needs now and in the future?
- What innovations have you tried recently? In the past twelve months? If so, what was the user feedback?

- Has frontline staff passed on any "uncomfortable" information about usage patterns or user comments recently? In the past three months or six months?

Barwise and Meehan (2010) concluded their article with the following: "Quality pioneer W. Edwards Deming is widely credited with the comment "In God we trust, all others must bring data." For those who are prepared to ask tough questions and *willing to hear* the answers, the potential benefits to the business are significant" (p. 68; emphasis added).

Differential advantages analysis

Once you understand the behaviors and needs of the various segments, it is possible to identify differential advantages for each segment. A differential advantage is one that exploits the reputation, services, or programs by creating or enhancing a special value in the minds of potential users. A public library example would be services for the visually impaired, such as large-print collections and reading machines. For service organizations such as libraries and archives, it is essential to reinforce the values and/or needs of the service community and the parent organization.

Multiple marketing approaches

In planning a marketing effort, it is advantageous, if not essential, to employ several different marketing tools. The selected tools (websites, social media, newsletters, flyers, advertisements, and annual reports, for example) should be those that best fit the lifestyle of the target segment. Receptions or open houses can be effective promotional tools, especially when there is a new service or product to demonstrate. In the case of a public library attempting to reach new immigrants, using the native languages of the target population is essential. One caution when preparing material in another language: it is imperative to have the material reviewed by a native speaker who understands both formal and colloquial usage.

Integrated market planning

When an organization implements an ongoing marketing program, there is the chance that, over time, different components of the program will be working at cross-purposes. An integrated program is the best insurance against ineffective use of marketing funds. One element in achieving an integrated plan is to have one person responsible for coordinating all marketing and promotional activities. Large libraries tend to have the resources to allocate one or more full-time persons to work solely on marketing or promotional activities. In the past, such positions often carried the title "public relations officer." Today, more often than not the title is "marketing director." Even when the level of staffing will not allow for a full-time marketing position, only one person (or, as a lesser second choice, a committee) should be responsible for coordinating all marketing and promotional activities. To make the work manageable, there must be a strategic marketing plan for the managers to review and update on a regular basis.

Continuous market feedback

To be effective, constant feedback from the service population is critical. In a sense it already is, or should, be an element in a library's ongoing monitoring of its environment. This is an example of how basic management activities intersect and are rarely truly completely independent from other operational functions. They are seamlessly intertwined.

Marketing audit

A marketing audit draws on feedback from the service community, library staff, and governing boards. Looking at what worked and why, what did not work and why, how the environment and community base has or has not changed, and what changes have taken place within the organization (in staff, services, resources, and facilities) all become important aspects in adjusting and maintaining a viable marketing program. Other elements include assessing the resources available to carry out the program, how well the people responsible for carrying out the program have performed, and how effective the program is in achieving long-term organizational mission, goals, and objectives. Darlene Weingand (1995) suggested that:

> The audit should also develop a "futures screen" that identifies trends and projections in both external and internal environments in order to develop contingency plans that will relate to alternative future scenarios. The futures screen places considerable emphasis on securing data on what "may be" in the next five years (and beyond); objectives can then be developed to reflect that informed projection. (p. 303)

Additional issues for an audit involve how certain factors have or have not changed since the program's inception. For instance, if the time frame is five years, staff members probably will have changed. Another factor is that small variations in organizational resources over the years may, in totality, be significant. A careful review of the operating environment may reveal that new or different competitors exist for the library. In essence, one should examine all relevant changes, both internal and external.

Such an analysis often helps to increase library usage (measured quantitatively or qualitatively), to increase attendance at important events, or to build a following for a valued program. The problem is that managers may be tempted to initiate promotional efforts on

---

||||| CHECK THESE OUT

An older but excellent article addressing library marketing is Deborah Lee's "Marketing Research: Laying the Marketing Foundation" (*Library Administration and Management* 17, no. 4: 186–88, 2003).

Another useful article is Jennifer E. Burke's "Top Marketing Tools to Know" (*Computers in Libraries*, 37, no 7: 28–31, 2017), which discusses a number of online resources that are great resources for library marketing efforts.

An example of a library marketing effort is described in Joy M. Perrin, Heidi Winkler, Kaley Daniel, Shelly Barba, and Le Yang's "Know Your Crowd: A Case Study in Digital Collection Marketing" (*Reference Librarian* 58, no. 3: 190–201, 2017).

an ad hoc basis to meet a particular need independent of larger or competing priorities. If such efforts succeed, they may become annual activities; the cumulative effect is a hodge-podge of disparate marketing efforts, which can consume massive amounts of time and energy but bear little resemblance to the strategic agenda of the institution as a whole.

BRANDING

The basic purpose of branding is the development of a symbol (a logo) that embodies the essence of a product, service, or organization. Deborah Lee (2006) defined branding as "a marketing concept that identifies a good or service through the use of a name, phrase, design, or symbol" (p. 94). Libraries have a generic logo, originally developed by the American Library Association, to draw upon when thinking about developing a brand: @ your library. This logo has been translated into many languages.

Branding is not always just a matter of a single library, as evidenced by the headline of a 2006 story in *American Libraries*: "Britain Launches Campaign to Transform Libraries' Image." In 2011, Subnum Hariff and Jennifer Rowley, writing about public library branding in the United Kingdom, noted, "There is increasing recognition that the future for public libraries is bleak, and that a major contributing factor is their failure to change the image or their 'brand' as their identity. This problem is not just prevalent in U.K. libraries but emblematic across the sector globally" (p. 347). They make the point that branding is more complex than "name, logo, strap-lines, and color schemes" (p. 347). They conclude the article with "branding can be used successfully to drive up borrowing and visits to libraries, and arguably to change brand image and perceptions of the library service" (p. 357).

Brands invoke both a physical and a psychological experience. When a powerful sense of service is developed in the staff, a manager can be confident that users will experience a positive psychological experience in almost every case and the best physical experience as the facilities allow. Both will be significant assets in establishing and maintaining a library's brand.

PUBLIC RELATIONS

Earlier, we noted that PR for some people has a negative image—"spinning a story" with a limited amount of factual material. Public relations as a profession, does have a set of core values and ethics. The core values are advocacy, honesty, expertise, independence, loyalty, and fairness. The Public Relations Society of America's ethical code provisions address free flow of information, competition, disclosure of information, safeguarding confidences, conflicts of interest, and enhancing the profession.

Few libraries, or other public sectors organizations, are able to employ a full-time communications manager or publicist. Large public sector organizations may have some staff with a little knowledge of the area. More often libraries rely on ALA and state organizations for guidance on PR activities. Larger libraries may retain a public relations consultant on an "as needed" basis. Public relations is about building relationships, making announcements regarding services and activities, and sometimes addressing controversial topics or major issues such as disaster.

A press release is a commonly employed PR communications method. If a release relates to a major event or issue a press conference helps highlight the importance of

---

|||| **CHECK THESE OUT**

The American Library Association's @ your library logo is a registered trademark. Visit the ALA website to see the different ways the logo can be used (www.ala.org/aboutala/contactus/rights/logo.rules).

An interesting article about a library branding effort is Amanda B. Albert's "Building Brand Love and Gaining the Advocacy You Crave by Communicating Your Library's Value" (*Journal of Library and Information Services in Distance Education.* 11, nos. 1/2: 237–50, 2017).

Another interesting article is Susan Wengler's 2018 "Branding Matters: Reimagine Your Library Services" (*College and Research Libraries News* 79, no. 3: 118–21, 2017).

---

the message. Such events usually entail taking questions and often the expectation is the chief operations officer will be available to answers questions—not just the PR person. An unfortunate fact is negative publicity seems easier to get than positive press. Based on experience, we know that academic libraries can expect to see a negative story once or twice a year in the student-run newspaper. Any allegation of fiscal mismanagement or labor problems easily makes the local evening news, the morning newspaper, or some website. What is unfortunate, but typical, is that none of the major publications ever publishes anything on the resolution of the problems. When negative stories hit the media, fast action is necessary, and a good relationship with a public relations expert is essential. Such an expert will have contacts and the experience to counteract the bad news. Knowing how, when, what, and to whom to communicate is essential during a crisis. Flexibility is a key component of this activity as the event develops. Social media is useful for speed but being too swift to communicate may create a bigger problem.

Public relations support is probably most needed when the library lobbies politicians and funding agencies about funding issues. Because politicians and agencies receive a large volume of mail and phone calls, skill and experience are necessary to catch their attention and make a convincing case. The American Library Association's website provides templates (www.ala.org/acrl/issues/marketing) that can be very useful for small libraries with limited funding. In addition, it is always useful to know a friendly PR person who might occasionally offer some pro bono advice. Positive publicity requires patient cultivation and careful packaging, which cost time and money.

A library's website serves as both a marketing and a public relations tool. Keeping the site "fresh" is important to retaining young people's attention. You have a variety of other social media tools as well. There are both technical and people issues to consider when you decide to move into such activities. Performing such activities well makes for wonderful marketing and public relations. Performing them not so well will send negative messages about the library and its services.

ADVOCACY

A related concept, advocacy, can assist you in striking a good balance in your marketing program. Susan DiMattia (2011) defined the concept: "Advocacy is neither marketing nor public relations. Simply put, it is the art of persuading or arguing in favor of something" (p.

14). Advocacy is a process for attempting to influence public policy and resource allocations; it differs from lobbying in that the focus is on policy and allocation issues, not on legislation. National PTA clarifies the difference between lobbying and advocacy:

> When nonprofit organizations advocate on their own behalf, they seek to affect some aspect of society, whether they appeal to individuals about their behavior, employers about their rules, or the government about its laws. Lobbying refers specifically to advocacy efforts that attempt to influence legislation. This distinction is helpful to keep in mind because it means that laws limiting the lobbying done by nonprofit organizations do not govern other advocacy activities. (https://www.macmhb.org/sites/default/files/attachments/files/Workshop%2028.pdf)

We noted earlier in this chapter that marketing and advocacy, while related, are different in purpose and practice. John Moorman (2009) wrote:

> Advocacy is a matter of perennial concern for today's librarians and library community as a whole. . . . As one who has been actively involved in library advocacy in four states for over thirty years and a registered lobbyist with the Commonwealth of Virginia, I know that without ongoing advocacy, libraries have no hope of receiving the resources they need to provide quality services to their user community. (p. 15)

Because advocacy is about supporting a cause or course of action, it is important that the library advocacy process become an integral part of a manager's responsibilities. It needs to be more than a recognized part of the marketing and promotion processes; it needs to be a "must do" for all library administrators. To become a successful library administrator, it is critical to develop advocacy skills. Pat Schuman, a past ALA President, emphasizes that part of all library administrators' jobs is to rally and organize library advocates to speak out for their libraries because they are the ones who lose when libraries are cut or closed. This is also supported in ALA's *Library Advocate's Handbook* (2010, 3rd ed.): "Library administrators are responsible for developing and coordinating an ongoing advocacy effort, one with well-defined roles for staff, trustees, and friends" (p. 3).

Because of the ever-increasing financial strain on public-supported organizations and agencies, library advocacy is now more critical than ever. In the past, advocacy

---

⦚⦚⦚ CHECK THESE OUT

ALA's Advocacy, Legislation and Issues website is extremely helpful for becoming advocacy proficient (www.ala.org/advocacy/). Two other ALA websites to take a look at are Advocacy University (www.ala.org/advocacy/advocacy-university) and Advocacy and Public Awareness (www.ala.org/advocacy/advocacy-public-awareness). They provide tool kits, packets, webinars, and online tutorials for your use.

Ken Haycock and Joseph R. Matthews's article "Persuasive Advocacy" provides an excellent overview of the process (*Public Library Quarterly* 35, no. 2: 126–35, 2016).

Jenna Nemec-Loise published another article about advocacy myths "Top Ten Advocacy Myths—Busted!" (*Children and Libraries*. 14, no. 1: 34–35, 2016).

efforts were focused on the stakeholders—community users, students, and faculty. These grassroots efforts have been effective when applied systematically. Engaging library employees—librarians and support staff—to become frontline advocates has added another layer of personal involvement. Who better than the frontline staff to influence the users whom they see regularly and probably know on a first-name basis? When referring to empowering frontline staff, Alire noted one frontline staff skill as the "[a]bility to advance the . . . library agenda by helping them to reflect on their personal circles of influence and the strategies that would be most persuasive" (ACRL 2006, p. i).

Writing about school library advocacy, Carl A. Harvey (2010) suggested you need to be tactical in your efforts. We have paraphrased his "tactical" concept into the following format to fit almost any type of library (read Harvey's article for the school perspective):

T = Target (know who and what your target people and issues are)
A = Action (have actions, not just words, to share)
C = Communication (choose the proper channels and approaches)
T = Time (timing is critical to getting your message heard)
I = Involvement (become active in the target group[s], if possible. It makes your message[s] more meaningful)
C = Change (talk about how your library has and is changing)
A = Attitude (be positive, upbeat, excited about your topic—it becomes contagious)
L = Leadership (demonstrate your and your library's leadership in providing effective and efficient services)

The above addresses formal efforts in the activities we covered and might seem to be beyond the interest of most library staff members much less any involvement. We suggest that every interaction between a user and a staff member is a mini marketing experience.

❶ KEY POINTS TO REMEMBER

- Marketing is an essential element in the strategic plan of a successful library.
- Marketing, like all managerial activities, requires time and careful thought.
- A sound marketing plan is based on generic product definition, target group definition, differential analysis, user behavior analysis, differential advantage analysis, multiple approaches, integration, feedback, and auditing.
- Internal marketing is essential.
- Branding a library is an important activity for projecting quality service.
- Public relations and communications management are related to, but different from, marketing activities.
- All marketing, promotion, and public relations activities should be monitored and evaluated.
- The library advocacy stage is set by the successful work completed through effective marketing, promotion, and public relations.

REFERENCES

American Libraries. 2006. "Britain Launches Campaign to Transform Libraries' Image." *American Libraries* 37, no. 5: 22.

American Library Association. 2010. *Library Advocate's Handbook*. 3rd ed. Chicago: American Library Association.

Andreasen, Allen, and Philip Kotler. 2008. *Strategic Marketing for Nonprofit Organizations*. 7th ed. Englewood Cliffs, NJ: Prentice-Hall.

Association of College and Research Libraries. 2006. *The Power of Personal Persuasion: Advancing the Academic Library Agenda from the Front Line*. Chicago: American Library Association.

Barwise, Patrick, and Sean Meehan. 2010. "Is Your Company as Customer Focused as You Think?" *MIT Sloan Management Review* 51, no. 3: 63–68.

Burke, Jennifer E. 2017. "Top Marketing Tools to Know." *Computers in Libraries* 37, no. 7: 28–31.

Cronin, Blaise, ed. 1992. *Marketing of Library and Libraries*. 2nd ed. London: Aslib.

DiMattia, Susan. 2011. "Advocacy and Image: Partners in Creating a Value Proposition." *Information Outlook* 15, no. 2: 14–16.

Gustafson, Julia Chance, Zachary Sharrow, and Gwen Short. 2017. "Library Marketing on a Small Liberal Arts Campus: Assessing Communication Preferences." *Journal of Library Administration* 57, no. 4: 420–35.

Hariff, Subnum, and Jennifer Rowley. 2011. "Branding UK Public Libraries." *Library Management* 32, no. 4/5: 346–60.

Harvey, Carl A. 2010. "Being Tactical with Advocacy." *Teacher Librarian* 37, no. 4: 80–90.

Kachel, Debra. 2017. "The Advocacy Continuum." *Teacher Librarian* 44, no. 3: 50–52.

Kies, Cosette. 1987. *Marketing and Public Relations for Libraries*. Metuchen, NJ: Scarecrow Press.

Lee, Deborah. 2006. "Checking out the Competition: Marketing Lesson from Google." *Library Administration and Management* 20, no. 2, 94–95.

McNeal, James U. 1992. *Kids as Customers: A Handbook of Marketing to Children*. New York: Macmillan.

Marketing Library Services. 2018. www.infotoday.com/MLS/default.shtml

Moorman, John. 2009. "Advocacy Today, Advocacy Tomorrow, Advocacy Forever!" *Virginia Libraries* 55, no. 4: 15–16.

Rowley, Jennifer. 2001. *Information Marketing*. Ashgate, U.K.: Aldershot.

Savard, Rejean. 2000. *Adapting Marketing to Libraries in a Changing and World-Wide Environment*. Munich: K. G. Sauer.

Schuman, Pat. 2012. E-mail Communication Sent to Camila A. Alire, April 3.

Smith-Butler, Lisa. 2010. "Overcoming Your Aversion to the 'M' Word." *AALL Spectrum* 14, no. 5: 7–8, 23.

Walters, Suzanne. 1992. *Marketing: A How-To-Do-It Manual for Librarians*. New York: Neal-Schuman.

Weingand, Darlene. 1995. "Preparing for the New Millennium: The Case for Using Market Strategies." *Library Trends* 43, no. 3: 296.

———. 1998. *Future-Driven Library Marketing*. Chicago: American Library Association.

Wood, Elizabeth J., and Victoria L. Young. 1988. *Strategic Marketing for Libraries*. New York: Greenwood Press.

PART III

Managing People

 Staffing

Human capital continues to be a guiding force in the effort to tap the potential of employees for organizational excellence. This is especially true of public organizations that are eager to attract the right persons for the right jobs in an increasingly competitive labor market.

Paul Battaglio, P. Edward French, and Doug Goodman, 2017

Libraries, like all employers, have requirements and guidelines for hiring related to federal employment and equal opportunity legislation.

Joan Giesecke and Beth McNeil, 2010

Since 2008, to both cut costs and improve performance within their public sectors, governments throughout the world have imposed new working arrangements, cut pay, altered radically the terms and conditions of employment, and initiated redundancy and severance schemes.

Edel Conway, Na Fu, Kathy Monks, Kerstin Alfes, and Catherine Bailey, 2016

Learning to give and receive feedback is difficult. Managers need practice in giving feedback, whether it's positive feedback, coaching, or constructive feedback.

Mary Jo Finch and Autumn Solomon, 2017

W e ended the prior chapter by suggesting everyone on the library staff can play a significant role in generating public support for the library. The starting point for achieving this is having the right people with the right skills in the right jobs working in a positive environment that maintains and enhances skills. Reaching such a state, and maintaining it, is challenging. There is a concept that serves as an umbrella label for working toward the goal—personnel management. As you might suspect, work culture is a component in attaining service excellence and engendering public support.

People are what make or break every organization, not grand visions, plans, money, or facilities. (We are not suggesting such elements are not important; rather, it takes people to translate such resources into an effective organization.) From a managerial leadership perspective, people issues take up far more of work time than do "things" (money or facilities, for example).

Hiring the best and brightest does not magically occur. You need to expend a significant amount of time on thoughtful planning. Effective personnel management programs rest on a thorough understanding of employment laws and regulations as well as a staffing process consisting of eight steps:

1. Determining needs
2. Designing each job
3. Recruiting
4. Selecting
5. Providing orientation and training
6. Giving appropriate evaluations
7. Coaching and disciplining
8. Handling resignations and terminations

STAFFING AND THE LAW

In chapter 3, "Legal Issues," we noted that we would cover additional legal concerns in later chapters; this is one of those chapters. There are a host of employment laws and regulations—federal, state, and local—that impact staffing. These legal constraints on personnel management cover most aspects of employment from recruitment to retirement.

Some legal employment issues, such as equal opportunity, rest on Constitutional grounds. The first federal legislation regarding employment equal opportunity in the United States was the 1964 Civil Rights Act. The Equal Employment Opportunity (EEO) act of 1972 deals with an individual's right to employment and promotion without regard to race, color, religion, sex, age, or national origin. The concept applies to all phases of employment—not just hiring but also promotion, training opportunities, and the like.

Many seemingly "fair" procedures, such as pre-employment tests, can be discriminatory if certain categories of applicants fail the test at a higher rate than the average (known as covert discrimination). Testing, evaluation, and selection of new employees must be done in terms of real job-related criteria or bona fide occupational qualifications (BFOQs). Generally, race, color, religion, age, sex, ethnic background, disability, and marital status are not valid criteria—we say "generally" because there may be circumstances, such as modeling or acting, when one or more of these criteria may be exempt from legal requirements. In the case of libraries, we are unaware of a circumstance in which any of these would be a BFOQ for a position.

Another employment law concept that is important to understand is affirmative action. Until very recently, affirmative action required employers to make an extra effort to hire and promote people in one of what are classified as "protected minorities." Under federal law (using current terminology), the protected groups are women, Latinos/Latinas, Asian and Pacific Islanders, African Americans, and American Indians. In essence, the goal is to have the workforce more or less mirror the composition of the population in the local job market.

A search of the web will turn up a daunting list of federal employment laws, rules, and regulations. A search of state and local laws, while less impressive in size, is still substantial in character. Federal legislation contains a national minimum wage. State and local governments often set higher minimums. This can be an issue for libraries that depend on part-time hourly workers. Regulations may also limit the number of hours that an employee can work per day or per pay period. Requiring someone to work beyond the legal amount requires paying higher rates (such as "time and a half" or "double time").

Workplace health and safety issues are frequently part of state or national employment laws and regulations. The Occupational Safety and Health Administration (OSHA) handles matters such as workplace air quality, exposure to and handling of materials that may pose a long-term health threat and required safety equipment.

You may encounter a variety of situations where libraries must work with unions or a collective bargaining unit. Many libraries have no unions, some have only staff unions, others have all nonsupervisory staff in a collective bargaining unit, and a small number have all but a very few of the top administrative staff in such groups. Regardless of what or how many staff are part of such groups, the contract or agreement adds another layer to HR activities.

By this point it is clear that there are indeed legal complexities to HR work. Also, it is why McDowell and Leavitt (2011) wrote:

> There is no question that the quantity and complexity of federal and state laws impacting the work of local government human resource departments has increased dramatically in the last few decades. . . . It would be fool-hardy for managers, supervisors, and human resource department personnel to set out through the minefield of employment laws and regulations without the competent guidance of attorneys who regularly practice in this area of law. (p. 240)

STAFFING PROCESS

Staffing is an eight-step process: defining need; designing each job; recruiting candidates for positions; selecting the right person; providing sound orientation, training, and development opportunities; giving appropriate assessments of job performance; coaching and administering fair discipline when necessary; and handling resignations and terminations.

Job design and description

Job design (JD) asks the question, "What activities are necessary to accomplish organizational goals?" Answers to this deceptively simple question can be multiple and complex at times. The goal should be to have a comprehensive list of all tasks, not merely a few broad phrases. For example, a task for a reference service desk worker should be more than "answer questions." It should cover all aspects of the work, such as providing answers to in-person questions, handling telephone questions, processing e-mail queries, and assisting users in finding information. Such detail is essential for creating valid job descriptions.

Once you have a list of tasks, it is possible to group them into logically related activities. The grouping of elements into related actions results in what HR officers refer to as *tasks*. The following is an example of elements grouped into the task "sort e-mail reference questions":

- log in to e-mail account
- read e-mail questions
- decide who can best answer the question(s)
- forward question(s) to appropriate person
- log off

The next step is grouping related tasks into a *position*—all the tasks performed by one person. (Note that everyone in the library occupies a position, and a position is not necessarily full-time.) Similar positions constitute a job category, such as archivist. Only in the smallest organizations will there be a one-to-one relationship of positions and jobs. In most cases there will be several people in a job category.

For HR officers there is another step—developing a classification system. The purposes of a classification system are to group jobs that require the same skill sets and to offer similar compensation in a given class. Because most libraries are part of a larger organization and other units within the larger organization are likely to have jobs calling for similar, if not identical, skills, HR creates a system that helps to ensure equal pay for equal work. An example is a library IT staff member who maintains servers probably has a skill set similar to that of a person working in a computer center doing the same tasks. Most systems establish *salary ranges* within a category, which means salary differences may exist for individuals in the same classification category. Such differences arise from experience and longevity.

Job success criteria

Job success criteria (JSC) are the key to selecting the right person for the right position. Establishing JSC is the most difficult and subjective of the steps in the model. While the goal sounds simple: "define what distinguishes successful from unsuccessful performance in the position," it can be difficult to determine what constitutes success. This will vary from library to library and, from time to time, within the same library. Many professionals would agree that these items could or should be on any list of JSC for a reference position:

- Accurately determine the nature of questions.
- Provide accurate answers to questions.

However, this view might change if any of the following were true:

- Accurate, but the person is abrasive to user.
- Accurate, but is "talkative" with selected users and therefore handles fewer questions.
- Accurate, quick, and pleasant with users but abrasive with colleagues.

Before starting to interview candidates, the search committee should understand what JSC are being sought. Also, it is essential that JSC are the result of agreement among those currently performing the work, senior management, and the parent body's HR office.

Job specifications

Job specifications (JS) are the skills, traits, knowledge, and experience that should result in successful performance. JS frequently appear in job descriptions and advertisements, for example, education required, years of experience, and the specific skills sought. From a legal point of view, you should be certain that the items listed are in fact BFOQs (bona fide occupational qualifications). Merely saying that it is so will not stand up in court; you must be able to prove it is true. Thus, you should not specify a master's degree in library or information science is required unless you are ready to prove that the degree is a *prerequisite* for success. When using the phrase "or equivalent" for a skill or background, you must be ready

> ### 💡 TRY THIS
>
> Look at four advertisements for library positions. What information is provided about (a) the organization placing the advertisement; (b) the position; and (c) the criteria for appointment? Compare the amount of information provided in the advertisements.

to clearly state what is and is not equivalent. Because the application form normally provides the basis for the initial screening of applicants to determine who will be interviewed, the form should provide space to list information about equivalent training and experience.

Selection tools

During the more than sixty years of legislation regarding equal employment and affirmative action, there have been numerous court cases that impact the selection process. Often the cases grew out of requirements that were not clearly associated with successful job performance. An example of an imprecise statement is "the successful applicant will have a lively personality." We don't know which would be more difficult to prove: (a) that a lively personality was essential for successful job performance or (b) what factors are present in a "lively" personality. A better way of getting at what the writers of such statements are looking for would be to seek individuals with a "demonstrated ability to work effectively with customers and staff in a highly service-oriented environment." Although wordy, it is much clearer about what the library is seeking and less open to question.

Recruitment

Recruitment takes time; a national search will probably require four to six months. This estimate covers the time from the development of the position description to the time the successful applicant begins work. The search could begin as an internal process; that is, an announcement of a vacancy goes to the library's staff. In some organizations, the policy is to interview any internal candidates before looking at outside candidates. More often, the search is both internal and external—with the internal applicants having the advantage of knowing more about the organization's issues.

Once there is a pool of applicants, the review or screening process begins. The process involves several elements: the application form, letters or statements of interest, the pre-employment test results (if required), a personal interview, and verification of qualifications and past work experience. Normally, you select only a few individuals for in-person interviews. The screening process relies on the applicant to supply the requisite information regarding her or his qualifications.

Application form

The application can provide a great deal of information about applicants, not only the data provided but also how they present it. It can reveal a lot about the individual's motivation, writing skills, maturity, and ability to understand and follow directions. Such forms usually provide the following information:

- the applicant's work history, including tenure in each position listed
- the applicant's educational background
- names of persons to contact regarding applicant's suitability for the position

There are questions you may not legally ask on the application or during the interview. These questions are those that could lead to discriminatory practices. Obvious questions about the applicant's race, religion, and age are not acceptable. Some forms have a space to indicate sex but often indicate this is optional information.

National searches present several challenges. Two significant challenges are cost and time. Few organizations have enough money to pay the travel and lodging expenses of every potential candidate. It is also unreasonable to expect candidates to pay their own way unless they have a very good chance of being selected. Interviewing at professional association meetings, such as ALA, are a partial means of reducing costs.

Cover letter and statement of interest

Application forms usually are very general; they seldom provide the applicant with an opportunity to demonstrate why he or she is suitable for the position. Requesting a cover letter stating the applicant's interest in the position and what special skills and experience she or he has helps bridge the gap between an institution-wide application blank and an in-person interview.

Letters of interest are useful, especially if the person has seen the full job description, not merely the advertisement text. Advertisements tend to be short because of cost concerns, and they seldom provide enough information for preparing meaningful statements. Posting the full description online gives the applicant a better understanding of the job's duties and what his or her chances are as well as what to include in a statement. Most applicants and screeners believe such documents are very helpful because they provide a fuller and fairer picture of the applicant.

Tests

Testing has been criticized on several grounds: invalidity, invasion of privacy, and discrimination against certain classes of applicants. The only pre-employment tests that are legal in library settings are those that assess common skills: typing, alphabetizing, numerical computation, or similar measurable traits. If a JSC is the requirement to type seventy words a minute error-free, there is no reason to interview a person who manages to achieve only thirty error-free words per minute. This, of course, assumes the 70-word error-free requirement is a valid JSC.

Interviewing

The interview provides the opportunity to explore the applicant's background, experience, knowledge, and expertise, as well as oral and social skills. From the applicant's point of view, the interview provides an opportunity to assess the position, potential coworkers, and the institution. Interviews—and how you handle them— are a key component in hiring the best and brightest people.

There are six considerations that ought to be part of any interview process. The first is planning. Beyond the obvious—such as when to conduct the interview—some of the key planning issues are where to interview, who should do the interview, what questions to ask, what the candidate ought to see, and how much time to build into the process for responding to candidate interests.

The second, and perhaps the most critical, aspect of the interview process is the set of interview questions. This part is crucial for ensuring that the library satisfies EEO requirements. Having a structured format is one of the best ways to ensure compliance as well as consistency and comparability of information about each candidate.

Third, your questions must be job related. You should be able to link each question to the job description. If there is no linkage, it is best not to ask the question. Asking some open-ended questions gives candidates an opportunity to respond more fully and demonstrate some of their skills. They also allow the interviewers to learn about oral communication skills and to assess a candidate's ability to respond to an unexpected situation.

The fourth consideration is the "personal impact" of both the candidate and the interviewers. Taking a few minutes at the start to create a friendly atmosphere helps candidates relax and be more effective during the formal interview. Things such as tone of voice, eye contact, personal appearance and grooming, posture, and gestures influence both parties.

The fifth consideration is related to impact—how the interviewers respond to the applicant. One trait interviewers must be careful to control is nonverbal behavior that may encourage or discourage an applicant in an inappropriate way. Another is to reflect interest in what the candidate is saying. Anyone with extensive experience with the interview process understands just how difficult controlling those two behaviors can be at times.

The final consideration is assessing the applicants' information equitably. These are some of the issues that can cause unfair assessment:

- overemphasis on negative information for one or two candidates
- stereotyping the "right" person for the position
- imprecise job information that leads to looking for irrelevant attributes in the candidates
- use of different weights for various attributes by different members of a search committee
- overuse of visual clues about the candidate that are not job related
- placing too much emphasis on the candidate's similarity—such as sex, race, values—to the interviewer
- not recognizing "contrast effects" (that is, when a strong candidate follows a very weak candidate, the contrast makes the stronger applicant look even stronger than she or he may be)

▌▌▌▌ **CHECK THIS OUT**

An older but comprehensive guide to job interviews is Susan Carol Curzon's *Managing the Interview: A How-To-Do-It Manual for Hiring Staff* (New York: Neal-Schuman, 1995).

Verification and evaluation

One of the more difficult and sensitive areas in any hiring procedure is verification of an applicant's education and work history. Letters of recommendation from former teachers and employers are often of questionable value because of the passage of time since the writer had direct contact with the applicant. It is not unheard of for present employers to write a glowing recommendation for a person they wish would leave. Dismissing an employee may lead to legal action, so some organizations "help" the person find employment elsewhere by giving less than accurate assessments.

Confidentiality issues may arise with references. Some public institutions allow candidates to see letters of recommendation. Some states (California and Colorado, for example) have open records laws that allow such examination, so letters of recommendation are being used less frequently. Another problem is fraudulent education or work history. Some people overstate their previous salaries. Only by checking can you determine whether the candidate has the claimed skills and background.

THE NEW HIRE

A new employee's first few days on the job set the tone for what follows. "Glad to see you; go to work" is not the best method for getting a new person to become a productive employee. By planning a formal orientation process, you create a solid beginning for both the person and the library.

A new hire's first day is frequently a combination of orientation, some training in the job, and time with HR to take care of all the new employee paperwork. During this orientation and training time, which may go on for some time when the tasks or duties are complex, the new hire should receive information about the significance of his or her duties. Early and frequent praise helps to develop a good working relationship. New employees often find their first several days confusing and unsettling. Spreading orientation out over several days helps make the new information, people, and duties less overwhelming. The training also should be flexible in order to adapt to various learning speeds as well as to the person's prior experience.

Most clerical jobs demand careful, specific instruction, as do manual and unskilled jobs. Group training programs are very efficient for such positions, but turnover seldom allows for this. Libraries that hire a significant number of part-time workers may be able to take advantage of group training.

▊▊▊ CHECK THIS OUT

A good article that explores the integrating of a new hire into the workplace is Jolie O. Graybill, et al.'s "Employee Onboarding: Identification of Best Practices in ACRL Libraries" (*Library Management* 34, no. 3: 200–18, 2013).

DEVELOPING AND RETAINING STAFF

For most of today's libraries, retention of their best people is a concern because of hiring freezes and the risk of losing a vacant position because of budgetary restraints. There are two basic training and development areas to consider: specific job-related skills and career development competencies and opportunities.

Libraries today face a rapidly changing technological environment. Keeping staff up to date on the technologies they use for their work is a major challenge, especially in times of "steady state" or declining budgets. Failure to maintain staff skills results in users receiving poorer service, which in turn leads to dissatisfaction with the library. You face a dual technological challenge: acquiring and upgrading the technology and finding training funds. (We explore staff development in more detail in the next chapter.)

Professional associations are an excellent source of training opportunities. Unfortunately, there are very few such organizational opportunities for support staff. The primary reason is that support staff members have few opportunities for paid travel, and their salaries are substantially lower, making it almost impossible for them to pay for such programs on their own. As more educational institutions and professional bodies extend the range of distance education programs, training opportunities will increase.

In addition to funding concerns, you face the problem of limited staffing, at least in most libraries. With limited staff, it becomes difficult to have staff out for training programs for any length of time. Some jurisdictions are so shortsighted that they refuse to give time off to attend training programs even when the staff member is willing to pay for the program—shortsighted because in time the libraries become less and less effective.

PERFORMANCE APPRAISAL

Management theory in the United States holds that performance appraisal is essential to the successful operation of any organization. In theory, it should help the worker to improve performance. There is a substantial list of beliefs about the appraisal process:

- It is essential to good management.
- It is natural, normal part of human activity.
- It ensures minimum performance at least.
- It is the only valid method for granting or withholding economic benefits.
- It is a means of maintaining control of production and service.
- It is essential for employee growth and development.
- It is essential for motivating employees.
- It assesses the quality or success of orientation and training programs.
- It is a means of objectively assessing an individual's work-related strengths and weaknesses.
- It reflects a continuous analysis of a person's daily work performance.
- It is an assessment of total performance, not just assigned duties.
- It reflects staff members' future and potential for advancement.
- It is essential for planning library personnel needs.
- It is key to successfully counsel staff members.

This is an impressive list of objectives for a single process. Everyone who writes about management—and everyone who practices it—knows that the process has many land mines. They also know that only sometimes does the actual procedure match the ideal. In reality, the process has two basic goals that are not congruent. One goal is administrative in character and the other is behavioral. Administrative goals relate to the employee, while the behavioral goals relate to the actions the employee takes. Saul Gellerman (1976) identified the features of appraisal that achieve the "best" results:

- Administrative purposes:
  - Secretive
  - Fixed
  - Bureaucratic

- Behavioral purposes:
  - Candid
  - Flexible
  - Individualized

The administrative aspect is designed to defend the decisions managers make about salary increases, promotions, and dismissals. Another goal is to create "comparable data" from a series of subjective judgments by a number of supervisors or managers.

Behavioral goals should help the individual identify areas where improvement is possible or necessary. These goals also identify where personal development might be desirable from the organization's point of view. Identifying exceptional performance is also part of the process. Statisticians will tell anyone who will listen that the bell-shaped curve is the normal distribution of data; that is, the vast majority of cases will fall into the middle-average category. On the other hand, anyone who reviews a significant number of appraisal forms knows that most organizations consist primarily of above-average or exceptional employees—perhaps mathematically impossible but managerially possible for annual assessments.

Attempting to achieve both sets of purposes in a single process verges on the ludicrous. It would be better to utilize two separate systems, one for each purpose. Many organizations claim they do this by calling the annual process an "annual development review" and asserting that there is no connection between that process and any later salary adjustments. Few employees believe this.

There has been something of a shift in thinking about the critical importance of performance appraisals that began around 2014. In part, it is a recognition of the difficulty in effectively achieving the dual goals. Another factor is the fact that many other countries (the Nordic countries, for example) have excellent organizational results without engaging in the appraisal process.

Regardless of what you may think about the process, it does exist as a managerial fact of life in many places. You must learn to make the process as useful as possible. A key factor is that you must make certain not to save feedback for scheduled performance reviews. Daily feedback—both immediate praise and correction—is the best way to ensure good work performance. It will also provide some assurance there will be few, if any, surprises at performance appraisal time.

> ▐▐▌▌ **CHECK THESE OUT**
>
> Two good articles about the current thinking about performance appraisal are Peter Cappelli and Anna Tavis's "The Performance Management Revolution: The Focus Is Shifting from Accountability to Learning" (*Harvard Business Review* 94, no. 10: 58–67, 2016) and Lori Goler, Janelle Gale, and Adam Grant's "Let's Not Kill Performance Evaluations Yet: Facebook's Experience Shows Why They Can Still Be Valuable" (*Harvard Business Review* 94, no. 11: 90–94, 2016).

CORRECTIVE ACTION

If you want good performance, you should make monitoring performance an ongoing process rather than an annual event. It also avoids many of the administrative aspects and focuses on the behavioral issues, a system that is corrective in character should produce effective performance from the staff.

A healthy supervisory system provides a two-way exchange between managerial leaders and their staff. Each should be free to voice satisfaction or dissatisfaction. Attempts to avoid stress or other matters will solve nothing. When it is necessary to take corrective action—for example, counseling sessions—there are some steps you can follow to make the time as productive as possible. Start by stating the purpose of the session. Even if the situation has the potential for confrontation, speak quietly and plan on letting the employee talk as much as possible. Listen to the person; do not spend time planning a rebuttal. Periods of silence, even long ones, can serve a good purpose—letting the parties think about what is taking place. Setting a time limit for the session often defeats the goal of the session, as it may take a long time to get to the central issue(s).

Expect the employee to be unhappy, probably argumentative, and, occasionally, ready to initiate a "personal" attack during the session. It is important not to take this behavior personally and not to respond in kind. Total resolution is not the only indication of a successful session. Sometimes it takes a series of sessions to reach a complete resolution. Try to end the session on a positive note and, if appropriate, schedule a follow-up session. We subscribe to the "Five Rs" of performance counseling:

- right purpose
- right approach
- right time
- right technique
- right place

We touched on some of the approach factors above: little advance notice, start the session quickly, come to the point immediately, state the facts, do not accuse, and try to keep calm. The right purposes include to strengthen, maintain, or restore a working relationship. Right times include only when necessary, not when you are upset, during low activity times, and not too far in advance. The right place is private and do not allow telephone calls or other intrusions to disrupt the process. After the initial statement, devote more time to listening rather than talking, and do not push the session. Finally, use one of two basic techniques, directive or nondirective. Directive sessions address issues such as rule or policy violations, correction of mistakes, and control of hostility. Nondirective meetings work best for concerns such as restoring a positive attitude or productivity, strengthening or restoring relationships, and motivating for greater teamwork.

There are occasions when more corrective action is called for—progressive discipline (PD). PD is a system that requires management and employees to address deliberately performance issues through a series of progressively sterner steps if the employee does not improve. Normally, the process starts with oral counseling followed by one or more written warnings that ultimately lead to termination if worse comes to worst. This does not mean that there are not circumstances that will warrant immediate termination. Most organizations and HR departments reason that it is helpful to identify types of conduct that are impermissible and that will lead to disciplinary action, possibly including immediate discharge.

GRIEVANCES

There is a chance a situation will arise in which a formal reprimand or dismissal are the only choices. When this happens, you might anticipate that the employee will file a grievance. Grievances can also arise when there is a union contract. It is important for you to maintain a solid paper record that documents what was done. Such a paper trail may include just a brief note on the desk calendar recording that a discussion with Employee X about Situation Y took place, or it may include memos or formal depositions.

A grievable issue is work-related and can be resolved through existing procedures. Very often the first formal step in the grievance process is for a person from HR or a grievance committee or board to meet with the parties, including the supervisor's supervisor, to attempt to resolve the matter without further delay.

Dealing with a grievance is like stopping a river. At its source, it is a small trickle that is easily blocked. Unchecked, grievances can become a small stream as additional complaints accumulate and resolution becomes more complex and difficult. As time passes without resolution, more and more baggage is attached to the original small issue. The grievance takes on a force of its own (a number of tributaries creating a river). Ultimately, it becomes a major river that is almost impossible to slow or stop.

The river analogy goes further, a grievance takes many forms. It will follow existing channels—if they exist—or cut its own channels. You can dam it up for a while (without resolving the issue), but this only applies constant pressure on the dam and eventually will cause a weak point to collapse. Once the dam breaks, it is impossible to stop the flood; it must run its course. After the course is run, many things will have changed. Having a grievance procedure helps control the river by providing a channel for addressing the issue.

Another step can be taken after the committee or board action, which is to bring in an arbitrator or mediator from outside the organization. Arbitrators or mediators will look at most of the same issues as the grievance committee.

COLLECTIVE BARGAINING AND MERIT SYSTEMS

Public sector libraries often must work within a civil service personnel system and/or a collective bargaining agreement (CBA). Both affect staffing activities from recruitment to promotions. They focus primarily on employee rights and benefits, although they cover other employment issues as well. In the case of collective bargaining, many agreements impact how you handle layoffs (seniority, for example). Grievance processes are a focus of both situations. CBAs almost always cover "working conditions;" what else is covered varies from contract to contract, even within the same organization. The phrase used in many job descriptions, "other duties as assigned," is usually missing in CBAs; which clearly assign all duties. Any change will require additional negotiations and inclusion in the new agreement.

A major challenge in a CBA is when a staff member can elect to join or not join the union. You must remember who is and is not a member when it comes to tasks, and you may have to deal with staff tension between union and nonunion members. That dual situation can also complicate your salary administration responsibilities. These few examples indicate the added complexity when a union and/or merit system is in place. You will need to quickly learn the ins and outs of what is and is not possible.

Merit, civil service, and public employee systems are special situations that apply in many government jurisdictions. Again, the details will vary from jurisdiction to jurisdiction, from the highly structured to relatively loose forms. Also, today there is a growing trend to make the merit system more like what you see in the for-profit sector. The concept of a government employee system based on merit (that is, ability to perform the work) rather than on political connections goes back to the late nineteenth century. The idea of merit led to the testing of a person's ability to perform the work which is still a key component for such systems—tests for getting the position and tests for promotions.

One issue for both unions and merit systems is employment security (sometimes tenure is another label). The issue is also a factor in efforts to "reform" employment practices, especially in governmental environments. Most organizations, including for-profits, have a probation period for new hires, often including those accepting a promotion. During that period, in theory, the employer can terminate the person for almost any reason. After passing probation the employee has greater job security. Under the merit system most employees are "classified"—they can be dismissed only "for cause," with the

---

⦀ CHECK THESE OUT

There are several older but still worthwhile reading articles about unions and collective bargaining units in libraries. Cameron A. Johnson's article "Library Unions: Politics, Power, and the Care of the Library Worker" (*Alki* 17, no. 3: 16–19, 2001) explores library-union dynamics. Hampton "Skip" Auld's piece "The Benefits and Deficiencies of Unions in Public Libraries (*Public Libraries* 41, no. 3: 135–42, 2002) explored the pros and cons of unions in public libraries. Carla McLean's 2005 "The Not-So-Odd Couple: Libraries and Unions" (*Alki* 21, no. 2: 11–12) examined the purposes of such associations. Finally, Deborah O. Lee, Kevin E. Rogers, and Paul W. Grimes looked at the salary impact of unions in academic library setting in "The Union Relative Wage Effect for Academic Librarians," (*Industrial Relations* 2006 45, no. 3: 478–84, 2006).

Two resources on merit system issues are Peter B. Broida's *A Guide to Merit Systems Protection Board Law and Practice* (Arlington, VA: Dewey Publications, 2015) and the U.S. Merit Systems Protection Board's *Prohibited Personnel Practices: A Study Retrospective: A Report to the President and the Congress of the United States* (Washington, DC: Merit Systems Protection Board, 2010).

criteria clearly spelled out. The other employment category is "at-will"—in such cases the employer has much more freedom to decide who to dismiss and when. Many government jurisdictions are shifting away from classified to at-will. New hires, after a certain date, are at-will, and older employees retain their classified status.

VOLUNTEERS

While volunteers have long been a staple in many libraries operations, the ongoing economic environment, especially for public and school libraries has increased their importance and use. There is a vast pool of talented, energetic, and motivated volunteers—especially retired librarians—to tap and retain. They also can become highly committed to a library's organizational goals, given the proper environment. Part of that environment is thinking about volunteers as just as important to quality service as paid staff members. Creating the proper environment calls for careful thought and planning.

A good starting point for thinking about volunteers is to consider a few basic questions:

- Should we use volunteers? (the key question to ponder)
- Where would we use volunteers?
- How would we use volunteers?
- Would the tasks be meaningful for volunteers?
- Who would supervise the volunteers?
- Do we have or can we create meaningful volunteer rewards?

Once you have decided you can make effective use of volunteers for work activities you, should employ most of the staffing concepts outlined earlier in this chapter. Often the decision that it would be nice to use some volunteers is made without a thoughtful plan for how to employee them. That approach sometimes works but is not recommended if you want long-term committed volunteers.

Start with volunteer job descriptions for each type of activity just as you would for paid staff positions. Doing so provides a solid base for both parties regarding the "whats" and "hows" of the position. Surprises, such as a volunteer announcing, "I don't want to make photocopies," are much less likely if the person reviewed a job description indicating photocopying was part of the expected job performance. As with paid positions, the job description should outline the position's duties and the experience and skills sought. After preparing the descriptions, it is wise to consult with the HR department to explore insurance issues, such as injury and liability coverage for volunteers.

‖‖‖ CHECK THESE OUT

Driggers, Preston, and Eileen Dumas. 2011. *Managing Library Volunteers*. 2nd ed. Chicago: American Library Association.

Volunteer Match. www.volunteermatch.org/.

Volunteers probably require more training and development than do paid staff. This is particularly true when the volunteer has retired from a somewhat similar paid position elsewhere. Such people may have to unlearn years of past practices and/or modify beliefs about "how things should be done." Often the managerial leader's assumption is that the person did this before and needs very little training, which sometimes also translates into inadequate orientation for volunteers.

There are some situations where tension can arise between volunteers and paid staff. One obvious area would be fear or concern on the paid staff's part about their job security, especially when funding is tight or hiring freezes are in place. We are not aware of any documented case of paid staff losing positions because volunteers were available. However, we do know of instances where layoffs took place because of funding problems, with the library operating solely on volunteer help. Thus, the concern is real and should be addressed openly and honestly.

A particular challenge is when volunteers and paid staff perform the same task(s). Whenever possible, you should avoid this situation. Performance assessment becomes a significant factor. Paid staff may resent the volunteer's apparent freedom to come and go with little or no notice. They may also think or observe that a volunteer receives encouragement or praise for work the staff believes is of a lower standard than they are expected to deliver. Your managerial creativity and ingenuity will face great challenges when you try to provide that extra level of encouragement to volunteers and retain their services while not undermining paid staff morale.

🔒 KEY POINTS TO REMEMBER

- People—the staff—are the essential element of a successful library.
- Attracting and retaining the "best and brightest" is a complex undertaking.
- Legal aspects impact all personnel activities, from recruitment to retirement.
- Assessing staffing needs involves position reviews and looking at labor force demographics.
- Recruiting and selecting the best person requires care and thought, including an understanding of legal issues.
- Tools for the selection process must be chosen with an eye on legal concerns.
- Selecting and landing a candidate can be a complex activity involving the library staff and the parent body's HR office.
- Proper orientation of new staff during the first few days or weeks is critical to good long-term work performance.
- Performance appraisal is a process that few people like and one that can have as many negative as positive outcomes unless handled thoughtfully.
- Discipline is a delicate activity that takes practice and skill to keep personal views at bay and objective data in the forefront.
- Unions contracts and merit systems can influence what you can and cannot do in terms of staffing.
- Volunteers can be useful but should be carefully considered.

REFERENCES

Battaglio, Paul, P. Edward French, and Doug Goodman. 2017. "Contracting Out for Municipal Human Resources: Analyzing the Role of Human Capital in the Make or Buy Decision." *Public Administration Quarterly* 41, no. 2: 297-333.

Conway, Edel, Na Fu, Kathy Monks, Kerstin Alfes, and Catherine Bailey. 2016. "Demands or Resources? The Relationship between HR Practices, Employee Engagement, and Emotional Exhaustion within a Hybrid Model of Employment Relations." *Human Resource Management* 55, no. 5: 901-17.

Finch, Mary Jo, and Autumn Solomon. 2017. "Antifragile Management and the End of the Annual Performance Review." *Public Libraries* 56, no. 3: 27-31.

Gellerman, Saul. 1976. *Management of Human Resources*. New York: Holt, Rinehart.

Giesecke, Joan, and Beth McNeil. 2010. *Fundamentals of Library Supervision*. 2nd ed. Chicago: American Library Association.

McDowell, Amy M., and William M. Leavitt. 2011. "Human Resources Issues in Local Government: Yesterday's Headlines Remain Today's 'Hot Topics.'" *Public Personnel Management* 40, no. 3: 239-49.

CHAPTER 14

Enhancing Performance

The concept of a learning organization has received considerable attention in the fields of organizational change, organizational development, human resource development and strategic management as the inducer of better organizational performance.

Mohan P. Pokharel and Sang Ok Choi, 2015

The importance of learning in and by organizations has since long been recognized by organization scientists.

Max Visser and Kim Van der Togt, 2016

We believe providing opportunities for interaction through team engagement-base projects nurtures a new generation of capable professionals with interpersonal skills and social capital, ready for action in the 21st century, building a bright future.

Kayo Denda and Jennifer Hunter, 2016

In the preface, we noted that management practice is a mixture of elements that interact in a variety of ways. Further, from a learning perspective, it is more effective to look at the elements as independent activities such as decision making instead of a mix of elements. This is a chapter, however, where we look at the intermixing of elements in terms of organizational performance rather than as an independent topic.

Successful organizational performance requires several elements to be in place simultaneously starting with the basics—mission, vision, and planning effectiveness. Effective environmental monitoring and its analysis also play a role in organizational performance. Organizational agility (ability to change) is another performance factor and, for public sector organizations, there are tight limits on how agile they may be (laws and regulations defining their activities for example). Moussa, Murray, and Muenjohn (2018), in writing about public sector innovation, made the point, "There exist a considerable number of barriers that hinder a culture of innovation particularly in the public sector" (p. 232). That comment applies to organizational change as well.

Additional performance factors include organizational climate and culture—both of which impact staff members' performance. Clearly staff performance is a key element in organizational outcomes and overall performance. Existing staff skills and commitment play into their performance. Facilities and financial resources are yet more factors that also limit public sector organizations to perform at higher levels.

Yesterday's knowledge, resources, and skill sets may still have relevance, but the constantly changing environment requires adjustments to the previous and the development of new capabilities. There is substantial literature addressing the values of lifelong learning. Certainly, the focus of such materials is on the individual rather than the organization. The fact of the matter is that ongoing learning is equally important to the organization. For an organization to succeed long term, its staff must learn and develop new skills on a continuing basis. We start with the organizational side and then move to the staff side.

ORGANIZATIONAL DEVELOPMENT

We explore two organizational performance enhancement concepts—organizational development (OD) and the learning organization (LO). OD is the older of the two. Its primary goal is increasing effectiveness and therefore enhancing performance. It is a top-down process which can present challenges for public sector agencies on occasions when the "top" is the overall organization—the city or state government. For example, a library may be hard-pressed to find ways to match the expectations of a mandated OD program as it may already be performing at the maximum that resources allow. OD draws on the behavioral sciences and is staff focused—organizations cannot change if its employees do not change.

An OD program is an approach that should allow an organization to respond better to a changing world. Donald L. Anderson (2017) described this approach: "While individual and organization learning is a part of OD and a key value we will discuss in a later chapter, OD work is not confined to training activities" (p. 10).

How does OD work? First, and foremost, it is intended to improve an organization's overall performance. The concept applies to both internal and external performance. The process begins when a performance problem arises, and management decides it is significant enough to address.

Second, OD focuses on improving an organization's ability to respond to a changing situation. It does so by developing a plan that management believes will best address the issue (an internal or external goal). An example of an internal goal could be to improve the staff trust in each other and of management. An external example might be to enhance the organization's environmental scanning process and problem-solving capabilities.

Third, it takes a total systems approach—culture, structure, and staff. An example of what this means would be a desire to create a work environment that is enjoyable to work in and in which learning is engaged, valued, supported, and recognized (i.e., developing one's full potential). The notion of full potential also applies to the organization as a whole.

Fourth, there is an emphasis on improving organizational collaboration—reducing the "silos" that often develop over time and become barriers to organizational performance.

▥ CHECK THIS OUT

If you are interested in learning more about OD, Donald L. Anderson's book *Organizational Development: The Process of Leading Organizational Change,* 4th edition (Thousand Oaks, CA: Sage Publications, 2017) is a solid choice.

〽 **CHECK THESE OUT**

In 2018, *The Learning Organization* devoted an entire issue (volume 25, no. 1) to the impact of gender on organizational learning.

Another article worth your time is Peter Critten's "A Radical Agenda for Enabling Organisation Transformation through Work-Applied Learning" (*Journal of Work-Applied Management* 8, no. 1: 65–78, 2016).

It is challenging to break down silos. One method of doing so is to have cross-training as a normal part of the workplace. Such training, if nothing more, exposes staff members to what other units do and the importance of those activities to the organization's ultimate success.

Fifth, it is not identical to the concept of change management, although there is overlap. The differentiation lies in the systems approach of OD rather than focusing just on the change process.

LEARNING ORGANIZATIONS

In a sense, the learning organization (LO) is an updated version of OD. Two differences in the concepts are that LO focuses on learning new skills and it is viewed as a collaborative process rather than top down. Visser and Van der Togt (2016) provide a good explanation of the difference in application of the LO:

> However, there are important differences between business and public sector organizations that impact the ways in which those organizations can learn. Business organizations generally work under market conditions. . . . PSO [public service organizations] generally work bureaucratic or hybrid conditions, in which departmental governance, political rules, regulations. . . . guiding decision-making and learning. (p. 236).

Staff members who are learning tend to be more motivated and committed to the organization and its well-being. That in turn usually results in improved organizational performance.

When it first appeared in 1990, Peter Senge's book *The Fifth Discipline: The Art and Practice of the Learning Organization* (2006, revised edition), it generated great interest in his concept of a learning organization. Learning organizations attempt to generate and acquire and pass on information and knowledge within themselves with the goal of adjusting their activities based on "new" knowledge in order to create a more effective organization.

Senge (2006) defined a learning organization as one "where people continually expand their capacity to create the results they truly desire" (p. 3). His five disciplines are personal mastery, mental models, shared visions, team learning, and systems thinking. *Personal mastery* is about your learning how to expand your ability to generate the best possible outcomes. It also helps create an environment where others seek to learn and develop their skills sets. *Mental models* is about your mental images of the world and how those images influence your actions and behavior. *Shared visions* is about developing group

---

▥ CHECK THIS OUT

Interested in learning more about mindsets? Carol S. Dweck's *Mindset: The New Psychology of Success* (Random House, 2006) describes her decades of research into the power of mindsets and their impact on learning.

---

commitment to current and future goals. *Team learning* is about building ever-stronger trust and effective communication and accepting team members' ideas as possible solutions to challenges with the objective of achieving ever greater team results. *Systems thinking* is about understanding and describing interrelationships in existing behavior systems in order to be more effective in changing those systems when necessary.

As a manager, you have important roles to play in a learning organizational environment. You need to actively bring new ideas to the staff and wider organization; the discussion of new ideas also will assist you when you need to institute change. Actively removing barriers to sharing new ideas is also something you should do. The sharing process is one technique for reducing the silo effect that often afflicts units in large organizations. You will also need to assist staff in modifying their behavior in light of the new information.

Part of the learning process is how you think about mistakes. An individual's mindset either enhances or stops learning. Gino and Staats (2017) discussed two types of mindsets—growth and fixed. The growth mindset views mistakes as a learning opportunity while the fixed sees a mistake as a lack of ability. Managerial leaders can create a work environment that fosters the growth mindset by treating mistakes as growth situations rather than placing blame. They can also do this by building it into their training and development activities.

TRAINING AND DEVELOPMENT

We touched on training and development (T&D) activities in the previous chapter. Here we explore the topic in more detail. Training programs focus on current and near-future organizational needs while development activities strive to enhance skills to meet potential organizational needs. It is also true that successful development efforts may lead to staff members leaving as a result of having new marketable skills.

An unfortunate fact regarding T&D in public sector organizations is the lack of funding to support such activities. Libraries have been particularly challenged in this area for some time. We are aware of some library systems that require staff to use vacation time to attend training programs and/or professional association meetings. Lack of managerial support for T&D activities will have a negative impact on organizational performance in the long run. Finding support for such activities is a test of managerial leadership skills. The most effective approach is to slowly get work funding for T&D efforts into the operational budget. We say slowly because it can be an uphill battle just to gain an initial nominal commitment to the idea from funding authorities.

Both management and staff benefit from training and development. They need to acknowledge this fact and support T&D efforts. In addition to full-time staff, there are two other categories of staffing to consider—part-time staff and volunteers. Part-timers may present special challenges because they may work schedules that make it difficult to include them in a planned activity. Volunteers present even more challenges.

Libraries frequently have volunteers performing important duties, sometimes even "core" library functions. In such instances, they may need training and development. That may be a more complex task than you might expect. Volunteers become volunteers for different reasons and come with a variety of expectations about what they will and will not do. Their expectations may not include developing new skills. Even when they are willing, finding a satisfactory time for doing so is often not easy. (There are a host of issues related to managing volunteers. One excellent guide on the topic is Matthew Allen Liao-Troth's *Challenges in Volunteer Management* [2008, Charlotte, NC: IAP-Information Age Publishing].)

Successful T&D programs are the result of the following basic steps. It is not surprising that the notion of success rests on careful planning and assessment of the training needs. Such planning should assess both the immediate and anticipated needs. Involving staff in the process is usually beneficial as they are often aware of small but important training needs. Once these needs are identified, establishing priorities, because the cost of addressing all needs is likely to exceed existing T&D funding resources. There may be occasions when an anticipated need will rank higher than an immediate issue, for example, when an upcoming technology upgrade will impact almost all the staff and the immediate needs affect only a few staff members.

Fully explaining the what, why, and when for the T&D program almost always improves the chances of success. Staff members may be less receptive or committed to learning if they are not clear why the training is necessary. Linking the activity to existing operations or well-known future needs also helps increase staff commitment to the process. If training performances are seen as being linked to the annual performance review, chances of a successful T&D fall sharply.

What are your options for training events? While there are a number of possibilities, finding one you need and can afford is not always easy. You can divide the possibilities into several broad categories—local, online, commercial/consultants, academic, and professional associations. Part of your decision rests on whether the necessary training is library-specific or pertains to general operational needs (for example, time management skills). Table 14.1 lists some of the common possibilities.

Each option has its own set of pluses and minuses. The obvious factors are cost and timing—when, for example, the cost of the training you need exceeds the T&D funds you have available. Some options are group-focused while others are individual (certificate

TABLE 14.1 T&D Resources

LOCAL	ONLINE	COMMERCIAL	ACADEMIC	PROFESSIONAL ASSOCIATION
• Library staff • HR department • Colleague dept.	• Vendor • Websites • HR paid	• Library consultant • For-profit firm • Consortium	• Day workshop • Certificate program • Continuing education	• Conference • Day sessions • Workshops

programs and conferences, for example). Vendor opportunities take several forms from online manuals to in-person vendor training. A staff member skilled in a particular system could coach or mentor less skilled personnel by making use of vendor material.

At the local level, many HR departments offer some training in topics that cut across many units. These sessions tend to be general operational topics such as effective handling of annual performance reviews, staff motivation, and workplace dispute resolution. Some HR units pay an online training firm to offer a variety of modules that individual employees can sign up for and work through in at their own pace. This approach can be cost-effective and can provide more flexibility for staff.

Another local possibility is T&D offered by other agencies within the parent organization. One obvious resource is the IT unit, which may offer some in-depth training for existing operating systems as well as software applications. Other possibilities include fire and police departments (for training on facility evacuation, fire extinguisher usage, and dealing with disruptive user behavior). Local T&D need not be a one-way street—the library can offer colleagues in other agencies training in activities such as effective use of online tools and offer training for useful databases that might not otherwise be available to them.

Library consultants are a source of library-specific training opportunities. There are two broad types of consultants—independent and state library staff. As you might guess, state library consultants tend to be less expensive; however, they may not have the expertise you need. There are also consultants that can resolve major issues that are beyond the local capabilities—a dysfunctional unit, for example. Needless to say, such consultancies are very expensive; however, they almost always achieve efficient results that make the expense worthwhile.

There are of course a number of commercial training firms. Based on the authors' experience, commercial training firms do offer some general workplace skill training that the library staff finds valuable. Again, it is a question of finding the training you require at the time it is needed.

👥 AUTHORS' EXPERIENCE

Evans was fortunate to have enough training funds to allow for each support staff member to have up to $500 for attendance at work-related workshops, seminars, and so forth. This was in addition to funds for the professional staff ($1,500). He was fortunate to have a supervisor who understood the importance of having staff who were committed to lifelong learning.

Greenwell has worked at several institutions that strongly value supporting professional development. While the cost of attending professional meetings continues to increase substantially (the $1,500 allocation librarians receive was once ample but is now difficult to stretch beyond a single conference), it's important that the institution continue to commit the maximum amount of funding possible. This is important for both lifelong learning and staff morale.

Mika also made sure that each annual budget included funding for attendance at professional associations, plus he would encourage and evaluate individual requests for attendance at professional-related workshops or educational opportunities, providing funding where it complemented a faculty member's teaching or research.

⦀ CHECK THESE OUT

Marcia Trotta's *Staff Development on a Shoestring: A How-To-Do-It Manual for Librarians* (New York: Neal-Schuman, 2011) is an excellent resource. As the title states, its focus is having a sound T&D event even in a limited resources environment.

A good article is Lisa Johnston's "Tech Expo: A model for emerging technology education for library staff" (*Journal of Library Innovation* 3, no. 1: 66–85, 2012). Technology-focused events can stretch limited funding, especially if the event is a collaborative effort (see the following Author Experience sidebar).

Academic institutions, especially those with LIS degree programs, frequently offer workshops, certificate programs, and leadership training. Some of these programs are for individual career development, which is not an immediate or foreseeable library need. (We look at career development in some detail in chapter 22.) Think carefully when using library funding for individualized development—drawing on these funds to pay for T&D for individuals often can generate discontent among staff who are not offered similar opportunities.

State and national library associations are other training and development resources. These may also be surprisingly expensive because of costs that go beyond the workshop fee—travel, room, and board are obvious additional costs. The authors believe supporting conference attendance is worth the effort as there are more than T&D opportunities that result from such attendance. Examples include learning about new technological developments, being able to meet with all the library vendors at a single location and hearing about what other librarians are doing.

STAFF DEVELOPMENT DAY

Many libraries address the lack of T&D resources by having a local annual staff development day (SDD). Results vary depending upon the degree of planning that goes into the event. Some SDDs are planned by the staff and others by management. Julie Todaro and Mark Smith (2006) noted "As library directors, we know that a single well-planned and executed training session can have a tremendous effect and is often all that is possible" (p. vii). Given limited resources for T&D, in-house efforts may be your best opportunities to achieve some success. One big challenge efforts is when to scheduling an event—for it to be effective you want most, if not all, of the staff in attendance. Having everyone at an event means there is no staff no service for the public. Closing the library during normal operating hours is frowned upon by funding authorities. Holding the event when the library is normally closed is frowned upon by the staff. Although more time-consuming for event planners and presenters, it is preferable to offer the content two or more times during the SDD. Another possibility is to record the event for those who do not attend in person. Yet another option is to get permission to provide "comp time" (time off at a later date) and have the event on a day the library is officially closed.

Successful SDDs require time and effort, especially in terms of assessment and planning. Having a standing committee or group helps ensure events reflect both library needs and staff interests. Assessment requires looking at what was and was not effective

👥 AUTHORS' EXPERIENCE

Evans has had extensive experience with a large-scale "Tech Expo" event that was consortium based ("Vendor Day"). The event grew from a small local event to a major three-day program with more vendors wishing to participate than the consortium could handle. Evans's university and library hosted the annual event as it had thirty-four "smart classrooms" and four twenty-four-seat computer labs in one building. The last event Evans participated in was in 2005 with just over three hundred librarians in attendance to learn about forty-seven vendors' products and to participate in vendor training sessions. The cost for attendees was very modest because the vendors were happy to underwrite almost all the costs. Unlike professional conferences, the vendors were the sole focus for the librarians.

    Obviously, this was a special, perhaps unique, situation. However, it is an example of something you might be able to organize, on some scale, with consortia partners.

and thinking about immediate training needs and development activities. Planning goes beyond identifying a topic and presenter and includes issues such as space for the event, perhaps food or snacks, and some decorations to create a space that is less work-like, especially when the event is in a library space. Atmosphere can make a surprising difference in what attendees take away from the event.

    The following are some of the major pitfalls to avoid when putting on an SDD event:

- failure to plan soon enough to secure space when needed
- failure to offer topics that appeal to staff members and/or do not clarify the benefit for the library and staff
- failure to understand the importance of making the event enjoyable, developmental, and worth the time spent
- failure to have a quality event while staying within budget constraints
- failure to keep the number of topics covered to a realistic level

TEAM BUILDING

Is it necessary to have a discussion of teams as part of a T&D chapter? There are at least two reasons. One is that effective team performance rests on behavioral factors that are not typical in many workplaces. Skills such as accepting conflict as part of the work process and group decision making are rarely part of traditional work groups. A second factor is that there is a need to help those who are not part of the team to understand the changes in operating practices (more meeting time for teams and team accountability, for example).

    Team structure was a hot managerial topic in the recent past. However, as *The Economist* suggested in 2016, teams often are a major managerial challenge; "Profound changes in the workforce are making teams trickier to manage. Teams work best if their members have a strong common culture" (p. 71). Effective organizations have a common hallmark—excellent unit cooperation, tightly integrated activities, a staff that trusts one another. The word *teamwork* could be used to describe this environment and its process. Teams in the workplace have been with us for a long time in one form or another. They are not a new concept, despite what you might think after reading the management literature. They are, however, playing an ever-greater role in how organizations get things done. Over the past twenty-some years, organizations including libraries have undergone a flattening of their structures, resulting in fewer layers of management. In many cases, they have experienced downsizing or at least received no increase in staffing even as workloads increased. As a result, the staff must be more productive and flexible, and also be eager to learn new skills, and take on more responsibilities.

Management writers use the term *team* in a variety of ways when referring to work-place groups. The following is one definition of a workplace team that seems to capture today's environment: "A work group is made up of individuals who see themselves and who are seen by others as a social entity, who are interdependent because of the tasks they perform as members of the group, who are embedded in one or more larger social systems, and who perform tasks that affect others" (Guzzo and Dickson 1996, pp. 308-09). Perhaps two more elements ought to be part of the definition—team or work groups develop a shared commitment to one another, and the group is empowered to make decisions regarding their work activities. In her introduction to an interview with J. Richard Hackman, Diane Coutu (2011) wrote:

> Over the past couple of decades, a cult has grown up around teams. . . . The belief that working in teams makes us more creative and productive is so widespread that when faced with a challenging new task, leaders are quick to assume that teams are the best way to get the job done.
>
> Not so fast says J. Richard Hackman, the Edgar Pierce Professor of Social and Organizational Psychology at Harvard University and a leading expert on teams. . . . Most of the time, his research shows, team members don't even agree on what the team is supposed to be doing. (p. 1)

Some of the differences that exist between a true team environment and the traditional workplace are significant. Work teams call for consensus rather than command and control. They require acceptance of the idea that conflict (both positive and negative) is a normal part of its operations, and that those conflicts should be addressed in an open, honest manner. Reaching decisions in a team setting depends more on the group's knowledge than on a single person's opinion. In teams, the emphasis is on the "whys" more than on the "hows." Essentially, it requires a collaborative process within the team in order for the group to succeed. The above characteristics reflect skills and behavior that are not always present in the workplace and therefore call for training for team members.

The decision to employ teams—temporary or permanent—is not one to make lightly. Teams and time go together like bacon and eggs. Teams require thoughtful planning, a careful assessment of staff capabilities, and an assessment of the organization's ability to adjust to team operations *before* starting the selection of team members. Teams require careful, ongoing nurturing from the time they are created until they are disbanded. They also require a different, and rather complex, assessment process to ensure sound and proper accountability.

There are two broad categories of teams: integrated and self-managed. Integrated teams receive one or more tasks from a manager, and the team works out how and who will do what to achieve the desired outcome(s). Self-managed teams receive goals rather than tasks. They generally have a "contact" manager they can turn to for guidance and assistance but overall operate very independently. Needless to say, the issue of coordination between teams is a major concern for successful team operations. Another challenge for team-based organizations is performance evaluation and issues of accountability.

Teamwork is effective when trust and delegation are present and when the staff understand the concepts of authority and responsibility. Given the flatter hierarchies and extended service hours of most libraries, teamwork is an effective way to organize staff. You can form teams to coordinate work across a service, to work on specific aspects of service, or to act as a facilitator to change management.

The team needs to have a clear understanding of performance expectations as well as the markers that will measure progress and achievement. In addition, all team members have to understand the boundaries of the authority that is delegated to the team and who has the responsibility to ensure that the team works effectively and efficiently.

An area where team-based work differs from traditional work is accountability. In the United States, most workers are accustomed to being individually responsible for their work outcomes. Group accountability may be one of the most difficult concepts for team members to understand and accept. Teams *must* be accountable, and success or failure is a *team* responsibility. Having to accept that "my performance assessment" may be negatively affected by someone else's actions often does not always sit well. (An important feature of self-managing teams and their accountability is that the teams must be allowed to address member performance on an ongoing basis rather than have the external leader handle any problems.) The question becomes: are there staff who already have a sense of team accountability or appear capable of accepting the concept?

Transitioning to teams requires everyone—managers and staff—to rethink roles and responsibilities. The transition requires some T&D effort because it can require almost a seismic shift in how we think about work. Caesar Douglas (2002) noted that the transition period is critical to success and can take twenty-four months or more to complete satisfactorily. One of the first managerial shifts must be from a "command and control" mode of behavior to one of acting as an advisor, which may not be an easy transition for some people. Another issue for managers is their self-monitoring ability. (Self-monitoring is the ability to strategically adjust your "influencing behavior" to fit the situation.) For the staff, adapting team behaviors and accepting those behaviors is critical. One behavior some people have difficulty with is group decision making and the amount of time that it takes. In group decision making, conflict and its resolution are a part of the process. For some people conflict is something to avoid at almost any cost, including conflicts involving strongly held views. A few individuals have significant difficulty having their performance judged on the basis of the group's performance.

One sound reason to employ a team is to address library projects (long- or short-term). Even members of short-term teams are likely to need some training for their first experience on a work team. Some of the common challenges for newcomers to team work are group decision making, the need to compromise, and the nature of team accountability. A major plus of team usage is that teams allow a managerial leader to bring together staff from throughout the library who have the skills for a specific need. Needless to say, creating a new work group requires time for the team members to establish working relationships and, significantly, to build the trust that is essential for a successful outcome.

There are two key areas where teams need T&D efforts—negotiation and compromising. Team members need to understand the whys and hows of these skills. Both are essential for the group decision making process that effective teams employ. Traditional work groups rarely need to exercise such skills, which is why there is a need for training.

To be truly effective, the team members should be cross-trained. That is, two or more members should be capable of performing any team task. Such training means that sick days and vacation leave will not disrupt team activities. Getting the right mix of members can be challenging both in terms of team members' interests and team requirements. Another area where training is almost always necessary is group accountability. Even individuals who have played team sports may not have experience with team accountability, because when a sports team has failures, more often than not, it is the coach rather than the entire team who becomes accountable. Accountability in teams is also a significant managerial challenge.

LIBRARIES AND TEAMS

Not too long ago, some libraries shifted to a team structure and even tried using "empowered teams." There was a belief that such a structure would produce better performance results. Today there are only a few such operations. Although teams are still an important tool in the managerial toolbox, the team structure is not frequently used. Some academic libraries, such as the University of Maryland Libraries, have tried the approach and since dropped the idea.

The best-known team-based library is the University of Arizona Library. The library received a great deal of attention in the early 1990s when it moved to a team-based structure. If you are interested, there are two articles about the Arizona model: Shelley Phipps's (2004) "The System Design Approach to Organizational Development: The University of Arizona Model" and Carla J. Stoffle and Cheryl Cuillier's (2011) "From Surviving to Thriving." (Note: Stoffle and Cuillier were lead individuals in moving to a team-based structure in academic libraries.) There is also an article about using the approach in a public library: Betsy Bernfeld's (2004) "Developing a Team Management Structure in a Public Library." In 2011, Lihong Zhu published an article discussing the team approach in a more limited fashion, "Use of Teams in Technical Services in Academic Libraries."

🔒 KEY POINTS TO REMEMBER

- Enhancing organizational performance is a never-ending process.
- Both organizations and their staffs must engage in lifelong learning if there is to be success long-term.
- Organizational development has a long history of helping organizations to adapt and learn from a changing environment.
- Learning organizations tend to be more responsive to a changing environment because they value and act upon new ideas.
- T&D can be a frustrating activity in an environment of limited resources.
- Team structures require special managerial skills and generate additional training and development efforts.
- Moving to team-based approaches brings with it the need to provide training about the team concept and its operations and assessment for all staff, not just potential team members.

REFERENCES

Anderson, Donald L. 2017. *Organizational Development: The Process of Leading Organizational Change*. 4th ed. Thousand Oaks, CA: Sage Publications.

Bernfeld, Betsy. 2004. "Developing a Team Management Structure in a Public Library." *Library Trends* 53, no. 1: 112-28.

Coutu, Diane. 2011. "Why Teams Don't Work." In *Harvard Business Review on Building Better Teams*, 1-18. Boston, MA: Harvard Business Review Press.

Denda, Kayo, and Jennifer Hunter. 2016. "Building 21st Century Skills and Creating Communities: A Team-Based Engagement Framework for Student Employment in Academic Libraries." *Journal of Library Administration* 56, no. 3: 251-65.

Douglas, Ceasar. 2002. "The Effects of Managerial Influence Behavior on the Transition to Self-Deleted Work Teams." *Journal of Managerial Psychology* 17, nos. 7/8: 628-35.

The Economist. 2016. "Team Spirit." 418, no. 8981: 71.

Gino, Francesca, and Bradley Staats. 2015. "Why Organizations Don't Learn: Our Traditional Obsessions—Success, Taking Action, Fitting In, and Relying on Experts—Undermine Continuous Improvement." *Harvard Business Review* 93, no. 11: 110-18.

Guzzo, Richard, and Marcus Dickson. 1996. "Teams in Organizations: Recent Research and Performance Effectiveness." In *Annual Review of Psychology*, edited by James Spence, 307-38. Palo Alto, CA: Annual Reviews.

Moussa, Mahmoud, Adela Murray, and Nuttawuth Muenjohn. 2018. "A Conceptual Framework of the Factors Influencing Innovation in Public Sector Organizations." *Journal of Developing Area* 52, no. 3: 231-40.

Phipps, Shelley E. 2004. "The System Design Approach to Organizational Development: The University of Arizona Model." *Library Trends* 53, no. 1: 68-111.

Pokharel, Mohan P., and Sang Ok Choi. 2015. "Exploring the Relationships between the Learning Organization and Organizational Performance." *Management Research Review* 38, no. 2: 126-48.

Senge, Peter M. 2006. *The Fifth Discipline: The Art and Practice of the Learning Organization*. Rev. ed. New York: Doubleday.

Stoffle, Carla J., and Cheryl Cuillier. 2011. "From Surviving to Thriving." *Journal of Library Administration* 51, no. 1: 130-55.

Todaro, Julie, and Mark L. Smith. 2006. *Training Library Staff and Volunteers to Provide Extra Ordinary Customer Service*. New York: Neal-Schuman.

Visser, Max, and Kim Van der Togt. 2016. "Learning in Public Sector Organizations: A Theory of Action Approach." *Public Organization Review* 16, no. 2: 235-49.

Zhu, Lihong. 2011. "Use of Teams in Technical Services in Academic Libraries." *Library Collections, Acquisitions, and Technical Services* 35, nos. 2-3: 69-82.

CHAPTER 15

Managing Diversity

Fostering diversity is seen as tool for enhancing a vibrant, post-nationalist society by governments favoring a liberal immigration regime; universities seek to create a faculty and student body that mirrors the diverse ethnic and racial composition of the population at large; and business organizations believe that enhancing diversity will lead to creativity and innovation.

Andreas Wimmer, 2016

Demographic trends indicate the United States will become a majority minority country in the near future. To help guide local communities during this time of rapid social change, libraries and librarians are developing programs, services and collections that are as diverse as the populations they serve.

ALA News, April 16, 2018

A diverse workforce is important to librarianship. As a result, the recruitment of librarians of color has remained a priority; additionally, ensuring that those individuals are retained and advancing is of equal importance because it speaks to the profession's ability to maintain a diverse workforce.

Kimberly Bugg, 2016

Because the vast majority of U.S. libraries are public sector institutions, they are open to almost anyone and also provide some level of service. Being open to almost anyone regardless of social, educational, and economic status (the status categories could fill the balance of this page) creates challenges for library services and collections as well as possible staffing concerns.

There are a variety of federal, state, and local laws and regulations that relate to diversity. Consider also the politics of diversity—there are strong and divergent views about how, or even if, society should engage with the issue. All of that makes managing diversity a challenge for any organization, but especially those in the public sector. As Khailova and Ladell (2018) noted, "With the changes in national leadership and the issuance of new policies aimed at reducing the number of newcomers in the country, 2017 was a divisive year. . . . Despite these actions, American libraries continue to state strongly that libraries are for everyone" (p.16).

Public sector organizations have broad-based service populations, most of which have very diverse characteristics. "One size fits all" simply does not apply. In this chapter, we explore how libraries may go about managing diversity. In 1999, Janice Simmons-Welburn

||||| CHECK THIS OUT

A good review of public sector diversity efforts is Jocelyn McGrandle's "Understanding Diversity Management in the Public Sector: A Case for Contingency Theory" (*International Journal of Public Administration* 40, no. 6: 526–37, 2017).

---

wrote, "Colleges and university libraries, their parent institutions, governments, and corporations have only begun to embrace and struggle with diversity in the workplace" (p. 205). To a large degree you could say that about 2019. Certainly, there has been some progress, but often there are strong sentiments against that progress in whatever aspect the efforts are addressing.

quote —

A diverse workforce obviously requires managers who are sensitive to and understand diversity issues. Legislation has brought some positive benefits in terms of diversity, but cultural experiences influence the way that we, as individuals, approach diversity. The politics of diversity are complex, contentious, and challenging. Culture influences the ways that people interact—sometimes consciously, sometimes subconsciously. Diversity touches on many managerial responsibilities relating to both the workforce and the community served.

From a library perspective, the matter might seem cut and dried—service to all. What seems straightforward becomes challenging when publicly funded libraries and the community providing the funding are deeply split about diversity. The ALA Office for Diversity (www.ala.org/aboutala/offices/diversity) offers a wealth of information about diversity issues.

One contentious issue is the question of how appropriate it is for libraries to provide collections in immigrants' native languages. *American Libraries* devoted much of its November 2007 issue to discussions of bilingual collections, in this case Spanish language materials. There was an essay for the pro and con sides of the debate. The content of the article sparked a number of letters to the editor reflecting the differences in opinion about the matter even within the profession. The discussion did, and probably still does, reflect the deep division in U.S. society regarding cultural diversity.

Almost every aspect of library operations carries with it the potential for raising a diversity issue. There are times when the divide is between the majority community's values and professional values. We believe there are good reasons for engaging in activities that support diversity:

- First, there is the very human reason that this affects everyone who interacts with the library, the staff, and the service community. Everyone

---

||||| CHECK THESE OUT

Alire, Camila A. 2001. "Diversity and Leadership: The Color of Leadership." *Journal of Library Administration* 32, nos. 3/4: 99–104.

Maurice Wheeler's *Unfinished Business: Race, Equity, and Diversity in Library and Information Science Education* (Lanham, MD: Scarecrow Press, 2005) is a useful, if slightly dated, title.

||||| CHECK THESE OUT

The citations for the material mentioned above are:

Kniffel, Leonard. 2007. "English Only Is English Lonely." *American Libraries* 38, no. 10: 3.

Quesada, Todd Douglas. 2007. "Spanish Spoken Here." *American Libraries* 38, no. 10: 41–42, 44.

Stephens, Julia. 2007. "English Spoken Here." *American Libraries* 38, no. 10: 42–43, 44.

"Opinion: English—Only Views Varied." 2008. *American Libraries* 39, nos. 1/2: 8–11.

---

has a need to achieve her or his individual goals. For staff, the goals may relate to their career or personal life and the users need to gain the greatest possible benefit from the service.

- Second, it makes good sense to create a collegial environment in which people are viewed as individuals. This encourages staff to become members of a team, and users are welcomed as valued members of the community. It optimizes both the potential of individuals and their productivity.
- Third, diversity is a factor in attracting and retaining the best talent among the staff. Staff turnover carries both visible and invisible costs.
- Fourth, when staff members know they are valued and take pride in the quality of their work, it influences how they interact with the community, which in turn, increases the comfort level of users and raises the overall performance of the service. As the business sector discovered, investing in good practice brings benefits for everyone and makes good sense.

DEFINING DIVERSITY

Some writers and organizations take a narrow view that relates diversity mainly to racial or cultural identification. We believe diversity encompasses far more than these two important areas. It can involve cultural, religious, language, age, disability, and sexual orientation

 SOMETHING TO CONSIDER

When talking about ethnic and racial diversity Camila Alire, the coauthor of the third edition of this book, noted that most of her colleagues would claim that they are not personally racist. She believed them. However, she makes a distinction between personal and institutional racism. Institutional racism is when the values, beliefs, and attitudes are so embedded in the institution or library organization that when someone who joins the institution has a different set of values, beliefs, and/or attitudes, he or she is discriminated against, either overtly or subtly. And, many of the well-established coworkers don't even realize they are doing it. Can you think of any situation where you have experienced this within an organization or library with which you are or have been affiliated?

||||| CHECK THIS OUT

Geert Hofstede's website (https://geerthofstede.com/landing-page/) is worth looking at.

---

in addition to racial and gender concerns. We also believe generational differences can be a diversity issue. You can probably understand how all these issues make defining diversity difficult and certainly not possible in a few short sentences.

We prefer the broader view as described by Geert Hofstede (1991) in his book *Cultures and Organizations: Software of the Mind*:

> Every person carries within him or herself patterns of thinking, feeling, and potential acting which were learned throughout their lifetime. Much of it has been acquired in early childhood. . . . As soon as certain patterns have established themselves . . . he [*sic*] must unlearn these before being able to learn something different, and unlearning is more difficult than learning for the first time. (p. 4)

By thinking about the way in which beliefs such as diversity are formed and the crucial issue of "unlearning," it becomes easier to understand why diversity is complex and sensitive. Each country develops its own unique immigration policies. Some encourage assimilation, while others encourage integration. Either policy will, or should, influence library services, particularly those in the public sector.

We expect you can understand why developing a short, comprehensive definition of diversity is not easy. Miriam Brewer (2011) provided an interesting way of defining diversity:

Diversity is:

D = different styles, disabilities
I = individuals, intelligence
V = variety, veteran status
E = education, economic status, ethnicity
R = race, religion
S = sexual orientation, social class
I = immigration status
T = thought processes, traits
Y = youth, years (p. 28)

HOW DO YOU VIEW CULTURAL DIVERSITY?

One way to begin to understand the complexity of cultural diversity is to discover your own viewpoint by examining the concept through the ten lenses proposed by Williams (2001). He identified the ways people may approach race, culture, nationality, and ethnicity (the approach was validated in a large-scale Gallup poll.) His categories are:

- Assimilationist favors nationalistic and patriotic ideals.
- Colorblind views people as individuals (ignoring race and color has an equalizing effect).

- Culturalcentrist improves welfare by accentuating history and identity.
- Elitist believes in the superiority of the upper class (keeps advantages through social ties).
- Integrationist believes in breaking down barriers by having people live and work together.
- Meritocratist believes dreams will come true if you have the abilities and work hard.
- Multiculturalist celebrates diversity and its contribution to national character and history.
- Seclusionist wants to protect oneself (different groups should live and work apart).
- Transcendent focuses on the human spirit (diversity contributes to the richness of humanity).
- Victim/caretaker feels one is suffering from oppression and deserves compensation.

In which of the categories do you see yourself? Self-awareness is a building block in emotional intelligence.

MANAGERIAL RESPONSIBILITY

There is a considerable body of legislation related to diversity, addressing issues such as equal employment opportunity, equal pay, and antidiscrimination. Sometimes, in addition to federal laws, each state has a slightly different approach. Learning the details of every change in the laws is not realistic for general managerial leaders. Keeping up-to-date on such matters is the responsibility of human resources and legal staff. It is also their responsibility to advise general managerial leaders of the changes that may impact them.

As a managerial leader, your responsibilities with regard to diversity are to:

- create an organizational culture that values diversity in all its manifestations;
- ensure that everyone has and demonstrates respect for the views and experiences of others; and
- implement practices based on sound policies so that diversity brings benefits to the library—for both staff members and users.

The key to success is to make flexibility a central component that will both support and retain staff and users.

You often read about organizations having to defend their staffing practices as they relate to hiring, promotion, and salaries. For example, many women have experienced sex discrimination. Institutional discrimination results in barriers to promotion if top management prefers to promote men to senior posts. Carlson, Kacmar, and Whitten (2006) conducted a study in 2005 that compared attitudes about female executives to those of 1965. Data showed that female respondents indicated steady support for the concept of women in management and a favorable attitude on the part of men had increased from 35 percent to 88 percent. Despite attempts to level the playing field when it came to abilities, however, only 32 percent of men thought women had to be exceptional to succeed in contrast to the 70 percent of women who felt that way. The researchers were unsure whether men were not seeing the barriers for women's advancement anymore or simply were providing politically correct responses. In the academic library sector, women hold the majority of directorships, and in some cases their compensation exceeds that of men in similar posts (Deyrup 2004).

INDIVIDUAL RESPONSIBILITY

Every staff member has a personal responsibility to recognize and value the differing attitudes of the people with whom they interact. Earlier we noted that individual values will vary, which creates different expectations when it comes to interactions. Unlike language, some differences are more subtle. For example, attitudes toward time vary: some people are relaxed about time, while others are rigid, which can cause conflicts. The rituals in meeting another person may vary from the warm smile, friendly handshake, and use of first names to great formality and using titles rather than names.

If you have lived in a different culture, you will better understand the degree of shock that a newcomer colleague or user experiences in a new society. For a newcomer, the challenge lies in identifying and understanding the values of the community. Often these values are not obvious or stated, and the newcomer has much to learn before adaptation takes place.

We mention culture shock because every staff member needs to understand how newcomers and new users feel during the process of acculturation. We all can experience frustration, helplessness, and perhaps hostility when faced with a new environment, as we compare the old and familiar life or organization with the new one. Remember that you don't have to move from one geographic location to another—the shock can happen when you simply change jobs.

ROLE OF PROFESSIONAL ASSOCIATIONS

ALA vigorously pursues programs to increase equal opportunities in the library workforce. Since the 1970s, ALA has recognized that people of color were underrepresented in the profession at large and adopted a leadership role to recruit and retain staff. Meetings and training sessions have been held at the national, regional, and state levels to exchange ideas and experiences about ways to improve the situation. ALA's Spectrum Initiative offers scholarships, mentoring, and leadership training (www.ala.org/advocacy/spectrum/)

ALA's Office of Diversity provides diversity statistics on topics such as gender, age, and race within the library profession (www.ala.org/advocacy/diversity/diversityresearch statistics). ALA also provides ideas for improving and maintaining a focus on diversity, but it is up to managerial leaders to make the library a more diverse workplace that serves all people.

PLANNING FOR DIVERSITY

The majority of libraries have a parent organization that holds the responsibility for developing a mission statement and policies to ensure that statutory diversity requirements are met. The responsibility of library managerial leaders is to ensure that these organizational policies become part of the library's planning process and to work with staff to ensure that good practice is observed. Two other responsibilities of the parent body are to commit funding to implement diversity policies and to monitor goals. Royse, Conner, and Miller (2006) discussed the design, methodology, and outcomes of a diversity climate assessment survey that produced benchmarks for measuring the progress and success of diversity programs. ALA provides examples of plans from large and small services that can be adapted to other types of information services (www.ala.org/advocacy/diversity/workplace/diversity planning).

Kendall (1994) made a number of useful points about successfully transitioning to a hospitable working environment, including the following observations:

- Top management must genuinely and seriously commit to an ongoing examination of its attitudes as well as its policies and procedures.
- The organization must view diversity as a long-term, multifaceted, continual process, not as an event or a quick fix.
- The organization must expect and be willing to deal with discomfort and resistance.
- The organization must not avoid discussions on institutional racism when addressing diversity and multicultural environments.
- The organization must develop a core staff willing to commit time and energy to bringing about a hospitable work environment for all people.
- The organization must know that its diversity activities will mirror its other activities.

There will be challenges in evaluating the process of making a successful transition to a hospitable working environment. As Kendall (1994) stresses, difficulties can arise when:

- measuring changes in attitude,
- there is a lack of a discrete beginning and ending to the tasks, or
- stress caused by other events in the library manifests itself as resistance to diversity.

We stress the importance of monitoring performance. Data on recruitment, promotion, and retention are available. Adding qualitative information gathered from exit interviews, appraisal interviews, or surveys also helps you monitor progress toward diversity goals.

R. Roosevelt Thomas wrote about what he labeled diversity and diversity management (D&DM). He identified five factors that are needed to create a sound diversity plan:

- Identify and adopt contextual definitions.
- Identify and develop the organization's mission, vision, and strategy.
- Address three key strategic decisions—type of diversity to address, using a "fish or teach to fish" approach with staff, in what areas to apply the plan.
- Plan for transition and application.
- Audit organizational culture to determine whether it supports the enterprise's D&DM aspirations (2011, pp. 22-25).

He also suggested that you build an infrastructure to support implementation of D&DM.

LIBRARY GOVERNANCE AND DIVERSITY

Appointments to governing boards or advisory groups should reflect the composition of the community served. This may sound like a statement of the obvious, but it can be tricky to achieve a balanced membership. It is often easy to identify regular users or those known to be supporters of the service, but it is useful to have representatives from groups who seldom use the services or who do not use them at all. Doing this can provide a more balanced view of stakeholders values and beliefs.

Board membership is one facet of the managerial leader's role. Being visible and known within the service community has many benefits. Political and social skills and networking help to achieve the vital balance. When writing about recruiting Latino public library trustees Alire and Ayala (2007, pp. 184–85) stated that the Latino trustee could be the liaison who could assist the library in the following:

- identifying potential Latino staffing prospects
- recommending effective programs to attract your underserved Latino community
- working on good public relations between the library and the Latino community
- developing library and Latino partnerships or networking with individuals and organizations

This advice could be adapted for other minority groups.

DIVERSITY PROGRAM AND STAFF

Many organizations in all sectors have diversity programs that attempt to address both internal (staffing) and external (service and customer) concerns. Careful examination of such efforts suggests they are more about avoiding lawsuits than they are about enhancing diversity (Dobbin and Kalev 2016; Morse 2016; Burrell, 2016). There is an organizational liability when there is a breach of laws or regulations and, at times, guidelines related to diversity and fair employment practices. Dobbin and Kalev in writing about their review of over 800 such programs and interviewing hundreds of front-line managers suggested that organizations "get better results when they ease up on the control tactics" (p. 54).

Diversity programs have two broad categories of concern—internal (inter-staff relationships and composition, for example) and external (services for diverse users and staff interactions with the service population, for example). On the internal side there are the employment aspects—hiring, promotions, and the like—and staff interrelationships. Likewise, the external side has two broad concerns: equitable service and customizing a service for a particular group (by providing resources in a language or topic, for example). Our example of Spanish language collections in public libraries earlier in this chapter illustrates making a special effort for a group is not always without controversy.

Program success usually results from taking a positive approach rather than a "don't do this" effort. Another success factor is working on biases; personal biases are difficult to change but the reality is that those biases are at the center of why advancing diversity is such a slow process. While programs may not succeed in changing personal biases, they can be effective in developing the ability to work more effectively with different cultures (both among staff and with users). A common label for this is "cultural competence." Essentially, cultural competence is the ability to respect cultural differences and work effectively with people of different backgrounds. Also, the notion of "culture" is generally broadly interpreted as "diverse," and goes beyond country of origin to include such characteristics as race and religion.

Ideally, a library's staff reflects the composition of the service community. In reality, this is more likely to be a goal than an achievement. Our earlier discussion of ALA's Diversity Counts illustrated the difference between the goal and the reality. Certainly, there are fewer minority graduates in the pool of potential recruits. Concern also extends to the question of identifying staff for promotion when there are fewer members of minority groups ready for the next step. It takes time to achieve diversity goals, and tokenism is a risk.

Regular training programs help ensure that existing staff—both paid and volunteer— are culturally competent and sensitive to all aspects of diversity. Offering an in-library program can provide additional support and assist in networking.

Communication styles differ among cultures and can impact both inter-staff relationships and as those with library users. Consider the contrasts between the Japanese and the American approaches to communication. The Japanese may be thought to communicate by not stating matters directly, while Americans often communicate in a very direct way. In some cultures, it is not usual to question a "superior" person, even for trivial matters. Making assumptions about the level of awareness of local practices and customs is not the wisest course of action. Personal space while in face-to-face conversation varies from very close to some distance apart. Eye contact while speaking to a person is another cultural variable. With a diverse work staff such differences can create small tensions.

An issue that can create staff concerns is religious observance. The organization may prefer that everyone conform to the holidays and dominant religious festivals of the country, but this practice can be problematic for those of other religious beliefs who observe the holidays of their faith. A positive, flexible approach works best in organizations open to the public. For example, within multicultural communities, some staff may be quite willing to trade holidays, thus allowing for more flexible service hours. It can be a win-win situation.

Today's libraries very likely have paid staff and volunteers from different generations. These generations have different general approaches to work such as employment expectations and work versus personal time. Often such differences create some tension.

The expertise of retired employees who serve as library volunteers can benefit a library. Generally, these individuals are self-disciplined, with a strong respect for orderly processes and a stable organization. Baby boomers (born between 1946 and 1964) comprise the largest of the generations. In their youth, many were rebellious and open-minded and were known for questioning authority. However, by middle age many had become more conservative in their approach to work.

Gen Xers (born between 1965 and 1979) often grew up in homes where both parents worked and thus were on their own sooner than the earlier generations. They tend to be very self-confident, individualistic, self-reliant, and often irreverent, especially about the older generations. In terms of work, they tend to focus on relationships and outcomes rather than on processes and organizational structure. Gen Y (born between 1980 and 1999) are considered the technology generation; they grew up with the web and all the other information technologies we take for granted today. They are more than adept at multitasking. They are a now-oriented generation, and they are not used to waiting long for anything (even responses from supervisors).

The newest generation, sometimes labeled Linksters, Gen Z, the Digital Generation, or Gen Next, is entering the workforce in growing numbers. The slow economic recovery may generate values that more closely resemble those who grew up during the Great Depression than the values of other generations.

SOCIAL JUSTICE AND DIVERSITY

There are a variety of definitions of social justice. However, they all share some common components. The first of these is that every person has a right to be respected. Another component is every person has dignity and value. A third component is that people have the right to achieve the maximum of their capabilities—not what someone else says their abilities are. Fourth, they have the right to equitable treatment. Associated with those rights is the idea that social organizations have a responsibility to advance social justice. Libraries of different types have greater or lesser amounts of responsibility to implement social justice into their operations (internally and externally).

In 2015, ALA incorporated the concepts of social justice and "public good" into its Core Values of Librarianship: "the foundation of modern librarianship rests on an essential set of core values which define, inform, and guide all professional practice. These are:

- Access
- Confidentiality/Privacy
- Democracy
- Diversity
- Education and Lifelong Learning
- Intellectual Freedom
- Preservation
- The Public Good
- Professionalism
- Service
- Social Responsibility
  (www.ala.org/aboutala/governance/policymanual/updatedpolicymanual/
  section2/40corevalues)

In a very real sense, the profession has been trying to implement social justice for a very long time. There are several ALA statements which have been in place for years that have reflected one or more of the components of social justice. These include the Freedom to Read, the Freedom to View, the Library Bill of Rights, and the Code of Ethics. There are a number of others, just search the ALA website using terms such as diversity and social justice.

PROVIDING SERVICE TO A DIVERSE COMMUNITY

In the hustle and bustle of daily work, members of the profession may sometimes forget that libraries, especially public libraries, play an important role in society. One of those roles is integration; that is, assisting newcomers as well as those of other marginal groups to become more comfortable in society. The second, almost opposite role, is assisting in identity formulation. Many individuals sense they are not the same as other people and have a sense of isolation. Through appropriate library resources, they can learn they are not alone and begin to identify with similar individuals.

Libraries have long worked to provide equitable treatment and service to the diverse members service population to the extent their resources allow. However, diversity needs far exceed the available resources. When you consider the staffing concerns, collection resources, and service needs for each of the varied groups that could benefit from special attention, it is clear that there is not enough funding. Sometimes it is possible to identify an activity that will serve the needs of two or more groups and thus reduce the number of unmet needs. However, those are few in number and many more unmet needs remain.

As an example of the challenges, think about reference service. A library may well have culturally competent staff, yet some of the people who could use its services don't for a variety of reasons. Some years ago, Liu and Redfern (1997) identified five common reasons why minorities did not use reference assistance in an academic library for the following reasons:

- They fear asking stupid questions.
- They fear that their English was not good enough.
- They fear that they won't understand the answers well enough.
- They did not think of asking questions.
- They did not understand the role of the reference librarian.

These findings are likely to be common in any culturally diverse community and perhaps even stronger in a public library setting. Public libraries may be forbidding to those who do not speak the language of the community, especially if they are first-time users. Without expending too much effort, you can probably rework the above barriers to fit almost any library service. Having respect for people and their culture is an important element in providing good service and promoting public good.

Staffing can be a big challenge, especially for public service activities. When one or more staff members do not respect certain categories of users, there can be substantial damage to the library's reputation in some segments of the service community—not just within the group that experiences the lack of respect.

It is a fact of life that individuals hold personal views, sometimes extremely negative, about those they consider "other." It is also a fact of life that such individuals have the right to hold whatever views they wish and, within certain legal limits, the right to express their views. Managerial leaders face the challenge of trying to control such expressions in the workplace. Managers have some laws on their side, but they are not lawyers, much less the police. Certainly, they can and should make legal guidelines clear to the staff. They can model expected behavior and provide sensitivity workshops. The human resources department may be of some help.

⦀ CHECK THIS OUT

Although it is an older publication, one of the best books on managing diversity remains *Achieving Diversity: A How-To-Do-It Manual for Librarians*, edited by Barbara J. Dewey and Loretta Parham (New York: Neal-Schuman, 2006).

One staffing approach can be very successful, if expensive. Hiring bilingual staff is one way to reduce user barriers. If the person is both bilingual and of a cultural heritage that reflects the community, so much the better, as people tend to more easily relate to "one of our own." Being able to do this is difficult even today. As Morales, Knowles, and Borg (2014) noted, "Given the extreme lack of diversity within the library profession efforts must be made to attract and retain members of underrepresented groups into librarianship. . . . Across the spectrum of library types (academic, school, special, and public) the demographic makeup of the profession has remained predominantly white female" (p. 440–441).

One member of our Advisory Board commented, "Good Luck" when it comes to managing cultural conflict. We agree that a little luck comes in handy when it comes to this challenge. We also believe that by following the ideas in this chapter you can reduce the amount of luck you'll need.

🔒 KEY POINTS TO REMEMBER

- Cultural diversity touches on many of the managerial leader's responsibilities.
- Cultural diversity affects everyone who interacts with the library.
- We each have a lens through which we view diversity.
- There are equal rights laws and regulations that must be observed.
- Everyone has the responsibility to value and recognize differences in society.
- An acknowledgment of cultural diversity must be embedded in planning.
- Developing and supervising a diverse staff presents challenges.
- Cultural diversity should affect service to users in a positive manner.

REFERENCES

ALA News. 2018. "Libraries Champion Nation's Diversity through Dia, April 30." April 16. www.ala.org/news/press-releases/2018/04/libraries-champion-nation-s-diversity-through-d-april-30.

Alire, Camila, and Jacqueline Ayala. 2007. *Serving Latino Communities: A How-To-Do-It Manual for Librarians*. 2nd ed. New York: Neal-Schuman.

Brewer, Miriam L. 2011. "Diversity and Cultural Taboos: What Your Recruitment Practices Say About You." *Franchising World* 43, no. 6: 28–30.

Burrell, Lisa. 2016. "We Just Can't Handle Diversity. *Harvard Business Review* 94, nos.7/8: 71–74.

Bugg, Kimberley. 2016. "The Perceptions of People of Color in Academic Libraries Concerning the Relationship between Retention and Advancement as Middle Managers." *Journal of Library Administration* 56, no. 4: 428–43.

Carlson, Dawn S., K. Michele Kacmar, and Dwayne Whitten. 2006. "What Men Think They Know About Executive Women." *Harvard Business Review* 84, no. 9: 28–29.

Deyrup, Marta Mestrovic. 2004. "Is the Revolution Over? Gender, Economic, and Professional Parity in Academic Library Leadership Positions." *College and Research Libraries* 65, no. 3: 242–50.

Dobbin, Frank, and Alexandra Kalev. 2016. "Why Diversity Programs Fail—And What Works Better." *Harvard Business Review* 94, nos.7/8: 52–60.

Hofstede, Geert. 1991. *Cultures and Organizations: Software of the Mind*. New York: McGraw-Hill.

Kendall, Frances E. 1994. "Creating a Multicultural Environment in the Library." In *Cultural Diversity in Libraries,* edited by Donald E. Riggs and Patricia A. Tarin, 76–91. New York: Neal-Schuman.

Khailova, Ladislava, and Kathy Ladell. 2018. "Partnering for Social Justice: Libraries Working with Other Organizations to Reach Out to Diverse Communities." *ILA Reporter* 36, no. 2: 16–19.

Liu, Mengxiong, and Bernice Redfern. 1997. "Information-Seeking Behavior of Multicultural Students: A Case Study at San Jose State University." *College and Research Libraries* 58, no. 4: 348–54.

Morales, Myrna, Em Knowles, and Chris Bourg. 2014. "Diversity, Social Justice, and the Future of Libraries." *portal: Libraries and the Academy* 14, no. 3: 339–451.

Morse, Gardiner. 2016. "Designing a Bias-Free Organization." *Harvard Business Review* 94, nos.7/8: 62–67.

Royse, Molly, Tiffani Conner, and Tamara Miller. 2006. "Charting a Course for Diversity: An Experience in Climate Assessment." *portal: Libraries and the Academy* 6, no. 1: 23–45.

Simmons-Welburn, Janice. 1999. "Using Culture as a Construct for Achieving Diversity in Human Resources Management." *Library Administration and Management* 13, no. 4: 205–09.

Thomas, R. Roosevelt. 2011. "Developing and Implementing a Diversity Plan." *Franchising World* 43, no. 6: 22–25.

Williams, Mark. 2001. *The Ten Lenses: Your Guide to Living and Working in a Multicultural World*. Sterling, VA: Capital Books.

Wimmer, Andreas. 2016. "Is Diversity Detrimental? Ethnic Fractionalization, Public Goods Provision, and the Historical Legacies of Stateness." *Comparative Political Studies* 49, no.11: 1407–45.

CHAPTER 16

Motivating Staff

Creating and maintaining a high-performance work culture that is flexible is essential. Creating a work culture where people love to work is even better.

Sara Rose, 2016

Job satisfaction is a global attitude that individuals maintain about their jobs based on perceptions of their jobs.

Edward Jernigan and Joyce M. Beggs, 2015

My experience is that staff can live through most changes as long as they understand why.

Mark Dehmlow, 2016

Encouragement and motivation go hand in hand, but they are not the same. Motivation is more general....Encouragement means pointing out a person's potential. . . . Top managers understand these basic truths about employee encouragement and motivation.

Harvey Mackay, 2018

A reality is organizational success ultimately rests on how well employees choose to perform their duties. The operative word is *choose*. All other aspects of managerial leadership will not lead to organizational success if employees choose to perform at a low level. In the absence of forced labor, workers do decide their level of performance, both short- and long-term. As noted in the Jernigan and Beggs quotation, the decision is based on personal perceptions of the tasks as well as the operating environment. Essentially, their performance reflects their level of job satisfaction or dissatisfaction. Also keep in mind that a satisfied employee tends to be more committed to the organization.

What are the factors that affect a person's decisions regarding work? We believe the overarching factor is the organizational climate. That climate reflects a number of interacting components—trust, respect, recognition, and organizational stability for example. Given the interacting character of such factors, it is not surprising that creating an environment like the one suggested in the Rose (2016) opening quotation is far from easy.

Job satisfaction and organizational commitment tend to vary by sector. On one level, public and nonprofit personnel usually have a high level of commitment to their organization. This is reflected in a least one clear way: they stay with their organizations even when they could earn more in the profit sector (think of librarians, teachers, and social workers, for example). Bradley E. Wright (2007) wrote about commitment and salary differences: "The existence of sectoral differences in reward preferences is not just a matter of purely academic interest; rather, it is assumed that these differences have a practical influence on performance of public sector organizations" (p. 54). In a way, organizational missions and professional values provide an intangible but real reward. Wright's article about his research supported this notion, "The intrinsic value that employees see in the mission of their organization was found to influence their work motivation by increasing the importance they place on their own work" (p. 60).

On another level, their job satisfaction can be lower than it might be due to lack of recognition of the value of their efforts by a goodly number of the general public. There is some perception that public agencies and their employees are bureaucratic, do as little as possible, and that what they do is ineffectual. Such articulated views in the press and elsewhere do little to enhance job satisfaction, the sense of being valued, and organizational commitment.

Libraries, like other public and nonprofit organizations, face some special challenges when it comes to creating the workplace for which people "love" to work. For example, rewards and recognition possibilities tend to be limited. The general public is often skeptical, if not hostile, views toward public sector employees in the broadest sense, which in turn can hurt staff morale. On the plus side for libraries, the public generally has a high level of regard and trust in their operations and performance. That makes it easier for managerial leaders to create a positive work environment and generate higher work satisfaction.

The vast majority of employee motivation research is conducted in the for-profit sector; only a small percentage has focused on nonprofit organizations and even less work has been specifically focused on libraries. However, public service motivation (PSM) research has a history of more than twenty years. The research focus is on why people choose to work in public service positions. Although the initial focus was on government employees, researchers have expanded their interest to most "helping" professions. Perry and Wise (1990) defined PSM as an "individual's predisposition to respond to motives grounded primarily or uniquely in public institutions and organizations" (p. 363). They suggested that the occupation choice (service work and helping others) and the relatively low salaries for such work indicate that what motivates service-oriented people might well be different from what motivates people in other job categories.

In 2010, Perry, Hondeghem, and Wise wrote an article reviewing twenty years of PSM research and the degree to which the three propositions they put forward in their seminal 1990 article stood up to research. The propositions were:

- "The greater an individual's public service motivation, the more likely the individual will seek membership in a public organization" (p. 683).
- "In public organizations, PSM is positively related to individual performance" (p. 684).
- "Public organizations that attract members with high levels of public service motivation are likely to be less dependent on utilitarian incentives to manage individual performance effectively" (p. 686).

They found that research strongly supported the first two propositions. The results for the third proposition, while positive, were mixed. They suggest the reason for the mixed results was because their original concept was based on U.S. culture; the idea has been picked up and studied in other societies. If they are correct in their assessment, this emphasizes the point that when you have a culturally diverse workforce your motivation challenges are even more complex.

People often think motivation is about management motivating workers. That is certainly true to a degree; however, first-level employee interactions are also important. In earlier chapters, we mention emotional intelligence (EI) and the importance of understanding your strengths and weakness as well as where "your head is today" and how that state may impact colleagues. Much of the EI literature focuses on managers; however, it applies to everyone in the workplace. Peter Salovey and John Mayer (1990) defined EI as a "subset of social intelligence that involves the ability to monitor one's own and others' feelings and emotions, to discriminate among them, and to use this information to guide one's thinking and actions" (p. 189). Being able to do so enhances the work environment regardless of one's organizational level.

Some managers think of motivation as a formula: ability + support + effort = performance. That view emphasizes the interdependence between managers and employees when it comes to productivity. An employee with all the necessary abilities who is making the highest effort will not perform well if the organization (or manager) fails to provide proper support. It is equally true that all the support in the world will not generate high performance if the employee lacks the skill or the willingness to make the effort. The idea of teamwork between management and staff in the workplace is more than just an abstract concept; it is essential for successful performance.

MOTIVATION THEORIES

There is still no single answer to the question: How can employees be most effectively motivated to achieve high productivity as well as quality without creating human-relations problems? Researchers, especially those focused on the for-profit sector, offer a number of ideas and concepts that assist in motivating staff. There are several motivation theories; however, they only go so far and rarely address the fact that behavior arises for a variety of factors that interact differently in different individuals. In many ways, the best advice is simply to treat people like people and not like cogs in a machine. We are *not* suggesting the motivational theories are pointless, but rather that you think of motivation as a combination of factors. Motivation theories fall into three broad categories: content, process, and reinforcement.

- **Content theories** provide methods for profiling or analyzing staff in terms of *needs*.
- **Process theories** provide insights into how people think about, and give meaning to, organizational *rewards*.
- **Reinforcement theories** provide guidance about the way that people learn patterns of behavior when that behavior is the result of environmental (workplace) *reinforcements*.

As we noted above, there is no single answer as to how you motivate staff. What the theories do is provide some insight in to some of the major drivers of workplace behavior. Table 16.1 provides an overview of the major theories. All of them have a number of variations on the major concept.

If you have taken a basic psychology course, two of the names in the table are probably somewhat familiar to you—Maslow and Skinner. The fact is that workplace performance is psychological in character most of the time. It is true that there are times when performance is driven by existing skills and/or experience and/or the lack of necessary

TABLE 16.1 Motivation Theories

CATEGORY	PROPONENTS	CONCEPTS
Contextual	Maslow (1943) McCleland (1961)	Hierarchy of needs; a satisfied need does not motivate
Process	McGregor (1960)	Theory X-Y (continuum of work attitudes - hate to love)
	Argyris (1965)	Growing to maturity (seven stages of increasing complexity)
	Herzberg (1959)	Motivators and hygienic factors are key to job satisfaction; hygienic factors merely maintain morale and efficiency)
	Likert (1958)	Manager-centered or employee-centered supervision
Reinforcement	Skinner (1938)	Positive and negative reinforcement
	Drucker (1954)	Management by objective

supplies and the like. If the performance is due to a lack of skills or experience, then that is a managerial shortcoming—due to poor employee selection, poor training, poor monitoring, for example. Even problems in the supply chain are basically a managerial issue.

Achieving high-quality work performance comes from understanding employee psychology and behavior. That is easy to state but challenging to do as almost everyone's behavior is the result of what she or he have learned and experienced. Essentially, that means we are each unique to some degree. Even identical twins will rarely, if ever, have identical life experiences. That is where the challenge lies. Shared time in the workplace is a key to understanding what does and does not drive staff performance; needless to say, the longer that shared time occurs, the easier it is to assess motivation.

The following briefly highlights the basic notions of the motivation concepts listed in table 16.1. Maslow's (1943) hierarchy of needs (physiological, security, social, self-esteem, and self-actualization) is focused on what drives peoples' behavior throughout life, not just in the workplace. The key concept is that the lowest unmet need drives behavior and that a met need does not do so. Another central idea is that there is cyclical pattern to the needs. Everyone needs to eat; when we are hungry, we go about getting something to eat (the need drives our behavior), once we've eaten, the need to eat disappears for some time, and other needs become the drivers. From a U.S. library perspective, the two lowest need categories (physiological and security) are not usually factors in a person's performance. The middle two categories (social and self-esteem) are the areas where library managers can influence staff behavior. The highest category (self-actualization) has only limited potential for managerial influence—perhaps through encouraging self-development by supporting advanced coursework, publishing efforts, and the like can be motivators.

Douglas McGregor's (1960) Theory X-Y is a broad-based look at work attitudes and behaviors. He proposed a continuum of assumptions about work attitudes (both managerial and employee) with the end points, X and Y, representing opposite views of worker motivation. Theory X assumes that employees' personal goals are incompatible with organizational objectives and that authority is the instrument of command and control. Theory Y asserts that people have much to offer an organization if they can fully accept its objectives.

Theory X assumes work is inherently distasteful to most people, and they will avoid it if they can. Because they dislike work, most people are not ambitious, have little desire for responsibility, and prefer direction from above. As a result, most people must be closely controlled and often coerced to achieve organizational objectives. Theory Y assumes work is as natural as play or rest. Depending on controllable conditions, work can be a source of satisfaction or a source of punishment. The average person learns, under proper conditions, not only to accept responsibility but also to seek it. The capacity to exercise a relatively high degree of creativity in the solution of organizational problems is widely, not narrowly, distributed in a population.

Libraries are generally closer to Theory Y than to Theory X, especially in terms of the professional staff. Donald Sager's (1979) research in libraries documented that management and managers treating staff as if Theory Y were operative tended to have higher productivity than those who operated on the Theory X premise.

A number of people built on the work of Maslow and McGregor. These include Chris Argyris, Frederick Herzberg, and Rensis Likert. Their work is considered process approaches due their focus on managers' expectations about employees.

Chris Argyris (1965) examined the effects of management practices on employee behavior and personal growth within an industrial work environment. He identified seven stages that take place as a person develops from childhood into a mature person. Further, he suggested that organizations have a built-in need to keep people in an immature state. In such situations, management views employees as interchangeable elements in the organizational machine. Argyris's idea was, that if senior management allowed employees to accomplish their tasks as necessary to meet performance goals (that is, treated them as mature individuals) performance would improve. His research supported that idea.

Frederick Herzberg (1959) and his colleagues looked at the job as the most important motivator in the work environment. They found that positive attitudes about work were highest when managers indicated to employees that they were doing a good job or let them know when they were considered to be experts (Herzberg's "motivator" category). Salary and fringe benefits did not produce positive feelings, as they generally produced negative thoughts when employees viewed them as inadequate ("hygienic" or maintenance factors). Negative thoughts and feelings resulted from the physiological and security aspects of the job; positive thoughts resulted from self-actualization, self-esteem, and social needs. One of the questions about the two-factor (motivators and hygiene) approach is, "Does a "satisfied" employee translate into a high performer?" In part, the answer to the question depends on three alternative assumptions—satisfaction causes performance, performance causes satisfaction, or rewards cause both performance and satisfaction. Satisfaction causes performance means that a manager's focus should be on improving job satisfaction. The second assumption means that the manager should emphasize performance. The only way this can work is to have adequate rewards for high performance. Often middle- and lower-level managers have little power to change or increase rewards. The third assumption has two managerial implications. If the concern is with both performance and satisfaction, the manager should provide high rewards for high performance and lower rewards for low performers. Most U.S. public sector managers, while preferring the third assumption, have only modest control over the reward aspect.

Rensis Likert (1958) classified managers' focus as being either production-centered or employee-centered. Production-centered managers advocate strict control of the work environment and view employees as instruments for getting the job done. Employee-centered managers consider supervision rather than production to be their primary task and provide information about production goals and general guidelines for doing the work. They then allow employees to determine individual work patterns, as long as those patterns fit into the overall process and employees ask for assistance as necessary. Likert concluded that high-production groups had employee-centered managers, while low-production groups had production-centered managers. He then described four systems of management that fall along a continuum.

System 1 is where management has no confidence in employees and excludes them from decision making. Top management retains most of the control, and an informal organization usually develops that opposes the formal organization's goals.

System 2 is a moderately good "master-servant" relationship with some degree of trust in employees and their ability to work independently. Major decisions and goal setting occur at the top, but middle- and lower-level managers make some decisions.

System 3 managers have substantial confidence in employees. Broad policy and general decisions take place at the top, but many decisions occur at all levels. Communication flows up and down, and rewards are common. Superiors and employees interact, often with a strong degree of confidence.

System 4 exists when management has complete confidence in employees. Decision making exists throughout, and top management works to ensure integrated decision making occurs. Communication flows upward, downward, and laterally.

Libraries tend to follow either system 2 or system 3, and a few employ system 4. The size of the library is a factor. Larger libraries are moving toward system 4. However, as discussion of participative management (later in this chapter) will indicate, this system also has challenges.

B. F. Skinner's (1938) research on positive and negative reinforcement, and how past experiences influence people's behavior, is also a factor in workplace motivation theory. The basic notion is that people learn from experiences and tend to want to repeat experiences that had good outcomes and avoid those that were bad experiences. In the workplace, managerial behavior and actions serve as the stimulus for conditioning employee behaviors and activities.

One of Skinner's terms was *operant conditioning,* which refers to the process of controlling or modifying behavior by manipulating the consequences of the behavior. In an organizational setting, the concept is better known as *organizational behavior modification.* There are four strategies associated with operant conditioning:

- Positive reinforcement results in increased frequency or strengthens behavior by providing a desirable (from the employee's point of view) consequence whenever the behavior occurs.
- Negative reinforcement results in increased frequency or strengthens behavior by providing an undesirable (from the employee's point of view) consequence whenever unwanted behavior occurs.
- Punishment results in decreased frequency or eliminates undesirable behavior by providing unpleasant consequences whenever such behavior occurs.
- Extinction results in decreased frequency or eliminates undesirable behavior by removing a desirable consequence whenever such behavior occurs.

Positive reinforcement calls for immediate reward when the desired behavior takes place. To use positive reinforcement successfully, you must perform the following actions:

· Identify desired behaviors for employees.
· Maintain a variety of incentives and rewards.
· Recognize that employees differ in what they consider to be an incentive or reward.
· Ensure that employees know what they must do to receive a reward or incentive.
· Provide the reward or incentive immediately after the desired behavior is manifested.

Negative reinforcement is most effective when used selectively—selectively in the sense that it is not the primary method of reinforcement. When using negative reinforcement, you should do the following:

· Tell the person what is wrong with what he or she did or is doing.
· Tell the person how to correct what is wrong.
· Implement the negative reinforcement in private.
· Implement the negative reinforcement immediately after the undesirable behavior occurs.
· Ensure that the negative reinforcement is appropriate to the behavior.

Management by objectives or results (MBO) is a reinforcement motivation method that gained attention due to Peter Drucker's (1954) research and consulting. When an employee behaves compatibly with organizational goals, that behavior usually results in the person receiving some form of reinforcement (a reward or recognition, for example). When the behavior is anti-organizational, the manager chooses from among a number of negative reinforcement alternatives (for example, reprimand, time off without pay, and even dismissal).

There are two approaches to MBO. One approach is for management to set performance objectives and communicate those objectives to employees who then have the right to determine how to best achieve the desired outcome. The second option differs from the first in that the employee is involved in the objective and/or results setting process. The second approach requires the employees know that the performance outcome is the key element when it comes to performance evaluation.

Careful definition of the boundaries of acceptable employee behavior is essential in this approach. The levels at which decisions may, and may not, be made must be clear. Yet freedom to act within those boundaries must be present because the result is what matters, not the performance of activities leading to the result. The great temptation is to judge the activities, but this can do more harm than good.

Both the manager and the employees must realize that this system requires a great deal of interdependence. Moving in this direction is risky for the manager, because ultimate responsibility remains with the manager. Trust is absolutely necessary on both sides, and the employees must realize that both parties are vulnerable.

There is no one person who is considered the "founder" of this approach. In some sense, Elton Mayo's work in the 1920s laid the foundation (see chapter 1 for a discussion of his work) with his emphasis on the social aspects of the workplace. Essentially, his focus on staff social interactions and the impact on performance suggested that more interaction and involvement the better the performance. The participative management concept is also a modified version of Likert's style 4 with ideas drawn from various researchers in the field of motivation.

For public sector organizations there are two types of participative management—internal and external. Clearly the internal (the employees) is or can be a motivational concern. However, outside stakeholders' positive or negative views of the organization are formed in part by the degree they believe they have a voice (through participation) in how the organization functions.

Ultimately, this process relies on group input for planning, policy formulation, decision making, and other organizational activities. Some years ago, Maurice Marchant (1976), wrote:

> Participative management requires group discussion, and each group should be small enough that all may take part. The group is concerned with issues of mutual concern. Thus, the director would not discuss cataloging changes without involving public services personnel. Nor would he allow the discussion to center on personalities but would hold it to resolution of the mutual problem. (p. 39)

Several of the key elements of participative management are implied in the above—small groups and respect for differing viewpoints. Small groups where all voices may be heard are important to positive outcomes, both internally and externally. Such groups also mean a substantial amount of time becomes committed to the process. Libraries are public-service oriented, and time is a precious commodity. Hours spent in meetings do not serve the users well. Striking a balance between stakeholder (internal or external) input and keeping services fully operational is a challenge.

How to handle accountability in a participative management environment is challenging. Decisions require accountability. Given the authority relationships in public sector agencies accountability must exist. So, how can both accountability and staff input be achieved at the levels desired?

If a manager solicits stakeholder input but reserves the decision making for himself or herself (i.e., the manager is accountable) this is not participative management. A better label for this approach is consultative management. When you label a process participative management, it should be made clear how the final decisions will take place, resulting in some form of consensus. When the final outcome is reserved for senior management, it is consultative management.

Manville and Ober (2003) outlined an approach that recognizes that motivating in a knowledge economy rather than in the for-profit sector is different. They suggested that people should be motivated by building organizations on an Athenian model, where "underpinning all the achievements was a system of governance based on personal freedom, collective action, and an open democratic culture" (p. 50). "People with expertise

---

||||| CHECK THESE OUT

The above is just a basic outline of the major ideas related to motivation. To gain a true understanding of the concepts read the original publications that we list in the reference section of this chapter.

came forward whenever their skills were needed, without becoming part of any standing bureaucracy" (p. 51). Also, there are generational differences when it comes to workplace expectations and motivation.

Teresa Amabile and Steven Kramer conducted a survey of 600 managers regarding the managers' opinions about what motivated knowledge workers. A companion multiyear survey looked at the workers' daily activities (including productivity), emotions, and motivation. Amabile and Kramer (2010) said:

> Ask leaders what they think makes employees enthusiastic about work, and they'll tell you in no uncertain terms. . . . "Recognition for good work" (either public or private) came out number one. Unfortunately, those managers are wrong. . . . On days when workers have the sense they're making headway in their jobs, or when they receive support that helps them overcome obstacles, their emotions are most positive and their drive to succeed is at its peak. (p. 44)

MOTIVATION IN PRACTICE

The above approaches to thinking about motivation are just that—food for thought. Certainly, MBO and participative management are employed as practical motivation methods. However, if you use them alone you may not get top-level performance. We will look at several elements that can enhance performance that are not part of the aforementioned approaches.

Organizational culture

We have touched on organizational culture several times in other chapters. Here we look at how it impacts staff and their work activities. In a sense, "culture" has become a synonym for environment (culture of trust, culture of fear, and culture of sports, for example). Organizational culture (OC), like societal culture, is something a person learns over time. The quicker a person learns OC, the more effective that person will be at work. Unlike societal culture, a person does not have much time to learn the beliefs, values, and attitudes regarding acceptable performance, and the like. Failure to learn can lead to being dismissed.

Does OC really matter? Michael Burchell (2018), a writer on the topic of OC, stated that "Our research has shown that great workplaces have lower voluntary employee turnover than competitors are able to recruit the best employees to fit their culture and needs, provide top quality customer service and create innovative products and services." All of the factors he mentioned ultimately related to better performance (less time training new staff, better employee fit and skill set with organization, and valuing innovation and change).

Managers, especially senior managers, are important, if not the key, players in creating OC. They also maintain and, occasionally, change the culture through their actions, behaviors, and communications. For example, they can create a static culture when they do not value employee initiative and innovation. Likewise, they will foster a dynamic culture when they do the opposite.

The other key players are the employees who observe and interpret management's actions and statements. Long-term employees are the primary source of influence as they have seen and heard a number of managerial pronouncements and the subsequent actions. Their perceptions of the culture are quickly communicated to new-comers who accept those views in order to fit in.

Incongruity is a significant concern in terms of OC. There can be differences between managerial pronouncements and action that can lead to a major difference between employee beliefs about the OC and those of management. That in turn will lead to conflicts and declining organizational performance.

Changing OC can be challenging, but more often than not very beneficial. Sara Rose (2016), who we quoted in the opening of this chapter, wrote about changing the OC of the Pueblo City-County Library District saying the following about the outcome:

> PCCLD's cultural change resulted in remarkable success for the district as seen in the four key results: circulation, library visits, program attendance, and computer & digital use. Between 2009 and 2014, circulation at the library district increased about 50 percent, the number of people visiting libraries grew nearly 40 percent, and the number of people attending library-sponsored cultural and educational programs and events increased 80 percent (p. 16).

Organizational climate

There is a close linkage between organizational culture and climate; however, there are also differences. The major difference resides in their relative stability. Organizational culture, like societal culture, is very stable, changes slowly, and efforts to change it are challenging. Organizational climate can change quickly and is susceptible to change efforts. The ease of change relates to the fact that workplace climate is a personal perception of the work environment rather than the dispersed nature of culture. In a sense, each staff member perceives the climate in a slightly different way although there may be a widely held view of the organization's culture.

Because of its personal nature, organizational climate is measurable, unlike culture that is a diffuse organizational characteristic. It is possible to measure strength and weaknesses in the climate and develop a plan for changing areas of weakness. Some of the perceptions climate surveys look at are:

• autonomy	• innovation
• cohesion	• cooperation
• trust	• atmosphere
• pressure	• diversity
• support	• rewards
• recognition	• participation
• impartiality	• facilities

The above are more or less generic labels that some libraries use; others employ terms such as teamwork rather than cooperation and benefits for rewards.

Martha Kyrillidou, Charles Lowry, Paul Hanges, Juliet Aiken, and Kristina Justh (2009) gave a presentation at the Fourteenth National Conference of the Association of College and Research Libraries in Seattle, Washington, on the use of a climate survey (ClimateQUAL) in the library setting. They noted that, "As organizational systems and

```
║║║║ CHECK THESE OUT
```

An article that discusses the use of ClimateQUAL to assess and address the impact
of organizational changes is Audrey DeFrank and Nora Hillyer's "ClimateQUAL and
Thinklets: Using ClimateQUAL with Group Support Systems to Facilitate Discussion and
Set Priorities for Organizational Change at Criss Library." (*Evidence Based Library and
Information Practice* 8, no. 2: 36–47, 2013).

In the same journal issue, Elizabeth Mengel, Judith Smith, and Elizabeth Uzelac's
"After the Data: Taking Action on ClimateQUAL Results" (48–59) discusses using the
data to plan staff development and training efforts.

procedures are adjusted properly to effect a "healthier" organizational climate, we expect
to see higher job satisfaction, less work conflict, greater organizational commitment,
engagement, empowerment and ultimately improved customer service" (pp. 162-63). You
can check out the methodology at www.climatequal.org.

Jennifer Vinopal (2016) provided a concise explanation of what the purpose and use of
the methodology when writing about its usage in terms of diversity:

> ClimateQUAL is clearly designed and described as a measure of staff *perceptions* about
> the organization's climate, including what they *believe* and how they *feel* about the orga-
> nization's fairness and how it values diversity. Because of its focus on perceptions about
> what the organization's values, ClimateQUAL can be a powerful tool for revealing and
> understanding fairness and bias within an organization. However, . . . as a proxy for or-
> ganizational health [it] might be problematic if not handled in an extremely thoughtful
> and well-informed way (p. 6). [italics in the original]

Her final point about the need to handle any survey results in a thoughtful informed
manner applies to any topic, not just diversity.

ENCOURAGEMENT AND RECOGNITION

Both of these actions appear on the list of areas that a ClimateQUAL survey can assess. In
many ways, both are low- or no-cost behaviors that motivate staff performance. Encouraging words cost nothing, and recognition may amount to little more than a few words. It
is also true that both are dual-edged—inappropriately used, either can damage or enhance
performance. Used with care, both are often the most effective tool in a manager's motivational toolbox.

Encouragement, support, recognition, and rewards relate to Maslow's social and
self-esteem needs. As such, they play a role in an employee's level of commitment and
performance. The danger lies in how a manger employs them. Part of their effective usage
resides in how well the manager reads the work environment. When there is a reasonable
chance that everyone, from time to time, can earn a "well done" or "keep it up" in public,
there will be both an encouragement-recognition value in doing so where both the recipient and others will hear. When that is not the case, such action will likely have a negative
impact on at least a few employees. That does not mean the person deserving of the feedback should not receive it. Rather, such compliments should to be private in character.

▶ **MOTIVATIONAL TIPS**

- Treat staff as valued individuals, not cogs in a machine.
- Share the maximum amount of organizational information.
- Involve staff as much as possible in decision making, policy development, and planning.
- Recognize cooperative efforts.
- Clarify performance standards and goals.
- Treat staff equally–no favorites.
- Celebrate staff successes.
- Encourage individuals to take on leadership roles.
- Demonstrate, through actions and behavior, the importance of organizational mission, vision, and values.
- Take the time to acknowledge good staff behavior.
- Use positive reinforcement and praise.

The notion of manager's favorite or teacher's pet is easy to create without realizing it is occurring and is surprisingly difficult to correct. Keep in mind that organizational and unit climate arise from individual *perceptions*, not necessarily from a reflection of reality or intent. Even just passing the time of day with someone may be perceived as favoritism if such behavior is not extended to all the staff.

A good time for generic encouragement and recognition is in staff meetings. Doing so, even when knowing there may be a person or two who do not deserve praise, still is likely to have an overall value for performance. Overuse of this behavior can over time become meaningless for the staff and cause a decline in performance.

Formal organizational recognition, such as employee of the month or the year's best employee, while less-dual edged than one-on-one encouragement and recognition, may have a downside. Employees' perception of the award process is the key to its positive or negative value. When the process lies solely in the hands of management there will be employees who have doubts. This is one time when a committee approach is worth the time it takes to reach a decision. Having more staff members than managers on the committee enhances the chances of favorable perceptions.

Motivational theories are the basis for understanding how to achieve top work performance. However, in the work-day setting some very simple actions can produce very good results. Assessing and analyzing the workplace culture and climate will help you decide what techniques to use, and when. The above tips will help you achieve great staff performance.

🔒 KEY POINTS TO REMEMBER

- There are three types of motivation theories: content, process, and reinforcement.
- The theories should be considered in relation to both staff and the user community.
- Motivation is inseparable from an individual's goals, values, psychological needs, and life experiences.
- What motivates one person may completely fail to strike a responsive chord in another.
- Most people modify their personal goals as they go through life.
- Salary can be a powerful motivator. Managers should treat employees equitably and provide recognition and rewards for superior achievement.

- Praise is a good motivator; be specific and note how individuals are performing well.
- Keeping communication channels open can often resolve an issue before it becomes a problem.
- Listen to the staff—they need to know that their ideas count and that you hear them.
- Flexibility is key in a good motivation system.
- Make sure all staff—from the most senior professional to the junior support staff person—knows what is expected of them; check that they understand.
- Give people the tools they need to do the job well.
- Provide opportunities for learning and extending skills, and let people shine.
- Motivators can be generation specific.
- A number of factors affect the performance of individuals working in a team environment.
- Motivating users encourages use of the service provided for them.

REFERENCES

Amabile, Teresa, and Steven J. Kramer. 2010. "What Really Motivates Workers?" *Harvard Business Review* 88, no. 1: 44–45.

Argyris, Chris. 1965. *Integrating the Individual and the Organization*. New York: Wiley.

Burchell, Michael. 2018. "How to Make a Great Place to Work: Company Culture." https://hiring.monster .com/hr/hr-best-practices/workforce-management/employee-performance-management/ great-places-to-work.aspx

Dehmlow, Mark. 2016. "Editorial Board Thoughts: The Importance of Staff Change Management in the Face of the Growing Cloud." *Information Technology and Libraries* 35, no. 1: 3–6.

Drucker, Peter F. 1954. *The Practice of Management*. New York: Harper and Row.

Herzberg, Frederick. 1959. *Motivation to Work*. 2nd ed. New York: Wiley.

Jernigan, Edward, and Joyce M. Beggs. 2015. "An Examination of Work Attitudes of Public Sector Employees." *Journal of Organizational Culture, Communication and Conflict* 19, no. 3: 103–17.

Kyrillidou, Martha, Charles Lowry, Paul Hanges, Juliet Aiken, and Kristina Justh. 2009. "Climate QUAL™: Organizational Climate and Diversity Assessment." *Proceedings of the Fourteenth National Conference of the Association of College and Research Libraries, March 12–15, 2009*, Seattle, WA: American Library Association, 150–64.

Likert, Rensis. 1958. "Measuring Organizational Performance." *Harvard Business Review* 36, no. 2: 41–50.

Mackay, Harvey. 2018. "A Word of Encouragement Can Change Anyone's Destiny." www.startribune.com/ mackay-a-work-of-encouragment-can-change-anyone-s-destiny/481804981/.

Manville, Brook, and Josiah Ober. 2003. "Beyond Empowerment: Building a Company of Citizens." *Harvard Business Review* 81, no. 1: 48–53.

Marchant, Maurice P. 1976. *Participative Management in Academic Libraries*. Westport, CT: Greenwood.

Maslow, Abraham H. 1943. "A Preface to Motivational Theory." *Psychosomatic Medicine* 23: 85–99.

Mayo, Elton. 1933. *The Human Problems of an Industrial Civilization*. Salem, NH: Ayer.

McGregor, Douglas. 1960. *The Human Side of Enterprise*. New York: McGraw-Hill.

Perry, James L., Annie Hondeghem, and Lois Recascino Wise. 2010. "Revisiting the Motivational Basis of Public Service: Twenty Years of Research and an Agenda for the Future." *Public Administration Review* 70, no. 5: 681–90.

Perry, James L., and Lois Recascino Wise. 1990. "The Motivational Basis of Public Service." *Public Administration Review* 50, no. 3: 367–73.

Rose, Sara. 2016. "Creating a Winning Work Culture." In Human Resources: A Look in the Cupboard," special issue. Edited by James Larue. *Public Libraries* 55, no. 4: 15–17.

Sager, Donald J. 1979. "Leadership and Employee Motivation." In *Supervision of Employees in Libraries*, edited by R. E. Stevens. Urbana, IL: University of Illinois Graduate School of Library Science.

Salovey, Peter, and John D. Mayer. 1990. "Emotional Intelligence." *Imagination, Cognition, and Personality* 9, no. 3: 185-211.

Skinner, B.F. 1938. *Behavior of Organisms: An Experimental Analysis.* New York: Appleton-Century-Crofts.

Vinopal, Jennifer. 2016. The Quest for Diversity in Library Staffing: From Awareness to Action." *In the Library with the Lead Pipe* January 13: 1-17.

Wright, Bradley E. 2007. "Public Service and Motivation: Does Mission Matter? *Public Administration Review* 67, no. 1: 54-64.

PART IV

Managing Things

CHAPTER 17

Managing Money

There is a significant gap in our knowledge about the relationship between the powers of politicians to set budgetary policies and the relevance of politically motivated budgets in governing the activities of public sector organizations.

Jean Claude Mutiganda, 2016

Not all budgets are the same, and libraries may employ a number of budgets to meet unique circumstances.

William Sannwald, 2018

The independent auditors who perform financial audits are also subject to standards known generally as accepted government auditing standards, of the Government Accountability Office.

Dennis Carrigan, 2015

Money may or may not make the world go around. What is very clear is that without money organizations would grind to halt. Securing adequate financial resources requires plans, and yes, budgets are one type of plan. The unfortunate truth is that libraries face uphill battles to secure even barely adequate funding. Without a sound budget plan, the chances of success are marginal at best.

Almost every library plan, especially strategic goals, objectives, and the like carry some degree of monetary implications, as may goals and objectives. Those implications feed into a budget plans, whether short or long-term. An example of a long-term budget plan could be to achieve a strategic goal several years in the future and which will be very costly. A library could break the cost down in several smaller incremental budget requests, thus making the reducing the overall sticker shock for the funding authorities. Budget plans require you to think almost as much about the future as you do about the present.

Money is the underlying resource upon which everything else in the library depends. A managerial leader's role is to utilize those resources effectively. To be successful in that activity, you must understand managerial and financial accounting, develop skills in raising funds from sources outside the library's primary funding source, and master the politics of the budgetary process. In this chapter we address these as well as other fiscal matters.

Securing adequate (or as close as possible to adequate) funding is challenging and calls upon all your managerial and political skills. You must realize that at times you'll fail through no fault of your own. Economic conditions may make it impossible for any library to receive funding at "normal" levels, and budget reductions may occur. However, by preparing solid requests, having a track record of careful and thoughtful stewardship of funds granted, providing high-quality service to the user community, and having realistic but forward-looking plans you will, more often than not, secure the maximum possible funding. Fiscal management consists of three broad activities: identifying and securing funds, expending the funds, and accounting for and reporting on how you spent the funds.

Being an effective steward of funds is complex regardless of the size of your library. It begins by assessing what needs doing (especially user needs) and the cost of the requisite activities, establishing priorities (with stakeholder input), creating a plan (the budget) that reflects the costs and priorities, and presenting the plan to the appropriate funding bodies. We know of few, if any, cases where the costs of desired activities were below the realistic amount of money likely to be received. Thus, setting priorities is a key element in fiscal planning.

No matter where you seek funding, you must have a well-crafted request. Preparing it takes time, effort, and a fair amount of creativity, as you will be in competition with other agencies and departments.

BUDGET AS A CONTROL DEVICE

A budget plan serves three interrelated purposes: planning, coordinating, and control. It represents choices made about alternative possible expenditures. Furthermore, it assists in coordinating work. As our opening quotation from Mutiganda suggests, funding authorities use budget requests and expenditures as a means of comparing what the library proposes and what the outcomes are. It is one of the parent body's most powerful tools for holding the library accountable.

While for-profit organizations begin budgeting by estimating sales and income, libraries start by estimating what income will be received from the parent organization. If there is a shortfall in what is deemed to be the minimum level needed, the library must seek funds from outside sources. There are few relatively predictable library-generated funds (user fees, endowment income, and other internally generated cash), while other sources are unpredictable (grant proposals and cooperative ventures, for example). Budgeting is essentially forecasting how much will you get and how much will it cost to operate over the budget cycle. Overly optimistic predictions lead to problems when funding falls short and/or there are unexpected costs. There can be cuts in the allocation during the fiscal year (FY) that are very disruptive. For libraries, about the only area to cut in such cases are those related to collection development (which is a library's only large pool of money other than salaries).

You rarely know what you will receive until near the start of the budgetary year (that is, the fiscal year). We know of cases where publicly funded libraries had to start a

---

||||| **CHECK THIS OUT**

An interesting article about politics, budgets, and libraries is Edith K. Beckett's "Influences on New Jersey Public Library Budget Requests" (*Bottom Line* 29, no. 2: 86–96, 2016).

cycle without an approved budget because politicians could not agree on how much to approve. This can create some serious scrambling when there are shortfalls. There have been a number of times when all of a community's agencies except emergency services had to close until the legislature or city council reached a compromise. Our experience has been that a conservative forecast is the safest and least disruptive to operations. Having a contingency plan also helps make managerial life somewhat easier for times when the politicians quibble over what and how much to fund.

Because budgets are estimates, to be effective you must make expenditure adjustments as circumstances change. Budgets need to be flexible in order to meet shifts in needs, but any major alteration requires careful thought and caution. Too many changes can damage the integrity and stability of both the budget and the organization. In most libraries, there is only a limited authority to make budget adjustments; asking before doing is the best approach when it comes to budgets.

Financial planning and control consists of several steps:

1. Determine ongoing and desirable programs and establish priorities.
2. Estimate the cost of plans for each unit in monetary terms.
3. Combine all estimates into a well-balanced program. This will require investigation of each plan's financial feasibility and a comparison of the program with institutional goals.
4. Compare, for a given time, the estimates derived from Step 3 with the actual results, making corrections for any significant differences.

A library's size does not materially affect the budgeting process, although in larger libraries each step is more complex. As a library grows, it may employ separate allocations for work units. A very large library may have many internal sub-budgets within the overall budget. Another complex step is combining and coordinating subsidiary allocations. It involves more than just totaling the smaller budgets. It must represent a total program that is consistent with the library's objectives. For this reason, very large libraries often have a person whose sole job is budget coordinator who must see the big picture.

Finally, budget officers compare the actual performance (what has been accomplished, the volume of work, and so forth) against the expected results. Managerial leaders must consistently assess existing circumstances in order to decide whether a major or a minor shift in budget allotments is necessary or desirable. This step is most important because budgets are often prepared twelve to eighteen months before they are approved and thus may represent predictions that are two years old at the time of review.

Library budgets are of two types: operating and capital. Operating budgets identify amounts of money the library expects to expend on basic activities; they cover a fiscal year, which is usually twelve months long. The fact that different organizations use different fiscal years (some examples are January 1 to December 31, June 1 to May 31, July 1 to June 30, and October 1 to September 30) can cause surprising problems for library consortia and their cooperative project funding.

Capital budgets are for expenditures on equipment (usually items expected to last two or more years). Expenditures for technology (hardware and infrastructure) usually fall into the capital expense category. The other major expense is for new construction or remodeling projects.

Funding bodies can, and occasionally do, change their fiscal year. This can cause the library difficulty, especially in maintaining subscriptions. The problem is not too great

👥 AUTHORS' EXPERIENCE

Evans worked at one private university where the institution changed its fiscal year three times in the space of five years, both lengthening and shortening the year. The library had great difficulty meeting its outside commitments—consortial, maintenance/service contracts, and subscriptions, for example. At the end of the all these swings, the institution returned to its original fiscal year as the assumed benefits of the changes were never realized.

when the funding body shortens the fiscal year by a month (although at some point in time it will be necessary to address any funding shortfall). When the funders extend the fiscal year by a month or more, the problem may be acute because of lack of funds.

BUDGET CYCLE

The budget cycle plays a role in the control aspect of budgeting. Budget managers normally deal with at least four fiscal years. Those are last year's, this year's, next year's, and the year after that. For the current year, the manager must monitor expenditures, compare what has occurred against expectations, and make appropriate adjustments. A common practice requires senior managers to provide additional justifications to the funding body for the requested budget for the coming fiscal year. As part of that process, the person is likely to have to respond to questions about expenditures in the current and past fiscal year.

Because budgets are estimates, funding bodies usually look at how well the requesting unit actually used its prior appropriations. Senior management must be ready to defend past expenditures, explain how the library is doing with current funding, and justify why extra funds are necessary for the coming fiscal year. During the latter part of a fiscal year, many organizations ask for your initial budget request for a fiscal year two years in the future.

PREPARATION

A library's senior manager is responsible for use of the budget as well as its preparation, regardless of how she or he delegated spending authority. Only in the smallest library is the senior manager solely responsible for spending the operational budget. In libraries with several units or departments, the senior manager usually delegates some discretionary spending power to them.

Such delegation accomplishes several things. First, it places the day-to-day budget decisions close to user services, making it easier to respond to changing needs. Second, it indicates to unit managers that the senior manager has a high level of trust in them. Third, it provides middle managers with an opportunity to gain an understanding of budgeting. It also presents senior management with an opportunity to assess middle managers' potential for a promotion that requires greater budgetary responsibility. Finally, it gives the senior manager more time to maintain overall budgetary oversight.

Early in your career, you are unlikely to have major budget responsibilities. You may be asked for information, even to provide dollar figures about what you think are the monetary needs for your area. As you progress in your career, you should take every opportunity to learn more and more about library budgeting and how the budget request process operates.

Initial budget preparation usually begins with unit supervisors. They provide their estimates of their funding needs and pass the proposal on to the next level or to senior managers. Each level further combines and adjusts the requests. Finally, senior management assesses the information and drafts the final request. For libraries, the process is essentially one of subtraction as the total amount requested by supervisors is almost always far larger than the library can reasonably expect. Thus, there is a need to pare down requests to a realistic amount. There is likely to be even further reduction during the next phase of securing a budget.

DEFENDING THE REQUEST

Preparing a budget request is often easier than defending it. This is because the library is one of many agencies competing for a limited pool of money. Needless to say, the total sought far exceeds what the funding authorizes have available. Each agency seeks to prove that its needs are the most urgent. Thus, the more care that you put into the preparation of a budget request and the reasons for requested increases, the more likely you are to secure the amount sought.

Those agencies who win the "battle of the budget" are usually the ones that recognize and act on the fact that budgeting is a very political process. All U.S. library managers ought to read the classic book by Aaron Wildavsky, *The New Politics of the Budgetary Process* (Wildavsky and Caiman 2011). Some librarians, especially students, have difficulty accepting Wildavsky's ideas, as the text deals with the U.S. federal government and, to a lesser extent, state governments. They see libraries as cultural havens somehow removed from the "ugliness" of politics. However, many librarians who read some or all of Wildavsky as students quickly see the connection as they gain practical experience.

In addition to the budgetary politics with external agencies, there are internal politics that arise from time to time. The elements are almost identical in the two instances; however, there is, very often, the added dimension of interpersonal relationships to take into consideration. Personal baggage makes it that much harder to resolve. "Why did special collections get the biggest increase?" "How come department X got the new FTE? We obviously need the help more than it does!" These are samples of the internal politics that can go on. Personal interests in gaining status, authority, and influence are often underlying issues. Such concerns go well beyond true budget concerns; they are very difficult to address, and senior managers must not let them get in the way of the overall budget process.

An incremental approach is present in most library budgets because of the long-term commitments (salaries, pension payments, database leases, and serial subscriptions). Also, if the user base increases, there will be pressure to hire additional staff. In jurisdictions with strong collective bargaining units, a workload agreement clause can cause a significant increase in staffing costs. Annual salary step and cost-of-living increases are difficult to control. Staff pressure will mount to make up for the losses they believe they have suffered.

Like it or not, lobbying is part of how the library presents its budget. To avoid the negative connotations of the word *lobbying,* some people label this *advocacy.* Both terms relate to the process of influencing people about the importance or value of an issue or cause. Gloria Meraz (2002) describes three areas that librarians can focus on in terms of lobbying—positioning themselves to be effective lobbyists, achieving the most from lobbying sessions, and understanding the lobbying arena. One of her points is that "decision makers tend to allocate funding to departments or agencies that are in trouble (crisis). . . . [W]ithout showing some sort of crisis, libraries are not likely to receive large allocations of resources" (p. 68). She notes that most libraries do not have to make up the crisis; all they need to do is show it.

One part of the advocacy process is to draw on the user base, which will be as vocal or as silent as the library leads users to believe they should be. A large user base is fine, but if users are silent during budget crunches, they are not politically useful. People who are willing to speak for the library at budget hearings can have a positive effect on funding agencies. The "letter to your legislator" approach can be very useful, especially if it occurs year-round and creates a strong positive attitude in funders' minds before they begin thinking about budgets. Some years ago, Jennifer Cargill (1988) wrote a short but to-the-point article about "getting the budget message out." At that time, and as it still remains today, one of the most difficult messages to convey to funding authorities, as well as to users, is the high rate of inflation of library collection resources. Finding a short, simple, accurate, way of explaining to non-librarians why such price increase percentages are so large is a challenge.

Developing a good working relationship with the staff members who work for those who have funding authority is an excellent idea. Make friends with staff members who work for the person who chairs the committee to which you submit the library's initial. budget request. If your relationship is year-round, it will be easier to maintain, and your chances of success improve further. Keeping in touch, finding out well in advance what will be needed for the hearings, identifying possible areas of concern, and offering assistance within reasonable limits are all methods of developing a good working relationship. You must be careful to keep the relationship on a professional basis so that there is no hint of personal favoritism.

When presenting plans for new programs, be cautious in what you promise. Do not promise more than you know you can deliver, even when you think you can do much better. It is better to under-promise and over-deliver. As tempting as it may be to make promises in order to get money, resist! Funding officers' memories are long, and failure to deliver on past promises raises serious doubts about current promises.

Does all of this sound too political for a library? It should not, because it reflects the unwritten rules by which governments and other funding bodies play the budget-politics game.

BUDGET TYPES

For libraries, the operating expense (OE) is the primary budget regardless of format (line-item, performance, etc.). Within the total operating budget, there is a series of accounts covering specific items of expenditure. These are generally interconnected and include the

- materials budget
- personnel budget

- distribution/expense budget
- administrative expense budget

A materials budget is for collection building and online access services. A personnel budget, which covers salaries and benefits, specifies the amount required for the staffing needed to meet service objectives. The distribution/expense budget reflects a library's allocating part of the overall budget to a specific area, such as branch operation or collection development. An administrative expense budget, as the name implies, details those expenses that result from performing general management functions.

What are the typical categories of expenditures included in an OE? For libraries, the largest category is staff salaries, often representing as much as 60 to 65 percent of the total budget. This is one category of expense that most libraries cannot move funds to or from or change during a fiscal year. Usually the only way you can use salary monies for some other purpose is by giving up an FTE (full time equivalent) or at least part of an FTE.

Funds for building the electronic and print collections are the second largest OE category. These funds may account for 25 to 30 percent of total budget. Like salaries, these expenses tend to grow more quickly than most of the other categories.

Generally, there is less than 15 percent of the budget left for all other expense categories. Office supplies, telephone, postage, and maintenance contracts are all essential and take substantial portions of the remaining funds. Other OE costs include facilities maintenance, printing or promotional activities, membership fees, staff travel, bindery charges, and insurance. Is it any wonder that few libraries have much money left for covering professional development and staff training and a host of other desirable expenditures?

Funds raised outside the parent organization for OE purposes are less constrained in terms of usage. There are times when a donor restricts funds for a special purpose. You are likely to encounter restricted and unrestricted funds. The OE is unrestricted; that is, you may spend OE collection funds for any appropriate item. A restricted collection development fund might require that you buy items only on Middle Eastern archaeology. It is not uncommon for a donor to restrict the expenditure of a gift to areas in which he or she has a special interest. As experienced fundraisers know, securing an unrestricted gift is difficult—no one wants to give money for "light bulbs and toilet paper."

Before exploring the major budget formats, we need to briefly mention two variations you will rarely encounter—lump sum and site budgets. A lump sum budget, as its name implies, is a single allocation, and the funds are not tied to any category of expenditure. You have the freedom to use the funds as needed or, at least, as your governing board deems appropriate. This freedom is wonderful until it comes to accountability, when it becomes akin to wrestling an angry bear with one hand tied behind you.

Site budgets are allocations tied to a specific location (a branch, for example) and cover all categories of expense. They can be a good method for giving more professionals early experience with managing an entire budget.

Another type is the formula budget. You most commonly encounter a formula budget in educational settings, where student numbers are linked to a funding amount—more students translate into more money. Some public libraries may use something similar that is based on a per capita figure or percentage of taxes.

In an academic library, you are likely to encounter a sub-budget that is formula based—acquisitions. Academic libraries have used a variety of formulas in an effort to help achieve some balance in spending in support of the teaching departments. Such efforts have never fully satisfied all the faculty members.

Line-item budget

The line-item budget is the most common format. It has a long history of use and allows for easy comparison of expenditure categories from year to year. Such budgets focus on classes of expenditures, with each class representing a "line" in the budget. Each major unit in a large organization, such as a library or a police department, has an identifying budget number. Within each budget number are individual lines representing the classes of expenditure the funding authority wishes to track. Whatever the label used for line items, the purpose is to allow for easy tracking of expenditures. If the funding body wants to know how much the organization as a whole spent on office supplies, all it needs to do is add up all of the XXX lines in the active account numbers. There is no standard number of expenditure classes in the budgeting system.

Line-item budgets are the least complex to manage and easiest to prepare. A budget request usually starts with last year's allocation and builds from there. More often than not you will have received some guidelines from the parent body about its overall increase target for the final budget. These will almost always indicate how much, if any, inflation you may add to which lines. You may be encouraged to shift monies from one line to another to better reflect your operating needs (an exception here is that you rarely have freedom to shift salary monies).

Performance budget

Some people view performance budgets as the best tool for fiscal control. Performance budgets focus on tasks rather than on classes of expenditure. A performance budget is an expansion of a line-item budget, but using it gives managers and funding authorities a means to assess the unit's performance in terms of quantity and unit costs.

The major drawback to the performance budget is that it is of little value in assessing quality. While it relates expenditures to the mission, goals, and objectives, it still does not clearly show the relationship of funds to quality. One reason you might want to employ a performance budget internally, regardless of what the parent organization's budget format is, is for staff development. In essence, you can give functional department heads their own budgets to manage. This will usually result in more realistic budget requests from the department heads as they gain an understanding of budgetary issues.

Program budgets

Program budgets relate expenditures to the programs the library provides, and links monies spent on them to the library's mission, goals, and objectives. Needless to say, such budgets require substantially more time to prepare. The extra time requirement may account for the lower usage of this format. A program budget takes more time to prepare because staff time has to be allocated to each activity (cataloging or reference, for example). While some staff may devote 100 percent of their time to a single program, others may have responsibilities in several areas. The question for such individuals is, how much time to attribute to each program?

How a library defines its programs will depend on how it defines its mission, goals, and objectives. Whatever the case may be, implementing a program budget requires introducing three major operational concepts:

- Develop an analytical ability for examining in-depth library goals and objectives and the programs designed to meet them.
- Create a five-year programming process plan combined with a sophisticated management-information system.
- Create a budgeting mechanism that can take broad program decisions, translate them into refined budgetary decisions, and present the results for action.

The following steps are necessary to accomplish the third task of identifying fiscally efficient operational programs that meet broad goals:

1. Identify library objectives.
2. Relate broad objectives to specific library programs.
3. Relate programs to resource requirements.
4. Relate resource inputs to budget dollars.
5. Relate inputs to outputs.

These steps not only provide a quick overview of the program budget process but also indicate the interrelated nature of management activities. Additionally, they provide another indication of why program budgeting is time-consuming.

The primary weakness of the program budget lies in its emphasis on the quantification of library activities. Comparative evaluations will involve qualitative judgments, which are difficult to reflect in the quantitative elements in the budget.

Planning programming budgeting

This approach is a combination of program and performance systems. Its focus is the planning aspect of the budget and is, in a sense, a long-term perspective budget as the library's goals and objectives are the driving elements.

Zero-based budget

The term zero-based (ZBB) comes from the first step in the process, that is, the agency is to assume that it is just beginning to operate (that is, starting from point zero). Thus, the focus of the planning and development of the ZBB is on the purpose and functions it should perform in order to meet its mission. In theory, an organization that uses ZBB would become more cost-effective by continuously reviewing its purposes and attempting to remove unneeded activities. From a taxpayer's point of view, if ZBB was practiced, the existing tax base would produce the maximum service at the lowest cost.

Several phases of ZBB are necessary in order to implement the system: construction, planning, budgeting, and control. *Construction* is a time-consuming part of the process. It is during the construction phase that the budget preparer assumes that the unit is starting at point zero activity. Decision packages are the ultimate goal of the construction and planning phases of ZBB. These costing activities are very similar to those of program budgeting. The outcome statement with costs becomes a decision package. The last step in preparing a decision package is to rank each option in terms of decreasing benefit to the organization. Clearly, the time necessary to prepare a comprehensive ZBB on an annual basis is enormous, and few organizations that still employ some variation of ZBB revisit the construction phase annually.

Something to keep in mind about the above is that libraries have little choice about which of the above approaches to employ. The parent organization makes that decision. Unlike what constitutes the FY, the parent body rarely changes the budget format.

ACCOUNTING SYSTEMS

The accounting system employed by the parent organization has a significant impact on the library's operations, especially in terms of collection building funds. There are three systems—accrual, modified accrual, and cash.

In the accrual system expenses are recorded when they occur (when an order is placed), not when they are paid (after the item is received). This approach is advantageous for libraries that encumber collection development funds as the encumbered amounts can carry forward into the next FY.

The cash method essentially treats expenses and expenditures as occurring simultaneously. Library encumbrances, in this system, do not carry forward in the sense that the monies involved remain available until the items are actually received. Any encumbered amounts at the end of the FY become a deduction for the next year, assuming the items arrive.

FUND ACCOUNTING

Because the majority of libraries are nonprofit organizations (nonprofit in the IRS sense rather than organizational sector) we include a brief section on fund accounting. This is a complex topic, and we can provide only some highlights. Fund accounting is peculiar to nonprofits. Accountants developed the system as a result of nonprofit characteristics of the users and the uses of information. Four of these special characteristics are:

- the focus on social benefits
- the relative absence of profit-motivated behavior on the part of resource contributors (public and private)
- the special government- and constituent-imposed constraints on their activities
- the lack of generating a profit (which is not the same as generating income)

Users of fund accounting information are a diverse group, both internal and external to the organization.

There are similarities between fund accounting and for-profit accounting systems. However, profit enterprises use a single-entry focus, while fund accounting usually involves many fragmented financial reports. Such reports focus on separate individual funds and the flow of liquid assets rather than income.

The general fund exists to account for the unrestricted resources as well as resources not accounted for in any other group of accounts. General fund operating statements show revenues, expenditures, and encumbrances, as well as changes in fund balances. Debit funds track resources segregated for paying interest and principal on a general obligation

👥 AUTHORS' EXPERIENCE

Evans had a firsthand experience with the cash approach. He was about to start a new job when he met with the library budget officer from the new institution. To say he was surprised to learn that he would have no collection development funds for the upcoming year is an understatement. The reason for the problem was because the amount allocated to the library was completely committed to cover existing encumbrances.

When a library places an order for an item it is in fact a small legal contract. That is, the seller could have a legal right to payment, even if the fulfillment took years to complete. The only legal approach is to formally cancel the order, which was the option Evans had to implement in order to free up some funds for current FY purchases. Accrual and cash systems do matter for libraries and determine some of the work in an acquisitions department during the final quarter of a FY.

debt. Many libraries have new facilities paid for in full or in part by bond issues—a general obligation debt. Capital project funds control resources for the purpose of acquiring major fixed assets. Reports on capital project funds seek to list sources, uses, and available resources for individual projects. Most library facilities projects are a combination of monies from public and private sources; such monies would be part of the capital project fund.

A special-revenue fund accounts for, and reports on, resources that come from special sources—for example, a library foundation—or that carry restrictions on their use. Some libraries have endowments that fall into this category. Some municipalities and some academic institutions engage in some form of commercial activities. Enterprise funds control activities that provide goods or services to the general public (Friends of the Library merchandise, for example) or user charges (photocopy charges are common). Library photocopy income would be part of the enterprise fund. Internal library funds are similar except the "customer" is part of the organization. You may encounter chargeback situations in which a non-library unit charges the library a fee for its services; two common chargeback areas are computing and building maintenance.

While library managers may have little direct involvement in fund accounting, they do have substantial indirect contact, whether they know it or not. Having some knowledge of fund accounting will assist in working more effectively with funding authorities.

AUDITS AND AUDITORS

Without question, fiscal accountability is a concern to supporters and budget officials. Essentially, an audit is a post-action review by an independent appraiser. There are several types of audit, not all of which are financial in character; however, the majority of audits do have finances as the underlying concern.

External and internal audits are the two broad categories. Almost every for-profit and nonprofit must have an annual external audit conducted by an independent auditor. Normally, an independent auditor is a certified public accounting (CPA) firm. The annual audit has two major purposes. The first is to ensure that financial accounts and statements are accurate. Second is to ensure that the organization is following generally accepted

---

||||| CHECK THESE OUT

Smith, G. Stevenson. 2002. *Managerial Accounting for Libraries and Other Not-for-Profit Organizations.* 2nd ed. Chicago: American Library Association.

Turner, Anne M. 2007. *Managing Money: A Guide for Librarians.* Jefferson, NC: McFarland and Company.

---

accounting principles. Such audits, because of their legal implications, are very thorough. A library that is part of an organization that must have an annual external audit may expect occasional, if not annual, visits from the independent auditor. You never know exactly what the auditors will want to review until they arrive; however, more often than not, it will be the collection development fund accounts. This is because there are so many financial transactions involved in acquisitions work.

Internal audits, or operational audits, may or may not be fiscal in nature. Some of typical audits are these:

- financial records (checks that records are accurate, proper, and in order)
- compliance (reviews both internal and external policies and procedures)
- operational (evaluates effectiveness and/or efficiency of an operation)
- performance (confirms whether purchasing, receiving, and payment records follow proper fiscal and accounting regulations)
- fact finding (determines if official job classifications and descriptions accurately reflect the work being done)

More often than not, parent body employees conduct the internal audit. These employees usually report to the chief operating officer of an organization in order to ensure their independence of judgment. Compliance and operational audits may use outside consultants who have the depth of knowledge needed to make judgments about a particular area.

Sound accountability is a major factor in receiving adequate funding for your operations. Jennifer Cargill (1987) offered good advice some years ago in an article titled "Waiting for the Auditor." She ended her article with, "Following the Ps—Proper Prior Planning and Preparation—will make them Painless" (p. 47). Doing so may not make it painless, but it will make it less painful.

BUDGET REPORTS

There are types of budget reports that you will need to become familiar with as your career moves forward. There is of course the annual budget form that shows the allocations. There are monthly reconciliation reports (often internal to the library) showing balances for what has been expended and encumbered and what remains. Acquisitions and collection development personnel, as well as senior managers, are interested in what these reports show. There is something similar from the parent financial office; the variance report shows the differences between allocated and expended amounts. Such reports are useful for many categories of expenditures, such as supplies and salaries. More important, they are extremely valuable for collection funds and other categories where encumbrances are key to knowing where you stand with the budget. G. Stevenson Smith (2002) illustrated the importance of variance when he wrote: "Variances provide different information for the manager. The *cost variance* is the difference between the legally approved budget appropriation and accrual-based expenses during the year. . . . The *expended variance* shows the effect of outstanding encumbrances on the cost variance" (p. 85). An advantage of the variance data is that at year end, assuming you have the authority to do so, you can think about shifting funds from an under-expended category to a different category in the coming fiscal year.

A final thought: the more you understand library budgeting, the more effective you will be in your career. Keep in mind that budgeting is not a once-a-year process. Effective managerial leaders know it is a daily issue.

🛈 KEY POINTS TO REMEMBER

- Fiscal management is about securing, expending, and accounting for the essential monies to operate the best possible library.
- Budgeting is more than managing this year's allocation; it is thinking about what you will need in the future as well as how well you managed previous allocations.
- Budgeting is a political process that involves careful monitoring of your library's environment if you hope to secure adequate funding.
- You seldom have a voice in the type of budget to use—line or performance, for example—so your goal is to make the most effective use of what type is in place. This requires some study of the budget type's theory and methodology as well as assessing the organizational culture of the parent or funding body.
- Gaining an understanding of accounting and financial terminology will aid in developing sound relationships with those who devote their full-time attention to money matters in the parent organization.

REFERENCES

Cargill, Jennifer. 1987. "Waiting for the Auditor: Some Interim Advice." *Wilson Library Bulletin* 67, no. 9: 45–47.

_____. 1988. "Financial Constraints: Explaining Your Position." *Wilson Library Bulletin* 68, no. 4: 32–34.

Carrigan, Dennis. 2015. "Understanding Your Library's Financial Audit." *Public Library Quarterly* 34, no. 4: 291–309.

Meraz, Gloria. 2002. "The Essentials of Financial Strength through Sound Lobbying Fundamentals." *Bottom Line* 15, no. 2: 64–69.

Mutiganda, Jean Claude. 2016. "How Do Politicians Shape and Use Budgets to Govern Public Sector Organizations? A Position-Practice Approach." *Public Money and Management* 36, no. 7: 491–98.

Sannwald, William. 2018. *Financial Management for Libraries.* Chicago: ALA/Neal-Schuman.

Smith, G. Stevenson. 2002. *Managerial Accounting for Libraries and Other Not-for-Profit Organizations.* Chicago: American Library Association.

Wildavsky, Aaron, and Naomi Caiden. 2011. *The New Politics of the Budgetary Process.* 5th ed. New York: Pearson/Longman.

CHAPTER 18

Generating Income

Charitable contributions are becoming a major source of revenue for many nonprofit organizations including libraries.

William W. Sannwald, 2018

Development activities, also known as fundraising, have long been an important part of the way cultural heritage organizations sustain themselves, in both the short and long-term.

Debra Riley-Huff, Kevin Herrera, Susan Ivey, and Tina Harry, 2016

To create success in these philanthropic activities, the organization must understand what it means to create a landscape that is desirable for potential donors and develop added value.

Michael A. Crumpton, 2016

Grants are an essential part of the library world, allowing librarians to undertake innovative and progressive projects that would otherwise not be realized without the necessary funding.

Grace Romund, 2017

In the previous chapter, we suggested that when it comes to library funding from its parent organization most allocations are marginally adequate. We also suggested there was a need for libraries to seek finds from sources other than funding authority if they hope to provide fully appropriate services. In this chapter, we explore the major sources for such monies.

It is a fact that libraries in the United States have a long history of some dependency on philanthropic support. The country's oldest university library (and today one of the richest) started with a donation of books from a man named Harvard. The idea that libraries should have support from tax dollars did not arise until the mid-nineteenth century. For more than eighty years a great many libraries have had some form of "Friends groups" that provide monetary support. Today, securing financial support beyond the base allocation means that the additional support is rarely supplemental but essential to maintaining service levels in many cases.

Whitchurch and Comer (2016) highlighted the need for academic libraries to raise money from outside sources; "Development work, i.e., fundraising, has been of interest to academic libraries for a number of years [actually close to 400 years], but with library budgets remaining static, or even shrinking, the importance of this work is increasing"

👥 AUTHORS' EXPERIENCE

Greenwell recalls something a successful development officer once told her. She had seen another library's newsletter listing items the library would like a donor to purchase. The wish list included things like backfiles of journal collections, a high-end scanner, a golf cart for library deliveries, and so forth. While the newsletter wasn't asking for "light bulbs and toilet paper," the development officer told her it wasn't the way their library should go, saying, "Success breeds more success." What he meant was that donors and potential donors want to hear stories about how the library (its personnel, spaces, collections) change the lives of students, researchers, and community members. A laundry list of things that couldn't be included in the library budget inspires no one, but stories about real people achieving their goals because of the library do.

(pp. 114–15). The issue of shrinking or static budgets applies to all types of libraries as does the necessity to seek more money.

There are several labels for the process of securing such support—fundraising, development, advancement, and philanthropic work. The concepts may differ slightly, but the bottom line is they all relate to gaining additional dollars for operations. Being successful in such efforts takes time and effort.

Developing and maintaining a positive image is important for all libraries—and it is essential for gaining outside support. As our opening quotation from Michael Crumpton notes, libraries need to create a "desirable landscape" (a positive vision) and demonstrate value. There will be little chance of securing additional funds if the library's image is not positive. However, having a positive image is not enough. You must communicate that image to users, the general public, and to prospective sources of new funding. Granting agencies are just as interested in the image of their grantees as are individual donors.

Finding sources of funding, other than the parent institution, for "light bulbs and toilet paper" is a challenge. Most foundations, donors, and grant-giving organizations are interested in funding only projects that have a very high probability of success. Securing funding for this activity may free up general operating funds for important activities that are underfunded or even the light bulbs that lack donor appeal. There will be competition from other libraries and other organizations seeking extra funding, and it will require an investment of time and collaboration within the library, if it is to be successful.

When thinking about securing more income and the time required to be successful, it is good to consider the broad categories of "charitable gifts." The primary focus should be on the percentage of gifts per category. In 2017, more than $410 billion in gifts occurred. Of that amount 70 percent came from individuals. (That percentage varies from 70 to 75 percent in most years.) Foundations—think grants—accounted for 16 percent of the giving. The balance was made up of bequests (9 percent) and corporate gifts (5 percent) (https://www.nptrust.org/philanthropic-resources/charitable-giving-statistics). Clearly the most likely donor category is the individual.

Fundraisers sometimes suggest that fundraising is akin to gold prospecting. You never know when you will strike it rich, but there is always hope. Your chances of doing so are enhanced if you understand the landscape of local giving so you can identify the best "prospects." Because libraries are short staffed in most instances and few can devote an FTE full-time to fundraising, it becomes essential to focus on the best possibilities.

Fundraising, although it may have to be solely a part-time activity, requires planning and leadership. It will not be effective if it is a matter of "I'll do it when I have time." Large libraries may have a full-time fundraiser; most depend on the efforts of several people who devote some of their time to fundraising—a team approach. As with any team, there needs to be one person in charge to call meetings, set agendas, propose ideas, implement plans, push the initiative forward, and monitor outcomes—in essence, provide the leadership. Generally, that person is the senior or next-most senior manager of the library. One reason for this is because donors want to know they are working with the decision makers.

Even if fundraising is a part-time activity, there is an institutional cost. Time spent on fundraising is time not spent on other library operations. The library's position as part of a larger whole usually means that it must get approval before undertaking fundraising activities. Senior managers may not approve such activities if they believe funds raised would not outweigh the time and effort or would be in conflict with other, "broader," fundraising activities. Additionally, many funding groups and agencies require matching funds. That is, the library has to demonstrate that it will provide a certain percentage of funds to the proposed project or program if funded. These funds can be actual dollars allocated, in-kind funds (volunteer time, for example), or a combination of both. Senior managers must be aware of these funding stipulations and be sure that the funds being proposed as matching funds exist before they approve a proposal.

REVENUE SOURCES

There are two broad categories of sources of additional income—internal and external. Some sources, in either category, are "iffy" in the sense they can be challenging to exploit. However, they are worth exploring as they can be very helpful.

Internal sources

Libraries generate revenue such as fees for services. There are two significant questions about such income. Does this income remain with the library? Often there are laws or regulations that require any such monies go to the parent organization's general fund. Yes, some of that money may come back to the library as general revenue budget allocations, but that is no different than saying a public library shares in the tax revenue. The second question is: if the library retains all or some share of the income, is that amount viewed as replacement or supplemental? If it is a replacement, then there is no gain for the library. Perhaps the most common situation where such questions come up is fine income. Many libraries

|||| **CHECK THESE OUT**

Two useful publications to read to get more in-depth information on library income generation are *Becoming a Fundraiser: The Principles and Practices of Library Development*, 2nd ed., by Victoria Steele and Stephen D. Elder (Chicago, IL: American Library Association, 2000) and "The Ten Principles for Successful Fundraising" by Gary A. Hunt and Hwa-Wei Lee (*Bottom Line* 6, nos. 3/4: 27–33 , 1993).

👥 FORMER AUTHOR'S EXPERIENCE

Camila Alire, while dean at the University of New Mexico, and her management team wanted to expand a coffee cart in the main library, much to the chagrin of some staff members who didn't want to give up valuable space. When doing focus groups, the library learned that while students appreciated 24/7 remote access to library materials, they also wanted a "library as place" where they could meet for group study and group projects and where they could enjoy a café atmosphere. The final result was the installation of the first full-service Starbucks located in an academic library in the United States. The goodwill between the library and the campus—students, faculty, and staff— far exceeded the concerns of the naysayers.

have fines for rule infractions as well as fees for lost or damaged items. As you might guess, not getting money for a lost or damaged items can become a drain on your budget when you must repair or replace the items. This in turn puts more pressure on you to raise monies from somewhere.

A similar situation may exist for fees charged for library services, although it is more common that the library retains all or most of that income. Such services include photocopying, printing, and space or room rentals. Those services have supply and/or maintenance costs that come from the library's operating budget. If the library is allowed to retain all such income and the service pricing is appropriate, there may be a slight monetary increase. This, of course, depends on the income not being treated as replacement funding.

Being able to retain such money as supplemental funding is not always easy, as funding authorities tend to try to keep overall increases as low as possible. To gain the necessary approval takes time and a well-designed strategy. Clearly, success will result in an ongoing increase, assuming the funding authority does not change its position on the nature of such funds.

Naming opportunities

Naming opportunities are one-time in nature and any monies realized almost always go into an endowment. A common time for naming opportunities is when there is a major library building or remodeling project. However, in many cases, not all the opportunities are taken. In some instances, there was no effort to seek such opportunities so that the library could engage in such an effort later. Perhaps a name becomes part of the building name or a room within the library for a fee. Such opportunities can generate large sums of money. Lower cost opportunities might be a special seating area, an information commons area, or even sections of the collections stacks.

An endowment should produce income in most years. Again, there is the question of how these funds are treated by the parent organization. A generalized picture of how an endowment operates is that the principal is invested and not touched in order to generate the maximum return. There is a percentage of the annual return on the investment that is dispersed for use. A very common percentage is 4 percent. Thus, assuming the endowment has a good year generating an 8 percent return with a payout of 4 percent, the library would get the 4 percent, and the balance, minus administrative expenses, increases the endowment principal. In theory, an endowment grows in size each year and lasts indefinitely while generating some spendable funds. The theory translates into reality when you average out a number of years. (Like all other endowments, those of libraries took substantial hits during the Great Recession and are only now recovering their losses.)

Another income possibility is a cooperative venture with a business, most often a coffee shop or fast food company. The idea is that the library will receive rental income for the space used by the business. Rent is often a percentage of sales rather than a flat rate, although there is usually a minimum annual fee if sales do not reach a defined level. It is even possible to have such a cooperative venture without giving up space in the library. To do so requires identifying a business owner who is a strong library supporter and convincing him or her to donate some small percentage of sales back to the library. A bookmark, sign, flyer, or similar item would provide information such as "Did you know the library gets X percent of every dollar spent at _____?" Clearly, such an effort requires substantial approvals and possibly generates some concern regarding "commercialization" of the library.

Bonds and millage increases

Two other one-time resources are very dependent on the library's public image because they require voter approval, at least for public and school libraries. Academic libraries may not face voter approval but will need senior management's approval for a bond issuance.

A millage increase would increase taxes (a mill is one one-thousandth of a tax dollar). Many states have laws that set the maximum allowable millage rate for library support. Only a few libraries have been permitted to reach the maximum. Any effort to increase the current rate requires voter approval. Getting voter approval hinges on public perception of the value of the library.

Conducting a successful library referendum takes careful planning and a substantial amount of work. A question is, does the effort pay off? The report on 2016 referenda (www.informedlibrarian.com) indicated that of 150 such efforts, 81 percent passed. The approved topics ranged from continued operating expense to constructing a new building. The referenda included bonds issuances and millage increases.

There are also some rare and, in the past, overlooked opportunities to raise some substantial amounts of money locally: wills, trusts, and planned giving. Obviously, bequests in a will become a source of funds only at death. Today many nonprofit groups actively work with people to have the library included in a will through an annuity or trust. Trusts come in many shapes and sizes. Some may generate income for the library only during the donor's lifetime; others may generate income for both the donor and library during the donor's lifetime, while others become effective only at the donor's death. Planned giving is likely to increase in importance for libraries over the coming years.

Partnerships with businesses are one of the newer fundraising approaches for libraries. Many libraries prefer to use the term "collaboration" as it seems less profit oriented. Glen Holt (2006) listed several reasons for seeking corporate partnerships. His last reason, in our opinion, is the most important: "Co-funding through sponsorships can be a great way to build and share current and potential audiences between the public and

> ### 👥 AUTHOR'S EXPERIENCE
>
> Evans served on the board of a public library district Friends group for six years. The primary fundraising was an ongoing book sale and a three-day annual sale. During his time on the board, the group raised about $35,000 annually. That money was distributed to various library activities such as the summer reading program, purchases for the bookmobile, and replacement furniture. Although the group provided most of the labor there was a substantial amount of library staff time for supporting the efforts.

private sector" (p. 35). You will need to think broadly or imaginatively to find sponsorship possibilities. Partnerships with business can be extended to acquiring expertise that is not available within the library. Local radio and TV stations may provide airtime, local newspaper reporters can brief staff on how to write good copy, and public relations companies may well be prepared to offer their help to nonprofit libraries.

External support groups

Library support groups have at least one clear advantage over internal sources of monies for operating expenses, that is, the funds they generate are less susceptible to the funding authority treating them as replacement funds. In part, because the amounts vary from year to year and, more importantly, the authority has less access to what those amounts might be. The amounts generated may be small, but often they are significant (see the sidebar above).

Friends

One long-standing revenue source for libraries is the sale of duplicate or otherwise unwanted gifts. "Gifts in-kind" to libraries are very common; how libraries dispose of such items varies. Publicly supported libraries need to be aware of any regulations regarding the disposal of public property. Donors may benefit from a tax deduction for cash donations or in-kind gifts to charitable or public bodies. Libraries are almost always 501(c)(3) organizations, which means gifts are tax deductible.

Individuals join Friends groups by paying a small annual membership fee that gives them a discount on items the group sells or some other modest benefit. Fundraising activities depend on members volunteering time to these efforts. One challenge for such groups is keeping up interest in its activities and maintaining library support for those activities.

Friends groups can raise money in a variety of ways other than book sales. A web search generates a substantial number of sites with ideas that go beyond the usual book sales. For example, see https://sparks.winnefox.org/2012/01/30/successful-fundraising -ideas/ and www.techsoupforlibraries.org/blog/creative-fundraising-ideas-for-libraries, which lists more 100 ideas.)

Foundations

Library foundations share with Friends groups the role of providing financial support for a library. Both may have 501(c)(3) status, but not always. The major difference is that the

AUTHORS' EXPERIENCE

After being on the Friends board, Evans became a member of the foundation board. One difference between the two was that monies raised by the Friends were dispersed in the year they were raised. The foundation generally had about half the Friends' distribution to make available. It takes a substantial endowment to generate income when the payout rate is 4 percent.

foundation handles the library's investments and has a long-term focus. Another difference is they have no members other than individuals on the board. Donors yes, members no. Board members may or may not be expected to make an annual contribution to the endowment.

The foundation seeks gifts, often through an annual solicitation that is similar to the ones we all receive during the year. As well, the board may be involved in securing a bequest or a planned giving gift.

As noted above, endowments generally have an annual distribution based on the endowment's investment's performance. The foundation allocates the funds to the library according to its own criteria. For example, it may invite library departments to submit requests for funds or perhaps there is a short-term project that could be funded with several years' worth of distribution. In the latter case, the board might purchase media with each year's income until all the money is spent.

Social media has become another fundraising venue for many organizations, including libraries. Friends groups and foundations almost always have a web presence that includes a mechanism for making a donation. How much money is raised as a result is less important than raising awareness about Friends groups and foundations. Making direct appeals becomes more effective as prospects learn more about the library's story.

A relatively new fundraising activity for libraries is crowdfunding. Almost all such efforts relate to a project and seek some portion of the funding by posting an explanation of the need on a website such as Kickstarter (https://www.kickstarter.com/). The goal is a specific dollar amount. In the case of Kickstarter, there is some expectation there is an innovative aspect to the project.

SOMETHING TO PONDER

501(c)(3) status is interesting from a library perspective. Such status means gifts to the entity are tax deductible. It also means the entity may not be politically active. The reality is, at least for public and school libraries, that libraries need help in both arenas— charitable giving and political influence.

If a library has both a Friends group and a foundation operation in place, might it be wise to have only one with a 501(c)(3) status? Since the foundation's focus is long-term and it (hopefully) receives large gifts, it makes sense for it to have 501(c)(3) status. The Friends group might be best employed as a politically active group.

Libraries have a built-in advantage that will help them reach their fundraising goals. People are often suspicious about online appeals, but as we have noted, libraries are among the most highly trusted organizations in the country. Thus, a library funding effort carries a high degree of donor trust and increases the chance of achieving the funding goal.

Crowdfunding, as is true of any fundraising activity, is hard work. The library's effort will be in open competition with a number of other "funding opportunities." Compelling stories are always a key component of any successful fundraising undertaking. Keep in mind that time devoted to creating a persuasive crowdfunding story can be useful in other library efforts such as advocacy and marketing programs.

FUNDRAISING PROCESS

Fundraising for nonprofit organizations has become a profession. Many of its practitioners specialize in a particular organizational type, such as education or health care. Such specialization allows the person to have a deeper understanding of the needs and operations of the organization. However, there are few fundraisers who specialize in information services, much less libraries. It is possible that it will take a significant amount of time to bring the fundraiser up to speed about what the library does and what its needs are.

Large libraries may have professionally trained fundraisers assigned to them on a part- or full-time basis. Many libraries depend on part-time efforts of various staff members to seek and secure outside funds. Very often these efforts take the form of writing a grant proposal. As we have noted, libraries tend to be marginally adequately funded and staffed. Given daily library operational demands is it any wonder fundraising is a part-time effort?

In addition to the part-time aspect, there is the fact that libraries are part of a larger organization and rarely are the only sub-unit in need of more funding. It is important to coordinate fundraising activities so that several units from the institution do not approach a single source with different projects. A proposal may already be in front of the source and therefore another proposal may raise questions about organizational priorities. Educational institutions typically have a development or philanthropy department that coordinates all campus fundraising activities.

Regardless of source, income generation is largely a matter of "the right person asking the right source for the right amount for the right project at the right time and in the right way." As you might imagine, getting all those "rights" right takes planning, practice, preparation, and practical experience. Workshops help, but real-world experience, and a few disappointments along the way, will translate theory and ideas into money in the library's bank.

||||| **CHECK THIS OUT**

A good article that reviews crowdfunding is Debra A. Riley-Huff, Kevin Herrera, Susan Ivey, and Tina Harry's "Crowdfunding in Libraries, Archives and Museums" (*Bottom Line* 29, no. 2: 67–85, 2016).

Another 2016 article worth reviewing is Joyce Garczynski's "#Donate: The Role of Social Media in Academic Library Fundraising" (*Bottom Line* 29, no. 2: 60–66).

Who gives?

The question of who gives is not easy to answer if you are looking to find a single donor type. Based on data collected by organizations such as the National Center for Charitable Statistics (https://nccs.urban.org/) and Giving USA (https://givingusa.org/), there is a very broad range in who donates. Certainly, large foundations and wealthy individuals contribute the most dollars. Basically, there are several different demographic elements that you might say are true of the average donor in that 70+ percentage category of donations mentioned earlier. The typical modest gift comes from a native-born married couple with children, who own their own home, and who have at least some post-secondary education. That description is based on data from sources such as those mentioned above. While that description is very broad, it does reflect the overall picture of charitable giving in the United States. Other factors are income and age. Older individuals with secure incomes are more likely to give than younger people. They also tend to give slightly higher amounts.

You must keep in mind that the composition of your service community is the key to successful fundraising for the library. For the public library, perhaps "married with children" will be significant in how the library goes about fundraising. Clearly it is critical in the school library context. However, it should not become the single focal point, as we will cover below.

While income may be a factor in the gift size, what may matter more is the number of gifts. In fact, the "small" donor is often the most consistent donor over time. A library foundation's annual fundraising generally contacts the same individuals while adding only a few new names to the list of prospects. It is rare for such efforts to see a gift greater than $100; nevertheless, the ongoing nature of such gifts builds an endowment.

What motivates giving?

Like the question of who gives, the reason why a donor decides to make a gift is complex. One reason for the complexity is that most gifts are rarely based on a single motive. Trained fundraisers are good at identifying multiple motivations and using them to secure a gift. Professional fundraisers often divide the motivators into one of two broad categories— self-interested and altruistic. Some charitable giving researchers suggest that even the most altruistic gifts are, at their core, based on self-interest.

What are the presumed altruistic motivators? Perhaps the clearest altruistic reason is seeing the gift as promoting a social good that has no connection for the donor beyond doing good. Two other categories seem to be even more a mix of altruism and self-interest.

One such motivator that some researchers place in the altruistic category is exchange theory. This type of motivation arises when a person receives something from a charitable organization and there is an implicit or even explicit implication the recipient should make a gift. An example of an explicit motivator would be a mass mailing of a calendar or greeting card accompanied by a return mail envelope and a form that lists suggested dollar amounts for donations. Another example is when a person receives some honor, perhaps an honorary doctorate. There may not be any overt suggestions that a gift, or assistance in securing a gift, is required, but the hope is that it will occur.

The second semi-altruistic motive is what some fundraisers refer to as the "warm glow." The glow arises in the donor when she or he gives to a cause they believe is important to social well-being and with which the person has no direct connection with beyond gift-giving.

Self-interest motivators are varied, but generally you can place them into one or more broad categories. Two of the most common are self-esteem and taxes. Almost every charitable gift has the potential for a tax deduction. Thus, it is linked to most other gift motivators; even if the deduction is not taken, the potential exists. Two variables in the impact of this motivator are the size of the gift (small amounts often are not deducted) and the "value" of the deduction. The larger the gift and higher that donor's tax bracket, the more likely it is to motivate a gift. Charitable giving researchers have evidence that changes in tax brackets and/or allowances for charitable deductions will increase or decrease the totals of charitable gifts (somewhere between 2 and 3 percent up or down for each 1 percent change in the tax).

Self-esteem is a strong motivator of charitable giving. Thinking "I can afford to do this" and then doing so gives the donor a sense of self-worth. Another motivator, recognition (such as a name on a plaque or listed as a donor in the annual report), when linked with self-esteem increases the chances of receiving a gift. One reason is that others who may know the donor may be impressed or encouraged to also donate.

Access to service is another self-interest motivator. This occurs when the donor will be given access to a service in return for a gift. A common example of this type of motivation is paying a membership fee to a charitable organization (a museum, for example). The membership amount may be deductible, which is one incentive to join. The organization gains a small amount but, more significantly, receives contact information for further fundraising efforts. A library example is where becoming a member of a Friends group gets the person a discount on items the Friends sell to raise money.

Another very common motivator is to memorialize or honor someone. Such gifts tend to be generous because the name of the person being honored will be displayed where others can see it. On a smaller scale, libraries for years offered named book plates at a very modest cost. In today's digital world, they are less common but still do exist.

A less common motivator, at least for libraries, is that donations can help clear a person's conscience. Occasionally, a library will get an envelope with a note and some cash saying something to the effect that the enclosed will make up for an item not returned.

Prospect identification and development

The discussion above painted the "who" and "why" of charitable giving in broad brush-strokes. However, until these elements are incorporated into a plan based on knowledge of the local charitable giving, they are of no real value. You need a plan of action to identify prospects and how to approach them. This is a time when library advocacy efforts are of help. These efforts should have identified individuals and business that, at some level, are empathic with library goals and operations. Fundraising professionals know the most likely donors are those already known to the organization. Certainly, that pool may be expanded over time, but it is the best starting point. When thinking about donation plans, there are three basic types of gifts that require plans of some type—irregular small gifts, modest annual giving, and major gifts.

Regardless of the giver type, there is a development process that varies. Gaining and holding potential donors' interest in the library is essential. Marketing and advocacy activities are part of that process. Securing favorable press is another means (e.g., about receiving a grant). Another tactic is to put on a program of broad community interest and invite potential donors. Especially effective is getting such individuals actively involved in some aspect of the library. When it comes to potential major donors, the development process may take years and a substantial amount of one-on-one "cultivation" (building the person's interest)—such as lunches, dinners, and the like. The goal is to get to "the ask" at a time when the answer is likely to be yes. Essentially it is the right person, asking for the right amount, at the right time and place.

Stewardship

Without question, once a positive outcome has been achieved, stewardship is the key to securing future gifts. Stewardship is a form of accountability. There are several components to effective stewardship, the most basic of which is sending a thank-you letter that mentions the dollar amount or type of in-kind gift. If nothing else, such a document provides donors with something for the IRS should they decide to take a tax deduction.

For moderate and large gifts, there are other elements, such as updates or communications about how the gifts had a positive outcome. For example, a donor who establishes a scholarship endowment usually receives at least two annual updates—the name of the scholarship recipient and statement of the endowment's performance. Often a thank you letter from the recipient is included. Another type of update is newsletters about the organization's activities and plans for the future. Seasonal greetings and communications of a personal nature (birthday cards and the like) and even small gifts (candy or a water bottle with the organization's logo, for example) are part of the stewardship tool kit. Donors deserve, and may expect, recognition and information about how their gifts are used.

Effective stewardship activities are essential when it comes to planned giving. Planned giving designates a gift that will come sometime in the future, most often when the potential donor's estate is settled. There is a document that spells out what the gift will be as well as how it may be used. *Potential* is the critical word. Planned gifts, unlike other gifts, are

---

⦀ CHECK THIS OUT

A good book to consult, regardless of library type, is Amy Sherman Smith and Matthew D. Leher's *Legacies for Libraries: A Practical Guide to Planned Giving* (Chicago: American Library Association, 2000).

👥 AUTHORS' EXPERIENCE

Evans has vivid memories of maintaining a long-term relationship with a donor who had a provision in her will that would give the proceeds from the sale of her home to the library when the estate was settled. He was told about the need to maintain this donor-library relationship as soon as he became library director: that he should go to her house twice a month on Sundays and further advised to take some bakery "goodies." Shortly after starting the visits, he decided to bake a cake for a visit. He was very surprised to find out that the donor had once supervised Julia Child and remained a close friend with Child. While she appreciated his cake-baking efforts, she suggested he buy one of Julia's dessert cookbooks. You need to do almost anything to maintain good donor relations.

provisional in character. A donor may revoke the agreement if there is negative news about the organization or there is poor stewardship. Also, there is the possibility there may not be the assets left in the estate to cover all or even any of the planned amount.

SEEKING GRANTS

Grants are another, if unpredictable, source of additional funding. As our opening quotation from Grace Romund suggests, such funds are not for everyday operational expenses. They are almost always for projects and specify specific time frames (most grants last twelve to twenty-four months) for expending the funds.

The art of grantsmanship is something you can develop, but like any art it takes practice, and then more practice, before you have consistent success. One way to start developing grant writing skills is to take one or two workshops on the topic. National and state library organizations offer such opportunities from time to time. State libraries often provide similar short courses, and some even provide one-on-one guidance. Once you have a handle on the basics, it is time to try the process.

Most libraries have several potential projects that need funding. Deciding what to put forward is a process of prioritizing library needs and assessing where the funding might come from. Clearly, there is little point in seeking money when you cannot identify a potential funding source. Likewise, careful thought should go into how much library priorities should change just because some funding *might* be available. "Might" is the key consideration; there are generally far more submissions made for funding than are granted. The odds of success are modest at best, especially for the first few submissions.

Where do you find information about potential organizations that fund library initiatives? An obvious first choice is a search for potential sources. Many state libraries have a site that lists major granting bodies along with their own grants program (for example, details of Maine's program can be found at https://www1.maine.gov/msl/libs/admin/funding/). The Institute of Museum and Library Services (IMLS) provides block grants to state libraries who in turn operate a grants program (https://www.imls.gov/grants/apply-grant/available-grants). This is, in a sense, a timesaving device for IMLS that also enhances a library's chance of securing a grant. A useful resource is The Foundation Center (http://foundationcenter.org/) which has a variety of information about philanthropic foundations.

A key step in developing a grant is to know what a foundation's or agency's current funding priorities are. Although their broad interests seldom change, their annual funding priorities within a broad area may vary from year to year. Do your research before making a call or sending a letter of inquiry. Most granting agencies have websites where you can do a substantial amount of research about the agency's mission, priorities of the current funding cycle, funding cycle timelines, proposal guidelines, deadlines, and much more. Most grant-giving agencies are willing to talk by phone to explore projects. This can save both you and the agency time.

Although grants are project-focused, they may offer some help with operating expenses. A common kind of relief is equipment, such as scanners, computers, and printers. Such items may be part of the grant and required to carry out the project. Equipment has a reasonably long life span, far beyond the project's life time, and they remain with the library, thus saving equipment money later.

Another potential area of income is the overhead that is part of the project's cost (the cost to administer the grant, use of physical space and equipment, and utilities, for example). Granting bodies set the overhead rate and what costs are allowed in the calculation of the overhead amount. For libraries, it can be challenging to retain some portion of the overhead funds as their parent organizations usually have first call on the funds. Libraries that have a solid record of generating overhead income often can work out a fund-sharing arrangement.

Many are matching grants. That is, the library is expected to cover some of the project cost. What will count as matching varies by granting bodies; however, almost all allow for some percentage of the salary of the library staff (the principal investigator or project leader, for example) carrying out the project. Another commonly allowed method of cost-sharing is the value of volunteer time contributed to the project. One of the authors is currently volunteering for a museum library and his "hourly value" is $28.83. Most nonprofit organizations use volunteer time in matching grants when appropriate.

■ KEY POINTS TO REMEMBER

- Income generation from sources other than the parent body will become an increasingly important part of a library's fiscal management activities.
- Fundraising requires time, thought, preparation, and effort.
- The vast majority of philanthropic giving comes from individuals.
- People give to causes they trust and believe will benefit society.
- Friends groups and foundations are an important source of donations.
- Major donors require cultivation and involvement before they donate.
- Online giving for libraries is likely to increase.
- Grants to libraries are often the key to funding a project and may provide some modest relief for the library operating budget.

REFERENCES

Crumpton. Michael A. 2016. "Cultivating an Organizational Effort for Development. *Bottom Line* 29, no. 2: 97–113.

Holt, Glen. 2006. "Economics: Corporate Sponsorship." *Bottom Line* 19, no. 1: 35–39.

Riley-Huff, Debra A., Kevin Herrera, Susan Ivey, and Tina Harry. 2016. "Crowdfunding in Libraries, Archives and Museums." *Bottom Line* 29, no. 2: 67–85.

Romund, Grace. 2017. "Collaborative Grant-Seeking: A Practical Guide for Librarians." *Journal of the Canadian Health Libraries Association* 38, no.1: 34–35.

Sannwald, William W. 2018. *Financial Management for Libraries*. Chicago: ALA Publications.

Whitchurch, Jesse, and Comer, Alberta. 2016. "Creating a Culture of Philanthropy." *The Bottom Line* 29, no. 2: 114–22. https://doi.org/10.1108/BL-02-2016-0012.

CHAPTER 19

Managing Technology

Libraries make major investments in strategic automation products, both
during the initial implementation period and in annual fees paid for support,
software maintenance, and other services.

Marshall Breeding, 2018

Librarians and archivists have made great strides in making collections
discoverable and accessible to a wide audience by creating electronic finding
aids, digitizing materials and using social media, but modern researchers
want more.

Nancy Richey, Amanda Drost, and Allison Day, 2017

Integrated library systems (ILSs) support the entire business operations of an
academic library from acquiring and processing library resources to making
them available to user communities and preserving them for future use. As
libraries' needs evolve, there is a pressing demand for libraries to migrate
from one generation of ILS to the next.

Shea-Tinn Yeh and Zhiping Walter, 2016

In today's electronic world, other than funding challenges, it is hard to imagine a more demanding management area for libraries than technology. Even personnel issues seem to be slightly easier. Had libraries not been quick to adapt technology and integrate it into daily operations, they would be more akin to dodo birds rather than being a valued part of society's well-being.

It's not unusual to hear claims that libraries are dead, unneeded anachronisms. Some people think that Google or Amazon could better fill the role libraries play in society. One thing that seems clear is that the people making such suggestions have only the vaguest idea what libraries do. Another frequently overlooked feature of libraries is their ability and willingness to adapt to changing technologies. In fact, they have over 4,000 years of successfully doing so. We expect they will continue to do so into the foreseeable future.

Libraries began using computers in the 1960s and have embraced new technologies as they develop and evolve. Today, there are very few daily activities in a library that do not involve some aspect of these new technologies. Almost every day, you can read about some new technological development that may have potential in a library setting. Libraries monitor technological developments and investigate how they might be useful in library operations.

There was a time, not all that long ago, when a five-year technology replacement cycle for the library seemed too short. Now it seems to have become nanoseconds. Finding

ADVISORY BOARD EXPERIENCE

As Mika has worked with libraries on strategic plans over the years, he has moved from creating ten-year plans, to five-year plans, and now often suggests to library boards that they view the strategic plan as a three-year plan. He recommends that the technology portion be part of that three-year cycle. In addition, where once technology hardware was seen as capital expenditure, he now suggests it be viewed as part of the supplies line. The costs have been dramatically reduced for computers in the past decade, and printers are inexpensive, with replacing ink cartridges being a larger expense than the printer itself.

the funding for that and to maintain other library services desired by our users tests our creativity and ingenuity.

Library technology also generates some collaboration challenges, as there is interdependency between the library and the parent organization's IT unit. Libraries are not self-sufficient when it comes to information and communication technology (ICT). Library managerial leaders must collaborate with IT colleagues to arrive at the best solution that meets the needs of the organization as a whole. It is also necessary to collaborate with other libraries in order to achieve maximum results from our digital dollars. (Note: we explore the managerial aspect of technology in this chapter and only comment in passing about how those technologies function.)

There are many components to libraries' use of technology; however, there are two broad aspects. From a daily work point of view, ICT has been fully integrated into library operations. Service to the users is equally dependent on ICT. Almost every library, from school libraries to the Library of Congress, employs technology for daily work activities and service and has been doing so for some time.

Offering the technologies is only part of the picture. They must be backed up by staff members who understand the needs of the user community, anticipate these needs, know the relevant sources, and deliver the required information in the preferred format at the right time. Information delivery still requires human intervention.

STAFF AND USER TRAINING

One aspect of managing technology involves ensuring that staff at every level have the necessary background and training to handle the technology in place. Funding for staff development opportunities for the professional side of information work is usually limited. The challenge is to decide how to allocate the funds available.

Library technology vendors usually offer some level of training on their products. It is often more effective to build training costs into the price of acquiring the system rather than try to secure separate funding. Some software vendors offer online training packages that are built into their applications.

There are three audiences for training: the entire staff, new staff members, and end users. Considering the range of training, it is evident why training costs should be an item in the annual technology budget. Sometimes it is possible to use a mentor approach for library-wide training. One advantage is that a mentor is better able to relate to the special needs of her or his coworkers than is a general trainer. Training in groups is more cost-effective than the one-on-one approach—this is true for both staff and end users. Two widely used training technologies are live webinars and recorded sessions.

Another training cost is the help desk function staff provide. With remote access, users will ask both information-related questions and questions about accessing the system. Bell and Shank (2004) have described the important role of blended librarians. There is a need for these specialists, who can handle the traditional requests for information and also assist users with technical problems. They must have subject knowledge, awareness of the many technical issues users may encounter, and strong communication skills. While the education of today's librarians provides a good background in basic areas such as database management and networking, support staff are less likely to have an educational background in ICT, so you will need to provide that background.

One other technology-related staff issue is "technostress." One of its factors is physical, as staff members spend more and more time at a computer all day. Poor posture, equipment, lighting, and physical arrangements can lead to a variety of physical or health problems, ranging from mild headaches and eye strain to carpal tunnel syndrome. Ergonomic factors are important as there are legal requirements that organizations must meet. Personnel need information about posture and exercises to release tension and must learn about how to plan their work so that they do not spend long uninterrupted hours at a workstation. Getting away, even for a few minutes every hour, reduces technostress.

Technostress' second component is mental. Managers know that changes in technology will result in tension even if there is no resistance to changing technology. Part of the stress-reduction process is to provide ample and adequate training for changes. Scheduling enough lead time and getting written information to the staff helps to reduce stress when a change actually occurs.

Working with vendors to produce user-friendly paper documentation and online manuals can reduce technostress. Nothing builds stress more quickly than facing some deadline that requires the use of a new technology and not being able to make it work after following every step in the documentation. Talking with other libraries about their impressions of the product and trying it out yourself before making the purchase decision are always good practices.

Mangers also face technological stress, especially related to leaving work at work. Some questions they should ask include:

- Is it really essential that I have the same technology at home as in the office?
- Is it really essential that I do this work at home?
- Is it possible that I could make better use of my time in the office so I do not have to take work home?

||||| **CHECK THIS OUT**

The American Library Association's *Library Technology Reports* (journals.ala.org/ltr) and *Smart Libraries Newsletter* (journals.ala.org/sln) are helpful for keeping in touch with developments in library technology.

- Is it really essential that I check my office e-mail from home at night, on the weekend, at a conference, or even on vacation?
- Can I turn my phone off when I leave the office?
- Is it necessary that I become the "techie of techies" in my organization when that is not my area of responsibility?

TECHNOLOGY PLANNING

Maintaining a successful library ICT program rests on careful long-range planning and the ability to adjust as circumstances change. Accurately predicting future changes is almost impossible much beyond twelve to eighteen months. Nevertheless, the best insurance for managing technology in the most cost-effective manner possible is developing a long-term plan.

By using a rolling plan that allows you to review and revise each year, you gain the benefits of long-term planning while maintaining the flexibility to adjust the plan in a changing environment. All of the planning elements discussed in chapter 7 apply. What makes long-term technology planning somewhat different from other planning is the almost certain knowledge that the plan will probably never be fully implemented—each passing year some element will be modified as technologies evolve.

There are several aspects of ICT planning. Most important are the strategic considerations. It is useful to think about technology both offensively and defensively. From an offensive viewpoint, considering how to achieve or realize maximum benefit from the use of ICT is vital. Defensively, think in terms of controlled growth and what is happening in other libraries. Finally, it is necessary to understand the underlying costs.

There are a number of planning models. We favor Emberton's (1987) holistic planning approach. The first step is to gain agreement on, or verify that, the current statement of the library's mission and goals reflects the actual desires of senior management and governing bodies. One advantage of starting here is that both are general in character, which means the uncertainty about future directions of technology is less of an issue.

👥 AUTHORS' EXPERIENCE

Greenwell can't emphasize enough how important it is to acquire and utilize technology to solve a problem, rather than purchase technology and then try to find some use for it. For example, when tablet computers first came on the market, many libraries felt they needed to acquire them, but not all had a plan in place for who would use them, how they would be used, or how such personal devices could be configured to work properly in a shared environment. Some libraries did the same with 3-D printers, not considering the skill level required to use modeling software or the ongoing cost of supplies and maintenance.

The desire to have shiny new toys can be strong, but without any sort of plan, they can be an incredible waste of funds and time. That's not to say that you shouldn't be looking at new technologies and how they could benefit library users and staff (really, all librarians should be doing this to some extent) but having a plan in place is important before making an investment.

Using objectives, which are much more specific, and which reflect the purposes of current functions and activities, allows you to plan technology requirements realistically.

Another step is to examine each goal, objective, function, and activity and ask the question, "Could ICT assist in its performance or achievement?" Related questions include, "What type and how much technology would, or could, be appropriate?" and "What problem does the technology address?" One example of a goal is "to provide twenty-four-hour access to library resources." By using a general statement, you can develop a long-range plan without too much concern about unexpected technological changes. You are not locked into a particular technology solution long term. It also makes it easier for the decision makers to look at today's state-of-the-art technology and consider experts' opinions about future trends when deciding what to do during the next twelve to eighteen months.

Basic technical issues also play a key role in a successful planning process. It becomes important to have answers to questions such as:

- Are there any organizational policies that influence decision making related to technology?
- What types of data are required to reach an informed decision?
- Which technology offers the greatest payoff in relation to service goals and objectives?
- What are the functional advantages, if any, of the new technology?
- What are the technical prerequisites for using a specific technology?
- If different objectives require different technologies, what are the compatibility issues?
- Does the library have the infrastructure to support the new technology?
- Is the technology open system or proprietary? If proprietary, how difficult would it be to migrate to another system in the future?
- How will staff and users be affected?
- What are the staffing and training requirements?
- What are the user education requirements?
- What are the short- and long-term implications?

Beyond technical considerations, there are some political and end user issues to consider:

- What is the parent institution's attitude toward expenditures on technology? Does it take a long-term or a short-term view?
- Is there an organizational policy to centralize ICT services, or are they decentralized?
- Will the expenditure for and implementation of the technology create relationship problems with other units in the parent institution or collaborating services?
- What is the library's track record with funding authorities when it comes to implementing technology?
- Will all end users be able to access and/or benefit from the proposed technology?
- Is there an issue about differing end user platforms or the average user's system capabilities?

- Does the proposed technology relate to or meet immediate- and long-term needs of end users?
- Does the proposed technology restrict or constrain end user creativity in using technology?
- Is the system flexible enough to meet all end users' needs?
- Are there any end user training implications?

The planning must involve functional, institutional, usage, risk, and staffing analyses as well as take into account implementation and hardware assessment. Remember that technology planning is about more than hardware and software; it requires understanding the organization, its purpose(s), and its customers. Your goal should be to create an information environment appropriate for the library while meeting the parent organization's needs.

CONTROLLING TECHNOLOGY COSTS

Controlling technology costs is a managerial leader's challenge and a budget officer's nightmare. Traditionally, libraries have had two categories of expense that are ongoing and always increasing: salaries and journal subscription costs. There are some techniques for controlling salary expenses, such as not granting additional staff positions, limiting annual salary increases, imposing hiring freezes, and, occasionally, cutting existing positions. Generally, there are fewer options for controlling subscription price increases, because they are outside the control of you and the parent institution. Many libraries have joined consortia to gain bargaining power with publishers in order to limit the size of price increases.

Today, technology costs are the third component in the ever-increasing costs for most libraries. They are also beyond your control. Unlike journals, you rarely are able to "cancel" technology. Today's libraries and their users are too dependent on technology to delay expenditures on upgrades and replacements. When a vendor no longer supports a product, you must either upgrade or face the costs and frustration of attempting to maintain the existing technology on your own. The two most effective tools for controlling technology costs are having a rolling five-year plan and developing a clear understanding of which functionalities are absolutely essential and which would just be nice to have.

A continuing trend in many organizations is to outsource services to control costs. Providers of specialist services are able to employ a wide range of expertise and amortize costs over a number of customers, perhaps moving some tasks offshore. ICT services have

👥 AUTHORS' EXPERIENCE

Evans worked at a university that struggled with controlling institutional ICT costs. The university president made a surprise announcement on a Friday afternoon that all of the ICT services were to be outsourced beginning on the following Monday. ICT staff had the weekend to decide if they would accept a position with the outsourcing firm. In any event, they would cease being university employees at 5:00 p.m. that day. The president also announced he had signed a seven-year contract with the company.

Four years later, the university canceled the outsourcing contract. That decision led to additional problems for campus IT users.

the potential for outsourcing, particularly in small organizations. This requires a clear understanding of expectations on the part of the customer and supplier, a consideration of what would happen if the supplier fails, a careful examination of internal costs and outsourcing, a legal contract, and close monitoring of the quality of service provided.

Technological security has both physical and intellectual aspects.

PHYSICAL SECURITY

You don't want the physical technology assets you've invested in to be stolen or its functionality compromised by malicious behavior. On the intellectual side, you must address concerns about personal privacy as well as intellectual freedom. To a degree, the physical security aspects are the easiest to manage.

There are four broad types of control that will help ensure quality and security:

- information system controls
- processing controls
- storage control
- physical facility controls

Information system controls attempt to ensure accuracy, validity, and propriety of system activities. Many relate to input as well as to output data. Some of the data entry controls are passwords for different levels of staff, formatted data entry screens, and audible error signals. Control logs preserve evidence of all system input.

Processing controls help ensure that correctly entered data goes through processing properly. Some processing controls identify errors in calculations, logical operations, or data not processed or lost. There are controls for both hardware and software. For hardware, these controls include malfunction detection circuitry, circuitry for remote diagnostics, and redundant components. In terms of software, checks for internal file labels, "checkpoints" within a program that assist in building an audit trail, and system security monitors are examples of processing control.

System output is another area of concern for processing controls. One example is logging of output documents and reports and where those reports went. Control listings are a means of providing hard-copy evidence of all output produced. Distribution lists help personnel responsible for control ensure that only authorized users receive output.

Storage control is equally important. Someone must be responsible for maintaining and controlling access to databases. You can control access through passwords assigned to end users or through identification verification. The typical system has a three-level security procedure: user logon, user password, and unique file name. Essential security measures for storage are file backup of data and programs and storage of backup material in another location.

Physical facility controls involve a variety of security measures, ranging from a locked room outside the public area to a high-security facility with elaborate environmental controls. In a distributed-technology environment, physical security of equipment becomes more difficult and complex, but you must attempt to provide some security, if nothing more than equipment "lockdowns."

Another important security element is the firewall that protects the network from unwanted access or intrusion by serving as a safe transfer point to and from other networks. Its function is to screen network activity and allow only authorized transmissions in or out. Unfortunately, firewalls are able only to deter, and cannot completely prevent, unauthorized access. Hacking continue to be a security challenge. One security solution comes from the growing area of biometrics. Security systems using biometrics assess physical traits that make a person unique: voice verification, fingerprints, hand shape, keystroke analysis, and retina scanning are some examples. A digitized biometrics profile is created for each user; special sensors then measure the person wanting access, and, if there is a match, access is allowed.

You must expect public-access PCs will have malware, viruses, and worms from time to time. All of these can be problems for staff machines; however, they are definitely problems for public machines. Some infections are just a nuisance, while others can destroy disk contents. They often migrate from one computer to another. Having effective and up-to-date virus checking software is important, as is using it on a regular basis. A virus-checking program that automatically scans any downloaded file is highly desirable.

INTELLECTUAL SECURITY

There are three major user privacy issues for libraries. One relates to personal information the library collects about a person as part of its normal business practices (such as basic contact information for borrowers and what they borrow). The second issue is who can access that information and under what conditions. The third issue is what vendors can collect from library users.

Although a much broader issue than technology, user privacy is part of managing library technology. Most libraries have a confidentiality policy, and ALA's "Policy on Confidentiality of Library Records" (www.ala.org/advocacy/intfreedom/statementspols/otherpolicies/poli cyconfidentiality) offers guidance in formulating or revising such a policy.

One part of library privacy relates to the personal information the library collects about its registered users, such as name and contact information. Making certain there are security measures to help ensure that only authorized individuals have access to this information is vital. Also, staff must receive training in understanding who may gain access without a court order. For example, can law enforcement officers, parents, or parent organization officials have access?

Another aspect of privacy is usage of library resources. In terms of borrowing records, most libraries require the staff to eradicate past circulation data in order to preserve user confidentiality. Today's ILS systems normally break the link between the borrower and borrowed item(s) upon return and payment of any required fees. If the circulation system

---

||||| CHECK THESE OUT

The following items explore in more detail the issues of privacy, libraries, and the digital environment:

Barnes, Susan B. 2006. "A Privacy Paradox: Social Networking in the United States." *First Monday* 11, no. 9. http://firstmonday.org/htbin/cgiwrap/bin/ojs/index.php/fm/article/view/1394/1312.

Woodward, Jeannette. 2007. *What Every Librarian Should Know about Electronic Privacy.* Westport, CT: Libraries Unlimited.

> ||||| **CHECK THIS OUT**
>
> A good article on protecting users' privacy is Greg Landgraf's "Data Collection and Privacy: Balancing Information Needs with Patron Protection" (*Public Libraries* 49, nos. 9/10: 14–15, 2018).

used in a library requires that the name of a borrower appear on a book card or some other traceable record, staff should render the name illegible as part of the discharging process.

Who may have access to information about what a person uses or has used has become complicated since 9/11. Police, government officials, ministers, parents, spouses, and others have asked libraries about the reading habits of borrowers from time to time. In the past, such access required a court order. After 9/11, there was a change regarding access to library records (at least for federal law enforcement officers). The USA PATRIOT Act authorized warrantless searches and the requirement that the library not communicate to anyone that such search occurred or was underway.

What data might be available from library records that law enforcement officials might not more easily access elsewhere? Actually, not all that much. Information about what a suspect might have been interested in that relates to law enforcement's concerns may well be available in more detail from those who know the person. As Karl Gruben (2006) wrote, "In actuality, the Department of Justice does not have as much interest in what Johnny is reading as it does in what he is looking at or e-mailing or Instant messaging on the internet, particularly since there is suspicion that the 9/11 hijackers communicated through internet terminals in public libraries" (p. 303).

Filtering access to the internet has been a hot topic for the general public, government officials, and libraries. Public and school libraries appear to be caught between a rock and a hard place if they offer internet access to the public and are short of funds for providing that access. Some members of the general public, governing boards, and elected government officials want libraries to use filtering software that will deny access to certain types of sites. Others, believing in free speech as protected by the First Amendment, do not support filtering. The primary reason for filtering is to keep children from having access to "unacceptable" sites.

The Children's Internet Protection Act (CIPA), enacted in 2000, requires public libraries and schools to install filters on their internet computers if they want federal E-Rate funds for internet connectivity. The penalty for not doing so is loss of federal funding. Public and school libraries have developed various policies on implementing CIPA, from installing filters on all public stations or installing filters on some stations designated for children to declining to install filters at all. Some public libraries take a middle ground, either designating certain stations without filters as "adults only" or disabling filters upon requests by adults (which is allowed by CIPA). A large number have chosen to forgo E-Rate funds in the name of intellectual freedom and professional ethics.

CLOUD COMPUTING

You have probably seen and read articles about cloud computing, which is another technology used in many libraries. Marshall Breeding (2011) stated that, "We're now entering into

---

▮▮▮ CHECK THIS OUT

A good resource on cloud computing is Marcus P. Zillman's "Grid, Distributed and Cloud Computing Resource Primer 2018" (http://whitepapers.virtualprivatelibrary.net/Cloud _Computing_Primer.pdf).

---

a new phase of the history of library automation characterized by new technology underpinnings, including cloud computing, fully web-based systems, and service-oriented architecture and fresh approaches to functionality that recognize current library realities" (pp. 33–34). For an update on the status of libraries and cloud computing, see https://statetech magazine.com/article/2017/07/libraries-expand-future-proof-services-cloud.

Cloud computing allows organizations to share technology online (hardware, software, and so on.). The basic concept of the "cloud" is to shift applications from local servers to remote servers that are used by many organizations—a form of collaboration in a sense. Perhaps the best library example of cloud applications is OCLC's World-Share Management Services (https://www.oclc.org/en/worldshare.html/). The website succinctly spells out the concept: "WorldShare provides a complete set of library management applications and platform services built on an open, cloud-based platform. World-Share offers integrated management of library workflows and creates new efficiencies as libraries share work, data and resources to save money and deliver value to their users." The page goes on to list various benefits, most of which relate to cost control and increased efficiency.

We believe that more and more libraries will include cloud applications in their regular technology planning process. Certainly, cloud technology will be examined carefully because of its potential for cost containment. All ILS systems have annual maintenance costs as well as staffing issues, even when much of the work is done remotely by the vendor.

SOCIAL MEDIA

Participating in social media is an important part of a library's activities. There are two primary reasons for libraries to make use of these media. The first reason is to increase awareness of services, programs, new resources, and other activities for users. The second reason is to build or create relationships with its service community.

This is not the place to explore all the current and potential uses of social media. However, there are some significant management issues related to the library's use of social media that we want to highlight. First, and perhaps foremost, there must be senior management support for the activity. A "let's try this and see what happens" approach is more than likely to lead to failure just as it would with any other project. Senior managers must have a commitment to succeeding. A lack of such commitment means there may not be enough resources, especially time, for the effort to be effective.

When the project is just the result of a staff person's interest in blogging or starting a library Facebook page, for example, the chances are it will be effective as long as that person remains an employee. Without a library commitment, the activity will wither away when that person leaves. We believe it is better not to start using social media than to do so intermittently or ineffectively—to create a positive library image takes time, money, effort, and commitment.

The small word *workload* is the key to most successful library activities. As we noted in chapter 13, job descriptions are important. The common phrase "other duties as assigned" can become a workload nightmare for employees. Getting a new position (full- or part-time), or even retaining an existing one, is often a great challenge, especially if the specific duties listed constitute a full workload for the position. Adding other duties later (such as looking after the library's social media) without taking some tasks away usually means something will get less attention. For the individual, there may be performance consequences if the time devoted to new duties causes poorer performance on one or more of the existing duties—or perhaps extended hours. A supervisor may not see the new duty as relevant to his or her unit's activities, which will add to the stress of everyone involved. This makes it imperative that you look at what the top priorities are for meeting the users' needs and consider what functions may no longer be needed or may be consolidated. Social media activities are important for libraries, but just adding them to existing workloads is not a good practice.

COLLABORATION

Library technological collaboration revolves around two broad categories—intra-organizational and extra-organizational. If you have to choose just one area to focus on it should be intra-organizational, as most libraries are dependent on the parent organization's ICT unit for the infrastructure that is necessary to provide web services. Working with library consortia is a means of helping control technology costs, including hardware, software, and digital content.

Costs and coordination of activities are critical. Positions such as Chief Information Officer (CIOs) are common. At times, a chief librarian might become the CIO; in other cases, it may be a computer science person. The critical and challenging role of the CIO is described by Broadbent and Kitzis (2004). (Broadbent is a former librarian now at Gartner Inc. and the Melbourne Business School). For example, how does a CIO balance the concepts of service and network security? A CIO often wants the tightest security possible, while the librarians want it as open as possible to encourage sharing.

As is true of budgeting, there are institutional technology politics. Most institutional CIOs face a host of competing demands. "We need new hardware and software for this project, *now*" and "We need you folks to modify this aspect of the system so we can . . . " are two examples of the many "we need it now" requests that come into ICT departments on a daily basis. Just like the library, ICT must prioritize its responses to such requests. The challenge for the library is to understand how the priorities are set and how to move up the list. We librarians sometimes do not fully understand just how complex the technology infrastructure is that underlies our activities. Working collaboratively is the best political approach. Taking time to understand at least the basic infrastructure is also a good idea. You can demonstrate some awareness of the fact that it is rarely just a matter of adding this or that software. The ultimate goal of the collaboration should be agreement that ICT supplies the means and the library provides the content for the end users.

There are signs of a growing trend in collaboration among independent software vendors in libraries rather than the fierce competition that formerly existed. The aim is to lower the cost and technical barriers for services, making it easier to share data more easily.

The new developments in collaboration bring together services across sectors, as government policies encourage linkages between archives, libraries, and museums. This will bring some exciting benefits for users crossing the boundaries—for example, between information and cultural services.

🔒 KEY POINTS TO REMEMBER

- Technology provides access to information for users and generates management information to aid decision making.
- Technology improves productivity and assists in data collection, analysis, and use.
- Technology can help free up staff time, and it can make a service operate more cost effectively.
- Managers require enhanced technology skills.
- The proportion of the budget spent on the initial investment and associated recurrent costs will continue to increase and dominate annual expenditures.
- A major investment is needed to train staff to work effectively and efficiently.
- Users benefit from coaching to help them access information effectively.
- Rapid change will continue.
- Increasing attention is being paid to legal and security issues.
- Technology requires careful planning and control.

REFERENCES

Bell, Steven J., and John Shank. 2004. "The Blended Librarian: A Blueprint for Redefining the Teaching and Learning Role of Academic Librarians." *College and Research Libraries News* 65, no. 7: 372-75.

Breeding, Marshall. 2018. *Perceptions 2017. An International Survey of Library Automation.* https://librarytechnology.org/perceptions/2017/.

_____. 2011. "A Cloudy Forecast for Libraries." *Computers in Libraries* 31, no. 7: 32-34.

Broadbent, Marianne, and Ellen Kitzis. 2004. *The New CIO Leader: Setting the Agenda and Delivering Results.* Boston: Harvard Business School Press.

Emberton, John. 1987. "Effective Information System Planning and Implementation." *Information Age* 9, no. 7: 159-62.

Gruben, Karl T. 2006. "What is Johnny Doing in the Library? Libraries, the U.S.A. Patriot Act, and Its Amendments." *St. Thomas Law Review* 19, no. 2: 297-328.

Richey, Nancy, Amanda Drost, and Allison Day. 2017. "To Scan or Not to Scan." *The Southeastern Librarian* 65, no. 1: 7-13.

Yeh, Shea-Tinn, and Zhiping Walter. 2016. "Critical Success Factors for Integrated Library System Implantation in Academic Libraries: A Qualitative Study." *Information Technology and Libraries* 35, no. 3: 27-42.

CHAPTER 20

Managing Facilities

Changes in the ways patrons use libraries over the last 20 years have affected library design requirements, and at the same time user groups have become increasingly diverse, with the result that design principles tend to be formulated at a highly abstract level and individual solutions need to be formulated on a case-by-case basis.

Paul Ojennus and Kathy Watts, 2017

The principles and practices of disaster recovery planning (DRP) and business continuity planning (BCP) while constantly evolving, are well established in the information technology community.

H. Frank Cervone, 2017

Modern buildings are almost like living organisms, with intricate systems for providing amenities and information.

Mathew B. Hoy, 2016

Sustainability in building planning is growing in importance, and in the awareness of designers and users. Focus is mostly on the macro-level of overall building design, with few efforts targeting micro-level aspects.

Edward Spodick, 2016

Libraries have been a "place" since their inception. Collections require physical space as do the users of those collections. Today, libraries remain physical facilities and are likely to be well into the future, despite what some pundits predict. Although they have always had a physical presence, today's libraries, in many ways, are unlike those your older siblings knew.

One example showcasing the changing aspect of libraries appeared in a newspaper article in 2011 that described new library design concepts for teenagers. It reported on a joint project funded by the Institute of Museum and Library Services (IMLS) and the MacArthur Foundation focusing on libraries and young people. It opened with, "Imagine walking into a public library filled with PlayStations, Wii game consoles, and electronic keyboards pumped up to maximum volume. . . . That is exactly how one enormous room on the ground floor of the Chicago Public Library's main branch functions" (www.edweek .org/ew/articles/2011/11/29/13thr_libraries.h31.html).

In this wired space, many questioned what the new role print materials may have. According to Amy Eshleman, an assistant commissioner at the library, there was a fight between the library staff and designers or funders over designing space for books. The library's desire to move its YA collections into that space prevailed, and "book circulation has gone up by about 500 percent since the space opened." The article also indicated that public libraries in Houston, Miami, New York, Philadelphia, San Francisco, and many smaller towns across the country would be designing similar spaces.

The above is an example of the evolving library space, both with new buildings and in refurbishing/purposing existing spaces, although the idea of having specialized spaces for particular groups or activities is not new. Public libraries have had children's' rooms for years and space for teenagers and young adults for some time as well. Some academic libraries have had undergraduate libraries for almost as long. What online resources have done is cause libraries to rework spaces, often called learning or information commons, in academic libraries. Even these spaces are being further refined as described in Diane Dallis' 2016 article "Scholars and Learners: A Case Study of New Library Spaces at Indiana University" (*New Library World* 117, nos. 1/2: 35–48).

The new spaces almost always involve a shift in services and training of staff, which can present its own share of challenges. We know of no LIS program that regularly offers coursework in creating "makerspaces" and other current trends, and this training is often needed in today's reworked library spaces. The need for new training creates further challenges for limited staff development funds. Such efforts reflect libraries' ability to respond to changing user interests.

Another managerial issue which we explore in some depth later in this chapter is "building efficiency" (that is, operational costs). That concept has been a design component almost from the inception of the library as a building. The issue has become increasingly important as energy costs escalate and the notion of sustainability has become a significant societal concern. The challenge for library design is that library purposes are not always an easy fit in terms of low energy use and sustainability concepts. We explore this issue later in the chapter.

LIBRARY AS PLACE

Library as place appears to be more viable than some have predicted. In fact, there is now an annual conference on the topic—the annual Institute on the Library as Place (www.access ola.org/web/OLA/Events/Signature_Events/Library_as_Place/OLA/Events/Signature_ events/Library_as_Place/Welcome.aspx). "The Annual Institute is great place to meet people who are also embarking on similar design and building projects." Throughout their existence, libraries have been places where people congregate, think, discuss, learn, and collaborate. That suggests there is a need for physical space. We like Terence Huwe's (2010) view of the issue:

> People love to study and commune together. With respect to understanding that basic human need, we have been remarkably effective in the battle for the hearts and minds of our communities. Of course, the digital era has revolutionized society's perception of space. Even so, against this backdrop, the struggle to preserve and enhance library space is a battle for the hearts and minds of communities. It is ongoing and will never end. (p. 29)

One library design function, especially in larger libraries, is to inspire people to think and learn. The notion of libraries as social places has been with us almost as long as libraries have existed. Having a café associated with or in a library is becoming more common in U.S. library buildings. As library collections become increasingly digital, there is less concern about having a "no food in the library" policy. The underlying reason for such policies is a concern about insect infestations and their potential health issues for both people and collections.

We agree with Alistair Black and Nan Dahlkild's (2011) statement regarding ongoing shifts in thinking about the library as physical space:

> Library domains have been rebranded—as idea stores, learning cafés, discovery centers, media spaces, and learning resource centers to give just a few examples. Further, while it is true that the emergence of and increasing sophistication of digital ICTs has sharply increased fears of a library- and print-culture Armageddon, the physical library build-ing has accommodated, with some success, the proliferation of virtual technologies. Indeed, the computer has in many respects enhanced the operations of the traditional library, bestowing upon it a new flexibility, not least in terms of greater opportunities and creativity in the organization of physical space, as materials are miniaturized and digitized. (p. 1)

A final thought, or caution, about the library as place is that some libraries, especially academic and school libraries, face the challenge of a senior institutional manager having the notion that "everything is digital, so there is no need for library space." Space always seems to be in short supply; just think about the last time you looked for a parking space. Senior managers receive more requests for additional space than is likely to become avail-able through construction. Fighting to keep what you have is hard, but there are ample resources available to help you win that struggle.

The issue goes beyond digital. One of the authors, when working on the design of a new library, had a facilities manager who was very upset at the idea that the building would have a substantial amount of empty shelving on opening day and for some time to come. "We can't have that. People will think we lied about what was needed." Eventu-ally, the notion that library collections grow annually, services and user populations also increase, and the reason for the new facility was the library had outgrown its current space was accepted—more or less.

MANAGING THE FACILITY

There are two broad aspects to managing the library as a building. First, there are the daily issues of keeping the facility safe, healthy, and inviting for users, as well as protecting in-vestments in collections and equipment. The second is something you may become involved in some time during your career—renovating or designing a new facility. As you might ex-pect, changes in the operating environment increase the responsibility and accountability you have for library space. Ames and Heid noted (2011) that, "A safe and clean facility is the responsibility of all the staff" (p. 10). Library service hours are generally longer than any individual staff member's workday. Often service is provided seven days a week, and sometimes twenty-four hours per day. Inevitably, some facility issues arise when few, if any, senior members of staff are on duty. You need to have plans in place for handling situations ranging from minor ones such as leaking faucets to major ones such as a fire or earthquake—and train the staff how to implement the plans.

HOUSEKEEPING MATTERS

With the exception of school and corporate libraries, most libraries are stand-alone facilities. This means that library staff has more responsibility for the space than in other types of employment. Today it is unlikely that a library will have full-time maintenance or custodial personnel on duty. Parent organizations usually find that sharing the services of such personnel is more cost effective than assigning full-time FTEs to a single facility.

Poor housekeeping can affect the health and safety of staff, users, and collections. It starts with basic questions about such tasks as who picks up litter and empties wastebaskets, cleans the restrooms, and how frequently. Does custodial staff have responsibility to dust the books and shelves? Who vacuums the floors and how often? Does anyone have this responsibility? These may seem like small problems, but there are health issues involved, especially for the staff.

Staff can become sick from extended exposure to "collection dust"—this is a medical fact. In extreme cases, a person may be unable to return to work. Beyond possible threat to the staffs' health, which is serious but not that common, there is collection health to consider. Dust and dirt on the shelves act as a fine abrasive as users and staff pull items off the shelves or replace them. Over time, that minor damage accumulates to the point where an item needs repair or replacement. You have to balance the annual cost of such repairs and replacement against the cost of having shelves dusted. (Note: custodial staff rarely has shelf-dusting duties; it is an extra cost activity.)

Other housekeeping issues include burned out lights, problems of temperature and

---

⊕ REAL WORLD EXAMPLE

An example of the joint responsibility for deferred maintenance and the high cost of failing to address a problem occurred in 2017 in Phoenix, Arizona. In this case a violent storm resulted in over $10 million in damage to the central public library. The actual storm only damaged the roof—it lifted the roof causing a cloud of dust that triggered the fire sprinkler system that was in need of maintenance. The repairs took a year to complete and the main library was closed throughout the restoration process.

Investigators found the sprinkler system problems were noted as early 2008, but never addressed. A total of eleven city and library employees were disciplined in the incident—demotions, suspensions, and even firings. The personnel actions resulted from their failure to report or follow up on the issues with the sprinkler system. Part of the lack of follow-up related to the lack of funds needed to repair the system and concerns over the level of disruption to library services (see www.phoenixpubliclibrary.org/AboutUs/Press-Room/Pages/Burton-Barr-Central-Library-Restoration-Updates-Archive.aspx). Insurance and library-reserve funds covered the cost of the repairs and remediation (Brenna Goth, "City Was Warned Library Could Flood," *Arizona Republic* August 19, 2017: 13A).

Evans has had several experiences with deferred maintenance. The most costly one related to asking for $32,000 to have some old shelving ranges seismically braced. The request was made for eight years. The standard answer was, "If there is enough money left after the high priority work is done, we'll address the problem." After an earthquake struck, repairs, replacement, and proper bracing cost the institution well over $250,000.

sun control, plumbing problems, leaky roofs, cracked sidewalks, and wet floors. The list could go on, but you can probably see our point. Any building component can cause a problem during in its lifetime. What happens when a user, late on a Saturday afternoon, reports that a water faucet in the restroom will not shut off and water is spilling over the floor? Is there someone or someplace to call? Will someone fix it before the start of the next shift? What does the staff do until the problem is resolved? In chapter 3, "Legal Issues," we noted the liability concerns regarding the library and users. You need to be certain that staff members understand how to handle facility problems and how to keep the liability exposure as low as possible.

Fixing matters related to housekeeping or to the building is a joint responsibility of the library and the parent organization. The library staff must report problems, but the actual repairs are done by the parent organizations. Almost every organization has a growing list of "deferred maintenance" projects. Mike Kennedy (2011), writing about educational institutions' maintenance issues, noted: "In the funding climate that schools and universities find themselves, building managers will be fortunate to hang on to the budget they have, let alone receive the resources they need to address short- and long-term maintenance requirements" (p. 32). This is still true.

Deferring maintenance is something we all do—even if it's nothing more than deciding to vacuum the floor tomorrow. Almost every library has some deferred projects, and almost every deferred project will cost a little more with each deferment. Most deferred activities are not all that costly, but in time some can become major funding or loss issues.

RISK MANAGEMENT

Risk management is an essential part of managing a building safely. Most parent organizations have some type of insurance that covers losses such as those resulting from fires and floods, but only to a degree. (It is rare for insurance to cover losses fully, as there is usually some type of deductible.) Insurance firms are usually happy to help you analyze a building's potential health and safety issues. If the insurance company can get the insured to address potential problems, there will be fewer claims to pay.

A risk management program identifies potential problems, possible solutions and their likely costs, and how to keep new problems from arising. In terms of potential issues, having a disaster or crisis management team prepare scenarios of possible events and how to address them will pay dividends should the worst happen. Crisis management recognizes that there is a "golden hour," the period during the earliest stages of managing a crisis when critical decisions are made.

Steve Albrecht (2018) discussed the top ten security risks for public and academic libraries. Many of the risks apply to any type of library.

- aggressive homeless people
- ransomware hackers
- malware
- improper internet usage
- hogging of internet access
- "entitled" students
- "entitled" faculty
- sexual harassment
- misuse of service animals
- opioid users

All of these risks carry both managerial and legal liability for libraries and how they address the challenges.

HEALTH, SAFETY, AND SECURITY

Library health, safety, and security are critical issues for staff and users, as well as for collections. A surprising number of hazards can emerge in operating a public facility such as a library. As a managerial leader, you have a duty of care for the staff, users, and collections. Involving all members of staff in identifying risks makes them aware of potential hazards.

One constant challenge is controlling temperature and humidity levels. Probably every manager has wondered from time to time, "Why, if they can send people into outer space and not have them freeze or burn to death, can they not design a building heating, ventilation, and air conditioning (HVAC) system for earth that works?" One reason for the complaints is the variations in people's inner thermostats: some people need cool temperatures, while others prefer warmer temperatures. In addition to individual preferences, systems break down, need to be taken out of service for maintenance, and simply wear out.

A great challenge is balancing concerns for people and collections in terms of both environment and safety. What is good for people is not ideal for the collections and equipment. Safety is divided into three major categories: safety from physical harm, safety of belongings, and psychological safety. You must address all these areas and balance the needs of people, collections, and technology.

For libraries with significant preservation responsibilities, such as archives and research libraries, it is a matter of balancing the needs of people, technology, and materials. Both staff and customers generally prefer a working temperature at or near 72°F (22°C) with 50-60 percent humidity. Ideal storage conditions for collections are 60°F (15°C) and 50 percent or less humidity. This means compromise, usually in favor of people and technology, when the goal is to mix people and materials. Separation may or may not be feasible or affordable, as it probably requires two HVAC systems or modification of a single system into the equivalent of two systems.

To gain an overview of safety issues, conduct a security audit as part of the risk management program. One way to do this is to create a security checklist that draws on expert advice from the parent organization's facilities manager, and then carry out a survey.

Unfortunately, people and "thing" safety concerns can also conflict. Except for one-room facilities, there are likely to be one or more emergency exits located in areas that are not visible to the staff. Emergency exits are usually mandated by fire protection and building codes. Their location is a function of distance between exits, the number of persons in an area, and the activities that go on in the area. While emergency exits provide for people's safety during a crisis, they also provide a means by which people who take library materials can leave unseen. One method of controlling this problem is to install alarms so that opening the emergency exit door alerts the staff. Usually the best that happens in this case is that staff are alerted to the unauthorized use of the exit, but by the time staff get to that door the person is no longer in sight. Higher levels of security may be necessary, such as CCTV (closed-circuit television) cameras, or designated security staff; you will have to weigh the benefits against the installation and operational costs.

User spaces in isolated or remote parts of the building are higher-risk areas than large open areas. Poorly lit and remote staircases are also high-risk areas. You must take action to protect both users and staff. Often at closing time there are only two or three staff members on duty to shut down the facility. Some libraries may be in locations where the crime rate is high and/or the building is geographically isolated, making the staff vulnerable, particularly during night shifts.

▦ CHECK THESE OUT

Cotts, David G., Kathy O. Roper, and Richard P. Paynet. 2010. *The Facility Management Handbook.* 3rd ed. New York: American Management Association.

Trotta, Carmine J., and Marcia Trotta. 2001. *The Librarian's Facility Management Handbook.* New York: Neal-Schuman.

Breighner, Mary, William Payton, and Jeanne M. Drewes. 2005. *Risk and Insurance Management Manual for Libraries.* Chicago: American Library Association.

Kahn, Miriam B. 2008. *Library Security and Safety Guide to Prevention, Planning, and Response.* Chicago: American Library Association.

EMERGENCY AND DISASTER MANAGEMENT

These two concepts relate to Frank Cervone's opening quotation for this chapter about the need to plan for infrequent but likely events for an organization. Certainly, emergencies and disasters are rare for any one library but occur in some library somewhere almost daily. Another reason for planning how to handle such events is they are highly stressful for staff, especially when they do not know what to do. With a plan, the library can rehearse what to do in various circumstances (by conducting practice drills, for example). Practice is unlikely to make perfect but certainly will reduce the chances of experiencing total failure. Fire and police departments are often willing to help create realistic practice drills—it helps their effectiveness when the real event occurs.

Of the two plans, emergency planning is the easiest. One reason is that emergency services are always willing to help develop such plans. Often there are some factors they want included that seem to go against what lay people might expect. Both authors learned this while developing such plans when the fire department said there needed to be a statement that staff should *not* attempt to rescue physically handicapped individuals, especially those not on the ground floor. They explained such efforts almost always lead to firefighters having two people to rescue. Instead, the staff should note the precise location of the person and report that to the firefighters.

Disaster preparedness planning attempts to identify major risks (fire, floods, earthquakes, etc.). During the course of your career, you are likely to have to deal with one or more facility disasters of some size (most will be small). Developing such plans requires time and effort but is essential. Using a steering committee composed of representatives from every department is an effective method for developing and, importantly, periodically updating the plan. A successful plan will include the following:

- a realistic assessment of potential disasters
- a consideration of the differences between handling a library disaster and handling one that is part of a larger local or regional disaster
- a determination of collection salvage priorities
- a determination of insurance coverage and authority to commit funds for recovery
- procedures to activate when a disaster or incident occurs
- staff training to ensure that the procedures work and that staff know about them

- a telephone tree for emergency telephone calls, starting with the person who will direct the recovery effort
- skeletal forms on the library's website that can be completed immediately upon the disaster occurrence that informs staff and users and updates them on a daily basis
- a list with telephone numbers of recovery resource vendors and service providers
- a schedule for regular review of the operation of the plan and updating information
- a partnership with another local library to which users can be directed when a disaster strikes

Perhaps the most common disaster is water damage—and not just from major storms or firefighting efforts. Water pipes and radiators break, and if this happen when the library is closed a day may pass before anyone notices the problem. Even an unremarkable rainfall can cause damage if building maintenance has been deferred for too long.

One thing is certain about a major disaster: not everything will be salvageable. Some documents will be destroyed, and many will have some damage, and there will not be time or money to save everything. Thus, the value of setting priorities before the disaster strikes becomes apparent. What is irreplaceable (first priority); what is expensive and perhaps difficult to replace but is replaceable (second priority); and what is easy to replace (last priority)? Setting these priorities may prove more difficult than you might expect, as staff members will have differing views depending on their primary responsibilities. Checking with users and perhaps with the parent institution may indicate that staff views and public views do not always agree. You may have to spend a substantial amount of time explaining and justifying the priorities and, eventually, reducing the scope of the first and second priority categories.

A recovery plan must also address the financial aspects of the situation. Time is of the essence in the recovery of documents. Waiting seventy-two hours or more to process wet paper materials may mean that there is little point in trying to recover them. Waiting to get approval to commit money to handle recovery efforts until after disaster strikes will probably mean missing the window of opportunity to save paper-based materials.

Having a plan and failing to review it at regular intervals or not practicing its implementation is almost pointless. Practice will mean some time lost from information work, but it will be well worth the investment. Also, copies of the plan—as well as appropriate insurance, police, fire, and security agency numbers—must be in the hands of all key personnel, both at home and in the workplace.

▌▌▌▌ CHECK THESE OUT

Kahn, Miriam. 2012. *Disaster Response and Planning for Libraries.* 3rd ed. Chicago: American Library Association.

Wilkinson, Frances C., Linda K. Lewis, and Nancy K. Dennis. 2009. *Comprehensive Guide to Emergency and Disaster Preparedness and Recovery.* Chicago: Association of College and Research Libraries.

SUSTAINABILITY

Sustainability is a word used widely in both the popular and the professional press. There is a variety of definitions of the word. We like the one mentioned by Edward Spodick (2016), "Sustainability is the ability to continue a defined behavior indefinitely." Although this is a very general definition, it allows the inclusion of a wide range of activities—recycling, electric cars, and efficient building designs, for example.

We placed our discussion of the concept in this chapter because it applies to both existing buildings and the design of new facilities. The concern about saving energy is not a new issue. As James Qualk (2011) noted, "The idea that a new or existing building can be capable of using very little, if any, grid energy or water while serving as a healthy place for people to live and work is now commonplace. But this is just one of many ways buildings still fall short of their true potential" (p. 75). Brian Edwards (2011), in writing about library building design, illustrated the overall issues in sustainability:

> Concerns over climate change and the consequent drive for energy efficiency is leading to new approaches to the design of libraries and reshaping of existing ones. Greater attention is being paid not just to fossil fuel energy consumption but to a wider range of environmental and ecological issues. In many ways the architectural approach to the twenty-first century library is returning to the roots of the modernist library found in Scandinavia with its emphasis upon high levels of daylight, natural materials, social harmony, and contact with nature. (pp. 190–91)

Parent organizations' facility managers have been engaging in energy-saving efforts for more than fifty years. Their efforts and the library's purpose, especially for libraries with major preservation responsibilities, can come into conflict. Earlier we noted that one of your challenges in managing a library building is that peoples' comfort levels in terms of temperature and humidity and what is best for collections are rather different. When facility managers turn off the heating or air conditioning during non-service hours to save energy, the library collections experience roller coaster swings in temperature and humidity.

"Smart buildings" and sustainability are closely linked. As Mathew Hoy (2016) stated, "Smart buildings take it a step further, beyond simply turning things on and off. Smart buildings also collect data about how and when a building is being used and provide a real-time picture of the status of a building" (p. 327). Such systems make it possible to improve substantially a building's operational efficiency and better balance user and collections' environmental requirements.

New buildings can be both environmentally appropriate and energy efficient. This is particularly true if the facility can become LEED (Leadership in Energy and Environmental Design) certified. The U.S. Green Building Council (www.usgbc.org/) developed the LEED rating system. It is a third-party certification process using a point system. The rating system has a maximum of a total 110 points from seven categories:

- Sustainable sites, 21 points
- Water efficiency, 11 points
- Energy and atmosphere, 37 points
- Materials and resources, 14 points
- Indoor environmental quality, 17 points

- Innovation in design, 6 points
- Regional priority, 4 points (this varies by region of the country)

A building that earns 40 points can be LEED certified; 80+ points gets a platinum rating, 60+ points earns a gold rating, and 50+ points gets a silver rating. It seems likely that this system will become a standard part of the design process over the coming years.

PLANNING FOR NEW SPACE

Only a few librarians will experience active involvement in planning a major addition, re-modeling project, or totally new facility. Many librarians look forward to such a project; only a few look forward to doing it a second time as it is time-consuming and, at times, frustrating work. Perhaps the major reason for this less enthusiastic view is that almost all building projects involve a series of compromises; the library wins some of these and many are won by the parent organization, architect, and/or budget managers. This is especial-ly true when attempting to plan a facility capable of handling growth for twenty years or more, which involves predicting the changes that may happen in that time. Perceived needs far exceed the funds available, resulting in a downsizing of the facility size or in the fit-out and equipment installed—and sometimes in all of them. The longer the time between fund-ing the project and its completion, the greater will be the downsizing, as costs generally es-calate. The process is often labeled "value engineering"—a fancy way of saying cost cutting.

Ideally, a new facility should be:

- flexible
- adaptable
- expandable
- accessible
- compact
- stable in climate control
- secure
- attractive
- economical to operate and maintain
- comfortable

We will address just a few of these. Flexibility is essential because the use of the space *will* change at some point. (See the opening paragraphs of this chapter for examples.) A modular building with few, if any, internal weight-bearing walls is a typical flexible design. Internal walls that are weight-bearing cannot be moved without causing structural damage or requiring very complicated and costly work.

Adaptability is not the same as flexibility. For example, public and special libraries and records management centers need to be located where their users gather naturally, but this can change over time as the parent organizations change. Therefore, the premises may need to be planned so that they can be adapted for other uses.

Given the inevitable growth of archives and libraries, a facility that can be expanded is highly desirable. Funds for an addition or remodeling are easier to raise than for an entirely new building. It is not uncommon for the area labeled "future expansion" on the original plans to turn out to be unsuitable, for various reasons, when the time comes to expand.

Ideally, the project consists of a primary planning team of five or more persons: archi-tect, library representative, specialist space planning consultant, interior designer, repre-sentative of the parent institution, and, in some circumstances, a user. Larger teams are possible, but the larger the group, the longer the process takes. Clearly, many people will

---

▦ CHECK THESE OUT

During the program writing stage it is well worth the time and effort to seek out user thoughts about the public service areas, as well as changes in services. Two sound articles about the value of such efforts are Camille Andrews, Sara E. Wright, and Howard Raskin's "Library Learning Spaces: Investigating Libraries and Investing in Student Feedback" (*Journal of Library Administration* 56, no. 6: 647–72, 2016) and Paul Ojennus and Kathy A. Watts's "User Preferences and Library Space at Whitworth University Library" (*Journal of Librarianship and Information Science* 49, no. 3: 320–34, 2017).

---

need to have input at different stages of the project but having everyone involved in every aspect of the project slows the planning activities.

The need for an architect is apparent. The library representative will most likely be a senior manager, if not *the* senior manager, because decisions need to be taken reasonably quickly, especially in the latter stages of the project. Parent institution representation is necessary if for no other reason than to monitor the cost of the project, and it is also helpful to ensure that the design will fit into any existing architectural master plan.

Planning any new building is a complicated task involving highly detailed data, down to the required nail and screw sizes. Few librarians have experience with designing a new library, and even fewer have been through that experience more than once. Also, there are few architects with library design experience, although the numbers seem to be increasing. Thus, having an experienced person (a library building consultant) is highly advisable. The consultant is usually the person with the greatest experience in developing effective designs for library operations. A consultant's role is to ensure that the interior design will be functional and includes the appropriate level of detail required for an effective and efficient building.

The input of an interior designer is useful, as he or she can take the vision, image, and ambiance that the library seeks to project and translate it into the finished space. The interior designer works closely with the architect and space consultant to ensure that the most effective use of space emerges at the fit-out stage. The building program is the key planning document. It is the outcome of the joint efforts of the library, the consultant, and the users. It provides the architect with the information needed to design the facility. Often it is also used to raise money for the project. To that end, it normally includes information about the existing services, collections, staff, and service population, along with data about the parent organization. At the heart of the program, and essential for the architect, are data sheets for all the activities and units to be built into the new facility. Data sheets cover not only the equipment and the people who will occupy the space but also the relationship of that space to other spaces in the facility.

There are several stages in the design phase of the project. The first phase yields conceptual drawings reflecting several different exterior designs and some blocks of interior space indicating work areas, collection space, and so forth. The second stage yields the schematic drawings reflecting the architect's interpretation of the building program. They start to reflect building and safety codes. Staff and user inputs are critical at this stage, as they will have to work in and use the space. The planning team should listen carefully to their comments and, whenever possible, incorporate them into the final design. It is at this stage that major adjustments in the location of this or that activity is the easiest to make, before the detailed drafting that follows later. An important consideration at this stage is the estimate of the operating cost for the facility and how it has been minimized.

Working drawings are the final stage. Here the drawings are complete to the last detail—which way a door opens, how wide it is, what it is made of, what color it is, and so forth. They reflect all aspects and specifications of the building, and they become the basis for the contractor's bid for construction. There is a review and approval process for the final working drawing by the "owners"—the library and its parent institution—that in essence states, "Yes, this is actually what we want built in all its detail." The reason this is important is because anything overlooked in the final drawing may be corrected or added, but for an additional charge. So, a thorough review of the construction documents is critical to the level of funding available to finish the planned project.

With the trend toward the development of joint-use libraries, for example, community libraries incorporating public and school libraries, or university and public libraries joining together, the planning of facilities includes even further considerations. The needs of all users and staff must be taken into account—and there can be conflicting interests. But good communication, a positive approach to planning, and goodwill can overcome difficulties, and a cost-effective solution can emerge.

Occupying a new facility is a major change for staff and users alike. There will be high expectations for the new facility; most will be realized, but a few will not. Change is stressful, and sometimes some of the compromises required generate staff unhappiness. The staff actively involved in the planning process must make a major effort to communicate quickly, frequently, and accurately to the rest of the staff about progress, changes, and the reasons for change.

🔒 KEY POINTS TO REMEMBER

- Library buildings, while continuing to adapt to changes in technology and user needs, are likely to continue being built for some time to come.
- Housekeeping matters—for both collections and people.
- Business continuity is vital.
- Risks must be assessed for the purposes of safety and insurance.
- Health, safety, and security are of growing concern.
- Disasters happen; all libraries need a disaster management plan that is regularly updated.
- Building and remodeling projects are complex and require professional assistance.
- The most successful new libraries are the result of a collaborative team effort that involves users' views about the new space.
- Sustainability will become an ever-growing factor in managing a facility.

REFERENCES

Albrecht, Steve. 2018. "Top 10 Security Risk Factors for Public and Academic Libraries. *Computers in Libraries* 38, no. 5: 4-7.

Ames, Kathryn, and Greg Heid. 2011. "Building Maintenance and Emergency Preparedness." *Georgia Library Quarterly* 48, no. 1: 10-13.

Black, Alistair, and Nan Dahlkild. 2011. "Library Design: From the Past to Present." *Library Trends* 60, no. 1: 1-10.

Cervone, H. Frank. 2017. "Disaster Recovery Planning and Business Continuity for Informaticians." *Digital Library Perspectives* 33, no. 2: 78-81.

Edwards, Brian W. 2011. "Sustainability as a Driving Force in Contemporary Library Design." *Library Trends* 60, no. 1: 190-214.

Hoy, Mathew B. 2016 . "Smart Buildings: An Introduction to the Library of the Future." *Medical Reference Services Quarterly* 35, no. 3: 326-31.

Huwe, Terence K. 2010. "Hearts, Minds, and the Library's Physical Space." C*omputers in Libraries* 30, no. 8: 29-31.

Kennedy, Mike. 2011. "Maintaining Perspective." *American School University* 83, no. 10: 32-35.

Ojennus, Paul and Kathy Watts. 2017. "User Preferences and Library Space at Whitworth University Library." *Journal of Librarianship and Information Science* 49, no. 3: 320-34.

Qualk, James D. 2011. "Building 'Shall Be Capable Of.'" *Environmental Design and Construction* 13, no. 11: 75-76.

Spodick, Edward. 2016. "Sustainability—It's Everyone's Job." *Library Management* 37, nos. 6/7: 286-97.

PART V

Managing Yourself
and Your Career

CHAPTER 21

Other Managerial Skills

By approaching a pending negotiation as a problem that needs to be solved rather than as a televised boxing match, you can not only manage your emotions at the table, but you can also free up mental bandwidth to think better on your feet.

Karen Cates, 2016

Collaboration is taking over the workplace. According to data collected by the authors over the past two decades, the time spent by managers and employees in collaborative activities has ballooned by 50% or more.

Rob Cross, Reb Rebele, and Adam Grant, 2016

Poking fun at meetings is the stuff of *Dilbert* cartoons—we can all joke about how soul-sucking and painful they are. But that pain has real consequences for teams and organizations.

Leslie A. Perlow, Constance Noonan Hadley, and Eunice Eun, 2017

There are a variety of skills that are important in both work and personal life activities that don't fall within the core concepts of management. Such skills become highly formalized when needed in the workplace. What makes them challenging to carry out effectively is our personal life behaviors in such situations underlie how we approach them at work. The personal approach is not always the effective method in the workplace. For example, how we handle conflict in our personal life—fight, flow, or flee—may carry over inappropriately at work. Often our personal life approach is so ingrained that we don't think about it, we just react as we always have. From a managerial perspective we need to understand our basic behaviors as well as which formalized method is likely the best for the work environment.

There are three broad skill sets that effective managers possess—technical, people, and conceptual. Early in your career, the technical skills are dominant—reference skills and database management, for example. Technical skills are what the employer seeks. Although technical skill importance tends to decline when you climb the managerial ladder, it never disappears completely. You should keep up to date on changes in methods, approaches, and applications of your technical skills. Part of a leader's credibility, especially in librarianship, rests on the follower's belief that the leader possesses the necessary technical skills to do the job correctly.

As you move up the managerial ladder, your conceptual skills become more and more important. Conceptual skills are those that help us see connections, visualize the big picture, create a vision, and foresee the implications and possible outcomes of decisions and the like. For example, "what should the library become in five years?" is a question of conceptualization.

People skills are always important, no matter where you are in the managerial hierarchy. Without some good people skills, you are unlikely to have a satisfying career. One fact of managerial life in the public sector is just how important people social skills are to personal and organizational success. Public sector organizations almost always have a highly heterogeneous service population that is diverse on almost all demographic metrics. Interacting effectively with such diversity requires high level people skills.

Beyond the service population people skill challenges, library managerial leaders face other people skill concerns. Public sector managers must work like politicians when determining overall policy. Unlike the service population, which is reasonably stable in composition, politicians change with some regularity. We have mentioned several times how political winds shift and vary in strength. Interacting with various political personalities requires both people skills and planning—planning in the sense of tailoring your approach for each person (one size really does not fit all in this case).

For libraries, another key area for demonstrating people skills is in collaboration and cooperative ventures. It is hard to imagine what librarianship would be like today if not for the variety of joint efforts they participate in. Where would we be without OCLC, which started as a cooperative effort by some libraries in Ohio? How would our online resources look if we did not have consortia to help control costs? The success or failure of such endeavors rests in large part on the people skills of the people involved. Perry and Christensen (2015) made the point that, "In a very real sense, the effectiveness of administrators may be a direct reflection of their effectiveness as collaborators" (p. 645). Most of the topics we cover in this chapter relate in some manner to people skills and to a person's career success.

COLLABORATION, CONFLICT MANAGEMENT, AND NEGOTIATION

Collaboration has become something of a buzzword the last few years. Cooperating with others may be most effective but is not something that comes about naturally; self-interest is strong, and conflicts may arise. Working through such situations takes behavior that requires a great deal of negotiating and compromising. Managerial leaders must hone these skills if they hope to be effective.

Organizational collaboration has two components—internal and external. From a managerial perspective, the internal side is the most controllable, and in some ways the most important. Sound internal collaboration, by whatever name you apply to the process—cooperation, working together, or teamwork, for example—is the underlying factor in organizational viability. Staff members within units must work together, and units must likewise cooperate to achieve organizational goals.

Creating a work environment that fosters teamwork is important to long-term operational success. That is easy to say but can be challenging to achieve and maintain. There is the basic issue of reducing self-interest in the workplace. One reason for the challenge is that most organizational performance assessment systems focus on individual performance and place less importance on teamwork. The result is a culture of self-interest: "Part of my financial well-being is linked to my doing well regardless of what my colleagues do." Thus, finding meaningful ways to reward cooperation regardless of what performance appraisal system exists is a step in creating a cooperative and collaborative work climate.

Knowing the staff at a professional level and having sound relationships with them goes a long way in creating a trusting work environment. Trusting others helps reduce the concern that cooperation may be detrimental to self-interest. Needless to say, a trusting work environment is helpful in a number of ways.

Involving the staff in such activities as planning and decision making generates a sense of "we are all in this together." That in turn promotes a feeling of shared goals. Shared goals tend to enhance collaborative efforts. All of the above work to enable a cooperative internal environment that almost always leads to better overall library performance.

Externally, libraries have a long history of joint efforts—almost 100 years of collaborative efforts. Early activities were of modest scale, for example, one library offering a service to other libraries for a fee. Perhaps the most successful sharing of work is seen in how the Library of Congress's sale of catalog card sets has morphed into what is today the world's largest bibliographic database, OCLC. There were and still are bumps and conflicts in that evolution, as is true of almost every shared library activity—document delivery, joint acquisitions, and reciprocal borrowing, for example.

Library collaborative ventures almost always involve senior managers in determining directions, funding, and other support issues. Just as self-interest is a factor internally with staff, so do library self-interests (bumps in the road) come into play in external collaborative ventures. Perhaps the most significant bump comes from the fact that the collaboration involves a group of senior managers who are more or less used to having the final say in most matters. Getting to a workable agreement and maintaining one rests on the next two topics—managing conflict and negotiation.

While we all engage in some form of conflict management in our personal lives, our personal approach may not work well in the workplace. Essentially, we do not manage conflict in our personal lives but react to it. Yes, you can say that reacting and managing are one and the same in terms of handling conflict, but we believe they are different; management implies an assessment and planning process in deciding how to respond to a conflict. In the workplace, such assessment, planning, and decision making are essential

IIIII CHECK THESE OUT

Four relatively recent and informative publications about public sector collaboration are:

Scott, Tyler A. and Craig W. Thomas. 2017. "Unpacking the Collaborative Toolbox: Why and When Do Public Managers Choose Collaborative Governance Strategies?" *Policy Studies Journal* 45, no. 1: 191–214.

Cuganesan, Suresh, Alison Hart, and Cara Steele. 2017. "Managing Information Sharing and Stewardship for Public Sector Collaboration: A Management Control Approach." *Public Management Review* 19, no. 6: 862–79.

Clarke, Susan E. 2017. "Local Place-Based Collaborative Governance: Comparing State-Centric and Society-Centric Models." *Urban Affairs Review* 53, no. 3: 578–602.

For an interesting article about collaboration in a library context, see Maggie Farrell's 2014 "Playing Nicely with Others." *Journal of Library Administration* 54, no. 6: 501–10.

for keeping disruptions caused by conflict to a minimum. Also keep in mind that all conflict is not necessarily bad.

Competition between ideas, approaches, methods, and so on, can be organizationally valuable. Assuming there is a reasonable level of negotiation between the competing positions, often the final result is better than any one of the competing positions. In many ways, library cooperative ventures are the outcome of such conflict or competition where library self-interests become melded into an overall approach that benefits all parties.

Professional arbitrators often divide personal behavior in dealing with conflict into three types—fight, flow, and flee. The first and last types are straightforward. "Flow" takes the form of assessing the situation and taking the course of least resistance (going with what will likely be the "winning side"). In some cases, the flow approach can lead to useful negotiations that are beneficial for all concerned.

Part of managing organizational conflict (where you become an arbitrator in a sense) is gaining some sense of each staff member's usual method of handling conflict (fight, flow, or flee). With such an understanding and experience with the staff you can begin to read signs of impending conflict and assess whether it can become a useful situation or one requiring resolution. When it is a matter of two or more staff members, it becomes fairly easy to make the judgment. When it is staff and a user, you only have half the picture. When it comes to interlibrary conflict, you have almost no clear picture or real power to manage the situation.

There is one almost guaranteed certainty—initially, the disputants will be fully convinced they are right, and the other party or parties are clearly wrong. When it comes to potentially disruptive differences, the sooner management steps in, the better for all concerned. The more time that elapses between onset and resolution is more time the disputants have to pull other staff on to "their side."

Fact finding is the key first step in assessing how best to try to resolve the situation. The more information you can learn from third parties, the better prepared you will be when talking to the disputants. Professional arbitrators recommend that the first step be a joint meeting with all the parties. The reason is if you meet with the first individual(s), the other person(s) will probably suspect, if not being certain, that you have already decided in favor of the first disputant(s). That often results in a loss of credibility in your role as a neutral third party, which in turn makes negotiations more difficult. Successful resolution revolves around compromise and negotiation.

We all engage in personal negotiation behavior without realizing that is what we are doing. Like personal conflict behavior, our personal style of negotiation is probably not the best method for the workplace. A few years ago, Deborah Kolb and Judith Williams (2011) noted, "Negotiation was once considered an art practiced by the naturally gifted . . . but increasingly we in the business world have come to regard negotiation as a science" (p. 39). Successful negotiation sessions, like so many managerial activities, hinge on the quality of the pre-session planning efforts. Going into a session without a plan rarely results in anything positive. You need to engage in two-faceted planning if you hope to have success.

One facet, as you might expect, is assessing what goals you and/or the organization have for the negotiation. What is the ideal outcome? What is an acceptable fallback position if the ideal is unachievable? What areas are acceptable to concede? Such questions are important as negotiation is a process of give and take. If you, or the organization, is unwilling to give up something (that is, my way or the highway), you are not negotiating but demanding. Establishing these points prior to the first session can reduce the anxiety and stress that is natural before and during the sessions.

> **||||| CHECK THESE OUT**
>
> A good book addressing negotiation from a library perspective is Beth Ashmore, Jill E. Grogg, and Jeff Weddle's *The Librarian's Guide to Negotiation: Winning Strategies for the Digital Age* (Medford, NJ: Information Today, 2012).
>
> A relatively recent article that provides a brief overview of the process is Karen Cates's "Negotiating Effectively: Getting to Win-Win" (*AALL Spectrum* 20, no. 3: 23–27, 2016).

The second facet may surprise you—think about the opposition's likely positions. Certainly, this will be highly speculative but not unimaginable. The fact there is to be negotiation means there has been some discussion of differing points of view that have not been resolved. Having some idea about the opposition's concerns and needs will also reduce anxiety and stress. And yes, the opposition more often than not has needs that must be met—no library vendor can lose money on too many transactions and remain in business.

As we stated above, taking an "I win, you lose" approach is not really negotiating. The notion of "win-win" is the goal of effective negotiation. Achieving such outcomes is not easy, nor very quick. Pre-planning will help speed the process as you will have already considered what you might concede.

There are some personal characteristics that you need to be a successful negotiator or arbitrator. A prime characteristic is patience. Negotiations take time and a good deal of discussion, so becoming impatient can lead to poor decisions. A related characteristic is physical stamina. Sessions often go on for hours, and sometimes weeks or months, if the issues are complex. And rarely do your other duties disappear. Attending to both activities is wearing and lack of stamina can result in poor decision making.

Persistence is a virtue in negotiations. It is one reason why most such efforts take a surprising amount of time; both parties will be persistent in making their points in order to gain concessions. Gaining a concession often requires many rounds of back-and-forth statements from each party's perspective. It is also why having patience is important.

Another essential characteristic is perspective—both you and the opposition need to keep an eye on the big picture. In a consortial situation where libraries are trying to work out a joint position, it is sometimes easy to forget that different libraries often have different priorities and needs despite sharing, more or less, common interests.

MEETING MANAGEMENT

Meetings, meetings, and more meetings—how much more productive could we be with fewer meetings? Harvey Mackay (2018) wrote about a study on organizational meetings in the United States. One startling finding was that there are 11 million business meetings *every day!* Two other findings are worth noting: 37 percent of all staff time is "meeting time," and 25 to 50 percent of that time is wasted. Another commentary on meetings appeared in an editorial in *The Economist* (2018). The writer noted that "meetings have been a form of torture for office staff for as long as they have pushed pencils and bashed keyboards" (p. 54). The answer to our question appears to be "a great deal."

As well as attending them, we also call meetings, but how many of those meetings were worthwhile in the sense of being productive? A few were probably very useful and, in a sense, remarkable for being so. Many only led to more meetings. Many others achieved minimal positive results. Some of the meetings made us wonder, "Why am I here?"

Why meetings matter when discussing productivity is straightforward—the time they take up. It is well known that some amount of time, even in productive meetings, will cause some loss of organizational productivity. Just getting to and from a meeting is non-productive time. There is the time spent socializing, as is typical of most meetings. How much organizational time is lost is dependent on how the chair handles the meeting. There is a productivity loss for each attendee; the more people, the greater the organizational loss.

It may surprise you to know that meetings may play a role in your career path. There are two aspects to this—what you contribute as a participant and how you manage the meetings you call. The participation aspect is relatively minor, although there could be times when your reputed behavior in meetings would impact an internal promotion— being a positive participant is always a plus consideration (this is why you list committee work on your resume or CV). Meetings you call and run play a bigger role. The more productive your meetings are, the more people will view you as an effective and valued person in the organization. Such impressions can become part of letters of recommendation when you apply for a new position.

When you think about calling a meeting, your first useful thought ought to be, "Is it really necessary to have a meeting? Could the matter be addressed online?" Even issues that require discussion might begin through some form of e-mail or online meeting. Some candidates for this approach are votes on a previously discussed topic, polling opinions, and distributing material for consideration and preliminary feedback.

Once it is clear an in-person meeting is necessary, plan it carefully, and send out the agenda well in advance. A key question is who should attend. Keeping that number as small as possible generally results in a more productive and shorter meeting and avoids loss of organizational productivity. When you plan a meeting, there are those you know must attend and some who would like to attend. A good approach, keeping in mind any political aspects, is to get in touch with the "musts" to determine the best time and place and set the meeting. Then, inform the "likes" when the meeting will occur; don't change the session's timing to meet their wants.

Another tip is to keep the number of topics to one or two. The more topics on the agenda, the more likely there will be more time wasted than used productively. Multiple topics also generally results in longer meetings—increasing the risk that some participants will lose attention. (The thought, "Well, my topic is covered" can lead to decreased attention to the other topics and wasted time.)

Even meeting space needs some planning, presuming you have options. In most libraries you will not have any choices and must use your office or whatever meeting room happens to be available. Squeezing too many people into a small space risks them becoming more concerned about comfort than they are with the subject. A space that is too large can also be distracting for attendees.

Running a meeting presents some challenges, for example, controlling the nonstop talker, the bully, and the ancient historian. You need people skills, experience, and diplomacy to keep meetings on track, on time, and productive. The following sidebar provides resources to help build strong meeting management skills.

|||||| **CHECK THESE OUT**

Forsyth, Patrick, and Phil Hailstone. 2017. *The Meetings Pocketbook.* 3rd ed. Alresford, England: Management Pocketbooks Ltd.

Song, Mike, Vicki Halsey, and Tim Burress. 2009. *The Hamster Revolution for Meetings: How to Meet Less and Get More Done.* San Francisco: Berrett-Koehler Publishers.

Perlow, Leslie A., Constance Noonan Hadley, and Eunice Eun. 2017 "Stop the Meeting Madness: How to Free Up Time for Meaningful Work." *Harvard Business Review* 95, no. 4: 62–69.

Bieraugel, Mark. 2017. "Never be Bored at a Meeting Again! Using Liberating Structures in Academic Libraries for Increased Productivity, Employee Engagement, and Inclusion." *College and Research Libraries News* 78, no. 8: 426–31.

TIME MANAGEMENT

Beyond meetings eating into your productive work time, there are a variety of other factors that can waste your time. Effectively managing the time you have available can help reduce the stress of what seems to be ever-growing demands on your time.

Time management is about managing yourself in order to maximize the time you have available. A careful look at how you go about doing your job will highlight just how much of your daily work time is unproductive. Evaluating your workload and style should help you to identify some areas that are relatively easy to change to more productive time. The following are some tips for increasing your productive working hours.

First and foremost, time management is a priority-setting process. One way to think about tasks is in terms of deadlines and sorting them onto one of two categories—important and urgent. Some deadlines are set by others (the submission date for your budget request, or your presentation for meeting date X, for example) and some are set by you (such as editing a memo or checking on progress of X). Not all urgent deadlines are really important, but they nevertheless must be met. Deadlines can also change over time. For example, at your annual performance review you agree to achieve a goal by the next review. That goal is important but not urgent for a good part of the year but becomes more and more urgent with each passing month. You also have the ability to set your own deadlines within the overall time frame.

There are some time wasters that many of us engage in, often on a daily basis. Perhaps the most common time waster today is checking e-mail. Checking the inbox may only take a few seconds per look; however, those seconds add up. It also diverts our focus from the task at hand. A good time saver is to set two or three times a day to check e-mail. Let colleagues know about your approach; that way they will not expect an instantaneous response, and there will be almost no organizational performance loss due to the delay. It may even increase productivity. Doing something similar with making and returning phone calls is also a time saver.

You should also look at how you handle business calls. How much time do you spend being social with the other party? Some is appropriate, but often it goes beyond being polite. Not many business calls really require more than fifteen minutes. If the matter is highly complex, perhaps a written communication is a better starting point.

Another area where you can save some time as a supervisor or manager is how you handle staff needs. You may like an open-door policy because it is a clear method of demonstrating your willingness to meet with staff. The fact is that each interruption stops what you were doing, and it takes some time to resume that work. One method to gain useful time is to employ a modified open door by setting defined times the door is open--perhaps an hour in the morning and another in the afternoon. During that time plan on doing work that requires little concentration and is easy to begin, stop, and resume.

A final tip is to lay out your priority work for the next day as you leave for the night. This will give you a head start on tomorrow; there will be no need to sort through things in the morning to decide where to begin. The following sidebar provides some resources for using your time more effectively.

▏▎▍ CHECK THESE OUT

The following are two resources that explore time management.

Williams, Kate and Michelle Reid. *Time Management*. New York: Palgrave Macmillan, 2011.

Institute of Leadership and Management. *Managing Time Super Series*. Hoboken, NJ: Taylor and Francis, 2012.

SELF-MANAGEMENT SKILLS

Workplace self-management is important regardless of your role and duties. Two of the key components in self-management are handling stress and office politics. Both issues are factors in productivity and can become potential time wasters if they become our work focus.

Stress

All of us experience some degree of stress in both our personal and work lives, and often the two interact with one another. A little stress is not always a bad thing, especially in the workplace. Stress has a way of focusing our attention. It becomes problematic when we become less and less able to cope. There are some early warning signs when our coping mechanisms are getting overloaded. A marked change in your sleep pattern can indicate stress is becoming a problem. Feeling anxious and not being able to identify why you feel that way is another signal stress may be getting too high. Still another sign that you have too much stress is when concentrating becomes difficult. Certainly, there are many more such signals (too many to explore here).

There are techniques that can help you to manage workplace stress. The most basic ways to reduce stress include exercising, eating properly, and getting enough sleep. Beyond those, having someone to talk to who understands the work context (a mentor or former colleague, for example) can be very beneficial. Establishing priorities and sticking to those priorities helps—shifting priorities can be very stressful. Delegating as much as possible is another tactic—trying to be the Lone Ranger all the time is a stress generator. A focus on perfection is also a bad thing in terms of stress if it leads to devoting too much time to one task while leaving other tasks unfinished. The consequence is that you become stressed about the undone. Another pitfall is trying to control the uncontrollable. Needless to say, managing work time effectively is a stress reducer.

Determining how much stress is too much is a personal matter. What is a major stress situation for one person is hardly a blip for another. You need to assess your stress tolerance and decide what, if anything, to do about how to manage it.

Political skills

We all have experienced some level of office politics. There are two broad categories of office politics: those that hinder organizational performance and those that move the organization forward. Yes, there is such a thing as good organizational politics. When we hear the words "office politics," we tend to automatically think it is a bad thing.

Someone who has the organization's well-being as their primary goal can achieve such a goal by being politically astute. If you understand where organizational power resides, how to secure some of that power (for non-personal use), and employ that power for organizational ends, then you are politically savvy in a positive sense.

Another aspect of being politically knowledgeable is understanding the nature of office politics or games—how they are played and how to combat them when they arise. Broadly thinking, there are three areas where such games occur—interpersonal, unit/departmental, and budgetary. When most people hear "office politics," they first think of interpersonal politics. Interpersonal politics are inevitable and can sometimes be ignored when they do not impact unit or organizational performance. Budget politics generate inevitable game playing. Not understanding how to play can have a long-term negative impact on the library.

Given that library work often involves working with other units, some games are likely from time to time. The most common games are ambiguity and flip-flopping. The ambiguity game arises when a unit wants to avoid accountability or blame for something while trying to appear cooperative. Flip-flopping gives the impression of cooperation while still protecting the unit's turf. Requesting more information is a classic method for delaying a decision or action. It also is an attempt to avoid any consequences of a poor or bad decision. A "yes, but . . . " or "sort of, if . . . " approach allows for the appearance of collaboration while leaving an option to dodge any blame for later problems.

Budget politics almost guarantee game playing. One constant in the library environment is politics surrounding collection development allocations, the second largest percentage of the operating budget after salaries. Collection development has few allies during budget preparation time. Thus, understanding the way budget politics operate in your institution is critical regardless of what unit you are in.

The above is a small sample of workplace politics that can impact library activities. The question is, what can you do to combat such situations? There are no one-size-fits-all solutions for addressing office politics and games, because variables such as personalities, motivations, circumstances will always exist. However, there are some general guidelines. Learning about the basic games that can arise gives you a chance to identify them early on, when they are easiest to combat.

The starting point for handling possible workplace games is to engage in some careful analysis of what is occurring. Why is it in play? Are there factors that negate the notion it is office politics? Why do you see this as office politics? (Sometimes we are wrong in our assumptions.) What are some other perspectives about what is going on? Discussing your perceptions of the situation with a neutral colleague or mentor can help sort out fact and fiction.

Diplomacy and tact

Tact and diplomacy are useful skills. We experience tact as children as we see adults say things to someone that seem slightly "off," but appear to make the person feel better. Over time most of us come to realize the benefits of being tactful, even if no one actually talked to us about being so.

There are several reasons diplomacy is a skill that takes time to develop, much less master. One reason is that being diplomatic is usually about achieving an organizational goal rather than a personal objective. Why organizational goals more often than personal? Over time, starting in childhood, we developed tactics for getting what we want which have nothing to do with being diplomatic.

Another reason diplomacy takes time to develop is because it requires tight impulse control, both verbally and behaviorally. Yes, we learned early on that outbursts are not always effective means to achieving our goal. Outbursts rarely, if ever, achieve organizational goals; if anything, they make the achievement all the more difficult. In terms of diplomacy, impulse control goes well beyond controlling outbursts. The physical control is relatively easy (no throwing up your hands when you are exasperated or starting to walk away, for example). Even words are controllable, if you plan your efforts. The big challenge is your nonverbal communication. Nonverbal cues often send a very different meaning than the words being said. We are often unaware of our nonverbal behaviors. One way to learn about "how you actually talk" nonverbally is to have colleagues tell you what they observe.

Diplomacy and tact share a common element: empathy. Most of us have the ability to feel empathy for others. We know of few libraries where all members have less than a full workload. It is hard to feel much empathy when a colleague uses a heavy workload as an excuse for non-performance. Lack of empathy can also make it more difficult to reach a satisfactory arrangement. If the problem stemmed from too many conflicting demands, a lack of empathy can only make it harder to resolve. What is left is a conflict situation, hopefully modest in scope, which requires resolution.

▥ CHECK THESE OUT

The following are good books that provide in-depth coverage of office politics and how to address the more common variations.

Clarke, Jane. 2012. *Savvy: Dealing with People, Power and Politics at Work.* Philadelphia, PA: Kogan Page Limited.

Goldstein, Mauricio and Philip Read. 2009. *Games at Work: How to Recognize and Reduce Office Politics.* San Francisco: Jossey-Bass.

Dillon, Karen, ed. *HBR Guide to Office Politics.* Boston, MA: Harvard Business Review Press, 2015.

PROFESSIONAL PRESENTATIONS AND PUBLICATIONS

The quality of your presentations will have some impact on your career development. (In a sense, even the way you handle meetings is a type of presentation.) While many of you may not publish, those in a managerial role will have some public speaking duties. Although individual presentations may not have much impact, in combination they play a surprisingly significant role.

There is a rather big word related to public speaking—*glossophobia*, or the fear of speaking publicly. Many of us don't enjoy public speaking and worry about doing so; however, few of us become speechless. We worry that we will make mistakes, lose our train of thought, and so forth. Keep in mind that even experienced public speakers stumble on occasion and are able to carry on. One reason they are able to do so is they have practiced and given the speech, often in different variations, many times. That is one of the keys to giving sound public speeches—practice, practice, and still more practice.

For all types of presentations there are some basic rules that apply—planning, preparation, practice, and performance. Planning begins with establishing the intended audience, purpose, and the time frame for your performance. The audience might be a group of fellow professionals attending a small meeting or a conference keynote address, or someone who will be interviewing you for a job, which is one of the most stressful situations. When you have a mixed audience, you need to decide who the target audience is; general public or professional, for example. There are a variety of other possibilities, each with its own implications for content, style, and level of detail. Clearly the purpose is another factor—are you hoping to inform, entertain, convince, or explain? The audience and purpose will focus the planning process. The time frame is a third factor in framing your content. There is a big difference between having fifteen minutes to explain and defend a budget request and a keynote presentation in terms of content packed into the time frame.

There is a general structure for most oral or written presentations. For short time frames the typical structure will not really work as you must get right to the matter. The structure for most presentations is introduction, overview, background, key points and results, supporting material (as necessary), summarization, and closing.

Once you have a draft, it is time to practice and test the timing. Usually, the first few run-throughs will show that you need to make some adjustments in content. This is also a time to have a colleague read the material—a different perspective almost always improves a presentation. Following the preceding steps will reduce some of the stress most of us feel before speaking in public. It will not get rid of all stress, but you will know that the material is properly prepared.

There is an important point to keep in mind about publishing—published materials last a long time, and people can read what you wrote years later. For better or worse, publications play a role in your career path. People have recognized this fact for centuries. The Roman writer Horace had this to say about the matter, "Let it be kept till the ninth year, the manuscript kept at home; you may destroy what you have not published; once out, what you've said can't be stopped" (*Oxford Dictionary of Quotations* 1980, p. 258). The work of the majority of librarians who publish will be read by their colleagues and they must therefore remember that what they write today may impact their careers in the long term. Writing takes time and effort; even academic librarians who have an expectation of publishing as part of their job receive little, if any, release time for writing. They write during their personal time—evenings, weekends, and even vacations. Writing for

---

||||| CHECK THIS OUT

An excellent article about writing for the library profession is Joan Giesecke's "Preparing Research for Publication" (*Library Administration and Management* 12, no. 3: 134–37, 998).

---

publication, regardless of the intended audience, is hard work. Writing for the professional audience requires careful research and thought, which adds still more time to the overall process. The need for research arises from the fact you are very rarely writing about something unique to the field. What others have said about the topic matters, and failure to note your predecessors' work will reflect poorly on your efforts. As Horace noted, once it is out there, there is no bringing it back, and the impact can last throughout your career.

Not all professional writing takes large amounts of time. Preparing a review of a potentially useful item for a library collection takes only a modest amount of time and provides a service to the profession. It also does not have much, if any, impact on your career path. Reviewing is the most common form of publishing for the majority of librarians who do publish.

Given the time commitment, does it matter what type of publishing you do? Probably not, if your job does not require you to publish. For those who are expected to do so, it matters a good deal. There is something of a hierarchy in the weight of a publication that more or less reflects the time commitment. That is, the greater the time commitment, the greater the value. Reviewing other peoples' publications is at the low end; being the sole author of a book is at the top. Being a columnist, an editor of journal or review section, and a chapter contributor for a book fall in between.

Knowing how to manage conflict, collaboration, negotiations, meetings, time, stress, organizational politics, and contributing to the profession through presentations and publication are important if you are to be a successful manager.

REFERENCES

Cates, Karen. 2016. "Negotiating Effectively: Getting to Win-Win." *AALL Spectrum* 20, no. 3: 23–27.

Cross, Rob, Reb Rebele, and Adam Grant. 2016. "Collaborative Overload." *Harvard Business Review* 94, no. 1: 74–79 .

Economist. 2018. "Taking Minutes, Wasting Hours." 427, no. 9098: 54.

Kolb, Deborah M., and Judith Williams. 2011. "Breakthrough Bargaining." In *Winning Negotiations.* Cambridge, MA: Harvard Business Review Press. (Originally published 2001 in *Harvard Business Review* v. 79, no. 2: 88–97.

Mackay, Harvey. 2018. "Advance Your Career with Every Meeting." *Arizona Republic* July 2: 8A.

Perlow, Leslie A., Constance Noonan Hadley, and Eunice Eun. 2017. "Stop the Meeting Madness: How to Free Up Time for Meaningful Work." *Harvard Business Review* 95, no. 4: 62-69.

Perry, James L., and Robert K. Christensen, eds. 2015. *Handbook of Public Administration.* 3rd ed. New York: Wiley.

CHAPTER 22

Creating Your Career

What is a career? It can be defined as a succession of related jobs, arranged in a hierarchical order, through which a person moves during their working life.

Jela Webb, 2016

Could your personality derail your career?

Tomas Chamorro-Premuzic, 2017

The keys to success are adaptability, keeping relevant and up to date through working and developing your network of contacts regularly.

Claire Laybats and Darron Chapman, 2016

How your career turns out rests primarily in your hands. Yes, unexpected events can and sometimes do play a role in your career path. However, we have more control over our careers than we sometimes believe, especially if we proactively plan rather than just let things happen.

Why bother thinking about your long-term career plans before you have your first position? A major reason for doing so is that it helps you decide what to seek in the first position. Often it sets the course for your career without your intending it to do so. Do you recall the scene from *Alice's Adventures in Wonderland* where Alice and Cat exchange views regarding directions? Alice: "Would you tell me, please, which way I ought to go from here?" Cat: "That depends a good deal on where you want to go." Alice: "I don't much care where." Cat: "Then it doesn't matter which way you go." So it is with your career; lacking a desired direction can well result in a less satisfying work life. It also means you have given up control of your career path.

One reason for planning ahead is that, in general, librarians can substantially increase their salaries through taking on greater and greater managerial leadership responsibilities. However, "up" is not the only way to do so, assuming you know such responsibilities are not something you're interested in. Also, the flattening of library organizational structures means there will be fewer upward opportunities.

Yet another reason for planning and periodically reassessing the plan is that we all know that technological knowledge and skills change rapidly; today's knowledge may be obsolete tomorrow. Monitoring the changes, even if not required in your current position, will help you assess what new skills to develop in order to meet long-term career goals. Elías Tzoc and John Millard (2011) listed twenty-one different categories of digital library career opportunities. While the categories are likely to remain constant for some time, the skills to perform the jobs are very likely to change. Keeping a watchful eye on such changes may well pay dividends down the road.

CAREER PLANNING PROCESS

There are five steps in creating a useful career plan: self-assessment, knowing career options, mentoring and networking, having a life plan, and having a professional development plan. Self-assessment is the first and, in many ways, the most important. It requires you to take a very hard look at yourself—where you currently are, not where you would like to be—and at your strengths and weaknesses. Ask yourself questions such as, "What is my personality (outgoing, shy, etc.)?" "Am I passive/assertive or rational/emotional?" "How do I prefer to learn (individually or in a group, hands on, academic, etc.)?" "What are my skills (both work and non-work related)?" "What do I value (friends, status, money, time, etc.)?" "What do I want in a job (learning opportunities, satisfaction in doing something well, etc.)?" "What did I like and dislike about past work situations?" Another key question is, "How much risk can I tolerate?"

Part of self-awareness is gaining an understanding of your preferred work traits and their potential long- and short-term implications for your career. One tool for doing this is the Hogan Development Survey (https://www.hoganassessments.com/assessment/hogan-development-survey/). It looks at eleven characteristics that can be good or bad in certain circumstances or over time. You may be surprised at what traits are among the eleven items.

- excitable
- skeptical
- cautious
- reserved
- leisurely
- bold
- mischievous
- colorful
- imaginative
- diligent
- dutiful

A web search for the survey will turn up a number of sites that discuss the methodology and interpretations of results.

Another part of the planning process is to assess what the available career options are, both for your existing LIS skill set and with the other knowledge and skills you possess. You may be surprised by the range of possibilities for MLIS skills outside of a library setting. Joanne Gard Marshall and colleagues (2009) looked at MLIS graduates from 1964 to 2005 and found that just over 14 percent were using the degree skills in non-library settings (some examples are jobs with database or content providers, ILS system vendors or developers, and database management firms). Your other existing skills and the MLIS may open unexpected opportunities as well, so investigating some of the possibilities will help you make an informed career plan.

Preparing a career plan may seem daunting. We suggest a good way to begin the process is to do the following by picking just your top three priorities for each category:

- your personal skills
- your professional skills
- your work values—"must haves"
- work areas of interest—"really like"
- work areas of low interest—"really draining"
- possible career options
- new skills you would like to have

As new challenges emerge, many of the older ones will remain. All these skills can apply to many non-library work environments. When you identify a subject area that

👁 FOR FURTHER THOUGHT

Think about what you do best, what you like doing best, what you do not like doing or avoid doing, what you hope to accomplish from your working life, and what your long-term goals are. Use this to start a first draft of your list of career goals. This is an important exercise to do throughout your career, and now is a great time to start.

looks interesting, try to locate people who are working in the field and see if they are willing to talk to you about opportunities and to provide a firsthand perspective of the work. Even better, assuming they are local, see if you might shadow them in their work-place for a day or two or volunteer to work alongside them. There is nothing like having experience in another area without having to leave your current position.

Part of the planning process is thinking about what you would like to be doing five or ten or more years from now. Another decision to make, once you have identified your long-term goal(s), is what you need—knowledge, skills, experience, and so forth—to achieve that goal. Professional development is your responsibility. Yes, your current employer may be willing to pay for some development activities, but almost always the activities will relate to your current position. Needless to say, few employers are willing to underwrite activities that are likely to lead to your going somewhere else. How you go about developing the requisite skills for the long-term objective is a matter of your preferred learning style.

Mentors

Finding a mentor is part of most successful career plans. A mentor provides help in a great many ways. However, to be effective, both of you must be willing and able to spend time getting to know one another. Developing trust is essential for successful mentoring. A mentoring relationship is relatively long-term. Mentors are great as "sounding boards" about

▶ TIP

When it comes to finding a mentor, you should not expect your supervisor to play that role. That person may do so but only rarely. It is up to you to find one. Two good places to start are with former teachers and people you meet through professional associations. A key to a good mentoring relationship is finding an individual who has similar work values, whom you respect, and who has achieved something you would like to achieve. Sometimes a mentoring relationship just develops. However, more often you will need to approach the person and ask if he or she would be willing to be your mentor. Have a plan in mind for what you are seeking in such a relationship so that the person can assess whether she or he has the knowledge, time, and so forth to undertake the desired activity.

Perhaps the biggest challenge for the mentee is being able to "hear" some things that are discomforting. However, a good mentor should and will point out areas where improvement would be beneficial.

current job situations: "I would think about doing that just now," "That sounds like an excellent plan," "I would sleep on that," and "Have you thought about . . . " are the kinds of comments mentors give to mentees. When the mentor gets to know you well, she or he can be very helpful in reviewing your self-assessment results. Mentors can be invaluable when it comes to job changes, and they may even push you to make a move when you are not sure you are up to the new responsibilities.

Keep in mind mentoring and coaching are related but different. They are related in the sense they both are focused on developing a person's skills. They are different in terms of time frame and purpose. Coaching is short-term and focuses on one or two areas for development. Mentoring is usually long-term and addresses overall professional development.

Beyond working with a mentor, you will want to follow Kristen Centanni's (2011) advice—start networking while in your MLIS program. Network contacts can be as helpful as your mentor throughout your career. They can be sounding boards, informants about job prospects, and more. Like mentoring, networking is about building relationships and trust. As is true of good work relationships, you need to be as good a listener as you are a talker. Certainly, social media is now a key part of networking and is a place where "me" can be dominant, unlike in face-to-face interactions where "me" should be less prevalent.

Social media

Something to keep in mind is what you put on your public social media accounts can impact your career. Prospective employers will likely check what you have posted. A CareerBuilder .com 2017 survey (Lauren Salm, "70% of employers Are Snooping Candidates' Social Media Profiles," https://www.careerbuilder.com/advice/social-media-survey-2017) found the number of employers doing such checking increased by 10 percent over the 2016 data. The odds are high that they will check yours.

The survey also noted an increase in the number of organizations that have at least one FTE devoted to conducting such checks. This could include what you have shared on Instagram, Twitter, and other platforms as well as what can be found via Google and other searches. If you are a member of LinkedIn, they may check what others say about you. They will try to verify qualifications you claim to have and assess your communication skills based on what they see.

Your social media persona will likely play an increasing role in your career. That persona is two-edged: it may keep you from getting a position, yet it may also make you stand out in a large pool of applicants. (Note: for some employers, a lack of a social media presence could be grounds to reject an application—they may feel the applicant may have something to hide.)

The Career Builder survey included some no-nos for social media in terms of job searching. We have added a few others to the list. Some may surprise you, but most are common sense yet are not always followed:

- poor or inappropriate word choices
- inappropriate images
- unprofessional persona
- claiming skills not held
- negative posts about current employer or colleagues

👥 AUTHORS' EXPERIENCE

We cannot emphasize enough how important it is to be involved in at least one professional organization during your career. Perhaps you will become involved in several organizations as your goals, interests, and job responsibilities change. We have both found this involvement to be a rewarding and essential aspect of our professional lives.

Most schools of library and information science offer student chapters of some of the major library professional organizations. While being a student places numerous demands on your time, becoming involved in these organizations while still a student provides you with achievements for your resume or CV, additional experience, and contacts, not to mention discounted membership fees for these organizations at the national level. This includes access to the organization's publications, discussion lists, and discounted rates to attend conferences. Many state organizations have similar arrangements for library school students, which are particularly valuable if you are seeking employment within the state. In any case, all of these opportunities will help you to build your professional network.

Greenwell has pointed out many times how her work with professional organizations early in her career helped her develop skills that she later used in the workplace. As an entry-level librarian, you may not have the opportunity to run a meeting or prepare a budget or plan a program. As a volunteer in a professional organization, you can develop and practice these skills in a somewhat low-risk environment. Building these skills is helpful as you take on additional responsibilities at work and perhaps consider job changes. This can be a good place to test out new skills and grow professionally.

- poor grammar
- sharing current employer's activities
- evidence of misuse of benefits such as sick time
- posting too often

It is becoming common for perspective employers to ask for candidate's social media accounts (Instagram, Twitter, and Facebook, for example). Some companies are more subtle about their requests. They ask the candidate to "friend" a particular company employee so that they can access the candidate's pages, or they ask the candidate to access his or her social media account on a company computer during the interview (Valdes and McFarland 2012). Many see this as an invasion of privacy; the potential employer sees it as a way to learn more about the candidate. The bottom line here, as with e-mail, is don't put up something that you would not want to see on the front page of the newspaper.

Finally, once you have thought through your long-term career goals, it is time to consider what you need to do to achieve those goals. Most likely it will entail some form of professional development. The vast majority of those of us in the field have a commitment to lifelong learning in all its forms, not just professional.

You have a variety of options for professional development. National professional association meetings are a major source that offer both general presentations and specialized workshops. Such meetings are also an important part of the professional networking process, so attendance need not always have a professional development motive. Local, regional, and online professional development opportunities also exist. Of course, there are course and degree program options as well as independent learning. Just remember, only you are responsible for your professional development.

MARKETING YOURSELF

Whether you are seeking your first professional position or a new job, you are marketing yourself to prospective employers. You probably know the basic components of a sound résumé (or curriculum vitae for academic positions). Just in case you don't recall the elements, here they are:

- Name, address, phone number, and e-mail address
- Education: high school, university—with distinctions and awards
- Professional courses: university, title of program, specialist papers, awards, and scholarships
- Courses that develop additional skills, such as IT, languages, or communication
- Work experience to date (remember that any work with the public, even in a supermarket, for example, will have helped you develop communication and team skills)
- Membership in relevant organizations, particularly professional bodies
- Attendance at professional conferences

As your career develops, adding attendance at professional development courses, papers presented at conferences, professional awards, and so forth may provide the essential pieces of information to get an interview. As a recent student, you may not have some of these accomplishments to include, and that is common. If you have some achievements in these areas—perhaps you presented a poster session, published a book review, or chaired a student organization—by all means include them. Your mentor can provide good advice on what to include and in turn will be better prepared to write references on your behalf. In a competitive job market, you could turn to a professional résumé writer. These writers know what employers expect and know what the current approaches are, and they are skilled in the design and layout of compelling documents.

Tailoring the résumé to the particular vacancy description can be effective; we strongly recommend you take the time to do so. In tight economic times, most job postings generate a large number of applicants. The search committee will look for applications that jump out because the applicant has skills matching the position's needs. A less tailored application may have the requisite skills embedded in it, but they are hidden in a wealth of other information. Ideally, that should not matter, but the reality is that being on a search committee is an added task that takes time away from other work activities, and thus a hasty first review may cause something to be missed. A targeted resume and cover letter is less likely to get overlooked.

Check with the people you list as references to be sure they are still willing to do so and that you have their current contact information. One way to do this is to send them the job announcement so they have a chance to assess what they can (or can't) do as a reference. A professor who you had for Children's Literature may be willing to

👥 AUTHORS' EXPERIENCE

Even while you are a student, it isn't too early to consider presenting or publishing. Some of the substantial papers you complete for your coursework might be suitable for publication in a state library association journal or other local venue. If your work is outstanding, you might consider submitting it beyond those publications. Greenwell has advised students in the past to approach their major papers and projects in library and information science programs with an intent to publish. Even if you choose not to publish them now, you may go back to the work in the future to uses as a starting point for a different publication.

A relatively low-stress opportunity to present your work is a poster session. Many state library organizations (and an increasing number of national and international ones) welcome excellent student work. With a poster session, you will be asked to prepare a large print poster describing your research in some detail. You will be expected to be available at designated times to answer questions about your research. In addition to gaining some presentation experience and creating something to include on your resume or CV, this will also help build your professional network and reputation.

be a reference, but perhaps may not be all that helpful when applying for an electronic resource librarian position.

Interviewing

So, you have an interview scheduled—what next? Do your homework on the institution and its location. You can gain a general sense of the employer online—but only a general sense. Ask your mentor and people in your network what they know about the institution. They may even know someone who worked there and who might be willing to talk to you. Most job interviews include or end with some variation of "Do you have any questions for us?" You should always have some questions prepared for your interviewers. Spend some time preparing a list of questions to ask that may not be covered during the interview.

In the past, libraries prepared a very short list of candidates—three or four—to invite for on-site interviews. The cost of bringing in more individuals was too high in terms of both money and time. Today libraries, like many other organizations, are using telephone interviews or video conferences to do an initial screening of a larger pool of applicants before making the final selection for on-site interviews. As Jahna Berry (2011) noted, "With video, companies can get an early impression of key factors, such as a job seeker's personality and communications skills, which helps narrow the applicant pool. But candidates must make careful preparation to ensure making a good on-camera impression" (p. D1).

Berry (2011) provided several tips for preparing for a video interview. One obvious need is not only to have the proper equipment and connectivity but also to test it well before the interview. It is a good idea to check that the room you plan to use is echo-free—echoes can be very distracting. Another room or space issue is the background; a cluttered or highly patterned background can be distracting and may send the wrong message. Lighting can be an issue; you may need to introduce more light that is out of the camera's line of sight. What you wear is also a bigger factor with video than it is with in-person interviews; patterned blouses or shirts are not recommended and check solid colors to determine how they come across on video. Keep family, friends, and pets out of the room and out of listening distance; they can be a distraction for you. Eye contact is always a factor in interviews but becomes critical in video interviews, as it is easy to tell when your eyes wander—look straight into the camera. If you can see yourself on the screen, try not to look at yourself or cover that part of the screen. Finally, and just as for in-person interviews, rehearse, rehearse, rehearse; if possible, record the rehearsal(s) so others can assess the performance and make suggestions for improvement.

Regardless of the interview format, thinking about and rehearsing your answers to some typical questions is worth the time and effort. Below are a few common questions:

- What interests you about this position?
- What are your work strengths?
- What are your work weaknesses?
- What do think your supervisor or friend would say about your work ethic?
- What was your favorite job, and what made it so?
- What was your least favorite job, and what made it so?

💼 SUGGESTIONS FOR INTERVIEWEES

- Research the library and parent organization ahead of time.
- Develop several questions to ask the interviewer(s) about the institution.
- Request a position description and develop a question or two about the position.
- Think about the answers you might give to questions that are likely to be part of the interview. (What interests you about this particular position? What do you consider your strengths and your weaknesses? What does the term "service" mean to you?)
- Dress appropriately.
- Be on time.
- Be certain to know the interviewer's or chairperson's name and learn the correct pronunciation.
- Remember that your body language reflects your interest and attentiveness.
- Brief pauses before answering complex questions are appropriate—thinking before speaking is always a good idea.
- Respond to all parts of a multipart question; asking for clarification or for repetition of a part of such questions is appropriate.
- Asking how any personal or potentially illegal question(s) relate to job performance is appropriate; however, ask it in a non-confrontational manner, as the question could be job-related.
- Thank the interviewer(s) for the opportunity to interview for the position.
- Asking about the anticipated time frame for deciding on who will be hired is appropriate.
- Send a follow-up thank you note to the individuals who interviewed you.
- Making post-interview notes about some of the high and low points of the interview can be helpful in the future.

👥 AUTHORS' EXPERIENCE

Greenwell used to trade business cards at professional conferences, but some years ago, she began connecting with new contacts via LinkedIn. In addition to creating a LinkedIn profile, you might wish to create your own website to share some information about your career goals, experience, and links to any relevant publications, presentations, online exhibits, websites, or other relevant work. There are many such platforms to do this.

A note about business cards: if you attend professional conferences or networking events as a student, create some business cards for yourself to exchange if you haven't already. You might be surprised at how much we still use them, even though we have phones, LinkedIn, and so on. You might include your name, contact information, where you are a student, your career goal, and expected date of graduation. This is a great thing to talk about with a mentor.

Networking

Networking is something of a mixture of mentoring, marketing, and expanding the range of your professional colleagues. For many people, social or professional networking is challenging. Nevertheless, doing this can be a significant factor in your career success. It is second only to mentoring in term of assisting you in your career development and advancement.

Professional networking is about creating, developing, and maintaining relationships with your peers. As is true with mentoring, the successful network is built on trust and on give-and-take, which involves such things as experience with a new library effort or system, news about job openings and information about the hiring library environment, and simple support.

For many of us approaching a stranger and saying something like, "Hi I'm _____. I work at X library and I saw your nametag indicates you're at Y institution. I hear your institution is doing _____. Could you tell me more about it?" is challenging. You will need to take some initiative when it comes to creating a professional network. Waiting for others to approach you is likely to result in a very narrow circle of professional friends. You can begin the process while you are in school; maintain contact with some of the colleagues who share your interests. It is unlikely many of those friends will be working at your library, and over time each person will develop new contacts, slowly expanding the network.

What are some of the major "dos" of effective networking? One very important one was mentioned in the above paragraph—introduce yourself and don't be shy. Develop a brief concise introduction with no "puffery"—simply your job and interests. If you have a business card, offer it; it is a good way to establish a means of communication without much effort. Assuming there are mutual interests, follow up. Developing trusting relationships takes time; be patient. Perhaps the simplest way to think of the process is like dating: keep it honest, develop trust, share, and so forth.

There is some good news for those of us who are really reluctant to introduce ourselves to strangers. Online professional networking sites exist. Some are a mixed bag of marketing, job seeking, and other services. LinkedIn is the best known such site in the United States—it is international in scope and is widely used by professionals in all fields.

LinkedIn is both a networking and employment site. Today, much of its income comes from selling access to its membership database to HR departments—old style "headhunting" has changed from person-to-person recommendations to bots searching databases. Both individuals and organizations are members of LinkedIn. According to a 2016 *New York Times* article ("New Item on the College Admission Checklist: LinkedIn Profiles," November 5), high schoolers applying for college are becoming members.

While high school students may not be suitable professional contacts, there is little doubt that LinkedIn and similar sites are becoming increasingly important in a person's career. Creating a profile is something to do upon graduation, if you have not already done so.

FLEXIBLE WAYS OF WORKING

Before taking your career in a new direction, examine the range of flexible working practices available in organizations today. Because libraries generally operate over extended hours, it is often easier to arrange flexible working arrangements than in many other types of organizations. Part-time positions may be available. A job-share is one way to retain professional expertise while moving into a new field. These arrangements can bring benefits to the employer by having a well-qualified and motivated staff member who works certain hours rather than losing the employee altogether.

Telecommuting may also be an option. Jassin and Moe (2005) discuss the ways in which librarians can compete with other workers by developing their own telecommuting jobs. Working from home on a freelance basis can be effective for an increasing number of fields of professional practice. It has been common for indexers and abstractors to work in this way for many years, and the practice now extends to handling inquiries, performing marketing and public relations tasks, and using information brokers, consultants, and editors. Working in this way requires good organization and communication skills and close attention to customer care. Professional associations are generally able to offer advice on the professional indemnity insurance that is essential to have when working independently in the information field.

▌▌▌ CHECK THIS OUT

If you are interested in learning more about becoming an independent information professional, Mary Ellen Bates' *Building and Running a Successful Research Business: A Guide for the Independent Information Professional* (Information Today 2010) is a classic guidebook to the field. Also check out the Association of Independent Information Professionals (AIIP) for more resources for independents https://www.aiip.org/.tip.

Another option is to take a temporary or contract post. Changes in the labor market have resulted in a greater number of people being employed on limited-term contracts. Contract work provides an opportunity to experience subject areas with a range of employers or in a variety of specialty posts. Employment agencies can help an individual to manage a career relying on contract posts, particularly in the private sector. A number of writers in the management field have suggested that all professionals will develop

> ▌▌▌▌ **CHECK THIS OUT**
>
> A good book that covers a variety of employment possibilities is T. Allan Taylor and James Robert Parish's *Career Opportunities in Library and Information Science* (New York: Ferguson, 2009).

portfolio careers in the future that involve greater flexibility and allow for them to switch between jobs. There are major precautions to take if stepping back from a permanent or full-time position: consider the vital pension plan, health insurance, insurance, and other benefits you will lose. This may not seem important to you when you are in your twenties or thirties, but it can have an impact later in life.

CAREER BREAKS

Career breaks benefit both the employee and the employer. In some occupations and countries, the need for a break is recognized in the conditions of employment (academics may be granted study leaves or sabbaticals, for example). The employer benefits because the person who enjoys a break comes back refreshed and reinvigorated. The staff development program also benefits because the staff member who covers the absence has an opportunity to demonstrate her or his skills in a different post. This helps the employer to assess that person's suitability for promotion.

Developmental internships or fellowships may be available for those designated as "high flyers"—for example, the developmental opportunities organized by the Association of Research Libraries. In some universities, staff may be eligible for a sabbatical to pursue their personal research in order to maintain subject knowledge.

Traveling overseas may be a choice at any stage in a career. Travel scholarships for short periods of time are offered by a number of organizations. Exchanges with professionals in other parts of the world can be set up with facilitators through exchange registers that list people in all types of organizations and in a number of countries around the world. Most are for three or six months and often involve a swap of job, house, and car. Voluntary service overseas was, at one time, the province of the new graduate, but now, as more people take early retirement or career breaks, their skills and experiences can be of value in other countries.

Breaks for family responsibilities, such as maternity or paternity leaves, are becoming part of established employment policies and practices. These leaves enable new parents to enjoy, and more fully participate in, the early stages of their child's life. The length of time available, and whether the leave is paid or unpaid, varies from one employer to another.

MOVING FORWARD

The general management literature demonstrates a continuing concern about the pressures that are being placed on managers and their staff as organizations strive to cut operating costs and as ICT changes the way in which work is done. Much has been written about the negative effects of stress, which can affect anyone within an organization, regardless of age, gender, or job level. Progressing in a career can increase the susceptibility to stress.

Learning a new job can mean taking work home and acquiring new knowledge, qualifications, or skills. E-mail and social media can add to the pressures of daily life, resulting in a situation where it is hard to break away from work, feeling there's always a need to "catch up." In the most serious manifestations of stress, excessive eating, drinking, or smoking may be the individual's answer to the problem. Stress can damage physical and psychological health and reduce the effectiveness of a person's performance, which, in turn, impacts on the work of their colleagues. Recognizing the symptoms may be unpalatable to the employee and difficult for the employer. Organizations that provide in-house counseling, such as universities, may have a better way to help staff. The remedy lies with the individual, who should limit the amount of overtime worked, take all of a leave allowance, enjoy a holiday, have a leisure-time interest, and enjoy time with family and friends for a full life.

Moving from a graduate program to a first job is likely to produce culture shock, as the fundamental purpose of professional education is not to train students for a first job but to prepare them for a career (Holley 2003). It is important to understand that the program's purpose is to prepare students for the long term by teaching the theory and principles to support them throughout their careers.

The direction your career takes is often conditioned by factors outside your control. These include economic, political, social, and technological changes and the state of the labor market. But there is a range of opportunities, and you have choices in deciding which direction to move. Career development depends on keeping well informed. Information-

TABLE 22.1 Factors Leading to a Successful Career

- Know yourself, both your strengths and weaknesses.
- Have high standards, both personal and professional, and demonstrate them in your daily work.
- Demonstrate commitment to whatever job you have.
- Cultivate clear thinking and maintain an objective viewpoint.
- Be reliable.
- Be adaptable.
- Cultivate your sense of humor and don't lose it.
- Understand the ways that others think.
- Show a concern for others in your professional and personal life, but in unobtrusive ways.
- Keep at the cutting edge of change.
- Develop good communication and influencing skills.
- Acquire political skills.
- Extend your managerial knowledge and know what the best practices in management. thinking are.
- Ensure that you are working effectively as a member of a team at all stages in your career.
- Know how to make decisions, and change them if the situation demands.
- Delegate.
- Maintain control over your own time.
- Recognize mistakes that you have made and learn from them.
- Understand that career development requires an investment of time and money.
- Enjoy the job you are doing. If you don't enjoy the one you are in, find another.
- Believe in yourself.

> ||||| **CHECK THESE OUT**
>
> Richard Nelson Bolles's *What Color Is Your Parachute? 2019: A Practical Manual for Job Hunters and Career-Changers* (New York, CA: Ten Speed Press, 2018) contains career and personality tests, articles, and practical advice for job seekers. His website is at http://jobhuntersbible.com/.
>
> Jeanette A. Woodward's *A Librarian's Guide to an Uncertain Job Market* (Chicago: American Library Association, 2011) is another helpful resource. For those of you planning to work in academic libraries, consider Teresa Y. Neely's *How to Stay Afloat in the Academic Library Job Pool* (Chicago: American Library Association, 2011).

handling skills are transferable skills, and they can be used in many occupations outside the mainstream of the information professions.

We have enjoyed our careers in library and information work and in management but couldn't have predicted the paths they would take when we started. We have both had wonderful experiences as librarians and library educators; however, it is also true that there have been one or two less-than-good experiences. So, we'd like to pass on some advice: monitor change and keep abreast of events, not only within librarianship and information work but also in what is happening in the wider world that might affect your career. (For example, where will librarians fit into the growing market for knowledge managers?) Continual self-appraisal and self-assessment will identify emerging education and training needs.

A mentor who knows you well will provide objective advice on your strengths and weaknesses. A mentor will also advise you on whether you should apply for that post that caught your eye—sometimes she or he will give reasons why you shouldn't.

Career goals are important, but flexibility is essential. Remember that realistic self-promotion will move a career forward. Finally, a key factor in any job is the level of enjoyment and reward, both extrinsic and intrinsic, that it provides.

REFERENCES

Berry, Jahna. 2011. "Get Acquainted with Your Future Boss: More Employers Using Internet Video Conferencing in Interviews." *Arizona Republic*, November 4: D1–D2.

Centanni, Kristen. 2011. "Making the Most of It." *Library Journal* 136, no. 16: 31.

Chamorro-Premuzic, Tomas. 2017. "Could Your Personality Derail Your Career? Don't Take These Traits to the Extreme." *Harvard Business Review* 95, no. 11: 138–41

Holley, Robert P. 2003. "The Ivory Tower as Preparation for the Trenches." *College and Research Libraries News* 64, no. 3: 172–75.

Jassin, Marjorie, and Tricia Moe. 2005. "The Flat Track to New Career Options for Librarians." *Online* 29, no. 5: 22–25.

Laybats, Claire, and Darron Chapman. 2016. "Career Management and Development, Where to Go When You Have Reached the Top." *Business Information Review* 33, no. 4: 228–31.

Marshall, Joanne Gard, Victor W. Marshall, Jennifer Craft Morgan, Deborah Barreau, Barbara Moran, Paul Solomon, Susan Rathbun-Grubb, and Cheryl A. Thompson. 2009. "Where Will They Be in the Future? Implementing a Model for Ongoing Career Tracking of Library and Information Science Graduates." *Library Trends* 58, no. 2: 301–15.

Tzoc, Elías, and John Millard. 2011. "Technical Skills for New Digital Librarians." *Library Hi Tech News* 28, no. 2: 11–15.

Valdes, Manuel, and Shannon McFarland. 2012. "Employers Ask Job Seekers for Facebook Passwords." *Associated Press*, March 22. http://news.yahoo.com/employers-ask-job-seekers-facebook-passwords-170500338.html.

Webb, Jela. 2016. "The Mid-Career Information Professional: Managing Your Own Career." *Business Information Review* 33, no. 3: 163–68.

ABOUT THE AUTHORS

G. Edward Evans, PhD, is a semi-retired, award-winning author and Fulbright Scholar. He holds several graduate degrees in anthropology and library and information science. Throughout his career, he has been an administrator, researcher, teacher, and writer. As a researcher, he has published in both anthropology and librarianship. He held a Fulbright Fellowship in librarianship as well as a National Science Foundation Fellowship in archaeology. His teaching experience has also been in both fields in the United States and the Nordic countries. Of note, he completed the faculty ladder (assistant to full professor) while teaching at the Graduate School of Librarianship and Information Science at the University of California, Los Angeles. Evans has extensive administrative experience in private academic libraries such as Harvard University and Loyola Marymount University. He retired from full-time work as associate academic vice president for libraries and information resources at Loyola Marymount University. Evans spends his semi-retirement years volunteering at the Museum of Northern Arizona, serving on the Foundation board for the Flagstaff City-Coconino County Library System, and doing professional writing.

Stacey Greenwell, EdD, has served the University of Kentucky Libraries since 2001 in several roles, including associate dean for academic affairs and research, head of the Information Commons, and head of desktop support. She recently began working with the information literacy and assessment department to provide instructional design support, teach, and work on research projects. Dr. Greenwell is a Fellow of the Special Libraries Association and has held numerous leadership roles in the organization, including chair of the Information Technology Division and founding chair of the Academic Division. She is a standing committee member for the Education and Training Section of the International Federation of Library Associations and Institutions (IFLA) and is a standing member of the Programme Committee for the European Conference on Information Literacy (ECIL). She is a frequent conference presenter and has taught an academic libraries course for the iSchools at Syracuse University and the University of Kentucky.

INDEX

Page numbers in *italics* refer to figures; those in **bold** refer to tables.